Peace
in the
Post-Christian Era

Peace
in the
Post-Christian Era

THOMAS
MERTON

Edited with an Introduction
by Patricia A. Burton

Foreword by Jim Forest

ORBIS BOOKS

Maryknoll, New York 10545

Library of Congress Cataloging-in-Publication Data

Merton, Thomas, 1915-1968.
    Peace in the post-Christian era / Thomas Merton ; edited with an introduction by Patricia A. Burton.
      p. cm.
    ISBN 1-57075-559-0 (pbk.)
    1. Peace – Religious aspects – Catholic Church. 2. Nuclear warfare – Religious aspects – Catholic Church. I. Burton, Patricia A. II. Title.
BX1795.P43M475 2004
261.8′73 – dc22

                                         2004008362

Contents

Foreword

Jim Forest

THE BOOK YOU HOLD in your hands was intended for publication in 1962. While Thomas Merton would be pleased that forty-two years later this labor of love is at last in bookshops and libraries, it would distress him that, far from being a poignant memento of a bygone era, it remains both timely and relevant.

1962: Culturally it was still the fifties. What would be known as "the Sixties" hadn't quite started. *West Side Story* had won the Academy Award for best film of 1961. The Beatles were unheard of.

John F. Kennedy was serving his second year as president of the United States. Nikita Khrushchev was in his fourth year as premier of the Soviet Union. It was three years since the revolution led by Fidel Castro had taken charge of Cuba. American military involvement in Vietnam was steadily building. The Cold War was still blowing its icy winds across every border. Russians *en masse* were regarded as godless Communists. The United States, the Soviet Union, Great Britain, and France were the only countries with nuclear weapons. It was ten years since the first hydrogen bomb had been exploded, seventeen years since the destruction of Hiroshima and Nagasaki by much less powerful atom bombs. Americans were spending hundreds of millions of dollars on fallout shelters as a means of surviving nuclear war.

Politicians, generals, and experts of the period spoke of "missile gaps" when they advocated building missiles that flew further and delivered bigger payloads.

Nuclear weapons were by no means the only systems of mass destruction. Both the United States and the Soviet Union had large programs for the development and stockpiling of chemical and biological weapons.

"Peace" was a suspect word. Those who used it risked being regarded as "reds" or "pinkos."

Yet profound change was underway in the United States. Racism was being challenged. Activists in America's Civil Rights movement were struggling to integrate schools, public transport, and restaurants. Martin Luther King had acquired an international reputation.

The Roman Catholic Church in America in 1962, after many years of struggle with anti-Catholic prejudice, could be relied on to have a supportive attitude regarding America's economic system and foreign policy. Over many a Catholic parish or school entrance were carved the words, *Pro Deo et Patria* — for God and country. Many Catholics had made a career in the military, the FBI and the CIA. For the first time, there was a Catholic in the White House.

One of America's most widely read religious writers was a Trappist monk, Thomas Merton. Orphaned in his youth, a convert to the Catholic Church while studying at Columbia University, in December 1941 he had given up a teaching job at St. Bonaventure's College in western New York State in order to begin monastic life at the Abbey of Our Lady of Gethsemani in rural Kentucky. When his abbot became aware of his talents as a writer, he was encouraged to write an autobiography. Published in 1948, *The Seven Storey Mountain* became a runaway best-seller. Merton, only six years a monk and only thirty-three years old, found himself a famous man. Every subsequent book he wrote was assured excellent sales both in English and in translation. For years his main themes were the monastic vocation, contemplation, prayer, sacramental life, the lives of saints and the quest for holiness, but there were also books that revealed his struggles as a monk. Though he occasionally revealed critical social views — there was a blast at racism in *The Seven Storey Mountain* — many of his readers were unprepared for his criticisms of the arms race and the Cold War that began appearing in Catholic journals in 1961.

There was also the Catholic Worker movement, led by Dorothy Day, another convert. Founded during the Depression in 1933, it had not only brought into existence many houses of hospitality to welcome the down-and-out but often took part in protests against preparations for war. While regarded as marginal by most of the hierarchy, it was a center of much ferment and enthusiasm. It was one of the few Catholic groups at that time deeply engaged in the Civil Rights movement. Its publication had many thousands of readers.

Thomas Merton was one of those who had a high opinion of Dorothy Day and the movement she led. In the summer of 1961 he submitted the first of a series of articles — "The Root of War is Fear"[1] — to the *Catholic Worker.* It appeared in the October issue. (At the time I was part of the Catholic Worker community in New York. Dorothy Day, aware of my interest in Merton's writing, asked me to prepare his essay for publication and also encouraged me to correspond with him. Thus began a relationship of letters and occasional visits that was to last until Merton's death in December 1968.)

In April 1962 Merton completed *Peace in the Post-Christian Era.* He had hoped it would be released by Macmillan in the Fall. Instead it was banned by Dom Gabriel Sortais, Abbot General of Merton's order: the Order of Cistercians of the Strict Observance, better known as the Trappists. Just days after completing work on *Peace in the Post-Christian Era,* a letter from Dom Gabriel was delivered to Merton which forbade him to do any further writing on the subject of war and peace.[2]

The following day, Merton sent me the most distressed letter that I ever received from him:

Now here is the ax. For a long time I have been antici-
pating trouble with the higher superiors and now I have
it. The orders are, no more writing about peace.... In
substance I am being silenced on the subject of war
and peace.

The decision, he said, reflected

an astounding incomprehension of the seriousness of the
present crisis in its religious aspect. It reflects an insensitivity to Christian and Ecclesiastical values, and to the
real sense of the monastic vocation. The reason given is
that this is not the right kind of work for a monk and
that it "falsifies the monastic message." Imagine that: the
thought that a monk might be deeply enough concerned
with the issue of nuclear war to voice a protest against
the arms race, is supposed to bring the monastic life into
disrepute. Man, I would think that it might just possibly
salvage a last shred of repute for an institution that many
consider to be dead on its feet.... That is really the most
absurd aspect of the whole situation, that these people
insist on digging their own grave and erecting over it the
most monumental kind of tombstone.

Beneath the surface of the disagreement between Merton
and his Abbot General was a different conception of the identity and mission of the Church. For Merton the monk was
obliged to be among the most attentive to what was going on
in the world at large and had a role to play in renewal:

The vitality of the Church depends precisely on spiritual
renewal, uninterrupted, continuous, and deep. Obviously
this renewal is to be expressed in the historical context,
and will call for a real spiritual understanding of historical crises, an evaluation of them in terms of their
inner significance and in terms of man's growth and the

advancement of truth in man's world: in other words, the establishment of the "kingdom of God." The monk is the one supposedly attuned to the inner spiritual dimension of things. If he hears nothing, and says nothing, then the renewal as a whole will be in danger and may be completely sterilized.

But these authoritarian minds believe that the function of the monk is not to see or hear any new dimension, simply to support the already existing viewpoints precisely insofar as and because they are defined for him by somebody else. Instead of being in the advance guard, he is in the rear with the baggage, confirming all that has been done by the officials. The function of the monk, as far as renewal in the historical context goes, then becomes simply to affirm his total support of officialdom. He has no other function, then, except perhaps to pray for what he is told to pray for: namely the purposes and the objectives of an ecclesiastical bureaucracy. The monastery as dynamo concept goes back to this. The monk is there to generate spiritual power that will justify over and over again the already predecided rightness of the officials above him. He must under no event and under no circumstances assume a role that implies any form of spontaneity and originality. He must be an eye that sees nothing except what is carefully selected for him to see. An ear that hears nothing except what it is advantageous for the managers for him to hear. We know what Christ said about such ears and eyes.

Merton wondered aloud if he should obey:

Now you will ask me: how do I reconcile obedience, true obedience (which is synonymous with love) with a situation like this? Shouldn't I just blast the whole thing wide open, or walk out, or tell them to jump in the lake?

But he was convinced disobedience would do more harm than good and that, in any event, it could not be his path:

> Let us suppose for the sake of argument that this was not completely excluded. Why would I do this? For the sake of the witness for peace? For the sake of witnessing to the truth of the Church, in its reality, as against this figment of the imagination? Simply for the sake of blasting off and getting rid of the tensions and frustrations in my own spirit, and feeling honest about it?
>
> In my own particular case, every one of these would backfire and be fruitless. It would be taken as a witness *against* the peace movement and would confirm these people in all the depth of their prejudices and their self-complacency. It would reassure them in every possible way that they are incontrovertibly right and make it even more impossible for them ever to see any kind of new light on the subject. And in any case I am not merely looking for opportunities to blast off. I can get along without it.
>
> I am where I am. I have freely chosen this state, and have freely chosen to stay in it when the question of a possible change arose. If I am a disturbing element, that is all right. I am not making a point of being that, but simply of saying what my conscience dictates and doing so without seeking my own interest. This means accepting such limitations as may be placed on me by authority, and not because I may or may not agree with the ostensible reasons why the limitations are imposed, but out of love for God who is using these things to attain ends which I myself cannot at the moment see or comprehend. I know he can and will in his own time take good care of the ones who impose limitations unjustly or unwisely. That is his affair and not mine. In this dimension I find

no contradiction between love and obedience, and as a matter of fact it is the only sure way of transcending the limits and arbitrariness of ill-advised commands.[3]

Behind the silencing, Merton wrote me a few weeks later, was the charge that he had been writing for "a communist-controlled publication," as the *Catholic Worker* was said to be by some of its opponents.[4]

Merton responded to Dom Gabriel's letter with the promise of obedience but also a defense of his book. In mid-May Merton received a reply in which the Abbot General renewed his order, stressing the difference between religious orders that teach and those that pray. "I am not asking you to remain indifferent to the fate of the world," Dom Gabriel insisted. "But I believe you have the power to influence the world by your prayers and by your life withdrawn into God more than by your writings. That is why I am not thinking about hurting the cause you are defending when I ask that you give up your intention of publishing the book you have finished, and abstain from now on from writing on the subject of atomic warfare, preparation for war, etc."[5]

Ironically, as Merton points out in *Peace in the Post-Christian Era*, Machiavelli's *The Prince*, an unabashedly immoral book, "has never been on the Index of books forbidden to Catholics."[6]

Merton obeyed Dom Gabriel, if in a limited way. Never given to a publisher nor vetted by Trappist censors, *Peace in the Post-Christian Era* remained generally unknown, yet was not altogether buried. Merton resorted to *samizdat* methods for putting his book in the hands of others, much as a Russian might in that same era. Dom James Fox, Merton's abbot, though far from a radical, decided that Dom Gabriel's ruling only barred publication in a widely distributed commercial form. He also saw no need for the order's censors to review material that wasn't being offered to the general public — thus anything mimeographed or offered to publications with a small circulation could be circulated with impunity.[7]

Dom James gave one of the abbey's young monks the job of typing the book on stencils for a mimeographed edition. In the first printing, several hundred copies of *Peace in the Post-Christian Era* were produced by this means. By June Merton began mailing copies to a wide variety of his correspondents, including Ethel Kennedy, sister-in-law of President Kennedy, and Cardinal Montini in Milan, later to become Pope Paul VI. Not long afterward, a second printing was run off. By the end of 1962 there were five or six hundred copies of the book in circulation. Hot item that it was, few of them stayed long at any one address. Merton's banned book must have reached thousands of attentive readers within a few months. Many of them were people of influence.

Part of the distribution of *Peace in the Post-Christian Era* was in my hands. In the course of the summer of 1962, by which time I was on the staff of Catholic Relief Services, Merton sent me at least twenty copies to distribute to others. I still have one copy that wasn't given away, though I can see from marginal notes in it that I shared it with at least one other reader.

I no longer have a carbon of my letter to Merton responding to the book nor has it survived in the Merton archives in Louisville,[8] but I see from a reply dated July 7 that I had put forward a number of suggestions for revision in the event he was ever able to do more work on the book. I expressed disappointment that Merton's own convictions about war, so similar to Dorothy Day's, were not expressed more explicitly, and proposed he add a section about Francis of Assisi, a saint particularly important to Merton. During the Fifth Crusade, Francis had given an example of unarmed peacemaking, traveling to Egypt to meet with one of Christianity's chief opponents, Sultan Malik-al-Kamil. Francis had also founded a "third order" for lay people whose members were forbidden to possess or use weapons of war. Merton wrote in reply:

> What a mess one gets into trying to write a book that will get through the censors, and at the same time say something. I was bending in all directions to qualify every statement and balance everything off, so I stayed right in the middle and perfectly objective ... [at the same time trying] to speak the truth as my conscience wanted it to be said. In the long run the result is about zero. . . . Certainly if I ever get to work over the book again, I will bear in mind your requests.[9]

Reading this again after all these years, I am struck by how the white-hot anger Merton expressed in his previous letter had either receded or been put under wraps. I'm also impressed by his reluctance to defend his book in the face of the criticisms I had voiced. There is a stunning modesty in his reply to a reader not half his age. Yet one sees in Merton's journal entries and letters to other friends how hard the struggle was to come to terms with being silenced on what he remained convinced was a crucial issue. Certainly he did not believe that he had been wasting his time in writing the book nor could he agree that it was just as well that it went unpublished.

Had publication not been blocked, perhaps there might have been a final round of revisions, but in its broad outlines I doubt the final text would differ significantly from the book as now published.

Fortunately much that Merton had been forbidden to say was being said by Pope John XXIII.[10] A succession of papal statements critical both of the arms race and nuclear weapons culminated in the publication of *Pacem in Terris* (*Peace on Earth*), issued in April 1963. It quickly became the most widely discussed papal encyclical of modern times. Addressed not only to Catholics but to all people of good will, Pope John stressed that the most basic human right is the right to life. John spoke out passionately against such threats to life as the arms race, said that war was no longer "an apt means for vindicating violated rights," and called for legal protection of conscientious objectors to military service. Far from sanctioning blind obedience to those in authority, the pope stressed the individual responsibility to protect life and uphold morality: "If civil authorities legislate or allow anything that is contrary to the will of God, neither the law made nor the authorization granted can be binding on the conscience of the citizens since God has more right to be obeyed than man."[11]

Writing to the Abbot General to say "it was a good thing that Pope John didn't have to get his encyclical through our censors: and could I now start up again,"[12] Merton asked if he might now return to work on *Peace in the Post-Christian Era* so that it might finally be published. Unmoved, Dom Gabriel renewed the prohibition. Merton commented in his journal, "At the back of [Dom Gabriel's] mind obviously is an adamant conviction that France [of which Dom Gabriel was a citizen] should have the bomb and use it if necessary. He says that the encyclical [*Pacem in Terris*] has changed nothing in the right of a nation to arm itself with nuclear weapons for self-defense."[13]

A Council of the Roman Catholic Church, the first one in nearly a hundred years, had been announced by Pope John in January 1959 and had gotten underway in October 1962 — the same month, as it happened, of the Cuban Missile Crisis, when the United States and the Soviet Union found themselves on the verge of nuclear war.

Seeking a way to play a role in the Council's discussions, in December 1962 Merton sent copies of *Peace in the Post-Christian Era* to Hildegard and Jean Goss-Mayr, secretaries of the International Fellowship of Reconciliation. The Goss-Mayrs were in close contact with Cardinal Ottaviani, secretary of the Holy Office and the member of the Curia most responsible for the process of preparing first drafts of Council documents. One of these was Schema 13, as it was known in the drafting stage — a document on the Church's role in the modern world, including the issue of war.

After two years of drafting and redrafting and many hours of debate, Schema 13 at last was published in 1965 as the Pastoral Constitution on the Church in the Modern World (*Gaudium et Spes*). The culminating work of the Council, it contained the only specific condemnation issued by the Second Vatican Council:

> Every act of war directed to the indiscriminate destruction of whole cities or vast areas with their inhabitants is a crime against God and humanity, which merits firm and unequivocal condemnation.

It was a sentence not very different than this passage in *Peace in the Post-Christian Era*:

> I wish to insist above all on one fundamental truth: that all nuclear war, and indeed massive destruction of cities, populations, nations and cultures by any means whatever is a most serious crime which is forbidden to us not only by Christian ethics but by every sane and serious moral code.[14]

Those who renounce violence altogether, choosing the tools of nonviolence instead, won the Council's approbation:

> We cannot fail to praise those who renounce the use of violence in the vindication of their rights and who resort to methods of defense which are available to the weaker parties too, provided that this can be done without injury to the rights and duties of others in the community itself.[15]

Supporting legislation for conscientious objectors, the Council urged all governments to make "humane provision for those who, for reasons of conscience, refuse to bear arms, provided that they accept some form of service to the human community."[16]

Echoing another major theme Merton had explored in *Peace in the Post-Christian Era,* the Council Fathers declared that orders which conflict with the "all-embracing principles of natural law" were criminal, stating further that "blind obedience cannot excuse those who yield to them," and that "the courage of those who fearlessly and openly resist such commands merits supreme commendation."[17]

How much Merton's writings played a role in the Council we may never know, but without a doubt he was a significant influence, mainly thanks to effective distribution of the mimeographed edition of *Peace in the Post-Christian Era.*

Now, forty-two years after it was written and thirty-six years after the author's death, the first copy of *Peace in the Post-Christian Era* bearing a publisher's imprint is coming off the press. These pages have slept even longer than Rip van Winkle.

How does a book addressing issues that were current in 1962 hold up in a world in which the Soviet Union is no more and the Cold War a chapter heading in history books? Despite many close calls, there has been no use of nuclear weapons in war since 1945. Indeed American and Russian stockpiles of nuclear weapons have been hugely reduced and nuclear tests have gone underground and become a rarity. We no longer hear an ominous phrase that was often repeated in the sixties to describe the lynchpin of deterrence strategy: "mutually assured destruction."[18] Few remember the names of Herman Kahn and Edward Teller, men mentioned repeatedly in *Peace in the Post-Christian Era.*

Yet the means of fighting nuclear war are still with us. Despite all the weapons that have been eliminated thanks to a series of treaty agreements of the past thirty years, the United States retains an estimated 10,400 nuclear warheads in its arsenal and Russia a similar number.[19] Meanwhile, in the United States, the Bush administration has called for development of a "new generation" of nuclear weapons "better suited" to battlefield use. The number of countries known to possess nuclear weapons has grown to include not only Britain and France but China, India, Pakistan, and Israel, while several other countries are suspected to have nuclear weapons or are known to have taken steps toward obtaining them. There is in addition the grave danger of nuclear weapons being procured by such terrorist organizations as Al-Qaeda. The issue of nuclear weapons and other means of mass destruction is not only still with us but the possibility of their use in war is growing.

Merton did not foresee the collapse of the Soviet Union and the disintegration of the USSR's Warsaw Pact alliance in Eastern Europe. Neither did he anticipate the current "War on Terror," as the Bush administration has defined its response to the events of September 11, 2001. Nothing similar to the Taliban or Al-Qaeda existed in 1962. Yet, as one reads *Peace in the Post-Christian Era,* it is striking how often the word "terrorism" appears — referring not to the activities of secret groups but rather to the acceptance by governments of tactics of war that result in large numbers of noncombatant casualties.

It is interesting how, when Merton speaks of Communism, references to terrorism often work well in its place. For example:

> The struggle against totalitarianism is directed not only against an external enemy — Communism — but also against our own hidden tendencies towards fascist or collectivist aberrations.[20]

The same would make sense today with only a slight alteration:

> The struggle against totalitarianism is directed not only against an external enemy — *such terrorist groups as*

Al-Qaeda — but also against our own hidden tendencies towards fascist or collectivist aberrations.

In many ways the world is hardly different than it was in 1962. Then as now, one need not have an overactive imagination to envision Doomsday. Death by nuclear explosion is only one of many grim futures we can all too easily imagine for ourselves.

Always sensitive to the language of propaganda, Merton would not be surprised with such current phrases as "the axis of evil," nor that Americans still take it for granted that evil is committed by their enemies, not themselves.

The willingness of the United States to participate in the United Nations and other international bodies only when doing so suits national interests would not surprise him. As he wrote in *Peace in the Post-Christian Era*:

> Indeed the big powers have been content to use the UN as a forum for political and propagandist wrestling matches and have not hesitated to take independent action that led to the discrediting of the UN whenever this has been profitable to them.[21]

The same mind-set is linked with the temptation to initiate preemptive war "based not on the fact that we ourselves are actually under military attack, but that we are 'provoked' and so 'threatened' that even the most drastic measures are justified."[22]

Also unchanged despite the passage of time is American bewilderment that so good-willed a people are the object of so much enmity:

> Faced by the supercilious contempt of friends as well as the hatred of our avowed enemies, and wondering what there is in us to hate, we have considered ourselves and found ourselves quite decent, harmless and easygoing

people who only ask to be left alone to make money and have a good time.[23]

One of Merton's still-relevant themes is the way that those moral restrictions which warriors pledge to apply to their conduct as they contemplate conflict in the abstract gradually recede and finally completely evaporate as events in actual war push them toward more drastic measures. In the early days of World War II America and Britain vowed not to replicate the city bombing committed by their enemies, but in the end didn't hesitate to regard entire cities as legitimate targets. As Merton writes:

> Moral thinking guided by pragmatic principles tends to be very vague, very fluid. Moral decisions were now a series of more or less opportunistic choices based on short term guesses of possible consequences, rather than on definite moral principles.[24]

When the first mimeographed copy arrived by post, I recall being startled with the book's title. Was I really living in a post-Christian world? After all, most Americans professed a belief in God and one didn't have to travel far to find well-attended churches. I couldn't deny, however, that our religious life in many ways resembled a Hollywood set: a thin veneer of impressive facades supported by scaffolding in back. As Merton put it:

> Whether we like it or not, we have to admit we are already living in a post-Christian world, that is to say a world in which Christian ideals and attitudes are relegated more and more to the minority. It is frightening to realize that the facade of Christianity which still generally survives has perhaps little or nothing behind it, and that what was once called "Christian society" is more purely and simply a materialistic neopaganism with a

Christian veneer.[25] . . . Not only non-Christians but even
Christians themselves tend to dismiss the Gospel ethic on
nonviolence and love as "sentimental."[26]

Yet not all is as it was when Merton finished writing *Peace in
the Post-Christian Era*. One of the changes that would greatly
please Merton is that among Christians the word "peacemaking" is no longer the suspect term it was in 1962, a profound
change in attitude that is partly thanks to him.

A striking sign of the times is the fact that several years ago
the Archdiocese of New York formally proposed that Dorothy
Day be recognized as a saint and placed on the calendar of the
Catholic Church. The Vatican has already given her the title,
"Servant of God."

The Catholic Church has been a consistent voice for peace
since Merton's time. Its commitment to seek peace has not
wilted despite such events as the terrorist attacks of September 11 or America's subsequent "preemptive" war in Iraq.

Were he alive and no longer hobbled by censorship, perhaps Merton would set to work on updating *Peace in the
Post-Christian Era*. But many paragraphs, even chapters, would
remain unaltered. He would remind us once again that Christ
waves no flags and that Christianity belongs to no political
power bloc. He would affirm once again that "an essential part
of the 'good news' is that nonviolent and reasonable measures
are stronger than weapons. Indeed, by spiritual arms, the early
Church conquered the entire Roman world."

NOTES

1. This was a chapter that would soon after appear in *New Seeds of Contemplation,* though the Catholic Worker version had some additional material,
the text of which is included in my biography of Merton, *Living with Wisdom*
(Maryknoll, N.Y.: Orbis Books, 1991), 135–39.

2. A book that Merton was editing at the time, *Breakthrough to Peace: Twelve Views on the Threat of Thermonuclear Extermination,* did make it into print, but when it went to press, Merton could not be identified by New Directions as the book's editor. Nonetheless his introduction was published under his name and the book also contained one of his essays, "Peace: A Religious Responsibility," a text similar to the first chapter of *Peace in the Post-Christian Era.*

3. Letter to Jim Forest dated April 29, 1962. The full text is included in *The Hidden Ground of Love: The Letters of Thomas Merton on Religious Experience and Social Concerns,* edited by William Shannon (New York: Farrar, Straus, Giroux, 1985), 266–68. Subsequent references cited as *HGL.*

4. Letter to Jim Forest, June 14, 1962; *HGL,* 268–69.

5. See Michael Mott, *The Seven Mountains of Thomas Merton* (Boston: Houghton Mifflin, 1984), 379, and Mott endnote no. 228, p. 623.

6. In the chapter "The Legacy of Machiavelli."

7. After his silencing, when publishing anything on war and peace even in small journals, Merton no longer used his own name. One piece in the *Catholic Worker* was signed Benedict Monk. In another publication, possibly *Commonweal,* I recall a letter to the editor that bore the signature Marco J. Frisbee.

8. The Thomas Merton Center, Bellarmine University, 2001 Newburg Road, Louisville, KY 40205; web address: www.merton.org.

9. Letter to Jim Forest, July 7, 1962; *HGL,* 269.

10. Merton's direct contact with Pope John had begun on February 11, 1960, when Merton received a packet from the Vatican that contained a portrait photograph signed by John as well as a blessing for the novitiate. Responding the same day, Merton told John that he had received permission "to start, very discreetly, a small retreat project" aimed at Protestant and Catholic theologians, psychiatrists, writers, and artists — something on the lines he had described in his previous letter to John, but to be held at Gethsemani rather than in Latin America. "Our goal," Merton wrote, "is to bring together . . . various groups of people highly qualified in their own field who are interested in the spiritual life, no matter what aspect, and who will be able to profit from an informal contact, from a spiritual and cultural dialogue, with Catholic contemplatives." A nonverbal response to Merton's letter reached Gethsemani on April 11 with the visit of Lorenzo Barbato, a Venetian architect who was a friend of the pontiff's. Barbato brought Merton an elaborately embroidered liturgical vestment, a stole, which had been used by Pope John XXIII. John wanted Merton to have it. Not long afterward, Dom James Fox received a letter from Cardinal Tardini, the Vatican secretary of state, expressing the particular interest Pope John had in the "retreats with Protestants which Fr. Louis was organizing at Our Lady of Gethsemani."

11. *Gaudium et Spes,* 51.

12. Letter to Jim Forest, April 26, 1963; *HGL,* 274.

13. Thomas Merton, *Turning Toward the World,* The Journals of Thomas Merton, vol. 4, 1960–63 (New York: HarperCollins, 1996), entry for May 10, 1963, p. 317.

14. In the chapter "Can We Choose Peace?"

15. *Gaudium et Spes,* 78.

16. Ibid., 79.

17. Ibid.

18. The initials, appropriately, were MAD. Secretary of Defense Robert McNamara defined mutually assured destruction as the ability to eliminate 25 percent of the enemy's population and 50 percent of the industry.

19. See the website of the *Bulletin of the Atomic Scientists:*
www.thebulletin.org/issues/nukenotes/jf04nukenote.html

20. In the chapter "Can We Choose Peace?"

21. In the chapter "The Dance of Death."

22. In the chapter "Working for Peace."

23. In the chapter "Can We Choose Peace?"

24. In the chapter "Justice in Modern War."

25. In the chapter "Religious Problems of the Cold War."

26. In the chapter "Beyond East and West."

Introduction

The Book That Never Was

Patricia A. Burton

THE AUTUMN OF 1961 was a time of great energy in the writing life of Thomas Merton. It was then that he drafted the articles on which he was to base *Peace in the Post-Christian Era*, his unpublished (and later notoriously banned) book about nuclear war. It was a new approach for Merton. He had tried to turn the ethical dilemmas posed by nuclear weapons into art, in such works as the prose poem "Original Child Bomb," but had hesitated for months about embarking on the next step, which was to write plain argument in the prophetic vein. He had set himself the task of "getting into contact with the others most concerned," and reading all the books and articles he could find on the subject of the Cold War and particularly nuclear weapons.[1] During this period, as his ideas developed, he also suggested a related project to James Laughlin at New Directions, the anthology *Breakthrough to Peace*,[2] edited anonymously by Merton and containing a long article which he also used as a foundation for his new book about nuclear war.

In treatments of Merton's life and writing, *Peace in the Post-Christian Era* is a rather shadowy piece about which certain ideas linger: the description "unpublished" and "forbidden" are the principal ones. There are oft-quoted self-deprecating remarks Merton made, as though he had given up on it, and a rather triumphant passage in his journal which has been interpreted to mean that he did get to publish the whole thing after all, in *Seeds of Destruction*. This is not the case: the story is much more complex. There is also a somewhat hazy notion that the ban on this facet of Merton's writing was lifted immediately after the promulgation of Pope John XXIII's encyclical *Pacem in Terris,* giving the story a happy ending. As we shall see, exactly the opposite happened.

Monk in a Time of War

Why was a monk (and famous spiritual author) commenting on social questions? Many have wondered why Merton's writing took this turn, but he did not have to search outside his own monastic tradition for a model. Throughout history, well-known monastics and mystics had written letters to the great and powerful, often with complaints about the ethics of their actions. Merton already had his exemplar: in 1953 he had written a foreword to a translation of letters of Bernard of Clairvaux addressed to a wide variety of people, including the politically powerful. Merton remarked that, although Bernard's letters were often angry, there was another side to his character, "gentle and longsuffering...tender as a mother," and concluded, "perhaps our own century needs nothing so much as the combined anger and gentleness of another Bernard."[3] Whether in imitation of Bernard or not, Merton began to write and collect letters which he ultimately published in mimeographed form.[4] It was one of the tactics which he had developed because his published articles and comments were meeting with increased resistance.

Whatever the hesitations and arguments against writing, there were equivalent forces pushing Merton to act. In many of his letters from the early 1960s, particularly those published in *The Hidden Ground of Love,* one theme repeatedly cropped up: his worry about what appeared to be the moral passivity of American Catholics, who were content to accept the lead of the Church even on questionable moral issues like the threat of nuclear annihilation inherent in the Cold War. To Etta Gullick:

> ... it is absolutely necessary to take a serious and articulate stand on the question of nuclear war. And I mean against nuclear war. The passivity, the apparent indifference, the incoherence of so many Christians on this issue, and worse still the active belligerency of some religious spokesmen, especially in this country, is rapidly becoming one of the most frightful scandals in the history of Christendom.[5]

A Place to Write

On December 2, 1960, Merton lit the first fire in the fireplace at the cinderblock cottage he called "St. Mary of Carmel," a building which had originally been intended as a meeting place for his discussions with groups from other Christian denominations. He was claiming the place, as part of an ongoing struggle to be allowed to live as a hermit. Still involved fully in the life at Gethsemani as Novice Master, Merton had received permission to spend some hours a day at the hermitage. Removal to another place, even one so near to the monastery, had given him a new perspective in what has been called his "turn toward the world." As he wrote on November 25, 1961:

> Yesterday afternoon at the hermitage, surely a decisive clarity came. That I must definitely commit myself to opposition to, and noncooperation with, nuclear war. (*TTW,* 182)

Undoubtedly as a result of those few hours of quiet and improved concentration each day, his production (especially of letters) increased, and continued to grow each year until his death.[6] By March 20, 1962, in the midst of the fray over his peace writing, Merton was celebrating his first full day at the hermitage (*TTW,* 212).

Contemplation and Activism

Finding a place to write involved not only a physical problem of geographic space but a search for a distinctive viewpoint from which to see the world. Merton was trying to discern what the activism of a contemplative writer would look like. There was always the assumption that his contribution would be "primarily, of course, by prayer. I remain a contemplative" (*TTW,* 175). His journals in 1961 are full of entries about using his primary talent and influence by writing in a time of crisis. On August 29, 1961, he wrote "have been considering the possibility of writing a kind of statement — 'where I stand'...There is no other activity available to me" (*TTW,* 156). By October 29, 1961, he was recording the first article:

> Yesterday I finished an article on Peace: Christian duties and perspectives. Discussed it a little with the novices, which was a good idea. It will certainly not please many people. (*TTW,* 174)

The article, later twice rewritten, was the first of several which were associated with the composition of *Peace in the Post-Christian Era.*

The title of the new book was an indicator of the process which was going on in both Merton the writer and Merton the contemplative. The term "post-Christian" is commonplace today, but it was relatively new when Merton used it. He attributed the term to C. S. Lewis, who had coined it in his 1954 inaugural lecture at Cambridge.[7]

Merton had used the term in his first published comment on nuclear war, sent to *Catholic Worker* in October of 1961. He had just reworked the 1949 spiritual classic *Seeds of Contemplation,* including the chapter "The Root of War is Fear," greatly expanding the chapter from the "old" *Seeds.*[8] It had originally been a series of austere aphorisms decidedly disapproving of what was called "the world" (a place from which the monk had withdrawn). The new version had become a passionate plea to Christians to work for the abolition of war in a world no longer seen from the outsider's viewpoint. The world was a place where everyone lived, even those in the most withdrawn monastic orders. For the *Worker,* Merton tacked on a few paragraphs of additional text at the end of the chapter, and it was there that he first used the term "post-Christian" (*PFP,* 11–13).

The use of the term automatically projected the viewpoint of Merton's book into a larger world, in which the Church was no longer seen as the focal point. He was earnestly hoping that Christians would be in the vanguard, setting an example as peacemakers in the frightening new Cold War world: that is the central idea of the book, as it is of the *New Seeds* chapter. For Merton, action had arisen out of contemplation: the renewed spiritual classic was the wellspring for the torrent of writing against nuclear war which he produced over the next year.

A Barrage of Articles

In a letter to Daniel Berrigan on December 7, 1961, Merton demonstrated that his internal struggles about this writing had continued to evolve into action:

> I am getting out an ingenuous, wide-eyed article on peace in the Christmas *Commonweal* [the article was later deferred to February 1962]...have been asked to write for *The Nation,* and may perhaps do something on "Christian Ethics and Nuclear War." Laying down a barrage all

around, and then when the smoke clears we'll see what it did. Probably not much. (*HGL*, 72)

In his journal, the interior debate was still going on:

About peace. Maybe the best is to say quickly and wisely and fully all that I have to say, all at once, and then let the blow fall. [. . .] No point in saving up the ammunition for later, there may be no later. (*TTW*, 187)

By the beginning of 1962, Merton's "barrage" was in place. In short order several essays made it through censorship and were published; one in particular (ominously) would be refused:

1. "Nuclear War and Christian Responsibility" in *Commonweal* in February, followed by controversy and a rewrite in the *Catholic Worker* in May–June 1962, called "We Have to Make Ourselves Heard." This version was later to be used as the basis for "Peace: A Religious Responsibility" in *Breakthrough to Peace,* and as a framework for *Peace in the Post-Christian Era*;[9]

2. "Christian Ethics and Nuclear War" in the *Catholic Worker* in March, before it had passed the censors (resulting in another rewrite, published as "Religion and the Bomb" in *Jubilee,* in May 1962);[10]

3. "Red or Dead: Anatomy of a Cliché" in *Fellowship* in March 1962, and included in a Fellowship pamphlet;[11]

4. "Christian Action in World Crisis" in *Blackfriars* in June 1962;[12]

5. "Target Equals City," a mimeograph Merton started mailing to friends in about February 1962, although it was not otherwise published in his lifetime. The censor returned it to Merton, indicating that he would not accept any further articles on the subject.[13]

By the spring of 1962 Merton had at hand carbon copies or mimeographs of various versions of all of these articles, which he used as a foundation for the book *Peace in the Post-Christian Era*.[14] The book had been requested: in a letter of March 4, 1962, to Jay Laughlin, Merton wrote "Macmillan offered me a ten thousand dollar advance for a book on peace, after the recent *Commonweal* article" (*TMJL*, 183).

On April 12 Merton wrote to the atomic physicist Leo Szilard that he wished "to devote a notable part of the royalties of a book I am currently writing, on peace, to your cause."[15] By April 29, he was able to write to Jim Forest, "I have been trying to finish my book on peace, and have succeeded in time for the ax to fall" (*HGL*, 266). The only direct mention of the book in Merton's journal at the time is an entry on April 26, 1962: "I read to the novices in a conference a bit of the Peace ms — on Machiavelli — and Teller" (*TTW*, 215).

How Merton Worked

The manuscript of *Peace in the Post-Christian Era* gives abundant evidence of the way Merton made use of, and added to, the text of the published essays. To construct the book, Merton used a carbon copy of one version of "Peace: A Religious Responsibility" (already subdivided with section headings, which he employed as chapter titles), physically disassembling it into parts, and then inserting parts of other essays into it as chapters. To this basic structure he added a great deal of new material. There are about 170 pages, held together by various numbering and lettering systems, bristling with inserts and even whole extra chapters developed on the fly, all bearing signs of haste and also a monastic thrift about both text and paper. A good deal of new text was written in on the blank left-hand pages of the carbon copies. Merton sometimes even used carbons of different versions of the same essay, and in the end nothing perfectly matches anything else (the carbons also vary from the final published versions).

In addition to recycling and augmenting material he already had, Merton also added long insertions of new material: five pages to further discuss theological views of war; a complete new chapter to examine nuclear scientists' views of the way their discovery was being used.[16] Towards the end of the draft he interpolated two whole chapters, comprising seventeen pages of text, using as a foundation the *Blackfriars* essay "Christian Action in World Crisis," which had probably been included late in the process because of censorship delays with the original essay.

The manuscript of *PPCE* shows Merton working fast and furiously, exploiting every free moment to update text he already had, to insert new material and to write entirely new chapters. At least three typewriters were involved; in the case of one manuscript page, Merton typed an initial paragraph on a rather rickety typewriter (perhaps a portable, at the hermitage), removed the page and put it into a different typewriter (which produced better copy) to continue, then edited the whole by hand.[17]

Merton did not simply string together and augment a few already-published essays to make the book. There is a particularly important central section of the manuscript which was not based on previously published articles, incorporating the selection Merton read to the novices, discussing Machiavelli and Teller. That this section was new is demonstrated by the quality of the copy in the manuscript, which is either in handwriting or in Merton's error-prone rough draft typing style. These new sections evolved under the following headings:

1. "Can We Choose Peace?"

2. "The Christian as Peacemaker"

3. "War in Origen and St. Augustine"

4. "The Legacy of Machiavelli"

These newly written parts of the book set the peace question in the framework of the Church's history and the traditional view of the just war. What Merton did subsequently showed that he had not forgotten these new chapters.

The manuscript also shows an organizing intelligence which kept the many seemingly disparate parts from collapsing into disorder. While it is evident that Merton carried file folders full of text up and down the hill to the hermitage, more importantly he must have carried the shape of the book in his head, putting it into writing only at those moments when his full-time job gave him the opportunity. It is hard to imagine how an author's working conditions could have been more difficult, especially for the task of writing such a complex piece, dense with argument as Merton's prose often is. That it still reads well forty years after the fact is a tribute to Merton's discipline, concentration and energy as a writer.

Obedience and Censorship

On April 27, 1962, Dom James Fox handed Merton a letter from Abbot General Gabriel Sortais, requesting that Merton no longer write on the issues of war and peace, particularly on nuclear weapons. The story of Merton's silencing has often been told, and it is hardly necessary to tell it again here. Merton was by 1961 fully experienced at dealing with Dom Gabriel's strictures. His experience with censorship had not been easy. All work had to go through a process of several levels before it received the final *imprimatur,* and it was often the Abbot General himself who withheld permission.[18] The Cistercian Order was facing a challenge of its own; the spectacular success of *The Seven Storey Mountain* had created a Trappist superstar, a contradiction in terms if ever there was one. In Merton's day monastic orders had carefully defined distinctive characteristics of life and practice, and the Trappists were not known for their writers. Whether or not it was a question of making Merton a special case, after *Seven Storey Mountain* (which had the usual *imprimi potest* from Merton's Abbot, Dom Frederick Dunne) all of Merton's further books were no longer signed off by the local Abbot, but passed up the line to the Abbot General, the Order's highest authority.

Although Merton understood that his work had to be free of doctrinal error, he found that censors often commented on whether or not a particular work was a fit subject for a monk. The French term "opportunité" cropped up, and the censors used it to cover a variety of situations. They often advised picayune changes which made no sense to Merton at all, prompting him to complain that the process was "deliberately designed to discourage writers."[19] In his repeated attempts to open up spiritual writing to a new personal level of experience, or to explore the wisdom of other faiths, Merton had repeatedly been stymied because these were thought not to be correct subjects for a Trappist to write about.

These difficulties had been building up over the years, and they had gradually eroded Merton's respect for the process. When censorship became particularly galling, his feelings spilled over into his journal and letters to friends he trusted. Merton believed that writing on the subject of the new threat of nuclear war was ethically essential. What he felt he was being told, however, was not that his opinions were necessarily wrong, but that it was not his place to express them: the *opportunité* argument again.

After a long series of battles in his two decades as a monastic author, Merton gradually developed a way of easing the frustrations. When the Abbot General told Merton not to write about Teilhard de Chardin's *The Divine Milieu,* Merton wrote in his journal

> I have no obligation to form my thought or my conscience along the rigid lines of Dom Gabriel. I will certainly accept and obey his decision, but I reserve the right to disagree with him. (*TTW,* 65)

An entry of May 10, 1963, sheds further light:

> I have never before seen so clearly that "agreement" with Superiors has little or nothing to do with it. They have their right to my obedience, but there is no need to be interiorly servile. One can be obedient and free, and even in a certain sense independent, at least interiorly. (*TTW,* 318)

Other writers caught under oppressive wartime regimes or behind the Iron Curtain called it "inner emigration": if they could not escape a difficult situation, they could maintain at least an interior freedom, hiding their writing and hoping for better times.

When confronted by Superiors, Merton had to give way if he wanted to remain in the Order. When he had assimilated a subject so thoroughly as this one, and believed in it so deeply, he could not automatically stop thinking about it, and it inevitably emerged both in his writing and in his actions. Events in the world were continually forcing him to rethink the writing he had promised to curtail.

Merton's struggles over the peace writing were not simply a matter of defiance of authority. His approach was filtered through the monastic practice of frequent examination of conscience; his own interior censor tried constantly to discern God's will, and applied equal doses of compunction which kept him more or less in balance, as this, in July 1961:

> I will stop making any kind of effort to justify myself to anybody. To prepare a place for myself anywhere, among any group. It is this that I have to face. This and the necessity to give up any activity that leaves the slightest

(intended) impression on the surface of the world. This and the necessity to renounce all surreptitious reaching for human immortality — that is, for being remembered. (*TTW,* 143–44)

The Price of Influence

Merton had never had any official power in the hierarchy of the Church or the Cistercian Order, but as a well-known author he had a great deal of influence: he wrote to two popes, to the sister-in-law of the U.S. president, to a U.S. secretary of state, to the mayor of Hiroshima, to a Zen master and several Muslims — in short, to anyone with whom he wanted to share communication. Merton's monastic solution to the censorship problem was to stay put and do what was possible from where he was. The irony was, of course, that he had to: leaving would have jeopardized his influence. Writing about criticism of his peace book from E. I. Watkin in September 1962, Merton painfully confronted these difficulties and said in his journal:

> [Watkin] asserts he would listen to no authority against conscience on this issue. But my position loses its meaning unless I can continue to speak from the center of the Church. Yet that is exactly the point: where is that true center? From the bosom of complacent approbation by Monsignors? (*TTW,* 244–45)

Even influence had its price, and Merton would come to know that more and more as time went on. To be most effective he had to stay put.

As to whether the ban had upset him or not: by June 4, Merton seemed to have adopted a sort of devil-may-care attitude and said in a letter to W. H. Ferry, "I am not sore, not even very much interested any more . . . have been going back to Origen and Tertullian" (*HGL,* 212).

When Merton went out of his way to say he did not feel something, it often meant that he did, but was too overwhelmed at the moment to be able to sort it out. His letters to Robert Lax were usually more honest, although couched in a private language:

> I have been silenced. I have been nacht und nebel for my war book. I have been put in the calabozo. I have been shut up in a tin can. I have been shrewdly suppressed at the right moment. I have been stood in the corner. I have been made to wear the cap. I have been tried and tested in the holy virtue of humility. I have been found wanting and tested some more. I have been told to shut up about the wars, wars is not for Christians except to support.
>
> Hence my dear Charlot the laments in the current *Jubilee* is my finale. It comes a little agent with too big an overcoat and false glasses with a copy of contraband war book in about six weeks. Nobody to print, nobody to show. Just read the damn war book.

Lax replied in kind:

> am thanking you for the book of thoughts on you-know-what, very good, strong, powerful, well-thought-out book. . . .
>
> ora (plenty) for nos intransigeants.
>
> it is the time of the mop.[20]

Merton went on to obey the direct order from the Abbot General in the most literal and careful manner possible, warning editors and friends not to publish any of his writing on nuclear war after the ban. He continued to hope, however, that the pieces which had been passed by censors would still be allowed because the ban had been a matter of timing. Although he felt he could distribute what he already had in hand, he knew that trying to rewrite it would be extremely risky.

Contact through correspondence with an ever-widening circle of friends had given Merton an informal channel which he would greatly need as time went on. Word of his silencing spread. It was a decade when people were demonstrating, marching in the street with banners, burning draft cards, spending time in jail. Ultimately Merton's "demonstration" consisted in enduring his silencing, meanwhile using any permitted means to send copies of his writing to so many places that some of it was bound to survive and be read.

The Propaganda Machine

In these days of word processors, personal printers and photocopiers with automatic collation, we have all but forgotten how hard it was a generation ago to cheaply produce multiple copies of a text. Carbon copies could only be made about half a dozen at a time, by retyping the article. Mimeograph text had to be typed on special stencils, and pages were often cranked out one at a time on the mimeograph machine, and collated by hand. The method may now seem cumbersome, but it had its advantages: stencils could be made by anyone with a typewriter, and the machinery was not expensive or complicated. With care, the stencils could even be used for more than one print run. It was thus both accessible and cheap, and in the 1960s it was the method of choice for underground or small-circulation publication of all kinds; school children, church congregations, street poets, social clubs, political movements, all were familiar with this populist medium. Whole magazines were mimeographed.[21] Even at Vatican II, mimeographs were the information weapon of choice, to the point that a Council official once tried to establish control over "the mimeographed sheets and booklets with which the Fathers were constantly bombarded in order to influence their voting."[22]

Merton's use of mimeographs started with his teaching notes as novice master. As he became more established as a writer, there were more demands on him, and also more friends he wanted to send articles to. He could command a certain amount of labor from the novices, to get the typing done. Having spare copies meant that he could easily mark up the next edit or recast an article for another use. He also knew that sending out mimeographs gave the material a fair chance of survival, whereas in the monastery it might wind up being used as scrap paper.

On the subject of mimeographs, and whether they constituted "publication," Merton astonished Jay Laughlin and Ping Ferry.[23] Laughlin seemed to think it was

> a kind of game, sort of like the taxpayer's relationship with Uncle Sam every March, where you don't do anything "dishonest" but try your darndest to find all the loopholes. (*TMJL*, 195)

Merton replied to Laughlin's letter with an earnest explanation, comprehensively expressing his own understanding of the rules, and also demonstrating a desire to justify the concept of monastic obedience to friends living in a secular culture, stating that

> mimeographed material [may] be circulated without censorship. This is the common practice.... As for private circulation, that is none of the censor's business.... Circulation of a couple of hundred mimeographed copies is not publication. (*TMJL*, 192–94)

There is an element of embarrassment in Merton's protestations. Whereas Catholics familiar with the procedure would have understood its use, Merton's secular friends might have concluded that censorship of writing was oppression pure and simple. Because of his genuine loyalty to the Order and the Church, Merton felt bound to defend them, even when he tended to agree in principle with the worldly friends. It was a delicate balance.

Flying under the Radar

Merton mentioned in letters to Catherine de Hueck Doherty and John Heidbrink that the mimeograph stencils had just been finished when the order to stop writing had arrived, saying, "I will run off a few copies anyway and friends can see it."[24] The mimeographed copies were ready in mid-June of 1962, and Merton sent copies immediately to many of his "peace friends," including Jim Forest, Daniel Berrigan, Etta Gullick, Dorothy Day, John Harris, Sister Emmanuel de Souza e Silva, and Charles S. Thompson, the publisher of *Pax Bulletin* in England.[25]

When he began to receive some critical comments from friends, Merton was as usual self-deprecating. The way Merton embraced the criticisms of *Peace in the Post-Christian Era* indicates that they may have been ironically comforting to him: recognizing that the book was not perfect made its suppression less painful for the author. At the time, he was only allowed one chance to get it right. If the book had gone through a normal editing and censorship process, its flaws would have been addressed. But as Merton said in a September 1962 letter to E. I. Watkin, "It did not even get to the censors, so I did not have a chance to find out if what I said accorded with the teaching of the Church" (*HGL,* 579).

For the Church's purposes, the book simply did not exist: as those who manned the guns at Fort Knox might have said, it flew under the radar. It also turned out that regardless of what Merton had said about the book, he did not stop mailing it, promoting it in letters, and trying to get another chance at rewriting it.

At Christmas 1962, more copies went off, to a wider circle of friends.[26] In February of 1963, when Merton sent one to Jacques Maritain, the accompanying letter made it evident that he was still smarting from the Abbot General's rebuke that his defense of peace

> "fausserait le message de la vie contemplative"... a hateful distraction, withdrawing the mind from the Baby Jesus in the Crib. Strange to say, no one seems concerned at the fact that the crib is directly under the bomb. (*CFT,* 35–36)

The tone is reminiscent of his Christmas message to Lax in their usual code, where humor hid despair:

> as for me my dear Charlot I sit in my hutch mimeographing forbidden books with the help of fifty-nine uncouth Albanian novices all highly irregular and dissipated ready for the most desperate acts. For the rest our situation is too awful to be described.[27]

Even when *Pacem in Terris,* Pope John XXIII's great encyclical on peace, was published in 1963 Merton was not allowed to reopen the subject by Dom Sortais, who turned down his request for permission to rewrite the book (*SCH,* 166). This was the third time the General had specifically stepped on Merton's peace writing. Merton consoled himself by exercising his influence in a letter, sending a copy to Ethel Kennedy, sister-in-law of the president of the United States, on May 4, 1963:

> I wrote a book on peace which the Superiors decided I ought to bury about ten feet deep behind the monastery someplace, but I still don't think it is that bad. I mimeographed it and am sending you a copy, just for the files, or, who knows, maybe the President might have five

minutes to spare looking at it. If you think he would, I
will even send him a copy. (*HGL,* 447)

Time went by. On June 3, 1963, Pope John XXIII, the author of *Pacem in Terris,* died. In August of that year, despite the
curtailment of his work, Merton was awarded the Pax Medal,
and wrote an acceptance speech minimizing his own role and
attributing the honor to *Pacem in Terris.*[28] On November 14,
Dom Gabriel Sortais also died, and the Order subsequently
elected a new General, Dom Ignace Gillet. Although he could
not surmise what effect these events might have, Merton still
had not forgotten about his unpublished book, and mentioned
it in a letter in January 1964 to Bishop John J. Wright, who had
been enthusiastic enough about it to circulate it among some
of the *periti* at Vatican II. Merton, encouraged, had offered
more copies and commented "even though the book was not
published, I am happy to think that the work was not wasted"
(*HGL,* 608–9). It had been more than two years since Merton
had started in on this work, and his efforts on its behalf had
resulted only in reinforcement of the ban.

Seeds of Destruction: **A New Crisis**

Merton did have hopes that at least some of his peace articles
and letters might be published in a new book of essays for
Farrar, Straus & Giroux, to be called *Seeds of Destruction.* In
March of 1964, however, he experienced yet another rebound
effect of the dispute with Dom Sortais in 1962. To Naomi
Burton Stone, he wrote on March 3:

> ... the unthinkable has happened.... A letter from the
> new Abbot General [Dom Ignace Gillet] came in concern-
> ing the articles on peace in *Seeds of Destruction.* ... [He] dug
> out the correspondence, had a meeting with the definitors,
> and said that these articles are not to be "republished" in

book form and implicitly in any other form. . . . Hence . . . we have to take out the articles on war. I am sick about this . . . (*WTF,* 142–43)

So sick, in fact, that Merton went on to question his own vocation and wondered if it was all "the most monumental mistake." The sorrow expressed in his journal entry of the day was clearly not just because of his own feelings but because the ban provided "a grim insight into the stupor of the Church, in spite of all that has been attempted, all the efforts to wake her up!" and once more stating, "I cannot leave here in order to protest since the meaning of any protest depends on my staying here."[29]

This was the low point in Merton's struggle. Within three days he had become more philosophical, and was able to write to Dom Ignace saying that he was "dropping this type of work" and assuring him of his "genuine loyalty and obedience" (*SCH,* 208). He was still sore and sad enough about it all to mention the problem in letters to Jim Forest, Leslie Dewart, and W. H. Ferry.[30]

What were the articles Merton wanted to use in *Seeds of Destruction*? A letter from Thomas Merton Center curator Robert Daggy, describes

the first "uncorrected proofs" of *Seeds of Destruction*. In the typescript Merton had inserted the mimeograph and cut pages from three articles written in 1962 — he makes it plain in the first proofs that these articles appeared almost without change just as they had appeared in journals. They were:

1. "Nuclear War and Christian Responsibility," *Commonweal* 75 (February 9, 1962)

2. "Religion and the Bomb," *Jubilee* 10 (May 1962)

3. "Christian Action in World Crisis," *Blackfriars* 43 (June 1962)[31]

So Merton had gone back to the original text of three published articles, hoping that what had passed the censors once
would still be acceptable. He had not attempted to use the
rewritten versions which appeared as chapters in *Peace in the
Post-Christian Era,* or any of the newer, uncensored material
there, but his care over the censorship issue had been for nothing. More than two years into the dispute there still seemed to
be no hope that Merton would ever be able to publish these
articles in a book of his own.

What saved the situation was the intervention of Robert
Giroux. Merton said in his journal:

> A call came from Bob Giroux in New York. It appears
> that the problem of publishing [*Seeds of Destruction*] is
> being finally resolved. (Giroux wrote to the General and
> got a settlement. One essay on war may be printed if I
> will "transform" it.) *(DWL,* 107)

What the "transformation" required is noted in Mott's biography: Merton "could write about peace, not war — he was
not to show pessimism" (Mott, 400).

"the real heart"

Over an astonishing ten days between June 2 and June 12,
1964, as he described to Leslie Dewart, Merton rewrote

> about a third of [*Seeds of Destruction*]. The earlier stuff on
> the bomb which had been permitted is now no longer licit
> and I have to do it all over, writing about peace without
> treating the question of the bomb. I suppose the next
> thing I can do is write about marriage without referring
> to sexual love. (*WTF,* 297)

When he needed a new, full-length article, Merton knew
just where to find the basis for it in the *PPCE* mimeograph.

By June he probably had only his personal copy left, and it is likely that he used that.[32] If he followed the same pattern with "The Christian in World Crisis" as he had with *Peace in the Post-Christian Era* (bearing in mind his usual thrift about paper and text) he would simply have pulled out pages from the central section of the mimeograph, most of which he knew had never appeared elsewhere. He would then have made his annotations, written new material around them, and handed the revised whole to the typist. The items he used were the section "Can We Choose Peace?" and those which treated of philosophical and theological tradition, "War in Origen and St. Augustine," "The Legacy of Machiavelli." The shape of these particular parts of the mimeograph had remained in Merton's mind over the two years of ups and downs about the book.

The way he used these sections was straightforward, but there was another section which, to the extent of a few paragraphs, appeared in *PPCE* and also overlapped with text in "Peace: A Religious Responsibility." This chapter was titled "The Christian as Peacemaker." One of the technical errors of the mimeograph is that Merton split the material he had into two parts, moving some from chapter 4 to chapter 10, neglecting to give the second part a new title. The fact that he maintained the text throughout three versions indicates how central it was to his idea of the Christian's role in achieving peace.

He did not extensively edit the recycled material, but fitted it up with new sections to change the focus, bringing in discussion of *Pacem in Terris,* and roughly doubling the length of the original text. He called the new article "The Christian in World Crisis: Reflections on the Moral Climate of the 1960s."[33] It contained an entirely new concluding section called "The Reply of *Pacem in Terris.*" He described the new article to Gordon Zahn in a letter as "a long rewritten piece on *Pacem in Terris,* basically the same as [*PPCE*] but without controversy on the bomb, just peace peace" (*HGL,* 653). The comment and others like it may have led to the idea that (as the Mott biography states) Merton published the whole of *PPCE* in *Seeds of Destruction* (Mott, 400). He had not managed that, but he had salvaged a part of the book which had never been published elsewhere, and which he seemed to care about particularly.

Finally, a month after he had submitted the new article for censorship, there was a jubilant entry in the journal. *Seeds of Destruction* was to go ahead with the new article, so "the real heart of the forbidden book, *Peace in the Post-Christian Era,* is to be published after all" (*DWL,* 127). The evidence of the text shows us that the term "the real heart" was literal. Merton had torn out of the mimeograph the crucial central pages which he needed.

New details of the censorship story have come to light recently, in an interview with Dom M. Laurence Bourget. Interviewer Jonathan Montaldo's questions pursued the story of the relationship between Dom Gabriel Sortais, his secretary Fr. Clement de Bourmont, and Merton. The interviewer asked whether Fr. Clement had been "an 'enemy' of Merton's literary career," as Merton and others had suspected (Mott, 374). Fr. Clement's better command of the English language meant he was in a position to comment to Dom Sortais about works in that language, and he was secretary to both Dom Sortais and Dom Gillet. What had been his involvement in the final chapter of the censorship story?

As it turned out, Dom Bourget had inadvertently intervened, without knowing what was involved, at a crucial moment. Called into Dom Ignace Gillet's office in July 1964, he was handed a manuscript, with the request:

> "Would you read this text of Merton and tell me if you find anything objectionable in it? We have no time to send it to the Censor because the printer is waiting for it to

complete a book." I did read the text very carefully and returned it promptly to the General with the comment, "Far from finding anything objectionable in it, I find what it says is pure Gospel!"

Dom Bourget finishes the anecdote with the comment

What still mystifies me, however, is that at that time (July 1964) Fr. Clement was still the General's secretary and I now wonder if I was only called in because he happened to be absent from Rome. The ways of Divine Providence indeed![34]

It is hard to imagine what Merton's reaction would have been if the new article had been rejected. He had certainly earned the right to a small session of rejoicing.

This new essay also developed a life of its own: a condensed version was reprinted in the *Saturday Review* in a special section on February 13, 1965, on *Pacem in Terris,* and also included in a pamphlet called *Therefore Choose Life,* published by the Center for the Study of Democratic Institutions, for the New York conference on the papal encyclical. The new essay was called "The Challenge of Responsibility."[35]

Aftermath

Merton's "peace demonstration" in the face of silencing had certainly exacted an emotional price, to the point that he had considered whether his vocation might be at an end. For a man who had thought and written so much about the authenticity of the interior life, the struggle which had put him into direct conflict with his Order had hollowed him out. The pain of living the internal conflict comes out in a remarkable passage in an August 1964 letter to Daniel Berrigan, where Merton describes himself:

As a priest I am a burnt-out case, repeat, burnt-out case. So burnt out that the question of standing and so forth becomes irrelevant. I just continue to stand there where I was hit by the bullet.... [W]ord will go around about how they got this priest who was shot and they got him stuffed sitting up at a desk propped up with books and writing books, this book machine that was killed.... When I fall over, it will be a big laugh because I wasn't there at all....

I am sick up to the teeth and beyond the teeth, up to the eyes and beyond the eyes, with all forms of projects and expectations and statements and programs and explanations, especially explanations about where we are all going... (*HGL,* 84)

Evolving away from the moment in history when the book had been written, Merton did not abandon his interest in the issues of nuclear war, and they cropped up repeatedly in his later work. In the end, the general ban was lifted in 1967 because the overall system of censorship was changed after Vatican II, and books no longer had to run the gauntlet of the old system which required approvals from every level of the Church hierarchy. Merton was finally assured that his work would no longer meet such obstacles (Mott, 490).

The Fate of the Mimeograph

The mimeograph form gave life to Merton's forbidden book, which would otherwise have had no existence at all. The general attitude (not just Merton's own) indeed seemed to be that sending out a few mimeographs did not constitute publication, so these copies were not thought to have any kind of official existence. Unfortunately, that meant that the mimeograph was never granted the status of "real" publication. The fatal flaw in the strategy of removing official attention from the book was that it worked all too well. "Unpublished" came to mean unpublishable. The controversy defined the book, as the suppression helped define the author. In the end, only relatively few readers were able to judge the full text for themselves. Later editors republishing Merton's peace material passed over *Peace in the Post-Christian Era*; after all, Merton had both criticized it and also said he had published the "real heart" of it. It was simpler to reprint the articles related to it.

In the end, time passed it by, and the work never found recognition in the Merton canon. References to it were generally vague or incomplete. The manuscript and the mimeograph faded into a kind of limbo, and lay there for nearly forty years, the one missing piece in the continuum of Merton's thought about nuclear war. The mimeograph has sometimes been studied, particularly in *Thomas Merton on Nuclear Weapons* by Ronald E. Powaski,[36] but it has not been readily available to readers interested in the peace movement of the 1960s, or for its continuing relevance today.

Who can now gauge the effect that this work had, even in mimeograph? In its time it had made its way to quite a few readers, some of them undoubtedly influential in the course of historical events. The appeal of a "forbidden book by Thomas Merton" must certainly have been a factor in making readers curious about it. Copies of the mimeograph travelled far and wide. There is a copy on file as part of Leo Szilard's papers at the University of California at San Diego.[37] Similarly, various other copies made their way into library collections.[38]

In spite of its rarity, *Peace in the Post-Christian Era* is part of history, not only of Merton's writing but also of the American peace movement, of Vatican II, and of the Cold War. Although flawed (since Merton had only one chance, under great pressure, to get it right) it deserves its historic place in the Merton canon. The careful "objectivity" for which the author's friends criticized him is more than offset by Merton's passionate involvement in the issues. He had been caught for a time between two forces: his peace friends outside the Abbey who hoped he would be more activist and extreme, and his Church connections who thought that nuclear war was not a proper subject for a monk to write about. As always he had tried to find the line by which he could communicate with everyone. In doing so he demonstrated an astonishing breadth of argument: who but Merton would have been comfortable discussing Origen, Augustine and Machiavelli in one chapter and Leo Szilard and Edward Teller in the next?

With the full text in print, readers will finally be able to trace Merton's thought on nuclear war through all its stages, and gauge Merton's effect on the outstanding question of his day. The voice which speaks from its pages is as clear and forceful as ever. It asks questions we still need to hear: Can we choose peace? What are our real intentions? The world has not solved the problem of nuclear proliferation, and recently the phrase "preemptive strike" has taken on a new meaning. Nuclear proliferation has continued despite the end of the Cold War. Merton's long-dormant book gives us a perspective from which to ask new questions about the unsolved issues it describes.

With this we have come full circle. Worry about the apathy of American Catholics and the need to make the issues clear had led to Merton's determination to write what he could, regardless of obstacles. His ability to publish had been severely limited, but he had done what he could. During the same time period he had written many other things, focusing on varied subjects, to the extent that this particular thread almost vanished into the fabric. Indeed it had not disappeared but rather had become part of him, and in the end, regardless of the ban, one of the primary things he is known for is his writing about peace.

The manuscript of *Peace in the Post-Christian Era* begins with the author's note to himself and his blessing on the book. This essay ends there:

+

Xtian Action

1) *Towards change — prophetism*
2) *That men may be masters of things and not mastered by them*
3) *Recognition of new situation — understanding meaning and creative value of crisis.*

NOTES

Works frequently cited have been identified by the following abbreviations:

Merton's Journals

DWL   Thomas Merton, *Dancing in the Water of Life: Finding Peace in the Hermitage.* The Journals of Thomas Merton, vol. 5, 1963–65, edited by Robert E. Daggy (San Francisco: HarperCollins, 1997)

TTW   *Turning Toward the World: The Pivotal Years.* The Journals of Thomas Merton, vol. 4, 1960–63, edited by Victor A. Kramer (San Francisco: HarperCollins, 1996)

Merton's Letters

CFT   Thomas Merton, *The Courage for Truth: The Letters of Thomas Merton to Writers,* selected and edited by Christine M. Bochen (New York: Farrar, Straus, Giroux, 1993)

HGL   Thomas Merton, *The Hidden Ground of Love: The Letters of Thomas Merton on Religious Experience and Social Concerns,* selected and edited by William H. Shannon (New York: Farrar, Straus, Giroux, 1985)

SCH   Thomas Merton, *The School of Charity: The Letters of Thomas Merton on Religious Renewal and Spiritual Direction,* selected and edited by Patrick Hart, O.C.S.O. (New York: Farrar, Straus, Giroux, 1990)

TMJL   Thomas Merton and James Laughlin, *Selected Letters,* edited by David Cooper (New York: W. W. Norton, 1997)

WTF   Thomas Merton, *Witness to Freedom: The Letters of Thomas Merton in Times of Crisis,* selected and edited by William H. Shannon (New York: Farrar, Straus, Giroux, 1994)

Reprints

NVA   Thomas Merton, *The Nonviolent Alternative,* ed. Gordon Zahn (New York: Farrar, Straus, Giroux, 1980)

PFP   Thomas Merton, *Passion for Peace: The Social Essays,* edited by William Shannon (New York: Crossroad, 1995)

Biography

Mott   Michael Mott, *The Seven Mountains of Thomas Merton* (Boston: Houghton Mifflin, 1984)

1. Thomas Merton, *Turning Toward the World,* The Journals of Thomas Merton, vol. 4, 1960–1963, edited by Victor A. Kramer (New York: HarperCollins, 1996), 176; subsequent references will be cited as *"TTW."*

2. Thomas Merton and James Laughlin, *Selected Letters* (New York: W. W. Norton, 1997), 183. Subsequent references will be cited as *"TMJL."* The published book was *Breakthrough to Peace: Twelve Views on the Threat of Thermonuclear Extermination* (Norfolk: New Directions, 1962). Merton was not listed as editor but only as a contributor: he was worried that difficulties with censorship would jeopardize publication (see also *TMJL,* 194).

3. Thomas Merton, Foreword to *St. Bernard of Clairvaux Seen through His Selected Letters,* edited and translated by Bruno Scott James (Chicago: Regnery, 1953), v–viii.

4. William Shannon, Introduction to *Passion for Peace: The Social Essays* by Thomas Merton, edited by William Shannon (New York: Crossroad, 1995), 6. Shannon marks the year of Merton's greatest activity against nuclear war as "The Year of the Cold War Letters" (October 1961 to October 1962). Subsequent references will be cited as *"PFP."*

5. Thomas Merton, *The Hidden Ground of Love: The Letters of Thomas Merton on Religious Experience and Social Concerns,* selected and edited by William H. Shannon (New York: Farrar, Straus, Giroux, 1985), 349; subsequent references will be cited as *"HGL."* See also letters to Dorothy Day, 139; Daniel Berrigan, 71; Jim Forest, 271.

6. Patricia Burton, *Merton Vade Mecum* (Louisville: Thomas Merton Foundation, 2001), 36–82.

7. Thomas Merton, "Loretto and Gethsemani," in *The Springs of Contemplation* (Notre Dame, Ind.: Ave Maria Press, 1992), 206. The date for the pamphlet is given as spring of 1962. Lewis's argument was that "Christians and Pagans had much more in common with each other than either has with a post-Christian. The gap between those who worship different gods is not so wide as that between those who worship and those who do not." C. S. Lewis, "De Descriptione Temporum," in *They Asked for a Paper* (London: Geoffrey Bles, 1962), 14.

8. Thomas Merton, *New Seeds of Contemplation* (New York: New Directions, 1962), 112–22. The original essay appeared under the same title in *Seeds of Contemplation* (New York: New Directions, 1949), 70–73.

9. "Nuclear War and Christian Responsibility" was reprinted in *PFP,* 37–47; "Peace: A Religious Responsibility" was reprinted in *PFP,* 99–123 and in Thomas Merton, *The Nonviolent Alternative,* ed. Gordon Zahn (New York: Farrar, Straus, Giroux, 1980), 107–28. Subsequent references will be cited as *"NVA."*

10. "Christian Ethics and Nuclear War" is reprinted in *NVA,* 82–87 and *PFP* 56–64; "Religion and the Bomb" in *PFP,* 65–79.

11. "Red or Dead" is reprinted in *PFP,* 48–52.

12. "Christian Action in World Crisis" is reprinted in *NVA,* 219–26, and *PFP,* 80–91.

13. "Target Equals City" was reprinted in *NVA,* 94–103 and *PFP,* 27–36.

14. The original manuscript is in the collection of the Thomas Merton Center at Bellarmine University, Louisville, Kentucky. There is also a photocopy in the John M. Kelly Library of University of St. Michael's College, Toronto. The author of this introduction examined both copies and did textual comparisons with the published essays in order to trace Merton's writing on nuclear war throughout its development.

15. Thomas Merton, *Witness to Freedom: The Letters of Thomas Merton in Times of Crisis,* selected and edited by William H. Shannon (New York: Farrar, Straus, Giroux, 1994), 49–50; subsequent references will be cited as *"WTF."* Szilard had been one of the physicists who developed the bomb, but afterwards campaigned against nuclear proliferation.

16. This section, "The Scientists and Nuclear War," which demonstrates the author's ease with contemporary material as well as traditional teaching, has never been published anywhere.

17. Thomas Merton, "Peace in the Post-Christian Era," unpublished manuscript, Thomas Merton Center, Bellarmine University, Louisville, Kentucky, 12.

18. Michael Mott, *The Seven Mountains of Thomas Merton* (Boston: Houghton Mifflin, 1984), 77; subsequent references will be cited as "Mott."

19. Thomas Merton, *The School of Charity: The Letters of Thomas Merton on Religious Renewal and Spiritual Direction,* selected and edited by Patrick

Hart, O.C.S.O. (New York: Farrar, Straus, Giroux, 1990), 133. Subsequent references will be cited as *"SCH."*

20. Thomas Merton and Robert Lax, *When Prophecy Still Had a Voice: The Letters of Thomas Merton and Robert Lax,* edited by Arthur Biddle (Lexington: University Press of Kentucky, 2001).

21. For example, a 1998 exhibit of mimeographed poetry and other writings in underground magazines at the New York Public Library is documented in the book by Stephen Clay, *A Secret Location on the Lower East Side: Adventures in Writing 1960–1980* (New York: New York Public Library and Granary Books, 1998).

22. Xavier Rynne [Francis X. Murphy, C.S.S.R.], *Vatican Council II* (Maryknoll, N.Y.: Orbis Books, 1968, 1996), 175.

23. Mott, 373–74. Mott notes that in this statement Merton was "ignoring the Copyright Act."

24. To Catherine de Hueck, June 4, 1962, *HGL,* 19; to John Heidbrink, May 30, 1962, *HGL,* 408. See also letter to James Laughlin, *TMJL,* 207–8.

25. All references in *HGL*: to Forest (June 14, 1962), 269; to Berrigan (June 15, 1962), 74; to Gullick (June 16, 1962), 353; to Dorothy Day (June 16, 1962), 145; to Harris (June 8, 1962), 398; to Sister Emmanuel (June 18, 1962), 188; to Thompson (July 19, 1962) 573.

26. To Abdul Aziz (December 26, 1962), *HGL,* 53; to Edward Deming Andrews (Decembr 28, 1962), *HGL,* 38.

27. Thomas Merton and Robert Lax, *A Catch of Anti-Letters* (Kansas City: Sheed and Ward, 1978), 7.

28. Thomas Merton, "In Acceptance of the Pax Medal, 1963" in *NVA,* 257–58.

29. Thomas Merton, *Dancing in the Water of Life* (New York: Harper-Collins, 1997), 84; subsequent references will be cited as *"DWL."*

30. To Forest (March 16, 1964), *HGL,* 279; to Dewart, *WTF* (April 24, 1964), 295; to Ferry (May 27, 1964), *HGL,* 217.

31. Letter to William Shannon from Robert Daggy, June 13, 1986. From the research files of William H. Shannon.

32. In October 1964 Merton told Jim Forest that he had "no more copies [of the mimeograph], but the essence of it is going to be in my new book…" (*HGL,* 282).

33. Thomas Merton, *Seeds of Destruction* (New York: Farrar, Straus, Giroux, 1964), 93–183.

34. Dom M. Laurence Bourget, O.C.S.O., "Thomas Merton: A Monk Who 'Succeeded': An Interview by Correspondence," conducted and edited by Jonathan Montaldo, *Merton Annual* 12 (1999): 48.

35. "The Challenge of Responsibility," *Saturday Review,* February 13, 1965, 19–30.

36. Ronald E. Powaski, *Thomas Merton on Nuclear Weapons* (Chicago: Loyola University Press, 1988). Powaski summarizes Merton's thought on nuclear weapons, drawing on the mimeograph and many other Merton materials.

37. http://orpheus.ucsd.edu/speccoll/findaids/science/szilard, at the Mandeville Special Collections Library, listed in the Register of Leo Szilard Papers among the items sent to Rare Books or General Collections.

38. There are two copies in the John M. Kelly Library at the University of St. Michael's College, Toronto. One is battered and grimy, anonymous (no cover label, not signed). The other belonged to St. Michael's professor Leslie Dewart, and it arrived as part of the second printing in August of 1962, as noted by Dewart on the cover. This copy, in considerably better shape, is signed by Merton.

Editor's Note

Merton's text is presented here with a minimum of editing, beyond a few obvious small corrections. The author's haste is witnessed by a few technical problems (as was often the case with his mimeographs), and these have been addressed as noted below.

Merton rearranged and renumbered his chapters so many times that the chapter numbering of the mimeograph was unworkable. In the text printed here, the chapters are numbered simply from 1 to 17, and the original numbers, which would only have caused confusion, are not included.

The manuscript indicated that during the writing process Merton removed part of the text of chapter 4 to a later position, as chapter 10; thus the mimeograph has two chapters titled "The Christian as Peacemaker." Merton had tried out and discarded chapter headings in several places, and one of these was "Working for Peace," which agrees well with the content of chapter 10.

Merton's few footnotes appear in the text where he placed them. Endnotes added by the editor comprise references left out or only sketchily done by Merton, with a few explanatory comments. It was not possible, more than four decades after the fact, to track down every quote if there were too few clues given in the text.

•

The book would not have been possible without the help and support of people along the way. Louise Girard, chief librarian at St. Michael's, suggested a trade of copies which brought the manuscript to light. Thomasine O'Callaghan, Merton Trustee, delivered the crucial copy in the summer of 1998. Years later, Merton collector Albert Romkema acquired the mimeograph; his vivid interest brought a new attention to the lost text. Robert Ellsberg read it and saw how it could speak to us anew in a year of war. Mary L. Stewart, as befits a staunch Merton-friend, provided love and encouragement, lending her own energy to help see the project through to the end.

Peace
in the
Post-Christian Era

1

Preamble: Peace —
A Religious Responsibility

BETWEEN 1918 and 1939 religious opposition to war was articulate and widespread, all over Europe and America. Peace movements of significant proportions were active in Germany, Britain, and the United States. Yet they were crushed without difficulty and almost without protest by Totalitarian regimes on the one hand, and on the other were silenced by the outbreak of what has been called a "classic example of a just or defensive war." Since 1945 there has been nothing to compare with the earlier movements of protest. Instead we have witnessed the enormous and crudely contrived fiction of the Communist "Peace Movement" which has been accepted with disillusioned resignation on one side of the Iron Curtain while, on the other, it has managed to make almost all efforts of independent civilian or religious groups to oppose nuclear war seem dishonest or subversive.

Yet never was opposition to war more urgent and more necessary than now. Never was religious protest so badly needed. Embarrassed silence, despondent passivity, or crusading belligerence seem to be the most widespread "Christian" response to the H-bomb. True, there has been some theological and ethical debate. This debate has been characterized above all by a seemingly inordinate hesitation to characterize the uninhibited use of nuclear weapons as immoral. Of course the bomb has been condemned without equivocation by the "peace Churches" (Quakers, Mennonites, etc.) But the general tendency of Protestant and Catholic theologians has been to reconcile nuclear war with the traditional "just war" theory. In other words the discussion has not been so much a protest against nuclear war, still less a positive search for peaceful solutions to the problem of nuclear deterrence and ever increasing Cold War obsessions, but rather an attempt to justify, at least under some limited form, this new kind of war which is tacitly recognized as an imminent possibility. In other words, theological thought has tended more and more to accept nuclear war, considering a lesser evil than Communist domination, and looking for some practicable way to make use of the lesser evil in order to avoid the greater.

But it would seem that a genuinely religious perspective, especially a Christian perspective, should be totally different. Therefore the purpose of the present book is to stand back from the imminent risks of the Cold War crisis, seeking to judge the problem of nuclear war not in relation to what seem to be our own interests or even our own survival, but simply in the light of moral truth. A Christian ought to consider whether nuclear war is not in itself a moral evil so great that it *cannot* be justified even for the best of ends, even to defend the highest and most sacrosanct of values.

This does not imply a purely pacifist rejection of war as such. Assuming that a "just war" is at least a theoretical possibility, and granting that in a just war Christians may be bound to defend their country, the question we want to examine here is whether or not the massive and unlimited uses of nuclear weapons, or the use of them in a limited first strike which is foreseen as likely to set off a global cataclysm, can be considered in any circumstances just. If it is true that this form of defense is unjust and inhuman, then we will have to completely change our way of thinking and abandon policies which ultimately *assume,* if they do not explicitly threaten, the massive all out use of nuclear weapons. And we have to do this quite apart from any consideration of political expediency.

And, this being the case, we inevitably come face to face with the question of war itself. Since any large scale war is likely to turn without warning into a global nuclear cataclysm, we can no longer afford to ignore our obligation to work for the abolition of war as a means of solving international problems. Yet how can we do this at a time when moral values have been to a great extent discarded as meaningless and when Christians themselves ignore or evade the compelling exigencies of Christian ethics in this matter? Unless it is possible to consider these urgent problems in a climate of tolerance, objectivity, restraint and respect for human rights, we will never come near solving them. And this climate of tolerance and justice will be frankly impossible where the atmosphere of Christian humanism and charity is lacking.

The great problem is in fact that both in the East and in the West, by Christians and non-Christians, nuclear weapons are taken for granted. Nuclear war is now assumed to be a rational option: or at least nuclear deterrence is accepted as a reasonable and workable way of "preserving peace." The moral issue is generally set aside as irrelevant. But if in all these cases, a use of nuclear weapons even to threaten total or quasi-total destruction of an enemy is immoral, then we are living in a completely noxious situation where most of our political, economic, and even religious thinking is inseparably bound up with assumptions that may ultimately prove criminal. And if this is so, we must be prepared to face terrible consequences. For moral rectitude and truth are just as much a necessity to man and his society as air, water, fire, food, shelter and all those things on which bodily life depends. More necessary! For the moral and spiritual life of man are specifically *human,* and without them he is better off dead!

This book therefore takes the stand that the *massive and uninhibited use of nuclear weapons,* either in attack or in retaliation, is contrary to Christian morality. And the arguments will be drawn particularly from Catholic sources. Recent popes have declared ABC warfare to be a "sin, an offense and an outrage" (Pius XII).[1] It may be quite true that these popes have also affirmed a nation's right to defend itself by *just means,* in a just war. It may also be true that a theological argument for the use of "tactical nuclear weapons" may be constructed on the basis of some of the popes' statements. But when we remember that the twenty kiloton A-bomb that was dropped on Hiroshima is now regarded as "small" and as a "tactical device" and when we keep in mind that there is every probability that a force that is being beaten with small nuclear weapons will resort to big ones, we can easily see how little practical value can be found in these theorizings.

"Tactical nuclear weapons" and "limited war" with conventional forces are of course proposed with the best intentions: as a "realistic" way to avoid the horror of total nuclear warfare. Since it is claimed that men cannot get along without some kind of war, the least we can do is to insure that they will only destroy one another in thousands instead of in millions. Yet curiously enough, the restraint that would be required to keep within these limits (a restraint that was unknown on either side after the early phases of World War II) would seem to demand as much heroism and as much control as disarmament itself. It would therefore appear more realistic as well as more Christian and more humane to strive for total peace rather than for partial war. Why can we not do this? If disarmament were taken seriously, instead of being used as a pawn in the game of power politics, we could arrive at a workable agreement for the gradual reduction of arms. It might not be ideal, but it would certainly be at once safer, saner and more realistic than war, whether limited or total. But we make ourselves incapable of taking either disarmament or peace with total seriousness, because we are completely obsessed with the fury and the fantasies of the Cold War. The task of the Christian is at least to make the thought of peace once again seriously possible. A step towards this would be the rejection of nuclear deterrence as a basis for international policy. The "balance of terror" is totally unacceptable. It is immoral, inhuman, and absurd. It can lead nowhere but to the suicide of nations and of cultures, indeed to the destruction of human society itself.

However, this tragic situation cannot be rectified in ten minutes.

If we fix our minds on total and immediate disarmament — a course which certainly recommends itself to abstract logic — we run into insuperable obstacles and perhaps end up by contributing even more to the climate of desperation and frustrated fury which is building up to war.

Yet we must keep disarmament in view quite seriously and objectively as an end to be attained through gradual steps. And we must then be willing to take such steps as appear possible, even if they imply a definite risk of error or failure. In other words disarmament must be something more than a pious front for political skullduggery. We cannot afford to go on with conferences in which proposals are made for propaganda purposes, and withdrawn as soon as there is any indication they will be taken seriously. There is no question that Communists have deserved their reputation for dishonesty in these matters, but the West is not without guilt either.

We have got to face the fact that war is not merely the product of blind political forces, but of human choices, and if we are moving closer and closer to war, this is because that is what men are freely choosing to do. The brutal reality is that we seem to *prefer* destructive measures: not that we love war for its own sake, but because we are blindly and hopelessly involved in needs and attitudes that make war inevitable.

2

Can We Choose Peace?

AMAN IS SAID to be "responsible" insofar as he is able to give a rational and ethically satisfactory answer, or "response," concerning his acts and the motives behind them. Cain, for instance, after the murder of Abel, was asked where Abel was — a question of primordial and typological importance. Cain's answer was not clear.

In discussing the fateful problem of nuclear war in terms of Christian responsibility, we must first discover what question is being asked of us, and by whom. If we are willing to face the question along with the questioner, we may eventually become able to give a true and clear answer.

The question is not merely "Where is the nuclear arms race leading us?" or "Can a nuclear war be avoided much longer?" or "Will the Communists take over the West?" or "Will the West win the Cold War?" or "Will the survivors of a nuclear war envy the dead?" From the standpoint of the present volume, such questions are irrelevant. Not that the issues they raise may not be vitally important, but the surmises and conjectures which might be offered as answers to such questions are really not answers to anything. They are beguiling guesses which seek to allay anxiety and which may well threaten to misdirect our best efforts if not to justify actions of which we ought to be ashamed.

The more important question is not "what is going to happen to us?" but "what are we going to do?" or more cogently,

"What are our real intentions?" This last question is probably seldom asked with sufficient seriousness. Let us suppose it is not simply something we ask ourselves. Let us hear it as a question that is proposed to us by the Lord and Judge of life and death. Let us bear in mind another such question: "Friend, whereto art thou come?" (Matt. 26:50). Judas, somewhat subtler and far unhappier than Cain, having learned some fundamental truths, happened to know that the acceptable answer to such crucial questions had something to do with love. So he kissed Christ. But his kiss was a sign of betrayal.

We are being asked the very same question, if not directly and openly by Christ, at least by history of which we, as Christians, believe him to be the Lord.

I do not say that our love of Christ, desperate and confused as it is, is little more than a gesture of betrayal. But let us be sincere about facing the question, and hope, through God's grace, to answer it better than Judas.

Quite apart from what the Communists may or may not do with the bomb, what are we, the dwindling and confused Christian minority in the West, going to do with it? Or at least, what do we *really want to do with it*? Get rid of it or use it on Russia? Have we anything left to say about it at all? Have not the decisions been taken to a great extent out of our hands? Not yet. Among our leaders, some are Christians. Others cling to humanitarian principles which should be relevant here. These leaders will (we hope) take kindly to suggestions and to pleas that are based on Christian ethical norms.

Yet it cannot be said that there is such a thing as specifically "Christian policy" in this, or in any other political question, however momentous. Theology does not dictate political or military strategy, and to identify a particular policy with Christian morality pure and simple is dishonesty and opportunism. Therefore we can neither say that a Christian is bound to fight Communism with every available weapon, nor that he may not fight Communism with any weapon. But we must say that whether in warfare or in pacifism the Christian is bound to act according to his Christian conscience. There are very strict limits set upon his exercise of the right to defend himself and his nation by force, and there are also strict limits upon his willing submission to evil and to violence.

The question of Christian responsibility is then concerned with these limits. But it is also concerned with something more positive. The Christian is not only bound to avoid certain evils, but he is responsible for very great goods. This is often forgotten. The doctrine of the Incarnation makes the Christian obligated at once to God and to man. If God has become man, then no Christian is ever allowed to be indifferent to man's fate. Whoever believes that Christ is the Word made flesh believes that every man must in some sense be regarded as Christ. For all are at least potentially members of the Mystical Christ. Who can say with absolute certainty of any other man that Christ does not live in him? Consequently in all our dealings with other men we must realize ourselves to be often, if not always, facing the questions that were asked of Cain and Judas.

We are, then, disciples of Christ and necessarily our brother's keepers. And the question that is being asked of us concerns all men. It concerns, at the present moment, the entire human race. We cannot ignore this question. We cannot give an irresponsible and unchristian consent to the demonic use of nuclear power for the destruction of a whole nation, a whole continent, or possibly even the whole human race. Or can we? The question is now being asked.

This is the question that forms the subject of the present volume.

Perhaps it is already being asked too late.

In this most critical moment of history we have a twofold task. It is a task in which the whole race is to some degree involved. But the greatest responsibility of all rests upon the citizens of the great power blocs which threaten to destroy one another with nuclear, chemical and bacteriological weapons.

On one hand we have to defend and foster the highest human values: the right of man to live freely and develop his life in a way worthy of his moral greatness. On the other hand we have to protect man against the criminal abuse of the enormous destructive power which he has acquired. To the American and Western European, this twofold task seems reducible in practice to a struggle against totalitarian dictatorship and against war.

Our very first obligation is to interpret the situation accurately, and this means resisting the temptation to oversimplify and generalize. The struggle against totalitarianism is directed not only against an external enemy — Communism — but also against our own hidden tendencies towards fascist or collectivist aberrations. The struggle against war is not only directed against the bellicosity of the Communist powers, but against our own violence, fanaticism and greed. Of course, this kind of thinking will not be popular in the tensions of a Cold War. No one is encouraged to be too clear-sighted, because conscience can make cowards, by diluting the strong conviction that our side is fully right and the other side is fully wrong. Yet the Christian responsibility is not to one side or the other in the power struggle: it is to God and truth, and to the whole of mankind.

This is not a political study. But the moral options of our times are necessarily involved in various interpretations of political reality. The different views of the situation prevailing in the West react upon each other, and all together they combine to create extreme difficulties and complexities. The question arises then whether man is really capable of choosing peace rather than nuclear war, whether the choices are ineluctably made for him by the interplay of social forces. The answer to this question must depend on many factors beyond the control of any individual or any one group. But the fact remains that we cannot face the moral issue as free and rational beings unless we can still assume that our freedom and rationality have meaning. If we are not able to choose to survive, then all discussion of the present crisis is pointless. If we are still free, then this book can be considered as a very imperfect contribution to the work of moral preparation which is absolutely necessary if we are to make significant use of our freedom.

At the present time it seems that there are three prevailing viewpoints in the United States, all with their own moral (and immoral) implications. A quick summary of these three points of view will necessarily be schematic and superficial.

At one extreme we have the "hard" and "realistic" view. It excludes all other considerations and concentrates on one inescapable fact: the Communist threat to western society. It considers that negotiation with Communism is for all practical purposes futile. It is thoroughly convinced that only the strongest pressure will be of any use in stopping Communism, and that the victory over Communism by any available means takes precedence over everything else. Hence this "hard" position is in fact favorable to nuclear war and makes no distinction between preemption and retaliation, except perhaps to favor preemption as more likely to succeed.

At the same time the "hard" school is convinced that the U.S. government is riddled with Communist agents and spies, and that all opposition to "hard" and conservative policies for building up our nuclear strength proceed from secret Communist plots. In fact they tend to regard anyone who strongly favors peace and disarmament as a Communist "dupe or fellow traveller," simply because of the worldwide propaganda given to the Communist "peace line."

The simplicity and ruthlessness of this view makes an immediate appeal to a very large proportion of the American middle class. It is simple. It is clear. It promises results. It has the advantage above all of permitting disturbed and frustrated people to discharge their anxieties upon a hated enemy and thereby to achieve a sense of meaning and satisfaction in their own lives. But unfortunately this kind of satisfaction leads to moral blindness and to stultification of conscience. The fact that this "solution" at the same time favors nuclear war, and considers it fully moral and justified by its "good cause," and *also appeals to certain types of Christians,* shows that it is a serious danger. To be succinct, it produces a state of invincible moral ignorance. It consecrates policies that have very dubious justice, blurring the ethical clarity of Christian thought, making base emotions and hatreds with the specious appearance of Christian zeal.

Such a judgment applies without doubt to the extreme "hard" position. There are however many gradations in the self-styled "realistic" view. Doubtless there is still much hesitation among conservatives to accept frankly uninhibited use of nuclear weapons. Certainly many of the clergy who are attracted to this kind of position (and they are numerous), would insist that they are thinking only in terms of conventional warfare and of nuclear deterrence. Knowing that total nuclear war, without any distinction between civil and military targets, has been strongly and clearly reproved by the popes, they would insist that they do not advocate such extreme measures. Yet perhaps they would be willing to accept the threat of massive nuclear destruction as a political weapon, and from there it is only a short step to the moral justification of genocide.

Even Edward Teller, "Father of the H-bomb" and a hardnosed nuclear "realist" if there ever was one, asserts that "the idea of massive retaliation is impractical and immoral" but this does not prevent him from being one of the most articulate and influential promoters of nuclear testing and of the arms race in general.[2]

At the same time it is disturbing to note real perversions of Christian ethical principles used to defend nuclear deterrence.

One writer says: *"the paradox of nuclear deterrence is a variant of the fundamental Christian paradox. In order to live we must express our willingness to kill and to die."* This is a falsification of perspective so gross as to be ludicrous. I look in vain for any hint that Christ may have said, "Unless the seed falling on the ground, *kill and die,* itself remains alone"!

Others who take the "hard" view simply ignore the moral issues involved and consider the whole thing with the dispassionate objectivity of the scientists. But unfortunately such objectivity, when it reduces human persons to statistical anonymity as "megapersons" and "megacorpses" and calculates how many millions we can lose "and still get along," has two disastrous effects: it contributes to the same blunting of humane and moral sensibility and it accustoms minds to stoical and indifferent acceptance of nuclear war. It is hard to see how the Christian moral sense can fail to be profoundly affected by the great popularity of writings by Herman Kahn who enjoys almost magical prestige as a prominent member of the Rand Corporation. We must remember that such individuals speak with more than their own personal authority. They have been operating in close conjunction with the highest military and governmental circles and their proposals carry considerable weight in Washington. In a sense, they speak in an aura of quasi-infallible finality. It is no exaggeration to say that the general atmosphere of the United States is one of reverent acceptance of views like these. Though there is widespread dissent among intellectuals and liberals, this very dissent, at a time of crisis, tends to make the dissenter himself appear irresponsible and subversive.

In a word, we confront a solid front of quasi-religious faith in the scientist secularism of the big men with computers. To question their decisions and to protest against the atmosphere of bellicosity they have given us to breathe is to invite contempt and the fury of two thirds of our fellow citizens. Therefore the atmosphere grows daily thicker. The free choice of peace, of disarmament, becomes more and more difficult, less and less probable.

A moderate and halfway position, which can be said to be that of the Kennedy administration and of the theologians, politicians and publicists who rightly enjoy respect for their sanity and depth (as opposed to the wild and superficial intransigence of the "hard" school) takes the view that we must accept the tensions, the risks and the pressures of the Cold War as facts from which there is no escape. The struggle with Communism must continue over a long period, but it must be prevented from exploding into a nuclear war. And yet "softness" and "defeatism" must also be avoided. Hence the thing to do is to build up one's military strength, not excluding the capacity for a nuclear strike, but also with emphasis on conventional forces. At the same time, peaceful and economic measures are to be taken and aid is to be given to underdeveloped countries in the hope that they will appreciate the opportunities and freedoms we enjoy and which we wish to share with them, thus making them our friends and persuading them to join us in resisting the blandishments of Communism.

Theologians and clergymen who adopt this position claim, quite rightly, that insofar as they favor conventional methods of resistance, they are in line with traditional Christian morality.

Finally there is a left wing idealistic viewpoint that favors more extreme measures for peace and appeals to some who remember the spiritual intransigence of past Christian ages or of Oriental religions. This wing is more or less pacifist, ranging from the "nuclear pacifism" of those who reject the use of all nuclear weapons as directly immoral or proximately leading to unjust destruction, to the total pacifism of those who uncompromisingly reject all war whatever. For practical

purposes this whole group may be considered as favoring unilateral disarmament, a policy that is not likely to be adopted
by either the United States, or still less by Russia and China.
In effect, then, this left wing is simply a minority movement
of protest and witness. It includes groups who strive to make
their point by civil disobedience and nonviolent action. In so
doing they irritate and disturb most of their fellow citizens, all
the more so because their intentions are often deliberately mis-
represented by the mass media and condemned out of hand as
Communistic by the "hard" conservatives.

In actual fact this left wing has a certain value, in its insistence on peace and on the uncompromising primacy of
spiritual and moral over political values. But at the same time
it can unquestionably lend itself to subtle manipulation and
abuse by really subversive elements, and in the long run may
even contribute to the danger of war by creating a false idea,
in the minds of the Russian leaders, that America might be
ready to revolt against the managerial autocracy that apparently
favors war.

Since the present volume necessarily implies that I myself
have adopted a particular view of this situation, I might as
well state what that view is.

It seems to me that these tensions, pressures and obsessions
all add up to an extremely serious danger of war. If this kind
of thing continues we are likely to be in a global war within
five years. The moderation of the "center" will hardly be able
to restrain the belligerency of those who take the "hard" view.
Indeed, the influence of the hard school is more and more
evident. Whereas President Kennedy used to assert that the
United States would "never strike first" he is now declaring
that "we may have to take the initiative" in the use of nuclear
weapons.

As our view of the world situation hardens and becomes
more rigid from day to day, our willingness and our ability

to take seriously any measure that might promote peace must inevitably weaken and die away. This is the problem. Without identifying myself with the left wing and with unilateralism, I must confess that their ideals cannot but win my heartfelt sympathy. However I believe that unilateralism pure and simple is a lost cause. There is no serious chance of unilateral disarmament and the amount of debate necessary to get the concept a fair hearing demands an amount of time and effort which would generally seem to be wasted, for even if it is understood it will be rejected by political and military leaders as totally unacceptable to the vast majority who cannot understand it at all.

I therefore align myself with those who take most seriously the need and the possibility of a strong, positive and uncompromising policy of multilateral disarmament.

I believe we cannot afford to renounce our efforts to negotiate a real disarmament agreement. However futile past efforts may have been, we must continue, hoping step by step to reduce our enormous expenditures for armaments, missiles and military installations. We should of course undertake this with the utmost seriousness, facing a real risk of possible error, but facing it with a good faith that cannot help but strengthen our position morally and psychologically all over the world. There is no question that we must avoid extreme and foolhardy risks. We have no moral obligation to render ourselves helpless in the face of an overwhelming enemy power. But we do have an obligation to take graded multilateral disarmament with the fullest possible seriousness.

We cannot take disarmament seriously if we do not believe it has a *positive* value in relaxing tensions and exorcising the menace of nuclear destruction. It is insufficient and delusory to imagine that we can *first* relax the tensions and *then* disarm. We must on the contrary take courageous initiative in disarming in order to reduce the tensions. If no one is willing to be the first to slow down the arms race, disarmament will never be possible.

It seems to me that policies which are content to create an "image" of a benevolent and peace-loving America are valueless, because they lack the depth and the seriousness of motivation which are absolutely necessary for constructive action in a world crisis. Confronted with the difficult task of "assuming world leadership" in a world from which it has remained traditionally and by preference isolated, America seems to have reacted with adolescent panic and truculence. Hostility, unpopularity and totally unsympathetic criticism have proved to be a serious test of the American political ideology.

Faced by the supercilious contempt of friends as well as the hatred of our avowed enemies, and wondering what there is in us to hate, we have considered ourselves and found ourselves quite decent, harmless and easygoing people who only ask to be left alone to make money and have a good time. The keystone of our admittedly nebulous optimism is that if everyone is left alone to take care of his own interests, the laws of economics will benignly take care of the needs of all, and anyone who is not a slacker can get rich. But this philosophy of life is questioned, and when it is questioned we also are forced to examine our beliefs. And when we examine them we find we are not too sure just what they are. We tend to operate on *sentiments* of good will or civilization rather than on deeply based convictions.

When asked what we mean by the "American way of life" we are brought up short, and have to wonder whether we mean more and better refrigerators, TV, Hollywood, Madison Avenue or what? The fact that Americans taken prisoner in Korea were very easily brainwashed while Turks were not, reveals something of the weakness and confusion of our inner motives.

Inability to face this weakness in a rational and mature way may prove one of the most disastrous of historic failures. It is even possible that frustrated and powerful Americans may play a large part in plunging the whole world into nuclear war simply because they cannot stand the tensions and confusion generated by their fundamental uncertainties, their ill-disguised emptiness, their diffuse and universal doubt.

The purpose of this book is not to bolster up a collapsing faith in anything, whether it be democracy or Christianity. I make no claim that the confusion and fury of modern man can be assuaged or better directed simply by obedience to a few religious or political slogans. On the contrary, I think that the adoption of poorly understood and emotionally loaded clichés can do enormous harm when it is brought into play to justify the belligerency of nuclear realists. Yet that seems to be what is most often happening to religious formulas at the present day, at least on the popular level.

It is principally against superficiality and extremism, at a time when war is, as I think, an imminent and serious danger, that I wish to insist above all on one fundamental truth: that all nuclear war, and indeed massive destruction of cities, populations, nations and cultures by any means whatever is a most serious crime which is forbidden to us not only by Christian ethics but by every sane and serious moral code. Policies which we tend to accept without question today, are policies which inevitably pervert our conscience and undermine our capacity for serious and constructive action. The chief reason why we are drifting into nuclear war is that we are confused, empty and discontented. We have no spiritual and ethical center. We do not have the motives which would enable us to build a peaceful world, because we do not have a sufficient reason to restrain our violence. At a time when another Hitler or Stalin is very likely to come on the scene, this is indeed a fatal deficiency.

3

The Dance of Death

N O ONE SERIOUSLY DOUBTS that it is possible for man
and his society to be completely destroyed in a nuclear
war. This possibility must be soberly faced, even though it is so
momentous in all its implications that we can hardly adjust ourselves to it in a fully rational manner. Indeed, this awful threat is
the chief psychological weapon of the Cold War. America and
Russia are playing the paranoid game of nuclear deterrence,
each one desperately hoping to preserve peace by threatening
the other with bigger bombs and total annihilation.

In this sick political maneuvering two things are abundantly
clear: first, the utterly defenseless and helpless civilian populations on both sides are being used as hostages. Naturally this
is more often insinuated than politically proclaimed. After all
this is not calculated to make any nuclear power popular in the
age of less favored nations. "Counterpeople warfare" is logically implied in any "balance of terror" (for after all, it is the
helpless civilian who is supposed to face terror, and does face
it). Secondly, it is quite seriously admitted that this enormous
threat may come to be and is in fact used in an absurd and irrational manner. The illogical logic of deterrence may and does
mean that the threat of annihilation can be brought into play
in a relatively trivial political issue which hardly concerns the
prospective millions of victims even in the most remote manner or in the smallest degree — except by implication in the
fabric of myths which preoccupy the power politicians. This is

what Herman Kahn calls "the Rationality of Irrationality,"[3] in which the objective is credibility at any price — or convincing the enemy that we fully intend to be completely ruthless in our recourse to nuclear weapons. Hardly a climate in which disarmament can appear either meaningful or serious! Has anyone reflected that someone might do well to make disarmament more "credible" than massive retaliation, and make convincing our intentions to keep peace?

There is no control over the arbitrary and belligerent self-determination of the great nations ruled by managerial power elites concerned chiefly with their own political obsessions, their world of war games, and pragmatic myths. The UN is proving itself unable to fulfill the role of international arbiter and powerless to control the pugnacity of the nuclear club. Indeed the big powers have been content to use the UN as a forum for political and propagandist wrestling matches and have not hesitated to take independent action that led to the discrediting of the UN whenever this has been profitable to them. Hence the danger that the uncontrolled power of nuclear weapons may break loose whenever one of the belligerents feels himself strong and sufficiently provoked to risk an all out war. Repeated threats to use the bomb have doubtless been mostly bluff, but one day somebody's bluff is going to be called, perhaps in a very drastic fashion.

Meanwhile Christian moralists have been debating in the background. Very much in the background. For though their judgments may receive a little polite attention from the general public, and may arouse genuine concern in the religious sector of the population, which is an articulate and significant minority, what they say has little direct effect on the policy of the western powers and none whatever on the decisions taken by the Soviets.

We repeat, the tendency of the "realists" and the "hard" thinkers in the United States is more and more towards discarding the moral question as completely irrelevant, if not confusing. The only thing that concerns them is political expediency, and when there is a debate about nuclear testing, or preemptive strike, we are told with finality that "morality has nothing to do with it." Doubtless this only reflects a general ignorance of the true nature of morality. It is probably thought that an ethical decision is one that gives one a good interior feeling of some kind, and naturally the policy makers are concerned with their policies and not with the way a few sensitive souls may *feel* about them.

But the fact remains that objective moral standards exist, whether people know them or not. Choices are made and judged in the light of objective moral laws, and violation of these laws brings disaster.

And so a few theologians and moral philosophers, Catholic, Protestant, and Jewish, have felt bound to express their opinion, and indeed many nonreligious observers contended that the religious spokesmen have been inordinately timid in speaking up. The moral sensibility of distinguished minds outside the religious context (for example, Lewis Mumford) has been notably greater than that of most theologians.

One senses, in the liberal comment upon our hesitancy and our silence, a kind of contempt for what is conceived to be opportunism and cowardice on the part of Christians. It is felt that we have, in general, contented ourselves with a sheepish conformity, a servile respectability which took care to see that our religious people did nothing to question or to oppose the maneuvers of the strategists. To put it bluntly, we priests and theologians are accused more or less explicitly of selling everybody down the river in order to maintain our own status and to protect the social advantages that have been acquired by our religious groups. Our "patriotism" tends to be discredited as the vociferation of publicists who know how to pick the right side and defend it hotly, since it is the side on which their bread is buttered. And, as a matter of fact, everyone more or less has a vested interest in the arms race. Without bombs, missiles, planes, satellites, our life would be somewhat less affluent than it is today!

Meanwhile the United States alone possesses a stockpile of nuclear weapons estimated at sixty thousand megatons. This is more than enough to wipe out the present civilized world and to permanently affect all life on the planet earth. These nuclear bombs can be delivered by some twenty-five hundred planes. It is no secret that such planes are constantly in the air, ready to strike. There are two hundred missiles available to U.S. forces, mostly of intermediate range, and this does not suggest the immediate likelihood of a purely push button war. But it is estimated that by 1963 there will be two thousand more, of which a large proportion will be intercontinental ballistic missiles based in "hard" installations. Attack on hard installations means ground bursts and therefore more fallout as well as more bombs. Hence even an attack concentrated on our missile bases is bound to have a destructive effect on many population centers.

An ICBM can carry an H-bomb warhead to a destination five thousand miles away, twenty times faster than the speed of sound. Intermediate range missiles can be fired from submarines and deliver H-bombs which could reduce the Eastern United States in a few minutes to a radioactive wasteland. H-bombs will soon be fitted to satellites and will be able to reach a target within a few minutes, without hope of interception.

It must be remembered that H-bombs are relatively cheap to produce, and it is not difficult to build and deliver the big ones. Poison gas can also be delivered by long range missiles. One such gas is manufactured in quantity by the U.S. Army Chemical Corps and it can exterminate whole populations of men as if they were insects. A similar nerve gas, originally developed by the Nazis, is manufactured in Soviet Russia. This gas is considered to be more effective against civilian populations than any nuclear agent. It leaves industry and property intact and there is no fallout! Shelters offer no protection against chemical agents.

In a word, the logic of deterrence has proved to be singularly illogical, because of the fact that nuclear war is almost exclusively offensive. So far there is no indication that there can be any really effective defense against guided missiles. All the advantage goes to the force that strikes first, without warning. Hence the multiplication of "hard" weapons sites, and of "deep shelters" becomes provocative and instead of convincing the enemy of our invulnerability, it only invites a heavier preemptive attack by bigger bombs and more of them. The cost of moving a significant portion of industry, business and the population underground is prohibitive and the whole idea is in itself nonsensical, at least as a guarantee of "peace." It makes sense only when one has completely renounced all hope of peace and committed oneself to the prospect of inevitable war. Even then, it offers no serious protection.

Far from producing the promised "nuclear stalemate" and the "balance of terror" on which we are trying to construct an improbable peace, these policies simply generate tension, confusion, suspicion and paranoid hate. This is the climate most suited to the growth of totalitarianism. Indeed, the Cold War itself promises by itself to erode the last vestiges of true democratic freedom and responsibility even in the countries which claim to be defending these values. Those who think that they can preserve their independence, their civic and religious rights by ultimate recourse to the H-bomb do not seem to realize that the mere shadow of the bomb may end by reducing their religious and democratic beliefs to the level of mere words without meaning, veiling a state of rigid and totalitarian belligerency that will tolerate no opposition.

In a world where another Hitler and another Stalin are more and more certain to appear on the scene, the existence of such destructive weapons and the moral paralysis of leaders and policy makers combined with the passivity and confusion of mass societies which exist on both sides of the Iron Curtain, constitute the gravest problem in the whole history of man. Our times can be called apocalyptic, in the sense that we seem to have come to a point at which all the hidden, mysterious dynamism of the "history of salvation" revealed in the Bible has flowered into final and decisive crisis. The term "end of the world" may or may not be one that we are capable of understanding. But at any rate we seem to be assisting at the unwrapping of the mysteriously vivid symbols in the last book of the New Testament. In their nakedness they reveal to us our own selves as the men whose lot it is to live in a time of possibly ultimate decision. In a word, the end of our civilized society is quite literally up to us and our immediate descendants, if any. It is for us to decide whether we are going to give in to hatred, terror and blind love of power for its own sake, and thus plunge our world into the abyss, or whether, restraining our savagery, we can patiently and humanely work together for interests which transcend the limits of any national or ideological community.

Someone may object here that this dark view of the contemporary situation reflects a lack of Christian optimism, and even a pessimistic abdication of Christian hope. But what is Christian optimism, and what constitutes Christian hope? Surely it must be something more than a vague, irresponsible conviction that whatever our sins, errors and mistakes God will prosper our *temporal* affairs and bring us unfailing security and happiness on *earth*. We are promised indeed a temporal as well as an eternal happiness. The good life is indeed available to us on earth in a truly just and well-ordered society. But when, as a result of the greed, folly and desperation of men who have rejected justice, the society of man falls apart, Christian optimism does not consist in hoping that God will put everything back together again exactly as it was before. This is nothing more than an expectation that God will indefinitely bless and protect the status quo. It seems to me that, considering some of the disadvantages of that situation, this is hardly an optimistic view. On the other hand, it is certainly right for us to hope that in spite of all our folly, God in his mercy can and may preserve the human race from global suicide. But surely we remain free to reject his mercy, and this is the terrible danger of the present hour. We are challenged to prove we are rational, spiritual and humane enough to deserve survival, by acting according to the highest ethical and spiritual norms we know. As Christians, we believe that these norms have been given to us in the Gospel and in the traditional theology of the Church. We must however live by these norms in all their depth and seriousness, and not merely invoke them to justify conduct which actually violates their true spirit. Calling upon God to bless nuclear war is a case in point!

4

The Christian as Peacemaker

C HRISTIANS BELIEVE that Christ came into this world as the Prince of Peace. We believe that Christ himself is our peace (Eph. 2:14). We believe that God has chosen for himself, in the Mystical Body of Christ, an elect people, regenerated by the blood of the Savior, and committed by their baptismal promise to wage war upon the evil and hatred that are in man, and help to establish the kingdom of God and of peace.

Indeed for centuries the Old Testament prophets had been looking forward to the coming of the Messiah as the "Prince of Peace" (Isa. 9:5). The messianic kingdom was to be a kingdom of peace because first of all man would be completely reconciled with God and with the hostile forces of nature (Hos. 2:20–22), the whole world would be full of the manifest knowledge of the divine mercy (Isa. 11:9) and hence men, the sons of God and objects of his mercy, would live at peace with one another (Isa. 54:13). The early Christians were filled with the conviction that since the Risen Christ had received Lordship over the whole cosmos and sent his Spirit to dwell in men (Acts 2:17) the kingdom of peace was already established in the Church.

This meant a recognition that human nature, identical in all men, was assumed by the Logos in the Incarnation, and that Christ died out of love for all men, in order to live in all men. All were henceforth "one in Christ" (Gal. 3:28) and Christ himself was their peace, since his Spirit kept them united in supernatural love (Eph. 4:3). Christians therefore have the obligation to treat every other man as Christ himself, respecting his neighbor's life as if it were the life of Christ, his rights as if they were the rights of Christ. Even if the other shows himself to be unjust, wicked and odious to us, we cannot take upon ourselves a final and definitive judgment in his case. We still have an obligation to be patient, and to seek his highest spiritual interests.

The Christian commandment to love our enemies was not regarded by the first Christians merely as a summons to higher moral perfection than was possible under the Old Law. The New Law did not compete with the Old, but on the contrary fulfilled it, at the same time abolishing the conflicts between various forms of obligation and perfection. The love of enemies was not therefore the expression of a Christian moral ideal, in contrast with Stoic, Epicurean or Jewish ideals. It was much more an expression of eschatological faith in the realization of the messianic promises and hence a witness to an entirely new dimension in man's life.

Christian peace was therefore not considered at first to be simply a religious and spiritual consecration of the Pax Romana. It was an eschatological gift of the Risen Christ (John 20:19). It could not be achieved by any ethical or political program. It was given with the supreme gift of the Holy Spirit, making men spiritual and uniting them to the "mystical" Body of Christ. Christian peace is in fact a fruit of the Spirit (Gal. 5:22) and a sign of the divine presence in the world.

Division, conflict, strife, schism, hatreds and wars are then evidence of the "old life," the unregenerate sinful existence that has not been transformed in the mystery of Christ (1 Cor. 1:10; James 3:16). When Christ told Peter to "put away his sword" (John 18:11) and warned him that those who struck with the sword would perish by it, he was not simply forbidding war. War was neither blessed nor forbidden by Christ. He simply stated that war belonged to the world outside the kingdom, the world outside the mystery and the Spirit of Christ and that therefore for one who was seriously living in Christ, war belonged to a realm that no longer had a decisive meaning, for though the Christian was "in the world" he was not "of the world." He could not avoid implication in its concerns, but he belonged to a kingdom of peace "that was not of this world" (John 18:36).

The Christian is and must be by his very adoption as a son of God, in Christ, a peacemaker (Matt. 5:9). He is bound to imitate the Savior who, instead of defending himself with twelve legions of angels (Matt. 26:55), allowed himself to be nailed to the Cross and died praying for his executioners. The Christian is one whose life has sprung from a particular spiritual seed: the blood of the martyrs who, without offering forcible resistance, laid down their lives rather than submit to the unjust laws that demanded an official religious cult of the Emperor as God. One verse in St. John's account of the passion of Christ makes clear the underlying principles of war and peace in the gospel (John 18:36). Questioned by Pilate as to whether he is a king, Jesus replies "My kingdom is not of this world" and explains that if he were a worldly king his followers would be fighting for him. In other words, the Christian attitude to war and peace is fundamentally eschatological. The Christian does not need to fight and indeed it is better that he should not fight, for insofar as he imitates his Lord and master, he proclaims that the messianic kingdom has come and bears witness to the presence of the *Kyrios Pantocrator* in mystery even in the midst of the conflicts and turmoil of the world. The book of the New Testament that definitely canonizes this eschatological view of peace in the midst of spiritual combat is the Apocalypse, which sets forth in mysterious and symbolic language the critical struggle of the nascent Church with the powers of the world, as typified by the Roman Empire.

This struggle, which is definitive and marks the last age of the world, is the final preparation for the manifestation of Christ as Lord of the universe (the *Parousia*) (Rev. 11:15–18). The kingdom is already present in the world, since Christ has overcome the world and risen from the dead. But the kingdom is still not fully manifested and remains outwardly powerless. It is a kingdom of saints and martyrs, priests and witnesses, whose main function is to bide their time in faith, suffering persecution in the furious cataclysm which marks the final breakdown of earthly society. They will take no direct part in the struggles of earthly kingdoms. Their life is one of faith, gentleness, meekness, patience, purity. They depend on no power other than the power of God, and it is God they obey rather than the state, which tends to usurp the powers of God and to blaspheme him, setting itself up in his stead as an idol and drawing to itself the adoration and worship that are due to him alone (Rev. 13:3–9).

The Apocalypse describes the final stage of the history of the world as a total and ruthless power struggle in which all the kings of the earth are engaged, but which has an inner, spiritual dimension these kings are incapable of seeing and understanding. The wars, cataclysms and plagues which destroy worldly society are in reality the outward projection and manifestation of a hidden, spiritual battle. Two dimensions, spiritual and material, cut across one another. To be consciously and willingly committed to the worldly power struggle, in politics, business and war, is to go down to destruction with the world. The saints are "in the world" and doubtless suffer from its murderous conflicts like everybody else. Indeed they seem at first to be defeated and destroyed (13:7). But they see the inner meaning of these struggles and are patient. They trust in God to work out their destiny and rescue them from the final destruction, the accidents of which are not subject to their control. Hence they pay no attention to the details of the worldly power struggle and do not try to influence it or to engage in it, one way or another, even for their own apparent benefit and survival. For they realize that their survival has nothing to do with the exercise of force or ingenuity. The ever recurrent theme of the Apocalypse is then that the typical worldly empire of Babylon (Rome) cannot but be "drunk with the blood of the martyrs of Jesus" (17:6) and that therefore the saints must "go out from her" and break off all relations with her and her sinful concerns (18:4ff.) for "in one hour" is her judgment decided and the smoke of the disaster "shall go up forever and ever" (19:3). Yet the author of the Apocalypse does not counsel flight, as there is no geographical escape from Babylon: the one escape is into a spiritual realm by martyrdom, to lay down one's life in fidelity to God and in protest against the impurity, the magic, the fictitiousness and the murderous fury of the worldly city (21:4–8).

What is the place of war in all this? War is the "rider of the red horse" who is sent to prepare the destruction of the world (6:4) for "he has received power to take away peace from the earth and to make them all kill one another, and he has received a great sword." The four horsemen (war, hunger, death and pestilence) are sent as signs and precursors of the final consummation of history. Those who have led the saints captive will themselves be made captive, those who have killed the saints will themselves be killed in war: and the saints in their time will be rescued from the cataclysm by their patience (13:10).

Translated into historical terms, these mysterious symbols of the Apocalypse show us the early Christian attitude toward war, injustice and the persecutions of the worldly empire, even though that empire was clearly understood to possess a demonic power. The battle was nonviolent and spiritual, and its success depended on the clear understanding of the totally new and unexpected dimensions in which it was to be fought. On the other hand, there is no indication whatever in the Apocalypse that the Christian would be willing to fight and die to maintain the "power of the beast," in other words to defend the pagan Empire.

Nevertheless, it must not be stated without qualification that all the early Christians were purely and simply pacifists and that they had a clear, systematic policy of pacifism which obliged them to refuse military service whenever it was demanded of them. This would be too sweeping an assertion. There were Christians in the armies of Rome, but they were doubtless exceptional. Many of them had been converted while they were soldiers and remained in "the state in which they had been called" (1 Cor. 7:10). They were free to do so because the Imperial army was considered as a police force, maintaining the *Pax Romana,* and the peace of the empire as Origen said (*Contra Celsum* II, 30) was something the early Church was able to appreciate as providential. However, the military life was not considered ideal for a Christian. The problem of official idolatry was inescapable. Many Christian soldiers suffered martyrdom for refusing to participate in the sacrifices. Nevertheless, some soldiers, like St. Maximilian, were martyred explicitly for refusal to serve in the army. Others, like St. Martin of Tours, remained in service until they were called upon to kill in battle, and then refused to do so. Martin, according to the office in the monastic Breviary, declared that "because he was a soldier of Christ it was not licit for him to kill." Christians were the first to lay down their lives rather than fight in a war.

The early Christian apologists condemn military service. Clement of Alexandria again takes up the theme of the Christian soldier as a "soldier of peace" whose only weapons are the word of God and the Christian virtues (*Protreptic* XI, 116).[4] Justin Martyr declares in his *Apology,* "We who formerly murdered one another (he is a convert from paganism) now not only do not make war upon our enemies, but that we may not lie or deceive our judges, we gladly die confessing Christ" (I, 39). St. Cyprian remarked shrewdly that while the killing of one individual by another was recognized as a crime, when homicide is carried out publicly on a large scale by the state it turns into a virtue! (*Ad Donatum* VI, 10). Tertullian declared that when Christ took away Peter's sword, "he disarmed every soldier" (*De Idololatria* XIX).

5

War in Origen
and St. Augustine

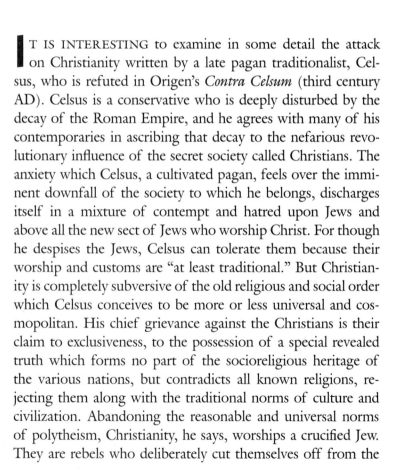

I T IS INTERESTING to examine in some detail the attack
on Christianity written by a late pagan traditionalist, Celsus, who is refuted in Origen's *Contra Celsum* (third century
AD). Celsus is a conservative who is deeply disturbed by the
decay of the Roman Empire, and he agrees with many of his
contemporaries in ascribing that decay to the nefarious revolutionary influence of the secret society called Christians. The
anxiety which Celsus, a cultivated pagan, feels over the imminent downfall of the society to which he belongs, discharges
itself in a mixture of contempt and hatred upon Jews and
above all the new sect of Jews who worship Christ. For though
he despises the Jews, Celsus can tolerate them because their
worship and customs are "at least traditional." But Christianity is completely subversive of the old religious and social order
which Celsus conceives to be more or less universal and cos-
mopolitan. His chief grievance against the Christians is their
claim to exclusiveness, to the possession of a special revealed
truth which forms no part of the socioreligious heritage of
the various nations, but contradicts all known religions, rejecting them along with the traditional norms of culture and
civilization. Abandoning the reasonable and universal norms
of polytheism, Christianity, he says, worships a crucified Jew.
They are rebels who deliberately cut themselves off from the

rest of mankind. They are undermining the whole fabric of society with their insidious doctrines. Above all, they are irresponsible and selfish, indeed antisocial. Instead of returning to the customs of their fathers and living content like the rest of men with the status quo, they refuse to take part in public life, they do not carry out their duties as citizens, and in particular they *refuse to fight in the army*. In a word, they remain callously indifferent to the service of the threatened empire, and have no concern with peace and order, or with the common good.

In a word, Celsus reflects the profound insecurity of one who is totally attached to decaying social forms, and who beholds in some of his contemporaries a complete indifference towards the survival of all that is meaningful to him. Christians not only believed that Celsus' world was meaningless, but that it was under judgment and doomed to destruction. He interpreted the otherworldly Christian spirit as a concrete, immediate physical threat. There was doubtless no other way in which he was capable of understanding it.

Origen replies first of all by vigorously denying that the Christians are violent revolutionaries, or that they have any intention of preparing the overthrow of the empire by force. He says:

> Christians have been taught not to defend themselves against their enemies; and because they have kept the laws which command gentleness and love to man, on this account they have received from God that which they would not have succeeded in doing if they had been given the right to make war, even though they may have been quite able to do so. He always fought for them and from time to time stopped the opponents of the Christians and the people who wanted to kill them.[5]

After this Origen takes issue with the basic contention of Celsus that there have to be wars, because men cannot live

ity. Origen announces the Christian claim that a
for all men to be united in the Logos, though
is most probably eschatological (realized only
after the end and fulfillment of world history). Nevertheless,
Christians are *not totally unconcerned* with the peace, fortunes
and survival of the Empire. Origen does not take the cate-
gorically unworldly view of the Apocalypse. He has a great
respect for Greek and Roman civilization at least in its more
spiritual and humane aspects. The unified Roman world is the
providentially appointed scene for the Gospel *kerygma*.

Origen as a matter of fact was far from antisocial, still less
anti-intellectual. A man who united in himself profound learning, philosophical culture and Christian holiness, Origen took
an urbane, optimistic view of classical thought. Indeed his
arguments against Celsus are drawn in large measure from
classical philosophy and demonstrate, by implication, that a
Christian was not necessarily a boor. The chief value of Origen's apologetic lay in his capacity to meet Celsus on the
common ground of classical learning.

Notice that Origen and Celsus have radically different notions of society. For Celsus, the social life of men is a complex
of accepted traditions and customs which are "given" by the
gods of the various nations and have simply to be accepted,
for, as Pindar said, "Custom is the king of all." Indeed it is im-
pious to question them or try to change them. The cults of the
gods, the rites and practices associated with those cults, are all
good in their own ways, and must be preserved. The Christians
who discard all this are plainly subversive and dangerous.

Origen on the other hand sees that human society has been
radically transformed by the incarnation of the Logos. The
presence in the world of the risen Savior, in and through his
Church, has destroyed the seeming validity of all that was in
reality arbitrary, tyrannical or absurd in the fictions of social

life. He has introduced worship and communal life of an entirely new kind, "in spirit and in truth."

The opening lines of *Contra Celsum* openly declare that it is not only right but obligatory to disobey human laws and ignore human customs when these are contrary to the law of God.

> Suppose that a man were living among the Scythians (cannibals) whose laws are contrary to the Divine law, who had no opportunity to go elsewhere and was compelled to live among them; such a man for the sake of the true law, though illegal among the Scythians, would rightly form associations with like-minded people contrary to the laws of the Scythians. . . . It is not wrong to form associations against the errors for the sake of truth. (I: 1, 7)

But among other things, the Christians are united against war, in obedience to Christ. This is one of their chief differences with the rest of society.

> No longer do we take the sword against any nations nor do we learn war any more since we have become the sons of peace through Jesus who is our author instead of following the traditional customs by which we were strangers to the covenant. (V: 33, 290)

Origen argues, then, that if Christians refuse military service it does not mean that they do not bear their fair share in the common life and responsibilities. They play their part in the life of the *Polis*. But this role is spiritual and transcendent. Christians help the Emperor by their prayers, not by force of arms. "The more pious a man is the more effective he is in helping the emperors — more so than the soldiers who go out into the lines and kill all the enemy troops that they can" (III: 73, 509).

This should not be totally unfamiliar to Celsus. After all pagan priests were officially exempted from military service so that they might be able to offer sacrifices "with hands unstained from blood and pure from murders." Christians both laity and clergy were a "royal priesthood," and did more by their prayers to preserve peace than the army could do by threats of force. "We who by our prayers destroy all demons which stir up wars, violate oaths and disturb the peace, are of more help to the Emperors than those who seem to be doing the fighting" (ibid.).

If at first Origen's claim that the Christians "helped the Emperor" by their prayers may have seemed naive, we see here more clearly what he is driving at. He does not mean that the prayers of the Church enable the Emperor to pursue successfully some policy or other of worldly ambition and power. He does not claim for the prayers of the Church a magic efficacy. He means that prayers are weapons in a more hidden and yet more crucial type of warfare, and one in which the peace of the Empire more truly and certainly depends. In a word, if peace is the objective, spiritual weapons will preserve it more effectively than those which kill the enemy in battle. For the weapon of prayer is not directed against other men, but against the evil forces which divide men into warring camps. If these evil forces are overcome by prayer, then both sides are benefited, war is avoided and all are united in peace. In other words, the Christian does not help the war effort of one particular nation, but he fights against war itself with spiritual weapons.

This basic principle, that love, or the desire of the good of all men, must underlie all Christian action, reappears even more forcefully in St. Augustine. But now we find it incorporated into a defense of the "just war," and the perspective has been completely altered.

Roughly two hundred years separate the two greatest apologetic works of early Christians against the classical world: Origen's *Contra Celsum* and St. Augustine's *City of God*. During these two hundred years a crucially important change has taken place in the Christian attitude to war. Origen took for granted that the Christian is a pacifist. Augustine, on the contrary, pleads with the soldier Boniface not to retire to the monastery but to remain in the army and do his duty, defending the North African cities menaced by barbarian hordes.

In these two hundred years, there have been two events of outstanding importance: the Battle of the Milvian bridge in 312, leading to the conversion of Constantine and his official recognition of Christianity and then, in 411, the fall of Rome before the onslaught of Alaric the Goth. When Augustine developed his theories of the "just war," the barbarians were at the gates of the city of Hippo, where he was bishop.

This is not the place to go into the crucially important question of St. Augustine's ideas of the human commonwealth, the earthly City, and its relations with the City of God. Suffice it to say that the question had become far more complex for him than it had ever been for the innocent and happy Origen.

For Augustine, the essence of all society is union in common love for a common end. There are two kinds of love in man — an earthly and selfish love (*amor concupiscentiae*) and a heavenly, spiritual, disinterested love (*caritas*). Hence there are two "cities" based on these two kinds of love: the earthly city of selfish and temporal love for power and gain, and the heavenly city of spiritual charity. It will be seen at once that this distinction throws the followers of Augustine's theology of war in contemporary America into a radically ambivalent position, for the Augustinian concept of society directly contradicts the optimistic American ethos. Indeed, the current American concept is that love of earthly and temporal ends is automatically self-regulating and leads to progress and happiness.

Every society, according to Augustine, seeks peace, and if it wages war, it does so for the sake of peace. Peace is the "tranquillity of order." But the notion of order in any given society depends on the love which keeps that society together. The earthly society in its common pursuit of power and gain, has only an apparent order — it is the order of a band of robbers, cooperating for evil ends. Yet insofar as it is an order at all, it is good. It is better than complete disorder. And yet it is fundamentally a disorder, and the peace of the wicked city is not true peace at all.

Cain is the founder of the earthly city (Gen. 4:17). Abel founded no city at all, but lived on earth as a pilgrim, a member of the only true city, the heavenly Jerusalem, the city of true peace. For Augustine, as for the Apocalypse and Origen, all history tends toward the definitive victory of the heavenly city of peace. Yet on earth, citizens of heaven live *among* the citizens of earth, though not *like* them.

This creates a problem. Insofar as the Christian lives in the earthly city and participates in its benefits, he is bound to share its responsibilities, though they are quite different from those of the heavenly city. Hence he may possess property, he marries and brings up children although in heaven "no one marries or is given in marriage" (Luke 20:34). *And also he participates in the just wars of the earthly city,* unless he is exempted by dedication to a completely spiritual life in the priestly or monastic state. A pagan, Volusianus, confronted Augustine with the same objection Celsus proposed to Origen. If Christians did not help defend the state, they were antisocial. Augustine replied not that they simply pray for the earthly city, but that they do in all truth participate in its defense by military action, but the war must be a just war and its conduct must be just. In a word, for the earthly city war is sometimes an unavoidable necessity. Christians may participate in the war, or may abstain from participation. But their *motives* will be different from the motives of the pagan soldier. They are not really defending the earthly city, they are waging war to establish peace, since peace is willed by God.

It is no accident that the Protestant thinkers of our own day who rate as nuclear "realists" and defend war as a practical and unavoidable necessity (like Reinhold Niebuhr and Paul Ramsay, for example) owe much, if not everything, to Augustine. But this is not a distinction belonging to Protestants alone. All Catholics who defend the just war theory are following Augustine. *St. Augustine is, for better or for worse, the Father of all modern Christian thought on war.*

Can we not say that if there are to be significant new developments in Christian thought on nuclear war, it may well be that these developments will depend on our ability to get free from the overpowering influence of Augustinian assumptions and take a new view of man, of society and of war itself? This may perhaps be attained by a renewed emphasis on the earlier, more mystical and more eschatological doctrine of the New Testament and the early Fathers, though not necessarily a return to an imaginary ideal of pure primitive pacifism.

What are the basic assumptions underlying Augustine's thought on war? First of all, there is one which Celsus the pagan proposed, and Origen rejected: that it is impossible for men to live without getting into violent conflict with other men. Augustine agrees with Celsus. Universal peace in practice is inconceivable. In the early days of the Church this principle might perhaps have been accepted as logical, but then discarded as irrelevant. The eschatological perspectives of the early Church were real, literal and immediate. The end was believed to be very near. There would not be time for an indefinite series of future wars.

But Augustine saw the shattered and collapsing Empire attacked on all sides by barbarian armies. War could not be avoided. The question was, then, to find out some way to fight that did not violate the law of love. And in order to reconcile war with Christian love, Augustine had recourse to pre-Christian, classical notions of justice. His ideas on the conduct of the just war were drawn to a considerable extent from Cicero.

How does Augustine justify the use of force, even for a just cause? The external act may be one of violence. War is regrettable indeed. But if one's interior motive is purely directed to a just cause and to love of the enemy, then the use of force is not unjust. This distinction between the external act and the interior intention is entirely characteristic of Augustine. "Love," he says, "does not exclude wars of mercy waged by the good" (Letter 138).

But here we come upon a further, most significant development in Augustine's thought. The Christian may join the non-Christian in fighting to preserve peace in the earthly city. But suppose that the earthly city itself is almost totally made up of Christians. Then cooperation between the "two cities" takes on a new aspect, and we arrive at the conclusion that a "secular arm" of military force can be called into action against heretics, to preserve not only civil peace but the purity of faith. Thus Augustine becomes also the remote forefather of the Crusades and of the Inquisition.

"Love does not exclude wars of mercy waged by the good!" The history of the Middle Ages, of the Crusades, of the religious wars has taught us what evil could have been expected from this noble principle. Augustine, for all his pessimism about human nature, did not foresee the logical results of his thought, and in the original context, his "wars of mercy" make a certain amount of sense. Always his idea is that the Church and the Christians, whatever they may do, are aiming at ultimate peace. The deficiency of Augustinian thought lies therefore not in the good intentions it prescribes but in an excessive naïveté with regard to the good that can be attained by violent means which cannot help but call forth all that is worst in man. And so, alas, for centuries we have heard kings, princes, bishops, priests, ministers, and the Lord alone knows what variety of unctuous beadles and sacrists, earnestly urging all men to take up arms out of love and mercifully slay their enemies (including other Christians) without omitting to purify their interior intention. This, in fact, has been carried to such incredible extremes as to constitute one of the more enormous scandals in the story of Christendom. The fact that it still goes on, without respite, without compunction, without the blessing of even the slightest awareness of implicit ironies, is one of the most depressing features of Christian justifications of nuclear war.

Of course when we read Augustine himself, and when we see that he imposes such limits upon the Christian soldier and traces out such a strict line of conduct for him, we can see that the theory of the just war was not altogether absurd, and that it was capable of working in ages less destructive than our own. But one wonders at the modern Augustinians and at their desperate maneuvers to preserve the doctrine of the just war from the museum or the junk pile. In the name of "realism" (preserving, that is to say, a suitable dash of Augustinian pessimism about fallen man) they plunge into ambivalence from which Augustine was fortunately preserved by the technological ignorance of his dark age. One wishes that his moderate followers had enough sense of proportion to realize what Augustinian pessimism really implies when the city of this world is no longer allied with the City of God, and when its citizens, restored to the plain state of respectable and efficient robbers, are armed in spirit with the cynicism of Machiavelli and Clausewitz, and armed in the flesh with devices capable of destroying continents. To ask such men to restrain their violence, to put a limit to their ambitions in the most unrestrained and unrestrainable struggle for power the world has ever known, and to ask them to please be so kind as to restrict themselves to a "just war" according to patterns in ancient authors they have neither read nor heard of . . . this would provoke despair if it did not first reduce us to a state of merriment.

Augustine kept a place in his doctrine for a certain vestige of the eschatological tradition. There were some Christians who would not be permitted to fight: these were the monks, first of all, the men who had totally left the world and abandoned its concerns to live in the kingdom of God, and then the clergy who preached the Gospel of Peace — or at least the Gospel of the merciful war. Yet as Christianity spread over Europe and the ancient Roman strain was vivified and restored by the addition of vigorous barbarian blood from the north, even monks and clerics were sometimes hard to restrain from rushing to arms and loving exuberantly with the sword. Do we not read that when a Frankish ship loaded with Crusaders ran into the Byzantine fleet in the first Crusade, the Byzantines were shocked at a Latin priest who stood on the stern covered with blood and furiously discharged arrows at them, clad in vestments, too: and he even went on shooting after the declaration of a truce.*

Still, there were recognized limits. Councils sternly restricted warfare. In tenth-century England a forty-day fast was prescribed as penance for anyone who killed an enemy in war — even in a just war. Killing was regarded as an evil to be atoned for even if it could not be avoided.[6] However, later theologians of the Middle Ages (Migne, 125.841) made clear that killing in a just war was not a sin and intimated that the soldier who did this required no penance, as he had done a work pleasing to God. We were then close to the time of the Crusades. But even then, especially in wars among Christians themselves, severe limitations were prescribed. War might be virtuous under

---

*This was in the First Crusade. Anna Comnena, "Alexiad" in R. H. Bainton, *Christian Attitudes to War and Peace: A Historical Survey and Critical Re-evaluation* (New York: Abingdon Press, 1960), 114.

certain conditions, but even then, good or bad, one must sometimes abstain from it at any cost. The truce of God in the tenth
century forbade fighting on holy days and in holy seasons.
The hesitation and ambivalence of the Christian warrior are
reflected in a curious oath of Robert the Pious (tenth century),
who wrote:

> I will not take a mule or a horse ... in pasture from any
> man from the kalends of March to the Feast of All Saints,
> unless to recover a debt. I will not burn houses or destroy
> them unless there is a knight inside. I will not root up
> vines. I will not attack noble ladies traveling without hus-
> band, nor their maids, nor widows or nuns unless it is
> their fault. From the beginning of Lent to the end of
> Easter, I will not attack an armed knight.*

It is easy to find texts like these which bring out the ridiculous inner inconsistencies that are inseparable from this view
of war and the constant temptation to evade and rationalize
the demands of the just war theory. The twofold weakness of
the Augustinian theory is its stress on a subjective purity of intention which can be doctored and manipulated with apparent
"sincerity" and the crucial importance of the way each situation is interpreted. Robert the Pious is characteristically naive
when he blandly assumes that traveling nuns might at any moment be "at fault" and give a knight such utterly intolerable
provocation that he would "have to attack them" — with full
justice. Expanded to the megatonic scale, and viewing as licit
the destruction of whole cities which are suddenly "at fault,"
this reasoning is no longer funny!

The history of this doctrine is not to be written here. Let
us remember, however, that in the sixteenth century, Christian Conquistadors felt themselves to be obliged by a kind of

---

*Robert the Pious, quoted in Bainton, 110.

divine mission to destroy civilizations "which carried out practices contrary to the natural law" (viz., the Aztecs and human sacrifices — or any other form of idolatry). This concept of Christian civilization with a mandate and obligation to punish and reform the lesser breeds without the law is still unfortunately prevalent in the west, even though the west is no longer Christian. It underlies the whole concept of the nuclear crusade against Communism.

A modern development has led to a very serious questioning of some assumptions underlying the just war theory. In 1944, in the heat of World War II with its annihilation "area bombing" of cities, Fr. John C. Ford, in a significant article rejected the opinion that an airman can bomb whole areas of a city indiscriminately, provided only that *he does not directly intend* to kill civilians.[7] There are certain acts which by their very nature are directed against the innocent, and no interior "purity of intention" can change their intrinsically evil character.

6

The Legacy of Machiavelli

I T SEEMS LIKELY that the doctrine of the just war and the moral inhibitions it implied did, at times, restrain barbarity in medieval war. We know that when the crossbow was invented it was at first banned by the Church as an immoral and cruel weapon.

However, in the Renaissance we find Machiavelli, one of the Fathers of *Realpolitik,* frankly disgusted with the half-heartedness and inefficiency with which wars were being carried on by certain Princes. It is instructive to read his grammar of power, *The Prince,* and to see how his pragmatic, not to say cynical, doctrines on the importance and the conduct of war are precisely those which are accepted in practice today in the international power struggle. It is difficult to say whether many of the more belligerent policy makers of our time have read Machiavelli, but one feels that he would be a man after our own heart: one who tolerates no nonsense about preparing wars that one does not intend to take seriously.

As Machiavelli is completely indifferent to all moral considerations, we can say that he implicitly discards the theory of the just war as totally irrelevant. And in a sense one can agree with his evident contempt for all the absurd mental convolutions that Robert the Pious had to go through to provide escape clauses for his belligerent needs. It is certainly more practical, if what you intend is war, simply to go ahead and wage war without first vowing not to fight and then creating exceptional cases in which your vow is no longer binding. Surely we can agree that this is a great waste of time and energy and it may lead to fatal errors and to defeat. In a world of power politics, there is no question that conscience is a great nuisance. But it is also true that in *any situation,* a conscience that juggles with the law and seeks only to rationalize evasions, is not only a nuisance but a fatal handicap.

One might almost say that the present power struggle presents man with two clear alternatives: we can be true to the logic of our situation in two ways — either by discarding conscience altogether and acting with pure ruthlessness, or else by purifying our conscience and sharpening it to the point of absolute fidelity to moral law and Christian love. In the first case we will certainly destroy one another. In the second, we may stand a chance of survival.

The Prince, says Machiavelli, should have "no other aim or thought but war." He should reflect that disarmament would only render him contemptible. And in order to guard against temptation to relax his vigilance and reconcile himself to peace, the Prince must learn how not to be too good:

> A man who wishes to make profession of goodness in everything must necessarily come to grief among so many who are not good. Therefore it is necessary for a Prince who wishes to maintain himself to learn how not to be good, and to use this knowledge and not use it, according to the necessity of the case.[8]

After all, the Prince must be practical. Not only must he create a suitable image of himself, as we would say today: not only must he be feared rather than loved (unless he is smart enough to be both loved and feared at the same time), but he must be feared with very good reason. He must not listen to conscience, or to humane feeling. He must not practice virtue when it is not expedient to do so, and he must not let himself be either too kind, too generous, or too trustworthy. Let him not waste time abiding by legalities or by his pledged word, unless it happens to be useful. Virtue, Machiavelli warns, has ruined many a prince. It is better to rely on force.

> There are two methods of fighting, the one by law and the other by force: the first method is that of men, the second of beasts; but as the first method is often insufficient, one must have recourse to the second. It is well then for a prince to know well how to use both the beast and the man (XVIII, 77).

This is the kind of practicality that is taken for granted but seldom stated so clearly in our age of power. It is refreshing to see it set forth with such primitive and pleasant frankness, free from all double-talk. Machiavelli goes on to justify this line of conduct, with reasons which constitute in their own way a kind of "humanism." Cruelty, he says, is after all more merciful than an indulgent softness which leads only to disorder and chaos in the long run. Better to be firm like

> Cesare Borgia. (Machiavelli has nothing but praise for the Borgias). Cesare Borgia was considered cruel, but his cruelty had brought order to Romagna, united it, and reduced it to peace and fealty. If this is considered evil, it will be seen that he was in reality much more merciful than the Florentine people who, to avoid the name of cruelty, allowed Pistoia to be destroyed (XVII, 72).

This is exactly the argument we hear today from the nuclear realists. The only hope of peace and order, according to them, is the toughest, hardest and most intransigent nuclear policy. This in the long run is "merciful" and peaceful. The difference is that in Machiavelli's time, though his arguments appealed mightily to certain powerful Christians, there was no effort made to say that his doctrine constituted a strict moral obligation. They were just accepted as the "reality" of political life and left at that. But today the man who is not ready to be ruthless with the enemy is considered by some a lax Christian and a traitor to the cause of freedom.

Incidentally, Machiavelli was not praising simply the *appearance* of cruelty, although this is a necessary minimum. He thought that one of the chief qualities of Hannibal had been his genuine inhumanity. It really kept his army together!

While St. Augustine transferred the question of war into the internal forum and concentrated on the intention of the Christian to wage a just war, Machiavelli ignores the internal situation as completely irrelevant. He is concerned with the brute objective facts of the power struggle — a struggle in which conscience generates only ambivalence and therefore leads to defeat. Morality interferes with efficiency, therefore it is absurd to concern oneself with moral questions which in any case are practically meaningless.

For Machiavelli power is an end in itself. Persons and policies are means to that end. And the chief means is war, not a "just" war but a victorious war. As Clausewitz was to say in our modern age of *Realpolitik:* "*To introduce into the philosophy of war a principle of moderation would be absurd. War is an act of violence pursued to the uttermost.*"

And this of course was a philosophy which guided the policies of Hitler. The rest of the world, for all its good intentions, was forced to learn it from Hitler in order to beat him. With nuclear weapons, the principles of unlimited destruction and violence has become in practice axiomatic. Deputy Defense Secretary of the United States Roswell Gilpatric declared in 1961:

> We are not going to reduce our nuclear capability. Personally I have never believed in a limited nuclear war. I do not know how you would build a limit into it when you use any kind of nuclear bang.[9]

Yet Machiavelli was not altogether typical of the Renaissance. Leonardo da Vinci, the exemplar of Renaissance genius, developed a plan for a submarine but destroyed the plan without making it known because he saw that the only serious purpose of an underwater craft would be treacherous and hidden attack in naval war. In his mind, this was immoral.

While *The Prince* is a clear and articulate expression of the principles of power politics, we must be careful not to assume that the present power struggle is purely and simply Machiavellian. This would be a grave error.

On the contrary, it is reasonable to suppose that in our day Machiavelli would have proceeded on different and more original assumptions, for this is no longer an age of warring princes or Italian city-states. He would doubtless be able to see through the romantic mythology with which the power struggle has been invested (for instance the ideas of proletarian, nationalist or racist messianism) and he would certainly recognize the importance of rational control over the vast technological developments which, in fact, dominate our policies.

It would above all be a mistake to imagine that Communism is Machiavellian. True, it has consistently followed the same line of objective pragmatism, discarding all moral considerations whatever. But it is nevertheless dominated by a mythology and in this mythology war is far from being the chief direct instrument of power. On the contrary, the Marxian dialectic is one of power through revolution and in this dialectic war appears as the fatal weakness of the capitalist system. According to the Marxian theory, capitalist imperialism necessarily exhausts and destroys itself in war, and when the structure of war-torn capitalist states collapses, then the revolution will take over. Consequently, the ideal situation for Communism is a state of war between two capitalist empires.

The fact that the state capitalism of Russia is now aligned against the private capitalism of the United States may indeed be a situation regarded as highly desirable by Red China which considers itself the true interpreter of the Marxian doctrine.

In view of the Marxist conviction, and it is an absolute conviction, that self-destructive belligerency is built into the capitalist economy, we would do well to reflect that the ever increasing velocity and expansion of our armament production can only be regarded in Moscow as a complete confirmation of Marxist theories. This is one of the chief reasons why Russia is as completely distrustful of the United States, as the United States are of Russia — indeed probably more so. The Russian conviction that America intends to destroy Communism by war is as firm as the American conviction that Communism intends to destroy capitalism by revolution. Both convictions are well founded, for each one rests solidly on the other. Only a really serious and profound change of policy can break this vicious circle. Unless both Russia and America are willing to prove their faith in the power of their respective systems by serious negotiations and turning their technology to peaceful uses, their ruin is assured.

To return to Machiavelli: though *The Prince* is a frankly immoral book it has never been on the Index of books forbidden to Catholics. We may suppose that it was read by many a Christian prince, and there is no doubt that the principle of "double effect" was developed and used in some measure to help keep the power politics of such princes in concord with at least a bare minimum of Christian morality. According to this principle, an end which is in itself not evil, and which is directed by means that are not evil, may be pursued even if evil side effects accidentally occur, provided they are not directly willed.

The classic example of double effect, given in the moral theologies of the seventeenth and eighteenth centuries, is this: You are fleeing for your life on horseback. To save yourself you must ride through a narrow place and there is a child lying in the path. Saving your life is a good end; there is nothing evil about riding a horse. There is no other avenue of escape. It is unfortunate that you have to ride over the child. This may mean injuring him or even killing him. You do not directly will his death but the fact that the child is there does not place you under any moral *obligation* to renounce your own safety. Hence you can go on, and even if the child is killed you are not held morally responsible.

This is of course an example of casuistry, and it obviously shows why casuistry has a bad name. We might ask if that bad name is not in some respects perfectly justified. The moral *casus conscientiae* was originally devised, in early manuals for confessors, as a guide to the solution of difficult cases *after they had occurred*. But a casuistical formation in moral theology tended to make confessors and directors of conscience consider these minimal and extraordinary cases almost as if they were ordinary norms. It is one thing to assert that in an extreme and exceptional situation a "lesser evil" may be "permitted" (though not "directly willed") and quite another to build a whole theory of Christian ethics on boundary line cases where the exceptional and the minimal becomes the norm.

What hope is there of a genuinely Christian conduct if it is *assumed a priori* as quite normal to regard the death of an innocent child as a "lesser evil" than one's own capture? What happens, in such circumstances, to the Christian emphasis in the Gospel and in the early Church, on the sacrifice of one's own interests for others? What, in a word, happens to the Christian emphasis on the greater good? It is replied that such emphasis is "only of counsel" and is "not demanded." This may be strictly true according to the letter of the law, but to live by such assumptions means in practice to live by totally unchristian and even amoral presuppositions.

It is precisely this climate of assumptions which has favored the development of ideas propounded in the "shelter panic" of 1961, about the morality of shooting a neighbor who tries to "invade" your fallout shelter. It seems our ethical thought has become entirely obsessed with rare, strange and one might add symbolic situations in which one is allowed to get by with something which, on the face of it, is a violation of the Christian law of love. It may be true that such exceptional situations exist: but why concentrate on them and forget the real norm of Christian justice and charity? The exceptional violence is now the norm of our thinking, while charity has become exotic.

Machiavelli wrote his advice for the individual monarch, in a day when men believed in the divine right of kings. But after Machiavelli, political thought underwent considerable evolution. The "Prince" was replaced by the "Sovereign State," and the revolutions which sought to liberate man from the tyranny of absolute monarchs brought them under the more subtle and more absolute tyranny of an abstraction. Just as mathematics, business and technology needed the discovery of zero in order to develop, so too political and economic power needed the faceless abstractions of state and corporation, with their unlimited irresponsibility, to attain to unlimited sovereignty. Hence the paradox that in the past ages usually regarded as times of slavery the individual actually counted for much more than he does in the alienation of modern economic, military and political totalism. At the same time it is the modern, irresponsible, faceless, alienated man, the man whose thinking and decisions are the work of an anonymous organization, who becomes the perfect instrument of the power process. Under such conditions, the process itself becomes totally self-sufficient and all absorbing. As a result the life and death not only of individual persons, families and cities, but of entire nations and civilizations must submit to the blind force of amoral and inhuman forces. The "freedom" and "autonomy" of a certain minority may still seem to exist: it consists in little more than understanding the direction of the historically predetermined current and rowing with the stream instead of against it. There should be no need to point out the demonic potentialities of such a situation.

Morality is the intelligent and ordered exercise of freedom not according to arbitrary and pragmatic interpretations of events but according to deeper and more fundamental principles which are dictated by the "nature" of things and persons themselves. Amoral decisions are those which do not take into account the objective underlying order of realities, in terms of means and ends, but which are moved simply by the impact of events seen and understood in the light of certain superficial assumptions.

Amoral conduct pretends to be more "realistic" than morality because it thinks itself to be more aware of the actual event in its concreteness. In point of fact, one of the greatest dangers of amorality is precisely its lack of realism. Not without reason did the Sapiential books of the Old Testament call the amoral and opportunistic man by the name of "fool." The very appearance of concreteness and objectivity in amoral conduct may be its greatest deception. The amoral man may think himself keenly aware of the actuality of objective facts, when in reality he is simply experiencing the pressure and urgency of his own assumptions. Indeed, he may purely and simply be projecting his irrational and symbolic obsessions on the exterior world and experiencing them as objective realities, in which case he is not only unrealistic but mentally ill.

So we come to a comparison between the so-called realism of the nuclear realist, his assumptions magnified and objectified beyond measure by electronic computers, and the realism of Machiavelli.

In a way the glib self-assurance of a book like *The Legacy of Hiroshima*[10] and its clear insistence, in short comprehensible words, upon a tough and transparent nuclear policy, may sound a little like Machiavelli. The resemblance is quite obvious in the systematic amorality of Teller's thesis.

Teller is dignified by the benign sounding title of "Father of the H-bomb." He is a Hungarian who fled from Europe in the thirties and worked on the atomic bomb project at Los Alamos during World War II. He describes the moral convulsions of fellow scientists over the use of the bomb, and even suggests that he himself might have toyed with the temptation to share them. He tells how, after Hiroshima, when all the other atomic scientists were "sick of the bomb" and all dispersed to various universities, he stayed at Los Alamos trying desperately to interest someone in his project to develop a thermonuclear device of immense destructive power.

The burden of this story is that the moral hesitations of atomic scientists were the great obstacle to the bomb and consequently to America's adoption of a suitable defense posture.

At a meeting of the General Advisory Committee of the AEC [Atomic Energy Commission] in 1949, unanimous decision against the H-bomb was summed up in a report stating: "We all hope that by one means or another the development of these (thermonuclear) weapons can be avoided. We are all reluctant to see the United States take the initiative in precipitating this development..." (*Legacy*, 43). At the same time, more succinct opinions were set down in two other reports which were not at that time made public. These two opinions represented more articulate modalities of opposition to the H-bomb. The majority declared, "In determining not to proceed to develop the super bomb we see an unique opportunity of providing by example some limitations on the totality of war and thus eliminating the fear and arousing the hopes of mankind." A minority report, signed by Enrico Fermi and I. I. Rabi, expressed outspoken moral opposition to the bomb. It declared:

The fact that no limits exist to the destructiveness of this weapon makes its very existence and the knowledge of its construction a danger to humanity as a whole. It is necessarily an evil thing considered in any light. For these reasons we believe it important for the president of the United States to tell the American public and the world that we think it wrong on fundamental ethical principles to initiate the development of such a weapon. (*Legacy,* 43–44)

In the eyes of Teller, on the other hand, these scientist were simply not facing facts: above all the fact that the Soviet Union would probably soon develop the superbomb itself. As a matter of fact in August 1949 it was announced that Russia had developed an atomic weapon.

Teller regards the problem of the bomb as a matter of policy rather than as a moral option. Though he is not totally unconcerned with the moral issue, and one feels that the moral arguments against total nuclear war are arguments to which he is certainly sensitive, his judgments are principally on the level of strategy. But even on this level, Teller rejects the "doctrine" of massive nuclear retaliation, and his rejection of the doctrine is not without moral overtones.

We should never have subscribed to this doctrine. We should never have declared that we would respond to limited Soviet acts of aggression with a massive all-out attack. Under no circumstances would we be justified in striking the first blow in an all-out war. If we had certain knowledge that the Russians would unleash the full fury of an atomic attack against us tomorrow, I still would say that in anticipation we should not strike the first blow today. My reason for saying this is not practical. I say it because I think it is right. But I believe to abstain from striking the first blow also happens to be the only practical policy. (*Legacy,* 261)

One can have nothing but praise for such an opinion.

7

Justice in Modern War

I N 1917, the poet Siegfried Sassoon, who had been fighting in the British Army since the opening days of World War I, wrote the following in a letter to the London *Times*.

> I believe that this war which I entered as a war of defense has now become a war of aggression and conquest. I believe that the purpose for which I and my fellow soldiers entered upon this war should have been so clearly stated as to have made it impossible to change them and that, had this been done, the objects that actuated us would now be attainable by negotiation.
>
> (from *The Listener*, February 8, 1962)

This raises a grave problem. When a war has been begun as a "just war," it may turn into an unjust war when clearly unjust means are resorted to and when the inhumanity of unlimited ruthlessness takes possession of the combatants and strategists. There is no denying that in the heat of war, the morality of the "just war" doctrine tends to be forgotten. This has been particularly true in modern warfare which has become more and more aggressive and offensive, and in which the overwhelming power of aerial bombardment has been unleashed against the enemies' cities and civilian populations.

The facts in this chapter are taken from a valuable study by Robert C. Batchelder, *The Irreversible Decision* (Boston: Houghton Mifflin, 1961).

In World War II, in which the Allied forces fighting Nazism undoubtedly had a just cause, judged by the traditional norms, the ruthless policy of demanding "unconditional surrender" led to greater and greater fury in their use of air bombardment and culminated in the atomic destruction of Hiroshima and Nagasaki.

At the end of World War II, many theologians openly began to discuss the question whether the old standards of the just war could be enforced in practice. It seemed to some of them at that time that the obliteration bombing of the cities on both sides, culminating in the total destruction of Hiroshima and Nagasaki by one plane with one bomb for each, had completely changed the nature of war. There was no longer any distinction made between civilian and combatant. Where this distinction was obliterated, or tended to be obliterated, how could one decide that the use of force was just?

The principle of double effect requires that there be no serious disproportion between the good one "intends" and the evil one "permits." Is this requirement satisfied when you "permit" the slaughter of fifty thousand civilians in order to stop production in three or four factories? (Investigation showed that even when there had been massive damage and countless deaths inflicted by obliteration bombing, the factories themselves were not always crippled very long, and soon resumed production.)

Could one appeal to the principle of double effect when the slaughter of civilians was explicitly *intended* as a means to "breaking enemy morale" and thus breaking his "will to resist"? This was pure terrorism, and the traditional doctrine of war excluded such immoral methods. Traditional morality also excluded torture of prisoners, murder of hostages chosen at random, extermination of racial groups for no other reason than race, etc. These methods were practiced by the enemy, and

after the war ended *they were bequeathed to the western nations.*
France in Algeria, for instance.

How did precision bombing (allowed by traditional standards of justice) turn into obliteration bombing? How did
ethical theory gradually come to defend obliteration bombing, and even mass destruction by atomic weapons? How is
it that we are now almost ready to permit any outrage, any
excess, any horror, on the ground that it is a "lesser evil" and
"necessary" to save our nation?

The deliberate terroristic annihilation of defenseless civilians
for military and political purposes, is perhaps not completely
new. In all ages there have been calculated terrorism, the
slaughter of innocents in war. It was never seriously considered
as either very necessary or very useful in the actual process of
winning a war. It was more or less a "bonus." (You remember perhaps the report on the raid that annihilated Dresden?
The city was full of refugees fleeing from the Russians in
the east. The death of several thousand extra victims was announced with sober joy as a "bonus" by those who commanded
the raid.)

Traditional Christian teaching, which deplored war itself
even under the best of conditions, never hesitated to condemn
terrorism in war as a very grave crime. Now terrorism is no
longer taken so seriously. We are seriously told that it is the
"duty" of our government to arm to the teeth with nuclear
weapons capable of wiping out whole cities, whole nations, or
even life itself. A conservative estimate declares that the United
States probably now stocks the equivalent in explosive power
of *ten tons of TNT for every human being on the face of the earth.*
We are going beyond the limits of strict duty, just in case.

Terror from the air, as a deliberately planned policy, was
characteristic of the Nazi and Fascist Axis. As a matter of fact
the honor of having initiated it in Europe belongs to Franco
Spain and Fascist Italy. The place? Guernica, a Christian city,

in the Christian province of the Basques, in Christian Spain. Date: 1937. Also please remember Nanking, China. Same year. Not so many Christians. We protested.

Poland was the next victim. Reduced to nothing in a few days by the Luftwaffe. 1939. England came next.

It is to the everlasting credit of the British that although the civilians of England suffered one crushing blow after another, and saw whole sections of their cities reduced to rubble, the government declared that the RAF would abide by traditional methods, and would confine itself to the strategic bombing of military targets only. But since daylight raids were very costly, most of the attacks had to be carried out at night. This made precision bombing very difficult, and in the end civilians suffered more than industry. So "area bombing," the destruction of the whole neighborhood that included a military target, was already in force by the time America came into the war. America determined to stick to the traditional ethical code. Roosevelt at first announced that the USAF would confine itself to strategic bombing.

It was Air Marshall Sir Arthur Travers Harris who opened up with obliteration bombing against German cities in 1942. Not only was this aimed at the "sure" destruction of factories and military objectives that might otherwise be missed, but frankly and explicitly the intention was to "destroy enemy morale." "There are no lengths in violence to which we will not go" to achieve this end, declared Churchill. And another government spokesman, unidentified, said, "Our plans are to bomb, burn and ruthlessly destroy, in every way available to us, the people responsible for creating this war."

Here we have already one complete cycle. A country begins a defensive "just war." It starts by declaring its firm adherence to the ethical principles held by its Church, and by the majority of its civilian population. The nation accepts unjust suffering heroically. But then the military begins to grow impatient, seeing that its own methods of retaliation are not effective. It is *the military that changes the policy.* The new, more ruthless policy pays off. The civilian protest is silenced before it begins. Those who might otherwise have objected, come to accept what they are told: "This will save lives. It is necessary to end the war sooner, and to punish the unjust aggressor."

The standards of justice are still in view — still *partially* in view. The injustice of the aggressor is very clearly seen. Justice in the use of means has been lost sight of, and what counts most is expediency.

We cannot lightly blame the courageous people who suffered so much and were so eager for the war to end. But . . . the Allies had come around to adopting the same methods precisely, the same ruthless inhumanity which made the enemy unjust. Injustice was now common to both sides. Needless to say, both were now strenuously arguing and convincing themselves, in exactly the same terms, that their war effort was just, that their methods were just, and that it was necessary to do all that they did in order to win the victory; end the war quickly and "save lives."

Note also, on both sides there were sincere Christians, encouraged by the clergy and by the Christian press to accept and support these claims. There were therefore Christians believing that each side was completely just. Christians on both sides "served God" by killing each other. . . . What had become of the meaning of the doctrine of the "just war"? What had become of Christian ethics in this situation? Did anyone stop to reflect on the total absurdity of this self-contradiction on the part of Christians? Not the least appalling contradiction lay in the fact that German Christians heroically sacrificed themselves to defend a government that cruelly persecuted the Church. In defense of Hitler's neopaganism, which advocated a totally immoral policy, they fought their fellow Christians of France, England and America.

America was obviously going to follow the tactics England had been forced to take over from the Nazis by the very logic of war. The USAF soon began obliteration bombing. A protest was published in *Fellowship,* the magazine of the Fellowship of Reconciliation, in 1944. Obliteration bombing was condemned by this magazine and by a group of Protestant ministers. The protest was taken seriously enough to get an official reply. Roosevelt said that these tactics were necessary to "shorten the war." There was a nationwide discussion of the issue. Americans were fifty to one against those who protested. They thought these moral scruples were ridiculous. To demand cessation of obliteration bombing was pure defeatism.

All distinction between precision bombing and obliteration bombing was forgotten in the general indignation. What mattered was to beat Hitler and right the wrong that had been done. Any methods that helped procure this end were justifiable.

One dissenting voice was that of a Catholic priest, Fr. John C. Ford, S.J., who argued that the obliteration bombing of cities was immoral and could not be defended by the principles of double effect.

Meanwhile the United States was working feverishly to develop the atomic bomb, believing that Hitler's scientists were on the point of perfecting this weapon that would multiply thousands of times the destructiveness of ordinary bombing.

However, before the atomic bomb was used, the B-29 bomber command in the Pacific had come to realize the failure of precision bombing of Japanese military targets. It was not possible to seriously slow down production by this means.

Early in 1945, General Curtis LeMay decided, on his own responsibility, to initiate a devastating new tactic of massive low-flying fire raids by night.

On the night of March 9–10 the whole of Tokyo was set afire with napalm bombs. The blaze was so furious that it boiled the water of the canals. Fire storms consumed all the oxygen and many who were not burned to death suffocated. So frightful were the effects of this raid that it claimed as many casualties as the atom bombing of Hiroshima.

Some apologists for all-out war point to this fact, saying that since there is in reality no difference between total war carried on by conventional weapons and total war carried on by nuclear weapons, there is no new moral issue involved. On the contrary, this calls for a clarification of the real moral issue. The issue is precisely this: not that atomic and nuclear weapons are immoral while conventional weapons are just, but that *any resort to terrorism and total annihilation is unjust, whatever be the weapons it employs.*

The Tokyo raid, followed by similar raids on more than fifty other Japanese cities, was justified on the grounds that much of the Japanese war effort depended on the "phantom industry," the detailed piecework on small parts carried on by individuals in their homes. Hence residential areas came to be just as "legitimate" a target as factories themselves. This fact contributed to the loose generalization, now widely accepted, without further qualifications, that in "modern war everyone is considered to be a combatant." Hence even residential areas became "military targets."

Already in May and June of 1945 the American High Command was considering the choice of an appropriate target for the new bomb.

In discussing the choice of the target, Truman and his advisers did not speak of this or that naval base, this or that fortress, this or that concentration of troops, this or that particular munitions plant. In Truman's own words: "Stimson's staff had *prepared a list of cities* in Japan that might serve as targets...." Later in the context Truman speaks of the entire city of Hiroshima as a "military target."

We must remember that in the list of cities originally considered was Kyoto, the religious capital of Japanese Buddhism. Kyoto was in no sense a military target.

There were of course industries in Hiroshima, but its "military" importance was so slight that it had hardly been touched so far. It had even been neglected by LeMay's incendiaries.

In other words, the "targets" considered for the atomic bomb were purely and simply cities. Any city at all, by the mere fact of being a city, was now a "military target." The fact that Kyoto was among them indicates that moral and psychological effect, in other words terrorism, was the dominant consideration in the minds of the high command.

Hiroshima was chosen in order that an "untouched" target might show the power of the bomb. The idea was to unleash the maximum destructive power on a civilian center, to obliterate that center and destroy all further will to resist in the Japanese nation. The word "target" and the word "city" had become completely identified.

Once again, moral thinking had gone through a full cycle in the short space of two or three years. The United States had entered the war with the conviction of the justice of its cause and with the firm intention to abide by just means.

However, it is possible that the notion of "just means" was much more nebulous in the American mind than it had been in the English. Moral thinking guided by pragmatic principles tends to be very vague, very fluid. Moral decisions were now a series of more or less opportunistic choices based on short term guesses of possible consequences, rather than on definite moral principles.

It is quite certain that though the American public conscience was characterized by a certain undefined sense of decency and fittingness in these matters, a sense more or less attributable to the vestiges of Christian tradition, this "moral sense" easily yielded to the more practical dictates of the situation.

The moral decision to use the bomb, without warning, on a Japanese city, was dictated by the urgent desire to end the war promptly, without having to sacrifice thousands of American combatants in the planned invasion of the Japanese archipelago. Once again, the idea was to "punish the unjust aggressor" and to "save American lives." Certainly few Americans before the bomb was dropped, would have questioned the validity of these considerations. The war had to be ended, and this was the way to do it.

It was not generally known that Japan was trying to establish diplomatic contacts with the Allies through Russia in order to work out a negotiated peace instead of the unconditional surrender relentlessly demanded by the Allies. Neither invasion of Japan nor use of the bomb was absolutely necessary for peace. However, the war mentality of the time made it impossible for policy makers to see this. They were convinced the bomb was necessary and their conviction overwhelmed all other considerations.

Nevertheless the use of the bomb on two open cities was a dire injustice and an atrocity.

Even after the war ended, a questionnaire conducted by *Fortune* revealed that half the respondents felt the decision to use the bomb on Hiroshima and Nagasaki had been right, while nearly a quarter of them *regretted that more atomic bombs had not been used on other Japanese cities!* Such was, and is, the general moral climate of the USA.

At the same time, the terrible effects of the bomb produced a moral shock and profound revulsion in certain quarters in America. Religious groups and publications protested more or less vehemently. Catholic voices, notably those of *Commonweal*, the *Catholic World* and of course *The Catholic Worker* were raised against the "sin" of the bomb. But it is to be noted that *America* already took a much more "realistic" and complacent view of the event.

In general, articulate protest against the bomb on moral grounds has been confined to a minority. The majority of Americans have "sincerely regretted" the necessity to use it, they have, in a word, "felt bad" about it. But that is all. These decent sentiments have very easily yielded to other, more "practical" considerations, and the foreign policy of our country since Hiroshima, while occasionally making perfunctory gestures of respect in the direction of the Deity, has been a policy of direct reliance on the threat of atomic and nuclear annihilation.

There have of course been repeated statements of unwillingness to carry out these threats, on the vague grounds that the consequences would be too awful. The American mind in general has however not questioned the fundamental propriety of using the bomb. This is practically taken for granted.

As the pressures of the Cold War become more intense, the fallout shelter scare has had a direct and intimate connection with the policy of nuclear deterrence. It has been clearly and explicitly part of a campaign to "engineer consent" and make nuclear war thoroughly acceptable, at least as a reasonable possibility, in the American public mind. This, in turn, is intended to convince our enemies that we "believe in" the bomb, and that, though we still utter pious hopes that it will never be necessary, we thoroughly intend to use it if we feel ourselves to be sufficiently threatened.

8

Religious Problems
of the Cold War

L ET US LOOK BACK over the ground covered so far in
our study of the war problem. The developments of the
last year have brought home to everyone that war will never
be prevented by the sheer menace of nuclear weapons. The
H-bomb is too powerful to make war a practical, let alone
ethical, solution to international problems. An all-out nuclear
war is something that simply cannot be "won." And yet even
though we must agree with the typically coy statement of Herman Kahn: "Almost nobody wants to be the first man to kill
one hundred million people,"[11] it turns out that quite a few
men, on both sides of the Iron Curtain, are not unwilling to
commit themselves to policies and objectives which may make
a nuclear war inevitable.

The "just war" theory, favored by theologians since the fifth
century, supposes a *defensive* war in which force is strictly limited and the greatest care is taken to protect the rights and
the lives of noncombatants and even of combatants. History
teaches us that these requirements were seldom met with in
practice. Nevertheless, before the invention of gunpowder, the
overwhelming advantage in a contest between equally matched
forces belonged to the defender in the walled city or castle.

But today the traditional idea of the "just war" becomes
fraught with ambiguities, since nuclear weapons are *purely*

offensive weapons. Not only that, but they are weapons which *cannot help but* annihilate noncombatants, open cities, and even neutrals, due to their enormous and uncontrolled destructive power. And finally these are weapons *against which there is no really effective defense.* Furthermore it seems that nuclear weapons are very likely to be used in a massive all-out first strike if they are to be used at all. If tactical nuclear weapons are used in a so-called "limited war" there is no guarantee whatever that the loser will not resort to massive and megatonic retaliation. To ask a belligerent to control himself in this matter would be requiring him to be far more heroically virtuous than he would have to be to disarm completely and trust in Divine Providence.

Hence the theologian is faced with a problem of fabulous complexity if he wants to justify nuclear war by traditional Christian standards.

Meanwhile, in the prevailing climate of uneasiness, with the growing realization that huge stockpiles of nuclear weapons and new missiles not only do not deter a nuclear strike but may well invite one, Christians are beginning to see that the first strike does not necessarily have to come from the Communist side. Though it is true that President Kennedy formally declared that the United States would "never strike first," he has since given in to the pressures of the situation and in the winter of 1962 said that the United States "might have to take the initiative." In any case there are fantastic possibilities of accident, miscalculation, misinterpretation, and plain confusion which might lead to a first strike in the name of Democracy, Liberty and — Christianity!

The mere suggestion of such a possibility still raises furious protest. One is asked immediately to "prove" it. Well, the United States has been doing a great job preparing for nuclear war, and has given special attention to making our nuclear strike capacity fully *credible.*

Our government clearly wants everyone to know that we have the biggest, the best and the most destructive nuclear weapons in the world and that we intend to use them whenever we feel sufficiently provoked to do so. The whole concept of deterrence, on which hopes of peace are still being based by "realists," depends on the *credibility* of this threat. The Russians on their own side are uttering even greater threats. When the full force of two huge mass societies and all their propaganda are devoted to putting this idea across, who am I to disbelieve? I find all that they *say* about their readiness and willingness to wage a nuclear war entirely credible.

When the preparations for the Second Vatican Council began to be discussed, a writer in the French magazine *Realités* produced an article which was not lacking in acute intuitions. It was called "The Last Chance Council." Doubtless this provoking title was dismissed by most of us Catholics as the flippancy of the irreverent mind. One feels nevertheless that the present Cold War crisis has brought home, at least obscurely, to many Christians, whether Catholic or Protestant, a sense that the Church is now facing a test that may prove to be decisive and perhaps in some sense "final." Christianity may be on the point of being driven back into the catacombs and losing, in the process, millions of the faithful.

Worse still, the destruction of civilized society and even the extinction of life on the planet might, if Christians themselves were deeply involved in responsibility for it, be in some sense on their part a disastrous failure and betrayal.

Though these fears have generated a climate of widespread uneasiness and even of implicit desperation, they are not without certain correlative hopes. We believe that the Church could not be brought face to face with any desperate situation which did not at the same time contain a challenge and a promise. For Christians to come "under judgment" in a historical crisis implies not mere blind doom, but rather a difficult choice, a "temptation" if you like, and one in which the future of Christianity and of the whole world may hinge on the heroism and integrity of the faithful. In other words, we find ourselves confronting the possibility of nuclear war with more than common and universal urgency, because we Christians are at least dimly aware that this may still be a matter of choice for us and that the future of Christianity on earth may depend on the moral quality of the decision we are making.

It is doubtless confusing to say the "future of Christianity" is now at stake. What is Christianity? Is it the Church? Is it Christian civilization? The mere clarification of terms would, if it were adequate, require an article to itself. Let us briefly note these most important points, and then pass on.

1. The future of the Church, the Body of Christ, is not in the hands of men. It is not subject to the vagaries of political history. There is and there can be no ambiguity and no uncertainty about the Church's fulfillment of her appointed task on earth. For the Church is Christ himself, present in the world he has redeemed, present in mystery, in poverty, in ways that are a scandal to human wisdom, in modes that confound the clever, the mighty, the affluent and the ruthless leaders of men. Just as "the world" defeated itself in condemning the Lord of glory, so now also worldly power works for its own confusion and for the establishment of the kingdom of God even when it attacks the kingdom most savagely and, it would seem, with the greatest chance of final success.

2. But taking "Christianity" in a wider sense, we are confronted with a far different situation. Christianity signifies the whole complex of Judeo-Christian attitudes, of beliefs, of culture, ways of life. It signifies all the basic and vital assumptions which have formed the worldview of the West, and on which Western civilization has been built. More than that, it can even be taken to include implicitly all that is rich and spiritual in all

the religious cultures and worldviews in so far as these riches can be understood to be "naturally Christian."

"Christianity" in this sense, has been the mother and protector of all that is good in Western humanism, in culture, in free society. Without Christianity the virtues, the tolerance, the humaneness, the philanthropy which have been taken to justify the liberal agnosticism of the nineteenth century, would hardly have been able to exist. Even the vestiges of humanism in Marxist society can be traced to a Judeo-Christian origin.

Without the broad, humane climate of true Christian culture the Christian faith and the full life of a member of the Church would be practically inaccessible to the average person.

In other words, if "Christianity" is destroyed, life in Christ will become a matter of extraordinary heroism, a venture and an unconditional commitment of which very few will be capable, particularly if it means going against the formidable tyrannic compulsions of mass-society.

3. Whether we like it or not, we have to admit we are already living in a post-Christian world, that is to say a world in which Christian ideals and attitudes are relegated more and more to the minority.

It is frightening to realize that the facade of Christianity which still generally survives has perhaps little or nothing behind it, and that what was once called "Christian society" is more purely and simply a materialistic neopaganism with a Christian veneer. And where the Christian veneer has been stripped off we see laid bare the awful vacuity of the mass-mind, without morality, without identity, without compassion, without sense, and rapidly reverting to tribalism and superstition. Here spiritual religion has yielded to the tribal-totalitarian war dance and to the idolatrous worship of the machine.

Christianity, in a word, is everywhere yielding to the hegemony of naked power.

Although since Hiroshima there has been a semblance of religious and spiritual renewal in the West, and even in some of the Iron Curtain countries, the reality and depth of the renewal can certainly be questioned. It is true that statistics show quantitative growth, but this does not necessarily imply a development in quality. On the contrary, it is often apparent that the religious aspirations of very many are confused, superficial, and pathetically insecure.

The Cold War has been playing on these feeble, inadequate religious sensibilities. It has aroused anxiety and the dread of imminent disaster. But unfortunately it has at the same time awakened very deep hatred and indeed it has revealed the profoundest tendencies to destructiveness and to suicidal despair.

Precisely the greatest danger of "Cold War religion" is that it provides these destructive tendencies with an apparent ethical and religious justification. It makes nuclear war look like spiritual heroism, and justifies global suicide as sacrifice and martyrdom. If we had not almost completely lost our innate Christian and religious sense we would be utterly aghast at the perversion of the deepest and most sacred of realities. We would be able to see the awful truth that in many ways the Cold War is *systematically perverting and eroding the Christian conscience.*

This is the climate in which all Christians are facing (or refusing to face) the most crucial moral and religious problem in twenty centuries of history.

It is doubtful for most Christians whether the real underlying religious issue is clearly visible. On the contrary, at least in America, the average priest and minister seems to react in much the same way as the average agnostic or atheist. The interests of the West, NATO, and the Church are all confused with one another, and even the possibility of defending the West with a nuclear first strike on Russia is sometimes accepted without too much hesitation as "necessary" and a "lesser evil."

We assume that Western society and Christendom are still identical and that Communism equals Antichrist. And we are ready to declare without hesitation that "no price is too high" to pay for our religious liberty. The cliché sounds noble to those who are not shocked by its sinister ambiguities.

"Paying the price" used to be equated with Christian sacrifice, or at least with some form of suffering or hardship in which one's own interests were set aside in view of a higher good. But now when we say "no price is too high" we are, it turns out, counting not only our own megacorpses (hopefully excluding our own sacrificial selves from the ghastly score) but also twenty, fifty, a hundred, two hundred million dead on the enemy side. No price is too high to pay! In an orgy of sacrificial ardor we will not hesitate to sacrifice their children. We will not hesitate to contaminate future generations. No price is too high! We will even annihilate neutrals. We will douse the whole hemisphere with lethal fallout. We will go the limit. We will let Europe and the Near East be immolated. We will sacrifice India (whose inhabitants have not, meanwhile, been consulted). No price is too high! We will sacrifice anyone and anything rather than go through the laborious, patient, humiliating process of change, adaptation and sacrifice that is necessary for world peace.

Should it really be necessary to spell out the fact that this slogan — "No price is too high" — somehow lacks nobility?

Even if it were perfectly certain beyond doubt that we were really defending religious freedom, this claim (at such cost) would still be absurd and immoral. But are we so sure that when we speak of defending our liberty, our rights, our personal integrity, we are not purely and simply talking about irresponsibility, good times, a comfortable life, the freedom to make a bit of money?

What are we defending? Our religion or our affluence?

Or have we so identified the two that the distinction is no longer possible?

9

Theologians and Defense

THERE CAN BE NO QUESTION that we have to defend in every way possible the religious, political and cultural values without which our lives would lack meaning. But these values cannot be defended by a passive capitulation to the meaninglessness of a nuclear policy that leads inevitably to the defeat and destruction of both sides. The arguments of those who are now trying to prove that an all-out nuclear war can be "won" lack even the semblance of plausibility. Their own most optimistic figures, based on extremely bland assumptions which they have fed into their computers, show that the America that "survived" a victory over Russia could easily become a victim of a determined aggressor like Red China, which in any case will soon have its own nuclear weapons.

While there can be no religious justification for a policy of all-out nuclear aggression, there is a strong and articulate body of theological opinion in favor of nuclear deterrence and an "adequate posture of defense." Fr. John Courtney Murray, who holds this view, hastens to qualify it by saying the following:

1. The uninhibited violence of nuclear war "disqualifies it as an apt and proportionate means for the resolution of international conflicts and even for the redress of just grievances."

2. To admit the right of war as an attribute of national sovereignty would "seriously block progress of the international community to that mode of political organization which Pius XII regarded as the single means for the outlawry of all war, even of defensive war." In both these statements he is practically paraphrasing the words of Pius XII.

3. While he quotes Pius XII to support his contention that the stockpiling of atomic weapons for defense is legitimate, he adds "this does not morally validate everything that goes on at Cape Canaveral or Los Alamos."[12]

In his book *We Hold These Truths* Fr. Murray devotes a chapter to this same question, clarifying and summing up the doctrine he had explained in his previous article.[13] In this chapter he has sketched out an intelligent approach to an understanding of the present power struggle and of its moral implications. He has emphasized above all the *unprecedented complexity and the depth of the disorder,* from an ethical and rational standpoint. He might have gone further and seen the crisis of our time in its spiritual dimensions, which are even more difficult to grasp and more frightful in their implications.

Fr. Murray believes that "coexistence in truth" between the great international power blocs is hardly possible where there is no common acceptance of a "norm recognized by all as morally obligatory and therefore inviolable" (Pope Pius XII), at the same time he warns that the exact line of rupture dividing the world is spiritual rather than geographic.

What, he asks, are the values to be defended? In what ways are these menaced — by war and by what other subtle pressures? What means are available for their defense? How far can war rationally be invoked as the *ultima ratio* or last resort in the conflict? What is the meaning of "aggressor" in the context of a weapons technology? Is there any real usefulness in the traditional Catholic doctrine of the just war?

Fr. Murray notes that the destructive force of war and the availability of modern means of communication should logically imply that war is pushed further back than ever as "last resort." Ideally, in the context of Pius XII's doctrine of war which Fr. Murray studies and summarizes, there is no *need for war today,* for our problems ought to be settled without it. He admits that "the whole Catholic doctrine of war is hardly more than a *Grenzmoral,* an effort to establish on a minimal basis of reason a form of human action, the making of war, that remains fundamentally irrational" (Murray, 263). And he admits at least implicitly the grave danger presented by this fact at a time like the present. The right of a nation to assume a "posture of defense" once again "does not morally validate everything that goes on at Cape Canaveral or Los Alamos" (Murray, 264). However, the threat of Communism is so great and so immediate, its aggressive pressures so unrelenting and so unnegotiable that an intransigent policy of nuclear defense is accepted by Fr. Murray as logical, necessary and moral.

He does not necessarily mean that this is not something to be decided for us by the Pentagon and accepted with ignorant, blind docility by the American public. It is on the contrary a matter of universal responsibility and concern, a burning question of public conscience.

Fr. Murray is to be praised for an aspect of his treatment of this question which is too easily ignored. At least he confronts the difficult problem of the sovereign state and the *jus belli.* What right has any state to plunge the whole world into war, merely because it wishes to avenge itself or recover a lost advantage? Fr. Murray believes that these are not just motives for a war. Only a strictly defensive war can be permitted. He lays down as fundamental the principle that "all *wars of aggression,* whether just or unjust, fall under the ban of moral proscription" (Murray, 255).

In particular he calls for a return of Catholic thought on war "to more traditional and more fruitful premises." And here he points out that the responsibility for the war "should not rest with the generals and the state department but with the people, who should have an active concern with the moral directions of national policy." He adds significantly, "My impression is that this duty in social morality is being badly neglected in America at the moment" (Murray, 257).

Once this has been said, however, he passes over the enormous problem of how the public is to acquit itself of this responsibility when it does not and cannot know the facts, when it is morally confused or in large part morally illiterate, when it submits passively to the enormous power of propaganda, and when in fact it accepts with complete docility a whole mass of unverified assumptions about the world situation which Fr. Murray himself also seems to accept without too much question.

One of the most crucial of these assumptions is that there is and can be no way to negotiate with the Communists. If we take this assumption for granted, then war becomes inevitable. But is it to be taken for granted? Anyone who has looked rather closely at the inextricable political tangle of the disarmament and other conferences can find, if he looks hard enough and honestly enough, real signs of concern and real efforts to advance workable proposals for peace. The fact is that those who are aware of the seriousness of the issue on both sides now *see* that East and West *must* find some way to negotiate or else they are doomed. To assume that no such negotiation can really make sense is then a fatal error.

Such assumptions tend to interpret and evaluate world events in a distorted perspective so that one reaches the painful absurdity of the crisis over West Berlin, itself the product of folly, blindness and ignorant presuppositions. Can it be said that a nuclear war over West Berlin would be justified as "defense"?

I do not know precisely where Fr. Murray stands on this question, but the affirmative opinion is certainly held and expressed. Doubtless when one is totally immersed in the flux of events and statements about events, threats and counterthreats, strategies and counterstrategies, then the idea of a nuclear war over West Berlin may come to seem logical and even necessary. In a larger perspective, from a detached viewpoint, the whole situation is seen to be at once tragic and absurd. Not that a great good is not at stake — but it has come to be at stake in a way that is totally irrational.

In any case Fr. Murray admits as a second basic principle that "a defensive war to repress injustice is morally admissible both in principle and in fact" (Murray, 258).

Here he quotes the well-known assertions of Pius XII. "Law and order have need at times of the powerful arm of force." "There are some [goods that are] of such importance for the human community that their defense against an unjust aggression is without doubt fully justified" (from an allocution to visiting members of the U.S. Congress Armed Services Committee, October 8, 1947). Force may and must be invoked if it is the only way to prevent "brutal violence and lack of conscience" in international affairs. After the Hungarian revolution and obviously in reference to the brave resistance of the freedom fighters, Pius XII said, "In this situation a war of efficacious self-defense against unjust attacks, which is undertaken with hope of success, cannot be considered illicit" (Christmas Message, 1956). Did the pope perhaps mean that armed intervention on behalf of Hungary, by Western nations, even at the risk of nuclear war, would have been licit? This is not totally improbable by any means.

It can be said that Pope Pius XII did not simply condemn atomic war as such or that all use of atomic weapons is evil. But they can only be used under certain very stringent conditions laid down by the traditional ethical doctrine.

1. The war must be truly a *defensive* war. The nation must be menaced in its "vital rights." War over a question of national prestige does not fulfill this condition, says Fr. Murray.

2. The situation must clearly be *beyond all negotiation* (Murray, 260).

3. The evil wrought by violence must not be out of proportion to the good to be attained by the war.

4. Force must be strictly limited so that it does not "entirely escape the control of man" (Murray, 262).

Here Fr. Murray declares that it should be *"obvious"* that massive and indiscriminate destruction by nuclear, bacteriological or other weapons is *never permissible*. "Who," he says, "would undertake to defend on any grounds, including military grounds, the annihilation of all human life within the radius of an ABC war that entirely escapes from the control of man?" (Murray, 262).

These are lucid statements of principle, but unfortunately the assumptions so widely accepted, so inescapable, and so all-powerful over the minds of men tend to vitiate our moral perspective so that men do not apply these principles correctly even when they want to apply them at all.

In the nation *menaced in its "vital rights"* is a defensive war justified? How many Americans would hesitate to say that the presence of a Communist state in Cuba was a deadly menace to "vital rights" and to the very "existence" of the United States? If the Russians wanted to make a moral option on war, they could just as easily say that they were gravely threatened in their very existence by American bases in Turkey and West Germany.

Yet we must be careful of propaganda that so easily confuses a threat to national prestige with a threat to the *existence* of a nation.

Is the problem *beyond all negotiation*? How easily we assume that all negotiation has become futile, that the Russians are simply crooks, that war cannot be prevented except by threats. Obviously there is some element of truth in all this, but perhaps we ourselves are not honest either, and perhaps we are looking for excuses to justify the use of violence. This could be a very grave matter indeed.

As to proportion between the evil of war and the good achieved by it: it is true that one can and should sacrifice material things for spiritual values. But the sophistry about being better dead than Red conceals a dangerous fallacy. In war, particularly nuclear war, the awful physical destruction is only one aspect of the evil. The spread of demoralization and crime, the tragic corruption and decadence of society, even the destruction of all social order, can follow from conventional war. How much more from nuclear war? There is every likelihood that a nuclear war would mean the total collapse of the social structure we are trying to defend. Would such a war be rational or just?

Fr. Murray concludes, as we ourselves have concluded in the previous chapter, that "Catholic doctrine has not been made the basis for a sound critique of public policies and as a means for the formation of right public opinion" (Murray, 265). And he adds that the "classic example" of this failure was the policy of unconditional surrender in World War II.

His solution is a return to the traditional doctrine, as a "solvent of false dilemmas" and as the middle way between the two extremes of pacifism and bellicism.

Hence his conclusion is that war must be understood as a rational moral possibility, and waged within moral limitations. And theoretically one need not quarrel with this solution. In practice, however, in a society that is largely immoral or amoral, in a situation utterly grave and utterly extreme, where all perspectives are distorted, where force is used without inhibition and without scruple, where power becomes an end in itself and the human person is merely a means to power, then one wonders what can be the effect of suggesting a "will to peace which bears within itself a will to enforce the precept of peace by arms."

We are back with Augustine and the fall of Rome, but with a difference. And it is a tremendous difference. We are not now facing a "war of mercy" and pure self-defense with swords and spears, but a war of inhuman cruelty and uninhibited massive destruction, waged with megatonic weapons.

We have seen two world wars waged with a "will to peace" in order to "end wars." We have seen the immoral doctrine of unconditional surrender invoked as a sure guarantee of peace. And now, with the "will to peace" we are not unwilling to undertake the total destruction of continents.

Reasonable as are his principles, and much as I agree with his motives and his theory, I am afraid many of Fr. Murray's readers may end up with the feeling that he has morally justified "everything that goes on at Cape Canaveral or Los Alamos."

An eminent Catholic theologian in England, Canon L. L. McReavy, declares without equivocation that the policy of nuclear deterrence, insofar as it relies on *a serious threat of massive nuclear retaliation* against the cities of the enemy, is *morally unacceptable*. "A positive intention to commit an immoral act in certain circumstances, however much one may hope they will never arise, *is in itself here and now immoral*."*

---

*L. L. McReavy, *Clergy Review* (1960), reprinted in *Pax Bulletin* #85.

However he adds that nuclear weapons may be stockpiled for possible use against "legitimate (military) targets." Here again we fall back into the same practical difficulty, for there is no indication whatever that military strategists are going to make the fine distinctions of the moral theologian. Bombs are bombs and it is utterly laughable to suppose that even a five megaton H-bomb would have been constructed for use against a "fleet at sea." And what about the fifty megaton bomb?

So Canon McReavy himself admits that it is probably that nuclear weapons "will not in fact be used with the discrimination required by the moral law, and *I regard it as morally certain that if megaton weapons are used at all, even as a last resort and in self-defense, they will be used immorally.*"*

Because of these practical ambiguities there is a strong tendency in favor of "relative" or "nuclear" pacifism, which admits the traditional doctrine of a just war by conventional weapons, but which insists that nuclear disarmament, or at the very least completely effective arms control, is of absolute moral obligation.

Fr. Murray says, without sufficient grounds, that the doctrine of "relative pacifism" is not to be squared with the public doctrine of the Church. We have seen that not all theologians agree with him. Quotations could be multiplied, but it should be sufficient here to cite the Pastoral Letter of the French Cardinals and Bishops, in June 1950. Asked if nuclear weapons use for indiscriminate destruction could be approved, the French bishops declared that the question *did not even need to be asked.* They added: "For our part we condemn (these weapons) with all our strength as we had no hesitation in condemning the mass bombing during the last war."

Pope John XXIII said in his first Encyclical (*Ad Petri Cathedram*):

---

*L. L. McReavy, Letter to the *Catholic Herald* (quoted in *Unity*, May 1960).

So monstrous are the weapons which this age of ours has brought into being that all nations, both vanquished and would-be victors, may expect nothing other than to be overtaken by immeasurable destruction, immeasurable ruin.

Surely a Papal Encyclical represents the public doctrine of the Church, and here, as elsewhere, we find a firm support for the contention that (in Fr. Murray's words) "war has now become a moral absurdity." That is precisely what the pope is saying of all-out nuclear war. Indeed, this truth is seldom questioned except, curiously, by theologians in West Germany and the USA. Can one's theology perhaps be biased by what we conceive to be our own political interest?

A recent manifestation of growing religious resistance to nuclear war is the collection *God and the H-bomb.*[14] This is an anthology of statements, declarations, articles and sermons, calculated to have popular appeal and brought together without too much critical distinction. Protestant, Catholic and Jewish leaders in Europe and America are represented here, all stating their conviction that total nuclear war is immoral, and all demanding that positive action be taken to prevent it. These statements of philosophers and theologians are supported by official declarations of Church groups and by a formal quotation from Pope Pius XII himself (see below). Bishop Sheen here goes on record with the statement: "Large scale nuclear warfare which denies all distinction between soldiers and civilians, and which makes nurses, doctors, lepers, infants, the aged and the dying objects of direct attack, is certainly immoral."[15]

One Protestant view of Christian nuclear pacifism is forcefully stated by Dr. Norman K. Gottwald of Andover Newton Theological College: "To call nuclear war Christian sacrifice is to reject all that Jesus stood for; it is merely to transfer orthodox terminology to the cult of the deified state. This is nothing more than western Shintoism."[16] Dr. Gottwald shows quite correctly that the theologian who stretches his theology so far that it supports so-called "nuclear realism" is, in fact, taking the next to last step before a final and complete justification of totalitarian autocracy.

Perhaps the most moving religious analysis of the situation, in this book, is the essay by Rabbi Samuel Dresner on "Man, God and Atomic War."[17] There is no question that the crisis of our time does not reveal its inner significance until it is examined in the light of Biblical revelation. Rabbi Dresner, speaking as one who is saturated with the Old Testament prophets, declares simply that the survival of man depends, now as always, decisively and without equivocation, on an inner revolution of man's spirit, and a full return to that God who, in the modern world, is singularly and terrifyingly "absent."

A veteran Catholic pacifist is the German Dominican Fr. Franziskus Stratmann, who, even in the days of the Weimar Republic and later when exiled from Nazi Germany, continued to write, speak and work for peace. Important books by him include *Peace and the Clergy* and *The Church and War,* now out of print.[18] He too is represented in *God and the H-bomb*. He shows that in the Middle Ages, the Gospel ethic was "supplemented — perhaps you may say stifled — by religiously neutral natural law," which encouraged elaboration of the theory of just wars, whose elastic principles were to be stretched indefinitely by later casuistry until they have now reached the breaking point. He admits nevertheless that even the natural law clearly repudiates total nuclear war.[19]

A much discussed English anthology of essays on nuclear pacifism is *Morals and Missiles,* edited by Charles Thompson, who is also editor of the *Pax Bulletin*.[20] As most of the articles in *Morals and Missiles* are in fact included in *God and the H-bomb,* the book does not require detailed discussion here. One may mention however a particularly good contribution on the just war theory by E. I. Watkin, which for some reason did not find its way into the American volume.[21] Watkin contends that in massive nuclear warfare the traditional norms of justice cannot be fulfilled.

A recent collection of essays by English Catholic intellectuals, *Nuclear Weapons and Christian Conscience,* frankly takes the stand that the immoral hypotheses of "realists" who seek to justify nuclear war are "doing more from within to undermine western civilization than the enemy can do from the outside."[22] These Catholic writers protest with all their strength against the "habitual moral squalor" of the prevailing opportunism, and remind the Christian who may have forgotten the Cross that in a situation like ours we may be forced to choose "the ultimate weapon of meaningful suffering" or deny the Christian faith itself (Stein, 39). It is absurd and immoral to pretend that Christendom can be defended by the H-bomb.

As St. Augustine would say in such a case as this, the weapon with which we would attempt to destroy the enemy would pass through our own hearts to reach him. We would be annihilated morally and no doubt physically as well. The H-bomb may possibly wipe out western society if it is used by the Communists, but it may destroy Christendom spiritually if it is used as a weapon of aggression by Christians.

It must be noted that these Catholic writers are not formal pacifists. They admit the traditional theory of the "just war" but feel that this concept is no longer viable. At the same time they attack the extreme argument that Christianity must be by its very nature pacifistic. One of the writers blames this idealistic view for encouraging the opposite cynical extreme, "doublethink about double effect."[23] The book questions the moral honesty of manufacturing and stockpiling nuclear weapons while "suspending the decision to use them." It questions the morality of using nuclear weapons even as a threat.

Another question: to what extent can the individual claim to remain uncommitted when his government pursues a policy that leads directly to nuclear war? One of the writers answers: "In modern warfare, responsibility for all that is not antecedently, clearly and publicly ruled out must be accepted by anyone who in any way participates in waging the war."[24] In brief this volume puts forward an articulate plea, based on Catholic morality, for unilateral initiative in disarmament.

Another symposium, by Dr. John C. Bennett of Union Theological Seminary, editor of *Christianity in Crisis,* brings together scientists, educators and Protestant theologians to discuss *Nuclear Weapons and the Conflict of Conscience.* Dr. Bennett reflects the growing anxiety of those nonpacifist theologians, like himself, Reinhold Niebuhr and Paul Ramsey, who formerly accepted nuclear deterrence as a guarantee against war. "Today," he says, "the dilemma [of force and Christian ethics] is much more difficult to live with because I do not have the same confidence that the deterrent during the next decade will prevent the war."[25] Hence the more urgent need for new perspectives which will not only prevent Communist aggression, but also prevent war. He rejects unilateralism, as well as the statistical and amoral calculations of Herman Kahn. He likewise clearly states the following principles, concerning the nuclear question.

1. *We must not deceive ourselves into believing we could ever justify the use of megaton bombs for massive attacks on the centers of population of another country, no matter what the provocation.* (Bennett, 101)

2. *We need to take more seriously than we do the effect of large scale nuclear war on the quality of life in the surviving community.* (105)

3. *We may be dehumanized by the very process (the arms race) which we defend as a protection of human values.* (105)

While differing on many points of detail and policy with Dr. Bennett, my own thesis in this present volume is in substantial agreement with these three principles which I regard as so obvious and so basic as to be inescapable.

This brief sampling of recent articulate religious opposition to nuclear war should encourage us. Religious spokesmen have not all abandoned themselves to silence or equivocation. Yet it remains true that there is still all too general an apathy and passivity among the clergy and the faithful. Perhaps it is exact to say that they are afflicted with a kind of moral paralysis. Hypnotized by the mass media, which tend to be aggressive and bellicose, baffled and intimidated by the general atmosphere of suspicion, bewildered by the silence or the ambiguity of their pastors and religious leaders, and remembering the failure of the peace movements that preceded World War II, people tend to withdraw into a state of passive and fatalistic desperation. There they have been literally run to earth by the shelter salesmen, and have set themselves despondently to digging holes in their back yards against the day when the missiles begin to fly.

10

Working for Peace

POPE JOHN XXIII pointed out in his first encyclical, *Ad Petri Cathedram,* that Christians are obliged to strive "with all the means at their disposal" for peace. Yet he warns that peace cannot compromise with error or make concessions to injustice. Passive acquiescence in injustice, submission to brute force, do not lead to genuine peace. There is some truth in Machiavelli's contention that mere weakness and confusion lead in the long run to greater disasters than a firm and even intransigent policy. But the Christian program for peace does not depend on human astuteness, ruthlessness or force. Power can never be the keystone of a Christian policy. Yet our work for peace must be energetic, enlightened and fully purposeful. Its purpose is defined by our religious belief that God has called us "to the service of his merciful designs" (John XXIII, Christmas Message, 1958). This does not mean we blithely assume that God has given the power of the bomb into our hands with a mandate to use it according to our fantasy. If we are now in possession of atomic power, we have the moral obligation to make a good and peaceful use of it, rather than turning it to our own destruction. But we will not be able to do this without an interior revolution that abandons the quest for brute power and submits to the wisdom of love and of the Cross.

It must however be stated quite clearly and without compromise that the duty of the Christian as a peacemaker is not to be confused with a kind of quietistic inertia that is indifferent to injustice, accepts any kind of disorder, compromises with error and with evil, and gives in to every pressure in order to maintain "peace at any price." The Christian knows well, or should know well, that peace is not possible on such terms. Peace demands the most heroic labor and the most difficult sacrifice. It demands greater heroism than war. It demands greater fidelity to the truth and a much more perfect purity of conscience. The Christian fight for peace is not to be confused with defeatism. This has to be made clear because there is a certain sophistry, given free currency by the publicists who want to justify war too easily, and who like to treat anyone who disagrees with them as if he were a practical apostate who had already surrendered implicitly to Communism by refusing to accept the morality of an all-out nuclear war. This, as anyone can easily see, is simply begging the question. And one feels that those who yield to this temptation are perhaps a little too much influenced by the pragmatism and opportunism of our affluent society.

There is a lot of talk, among some of the clergy, about the relative danger of nuclear war and a "Communist takeover." It is assumed, quite gratuitously, that the Communist is at the gates, and is just about to take over the United States, close all the churches, and brainwash all the good Catholics. Once this spectral assessment of the situation is accepted, then one is urged to agree that there is only one solution: to let the Reds have it before they get our government and our universities thoroughly infiltrated. This means a preemptive strike, based not on the fact that we ourselves are actually under military attack, but that we are "provoked" and so "threatened" that even the most drastic measures are justified.

If it is argued that there can be no proportion between the awful destruction wrought by nuclear war and the good achieved by exercising this largely imaginary specter of Communist domination, the argument comes back: "better dead than red." And this, in turn, is justified by the contention that the destruction of cities, nations, populations, is "only a physical evil" while Communist domination would be a "moral evil."

It must be said at once that this fantastic piece of nonsense has no basis in logic, ethics, politics or sound theology. It is a sophistry pure and simple. The quotations from Pope Pius XII will suffice to establish the true Catholic perspective on these points.

The destruction of cities and nations by nuclear war is "only a physical evil"? Pope Pius XII called ABC warfare a "sin, an offense and an outrage against the majesty of God." And he adds: "it constitutes a crime worthy of the most severe national and international sanctions." (Address to the World Medical Congress, 1954). Fr. John Courtney Murray, S.J., whom no one can accuse of being a "pacifist," has stated, "The extreme position of favoring a war . . . simply to kill off all Communists, cannot be a legitimate Catholic opinion."

The real issue here is not actually a moral principle so much as a state of mind. This state of mind is the one which we find in the mass media. It is made up of a large number of superficial assumptions about what is going on in the world and about what is likely to happen.

A "state of mind" is something indefinite and intangible, and for that very reason it tends to be ignored or underestimated. One can hardly come to grips with it, once it is barely reducible to discourse. And yet this does not mean it is incommunicable. On the contrary, it spreads like fire and catches hold of every mind and heart. One is not protected against this moral combustion merely by rational statements of principles or of fact. Something much deeper is required. One must have profound and solid grounding in spiritual principles, one must have a deep and persevering moral strength, a compassion, an attachment to truth and to humanity, a faith in God, an uncompromising fidelity to God's law of love. Failing this, a nebulous and all-pervading "state of mind" will take over the role of morality and conscience, and will rationalize its prejudices with convenient religious or ethical formulas. The result will be a fatal turning away from truth and from justice.

The present "state of mind" is one of truculence and suspicion, based on fear. In such a mood, it becomes difficult to see any other solution than violence. War becomes more and more logical as the "last resort" and the more one is persuaded that the situation is critical, the more he believes that the extreme measure, recourse to the bomb, is demanded. Hence all thought of rational, pertinent negotiation is dismissed as impractical and absurd. We are rapidly reaching the point where we will completely despair of those peaceful measures on which our salvation depends. We are coming to believe in war as the "real solution." It would be tragic indeed if our survival and indeed our Christian faith itself were left entirely at the mercy of such assumptions!

To protect ourselves, we have to stand back and try to recover our Christian perspective, instead of rationalizing, in moral terms, the familiar mental clichés that are dinned into our ears by the mass media.

We have to recognize that a spirit of individualism and confusion has reduced us to an ethic of "every man for himself and the devil take the hindmost." This ethic, unfortunately sometimes consecrated by Christian formulas, is nothing but the secular ethic of the affluent society, based on the false assumption that if everyone is bent on making money for himself the common good will automatically follow, due to the operation of economic laws.

An ethic of barely disguised selfishness is no longer a Christian ethic. Nor can we afford to raise this to the national level and assume that the world will adjust itself if every nation seeks its own advantage before everything else. On the contrary, we are obliged to widen our horizons and to recognize our responsibility to build an international community in which the right of all nations and other groups will be respected and guaranteed. We cannot expect a peaceful world society to emerge all by itself from the turmoil of a ruthless power struggle — we have to work, sacrifice and cooperate to lay the foundations on which future generations may build a stable and peaceful international community. Every Christian is involved in this task, and consequently every Christian is obliged to seek information and form his conscience so that he may be able to contribute his own share of intelligent political action toward this end.

As Cardinal Meyer of Chicago said in his Lenten Pastoral for 1962: "The charity of Christ which makes us solicitous for our families and for our American society must also make us solicitous for the welfare of the whole world....We are overcome by evil not only if we allow Communism to take over the world but if we allow the methods and standards of Communism to influence our own. If we adopt a policy of hatred, of liquidation of those who oppose us, of unrestrained use of total war, of a spirit of fear and panic, of exaggerated propaganda, of unconditional surrender, of pure nationalism, we have already been overcome by the evil."

11

Beyond East and West

WE ARE NO LONGER LIVING in a Christian world. The ages which we are pleased to call the "ages of Faith" were certainly not ages of earthly paradise. But at least our forefathers officially recognized and favored the Christian ethic of love. They fought some very bloody and unchristian wars, and in doing so, they also committed great crimes which remain in history as a permanent scandal. However, certain definite limits were recognized. Today a non-Christian world still retains a few vestiges of Christian morality, a few formulas and clichés, which serve on appropriate occasions to adorn indignant editorials and speeches. But otherwise we witness deliberate campaigns to oppose and eliminate all education in Christian truth and morality. Not only non-Christians but even Christians themselves tend to dismiss the Gospel ethic on nonviolence and love as "sentimental." As a matter of fact, the mere suggestion that Christ counseled nonviolent resistance to evil is enough to invite scathing ridicule. One Catholic writer declares in so many words that he will stick to natural law and abandon the Sermon on the Mount to "Protestant ministers and *Jewish Rabbis.*"

It is therefore a serious error to imagine that because the West was once largely Christian, the cause of the Western nations is now to be identified, without further qualification, with the cause of God. We must certainly oppose the tactics by which Communism seeks to attain world power, but a policy of nuclear extermination will do more harm than good to our own cause. It may well be an apocalyptic temptation. It may indeed be the most effective way of destroying Christendom, even though man may survive. For who imagines that the Asians and Africans will respect Christianity and receive it after it has apparently triggered mass murder and destruction on a continental scale? Neither faith nor sanity can imagine that Christianity could defend itself by nuclear preemption. The mere fact that we now seem to accept total nuclear war as reasonable and Christian is a universal scandal.

True, Christianity is not only opposed to Communism, but in a very real sense, at war with it. However, this warfare is spiritual and ideological. "Devoid of material weapons," says Pope John, "the Church is the trustee of the highest spiritual power."

This means not only that the Christian fights for peace and justice by prayer and faith, but that Christian social action is the most important weapon of the Church against Communism. The encyclical *Mater et Magistra* makes this quite clear. Christians should give their wholehearted support to all reasonable plans for aid to underdeveloped countries, but of course we do not have to yield to starry-eyed utopianism in this ideal. Foreign aid must be effectively channeled so that it really benefits the people of the nations concerned and is not diverted into the pockets of corrupt political and military cliques or, worse still, misused by the enemies of freedom. We must furthermore not be deluded into thinking that economic aid and a higher standard of living are a satisfactory solution to all the problems of the "Third World."

In a word, to place our trust in the power of money is no more Christian than to rely on the bomb. In either case the aim is domination, not reconstruction, and Christian social action must work for a complete renewal of social structures wherever they have ceased to function adequately.

Victory over Communism can be achieved not by threats, still less by bribery, but only by a fully convincing demonstration of the constructive and creative capacities of the society that still appeals in great measure to classical and Christian standards of social justice. But if our society proves itself to be a system of organized and belligerent irresponsibility, then we have no other solution than a recourse to violence. And this will be no solution. It will be an immoral evasion of the problems created by our infidelity to our own Christian heritage.

Whatever we may think of the ethics of nuclear war, it is clear that the message of the H-bomb is neither salvation nor "good news."

But we believe, precisely, that an essential part of the "good news" is that nonviolent and reasonable measures are stronger than weapons. Indeed, by spiritual arms, the early Church conquered the entire Roman world. Have we lost our faith in this "sword of the Spirit?" Have we perhaps lost all realization of its very existence?

Of course we must repudiate a tactic of inert passivity that purely and simply leaves man defenseless, without any recourse whatever to any means of protecting himself, his rights, or Christian truth. We repeat again and again that the right, and truth, are to be defended by the most efficacious possible means, and that the most efficacious of all are precisely the nonviolent ones, which have always been the only ones that have effected a really lasting moral change in society and in man. The Church tolerates defensive use of weapons only insofar as men are unable to measure up to the stricter and more heroic demands of spiritual warfare. It is absolutely unchristian to adopt, in practice, a stance which practically rejects or ignores all recourse to the spiritual weapons, and relegates them entirely to the background as if they had no efficacy whatever, and as if material weapons (the bigger the better) were the ones that really counted.

It seems that a great deal of the moral discussion about nuclear war is based, in fact, on the assumption that spiritual weapons are quixotic and worthless and that material weapons alone are worthy of serious consideration. But this attitude is precisely what leads to a fundamental vitiation of the Church's traditionally accepted doctrine on the use of violence in war: it seeks in every possible way to evade the obligation to use war *only as a last resort,* purely in *defense,* and with the use of *just means only.*

Once again, the question of the "last resort" is of the most crucial importance. Among Christians there is really not much dispute over the basic ethical principles concerning war. Where the discussion really generates heat is in the application of these principles to concrete cases. And here once again we return to the problem of basic and unspoken assumptions.

If one takes it for granted that all negotiation has become futile, that the enemy is so fundamentally and utterly corrupt that he cannot in any event be believed and that he will never seriously cooperate in an effort to disarm, then one will be permanently disposed to see, in every new crisis, a more evident justification for recourse to the "last resort" of war. And as tensions mount, and the conviction of the inefficacy of all but brutal means becomes more firmly established, one will at the same time be more firmly convinced of the *need* for *total* and *ruthless* use of the bomb in an annihilatory strike.

At the same time, of course, identical attitudes are found among extremists on the other side, equally convinced of our irreformable wickedness, our totally unscrupulous desire for power, to be achieved by the most violent means.

The truth is that the extremists on both sides are quite right. They are contemplating, in one another, the mirror image of their own hatreds, fears, suspicions and murderous intentions.

Each one assumes and takes as axiomatic the violent purpose of the other. The assumption is correct: it is based on the experience of his own indubitably violent intentions.

The Christian problem is not to decide which one of the two sides has the moral right to throw the first bomb but to dissipate the poisonous and blinding smoke of bellicose assumptions. The task begins in ourselves. But we are afraid to begin it because we are convinced that if we once let down our guard we will immediately be knocked out.

The question is then to study the problem and possibility of a gradual and rationally negotiated disarmament plan (which has long since been under way) and to create an *atmosphere of hope and confidence in negotiation*. This is a task of supreme urgency, and it is a Christian duty.

Inevitably, as soon as the obsession with bigger and bigger weapons takes hold of us, we make it impossible for ourselves to consider the just rights of noncombatants. We tend to twist the truth in every possible way in order to convince ourselves that noncombatants are really combatants after all, and that our "attack" is in reality "defense" while the enemy's "defense" really constitutes an attack. By such tactics we disqualify ourselves from receiving the light and grace which alone can enable us to judge as spiritual men and as members of Christ. Obviously, without this special gift of light, we remain utterly incapable of seeing or appreciating the superiority of spiritual weapons, prayer, sacrifice, negotiation, and nonviolent means in general.

This results in the unhappy situation that non-Christians with rather dubious doctrinal support in irreligious philosophies, have been able to take over characteristically Christian spiritual methods, appropriating them to themselves and thus further discrediting them in the eyes of the orthodox believer who is already confused by the now instinctive justification of war and weapons as the "normal" way of solving international problems.

We must remember that the Church does not belong to any political power bloc. Christianity exists on both sides of the Iron Curtain and we should feel ourselves united by very special bonds with those Christians who, living under Communism, often suffer heroically for their principles.

Is it a valid defense of Christianity for us to wipe out those heroic Christians along with their oppressors, for the sake of "religious freedom"?

Let us stop and consider where the policy of massive retaliation and worse still of preemptive strike may lead us. Suppose we plan to annihilate huge population centers, at the same time showering vast areas around them with lethal fallout. We believe it is necessary to do this in order to protect ourselves against the menace of world Communism.

In these countries which (it is supposed) we will not hesitate to annihilate, the vast majority is not Communist. On the contrary, while the people have resigned themselves passively to Communist domination, and have become quite convinced that there is no hope to be looked for from us because we are their declared enemies, and intend to wipe them out, they are by no means Communists. They do not want war. They have, in many cases, lived through the horrors and sacrifices of total war and experienced sufferings which we ourselves are barely able to imagine. They do not want to go through this again.

We, in the name of liberty, of justice, of humanity, are not unwilling to pursue a policy which promises to crush them with even greater horror, except that it may perhaps be "merciful" that millions of them will simply be blown out of existence in the twinkling of an eye. Merciful? When many of them have a Christian background, many of them are faithful Christians? Can we, in the name of faith, and of the Church, be willing to exterminate other believers in Christ, other members of our own Church, without even giving them the opportunity to make an act of contrition?

What good will our bellicosity do us in those countries? None at all. It will only serve to reinforce the fatalistic conviction of the necessity of armament and of war that has been dinned into these populations by the Communist minority which dominates them.

Thus in order to get at a small minority of fanatics, we will not hesitate to threaten most frightful terrorism to crush their innocent victims. The populations of the Iron Curtain countries will then be the victims twice over. Already prisoners of our enemy, we are making them at the same time our hostages. We can consider killing them in the most barbarous manner in order to make their captors feel our power. Is this Christianity? Is this even sane logic?

I say that "we" are willing to do all this. Of course we do not want these effects: but if we want what makes them inevitable, how can we disclaim responsibility for them? Must we continue to insist on stretching our moral principles to the breaking point in order to accommodate unprincipled and irreligious men who calculate in such terms?

How do we justify our readiness to wage a war of this kind? Let us face the fact that we feel ourselves terribly menaced by Communism. Certainly we believe we have to defend ourselves. Why are we menaced? Because, as time goes on, the Communists have gained a greater and greater advantage over us in the Cold War. Why have they been able to do this? This is a question of historical fact, which however is not absolutely clear, but anyone will admit that our very reliance on the massive power of the bomb has to a great extent crippled us and restricted our freedom to maneuver, and the Communists have been operating under the *protection* of this massive threat that is too enormous to let loose for any but the most serious causes. Hence, instead of the serious provocation, the massive attack, we are confronted with a multiplicity of little threats all over the world, little advances, little gains. They all add up, but even the total of them does not constitute a sufficient reason for nuclear war.

Hence we come face to face with the paradox that the power of the bomb itself has handicapped us. We are perhaps still thinking in terms of World War II, just as the French, in 1939, were thinking in terms of trench warfare of World War I and built themselves the Maginot line, a supertrench complete with everything including subway trains: but it only served to immobilize them in the face of Hitler's fast-moving Panzer Divisions supported by the Luftwaffe.

It is because of our reliance on the bomb above all that we have been so sadly handicapped and inert in the Cold War. We cannot help but realize this: and at the same time our improvisations of a more positive and peacefully constructive policy leave us uncertain of success because they have no context in a logical, systematic long-range plan.

Once again, the trouble is to be sought in our mental and spiritual confusion, our lack of imagination, our inner doubts, our opportunism and our lack of principle. All of these are revealed in the assumptions, the "axioms" that underlie our assessment of the world situation.

12

Moral Passivity
and Demonic Activism

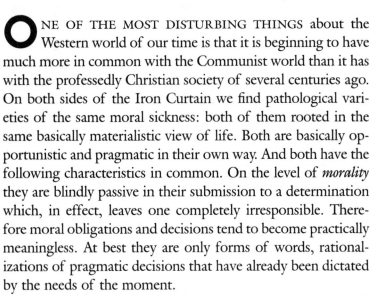

ONE OF THE MOST DISTURBING THINGS about the Western world of our time is that it is beginning to have much more in common with the Communist world than it has with the professedly Christian society of several centuries ago. On both sides of the Iron Curtain we find pathological varieties of the same moral sickness: both of them rooted in the same basically materialistic view of life. Both are basically opportunistic and pragmatic in their own way. And both have the following characteristics in common. On the level of *morality* they are blindly passive in their submission to a determination which, in effect, leaves one completely irresponsible. Therefore moral obligations and decisions tend to become practically meaningless. At best they are only forms of words, rationalizations of pragmatic decisions that have already been dictated by the needs of the moment.

Naturally, since not everyone is an unprincipled materialist, even in Russia, there is bound to be some moral sense at work, even if only as a guilt-feeling that produces uneasiness and hesitation, blocking the smooth efficiency of machinelike obedience to immoral commands. Yet the history of Nazi Germany shows us how appalling was the irresponsibility which would carry out even the most revolting of crimes under the cover of "obedience" to "legitimately constituted authority" for the sake of a "good cause." This moral passivity is the most terrible danger of our time, as the American bishops have already pointed out in their joint letters of 1960 and 1961.

On the level of political, economic and military activity, this moral passivity is balanced, or overbalanced, by a *demonic activism,* a frenzy of the most varied, versatile, complex and even utterly brilliant technological improvisations, following one upon the other with an ever more bewildering and uncontrollable proliferation.

The fantastic rapidity of technological progress can be estimated by Herman Kahn's remark that "We are having a complete technological revolution in the art of war approximately every five years."[26] In the past history of the human race, such technological revolutions have been spread over centuries. We are simply not able to make adequate moral, spiritual and intellectual adjustments to the proliferation of force. Politics pretends to use this force as its servant, to harness it for social purposes, for the "good of man." This intention is good, but its confidence is naive. The technological development of power in our time is by no means intrinsically evil. On the contrary, it can and should be a very great good. In actual fact, the furious speed with which our technological world is plunging toward disaster is evidence that no one is any longer fully in control — least of all perhaps, the political leaders.

A simple study of the steps which led to the dropping of the first A-bomb on Hiroshima is devastating evidence of the way well-meaning men, the scientists, generals and statesmen of a victorious nation, were guided step by step, without realizing it, by the inscrutable yet simple "logic of events" to fire the shot that was to make the Cold War inevitable and prepare the way inexorably for World War III. This they did purely and simply because they thought in all sincerity that the bomb was the simplest and most merciful way of ending World War II and perhaps all wars, forever.

The tragedy of our time is then not so much the malice of the wicked as the helpless futility of the best intentions of "the good." There are war makers, war criminals, indeed. They are present and active on *both sides.* But all of us, in our very best efforts for peace, find ourselves maneuvered unconsciously into positions where we too can act as war criminals. For there can be no doubt that Hiroshima and Nagasaki were, though not fully deliberate crimes, nevertheless crimes. And who was responsible? No one. Or "history." We cannot go on playing with nuclear fire and shrugging off the results as "history." We are the ones concerned. We are the ones responsible. History does not make us, we make it — or end it.

In plain words, in order to save ourselves from destruction we have to try to regain control of a world that is speeding downhill without brakes because of the combination of factors I have just mentioned: almost total passivity and irresponsibility on the moral level, plus demonic activism in social, political and military life.

First of all we must seek some remedy in the technological sphere. We must try to achieve some control over the production and stockpiling of weapons. It is intolerable that such massive engines of destruction should be allowed to proliferate in all directions without any semblance on a long range plan for anything, even for what is cynically called "defense." To allow governments to pour more and more billions into weapons that almost immediately become obsolete, thereby necessitating more billions for newer and bigger weapons, is one of the most colossal injustices in the long history of man. While we are doing this, two-thirds of the world is starving, or living in conditions of unparalleled and subhuman destitution.

We speak of the "spiritual desert" and the decline of morality that would result from Communist conquest. What about our western world, where on the one hand an affluent society, glutted with profits made out of weapons, is sinking into depths of moral degradation comparable to those of the late Roman Empire, while on the other hand an underdeveloped society reduced to pauperism, robbed of its primitive order and culture, lives the vicious and despairing life of an enormous worldwide slum. Is this combination by any chance to be regarded as a spiritual Eden?

Far from demanding that the lunatic race for destruction be stepped up, it seems to me that Christian morality imposes on every single one of us the obligation to protest against it and to work for the creation of an international authority with power and sanctions that will be able to control technology, and divert our amazing virtuosity into the service of man instead of against him.

It is not enough to say that we ought to try to work for negotiated disarmament, or that one power bloc or the other ought to take the lead and disarm unilaterally. Methods and policies can and should be fairly considered. But what matters most is the obligation to travel in every feasible way in the direction of peace, at all costs, using all the traditional and legitimate methods, while at the same time seeking to improvise new and original measures to achieve our end.

Long ago, even before the A-bomb, Pope Pius XII declared it was our supreme obligation to make "war on war" (1944). At that time he stressed our moral obligation to ban all wars of aggression, stating this duty was binding on *all* and that it "brooks no delay, no procrastination, no hesitation, no subterfuge." And what have we done since then? The A-bomb, the H-bomb, the ICBM, the further development of chemical and bacteriological weapons, and every possible evasion and subterfuge to justify their use without limitation as soon as one or the other nation declares that it may be expedient!

Therefore in his Christmas messages of 1954 and 1955 Pius XII renewed his pleas to nations to outlaw ABC warfare:

> For our part we will tirelessly endeavor to bring about by means of international agreements — always recognizing the principle of legitimate self-defense — *the effective proscription and banishment of atomic, biological and chemical warfare.* (1954, italics added)

In 1955, with greater detail, the Pontiff spoke out against nuclear testing and nuclear armaments as well as against the arms race in general. He demanded that nuclear testing be given up, nuclear armaments renounced, and arms in general subject to strict control.

> We do not hesitate to declare as we have in previous allocutions, that the sum total of these precautions *is an obligation in conscience of nations and of their leaders* (italics added).

Therefore a Christian who is not willing to envisage the creation of an effective international authority to control the destinies of man for peace is not acting and thinking as a mature member of the Church. He does not have fully Christian perspectives. Such perspectives must by their very nature, be "catholic," that is to say worldwide. They must consider the needs of mankind and not the temporary expediency and short-sighted policy of a particular nation.

To reject a "world-wide" outlook, to refuse to consider the good of mankind, and to remain satisfied with the affluence that flows from our war economy, is hardly a Christian attitude. Nor will our attachment to the current payoff accruing to us from weapons make it any easier for us to see and understand the need to take the hard road of sacrifice which alone leads to peace!

Equally important, and perhaps more difficult than technological control, is the restoration of some moral sense and the resumption of genuine responsibility. Without this it is illusory for us to speak of freedom and "control." Unfortunately, even where moral principles are still regarded with some degree of respect, morality seems to have lost touch with the realities of our situation. Modern warfare is fought as much by machines as by men. Even a great deal of planning depends on the work of mechanical computers.

Hence it becomes more and more difficult to estimate the morality of an act leading to war because it is more and more difficult to know precisely what is going on. Not only is war increasingly a matter for pure specialists operating with fantastically complex machinery, but above all there is the question of absolute secrecy regarding everything that seriously affects defense policy. We may amuse ourselves by reading the reports in the mass media and imagine that these "facts" provide sufficient basis for moral judgments for and against war. But in reality, we are simply elaborating moral fantasies in a vacuum. Whatever we may decide, we remain completely at the mercy of the governmental power, or rather the anonymous power of managers and generals who stand behind the facade of government. We have no way of directly influencing the decisions and policies taken by these people. In practice, we must fall back on a blinder and blinder faith which more and more resigns itself to trusting the "legitimately constituted authority" without having the vaguest notion what the authority is liable to do next. This condition of irresponsibility and passivity is extremely dangerous, and also it is hardly conducive to genuine morality.

An entirely new dimension is opened by the fantastic processes and techniques involved in modern war. An American president can speak of warfare in outer space and nobody bursts out laughing — he is perfectly serious. Science fiction and the comic strip have all suddenly come true. When a missile armed with an H-bomb warhead is fired by the pressing of a button and its target is a whole city, the number of corpses is estimated in "megacorpses"—*millions* of dead human beings. A thousand or ten thousand more here or there are not even matter for comment.

It is well known that there have, in recent years, been several false alarms in which the whole striking force of the Strategic Air Command was alerted and stood in readiness to take off for the annihilation of predesignated targets (including *cities*). In each case disaster was fortunately averted. But the risk is enormous. Even if it were possible for us to assume that military men in possession of this awful power would use it only according to Christian and ethical standards (and this is not a valid assumption) there would still be the totally irrational situation which leaves the fate of the entire civilized world at the mercy of some unpredictable mechanical or psychological failure.

We may, and we must, learn to live with this absurd and awful menace for the time being. But to accept it as permanent, to "adjust" to it, and to build future policies upon it would not only be immoral but insane.

Hence the need for strong peace movements, both as a protest and a "brake" to slow down the accelerated rush toward war, and as a preparation for more positive and constructive steps to establish peace.

13

The Scientists
and Nuclear War

IT SHOULD NOT BE NECESSARY to remind the reader that peace is normally and logically the work not of peace movements but of governments. The responsibility of preserving the world from nuclear disaster rests principally with the leaders of the nuclear powers and with their collaborators in international politics. Particularly immediate and urgent is the responsibility of those who represent these governments in disarmament conferences. Yet the efforts at negotiation have bogged down in double-talk. Many intelligent proposals have been made by either side, but it does not seem possible to make any headway in adopting them. The whole question of negotiation for peace is infinitely complex, and the mere effort to master the thousands of pages of reports and analyses would appall even someone who thought the effort would really help to promote true peace. Actually, in all the skirmishes and debates, the real issues are the ones that seem to evade formulation. One is easily left with the impression that the whole effort is futile and that negotiation itself is a farce. This is a very dangerous state of mind, because there is no alternative to intelligent negotiation except war itself. We must agree or blow one another up. Hence it is vitally important that the negotiations be continued, not as a pure matter of form, or as an exercise in political maneuvering, or as a forum for the platitudes of propaganda, but in deadly earnest. The earnestness must however prove itself by real concern for the interests of humanity, and not for the prestige of this or that portion of it.

The pressures of public opinion can and must play a part in stimulating intelligent governmental action. That is why it is important first of all to clearly state the moral limits which the enlightened conscience will refuse to violate. This statement of principle and of the firm intention to abide by principle must be made known without ambiguity, so that it will have a decisive effect upon the direction of policy.

It must be made perfectly clear that we believe in safeguarding objective truth and rights more than in the achievement of short-term political advantage. It must also be made clear that we believe that if we are loyal to our deepest moral obligations, even when that loyalty may seem to place us temporarily at a disadvantage, we are convinced that truth itself will be the most powerful safeguard of our own deepest interests and those of the world.

The natural law has not been and cannot be abrogated. It is written in the hearts of all men, including Communists. It can of course be violated and silenced. And indeed it is frequently and systematically violated, and has been for centuries in numberless ways both by societies and by individuals. Still it must be recognized that the voice of conscience cannot be permanently silenced. Men will be continually confronted with truth. Even if natural ethics do not guarantee protection against the danger of nuclear war there should be at least a vestige of sanity and common sense that would make us all realize that massive nuclear destruction should be avoided, simply because the objective facts are so obvious and so inescapable. Even when men dishonestly tamper with the facts and try to manipulate the truth, they have to try to justify their actions in the name of truth and right. Even a dishonest appeal to truth will

call the attention of men to truth and reality, and some will
have to admit objective facts whether they want to or not.

Ever since the atomic bomb was developed, the atomic scientists themselves have had to confront their moral obligations
and, in the main, have tried to live up to them. From the very
first the scientists pointed out what the possible effects of the
bomb might be, and attempted to help politicians guide their
policies in the direction of just and humane ethical standards.
From the first, though the atomic scientists have been listened
to with respect their advice has generally been set aside for
the sake of political advantage. The politician and the publi-
cist usually win out — that is to say ignorance and expediency
triumph over knowledge and moral concern!

The scientists themselves are divided. Not all of them want
to commit themselves fully in an issue which is dangerous and
might invite serious consequences. The public does not listen
to the voice of the scientists with equanimity. Politicians and
business men have not been ambiguous in signifying what ora-
cles they will consider acceptable. The mass media do not tend
to encourage an expression of the less popular view, even when
that expression comes from one of the high priests of nuclear
physics.

At present the prophet who is at once politically most "orthodox," most "acceptable" and most widely "heard" is the one
who proposes newer, bigger and more sophisticated weapons
systems, and who espouses the cause of the fallout shelters
for everybody. The weapons systems and the shelters fit obviously into a plan for an accelerated arms race, and the
most vocal spokesmen for this policy are Edward Teller and
Herman Kahn.

Why are these men the accepted and approved authorities?
Because their message is the one that is most propitious to the
aims, the fears and the concerns of big business, the military
and the nervous public of the "garrison state."

Edward Teller, in his book *The Legacy of Hiroshima,* complains not without an underlying bitterness that the moral scruples of other atomic scientists slowed down the development of his invention, the H-bomb. Teller certainly does not agree with the outspoken group of his colleagues whose views are published in the *Bulletin of the Atomic Scientists.* Whereas a very significant proportion of the atomic scientists would seem to favor a positive and concrete disarmament policy, and to have a genuine confidence in the possibility of a multilateral reduction of arms at least to the proportions of the "minimum deterrent," Teller is considered one of the major instigators of the all-out arms race.

In actual fact, Teller goes to some effort to assure us that his real goal is "the clean tactical nuclear weapon." He believes that peace can be preserved by a policy of limited nuclear wars, fought by specially trained troops. In these wars, according to him, cities would be spared and the "clean tactical nuclear weapon" would come into play to break up concentrations of troops, to smash the resistance of guerrillas, and to flush out Communist penetration. In order to prevent recourse to the megatonic weapon, and massive retaliation or even preemptive strike, he would have us rely on the "invulnerable deterrent" and on civil defense. But of course the invulnerable deterrent involves thousands of missiles. This philosophy of nuclear war says, in so many words, that there are ways and means of waging wars intelligently and efficiently. Efficiency means preparedness. Total preparedness is in fact the only guarantee of the survival of capitalism against Communist penetration.

Whatever may be the merits of this theory, I would like to draw attention to a few very significant facts, which have a direct bearing on the moral thesis of my book.

First of all, even though he sponsors an arms race at full speed, Teller insists repeatedly that he considers the preemptive strike policy to be both immoral and inefficacious.

I think a rather lengthy quotation is advisable here. Although Teller says nothing that should not be perfectly obvious, what he says is by no means obvious to the public of the United States at the time of writing. Least of all is it obvious to those for whom the name of Teller represents the ultimate in wisdom. Coming from the Father of the H-bomb the following sentiments should have a particular significance.

Our national purpose is peace, coupled with freedom and a decent livelihood for peoples throughout the world. *To preserve world peace we have adopted a policy in which I believe strongly and which I share fully: we must never strike a first blow. We are firmly convinced that it would be morally indefensible to start an atomic war.* We have held to this policy. Even when the United States had a monopoly of nuclear weapons, we did not seriously consider using them although Communism used the force of arms to suppress freedom in Eastern Europe and to conquer China.

The policies of both massive retaliation and mutual deterrence carry the threat that the United States will fight if our allies are attacked. This is basically inconsistent with convictions which are strongly upheld by many Americans. It is also exceedingly dangerous. This threat, carried out, would expand a localized conflict into a worldwide nuclear war. *I do not believe that the United States should unleash an all-out atomic attack for any lesser reason than to return a full scale attack made upon us.* (*Legacy,* 234, italics added)

This quotation makes two serious moral contentions: that preemptive strike policy is out of the question and that massive retaliation is also out of the question except as the ultimate resort in the event that the United States was subjected to a massive first strike. Teller also takes it for granted that the Russians do not want a nuclear war, at least not now. This is not by any means the common doctrine of the "hard" school of thought. Nor do the "realists" take kindly to another thesis adopted by Teller: *"we must create a world community. This is the central problem of our age"* (*Legacy,* 290).

The reason for dwelling at some length on this statement is the fact that it is quite extraordinary in the context of his definitely bellicose assumptions. We are to build weapons to the point of saturation, but never use them. One feels that Teller has gone out of his way to insist on these points in order to allay moral anxieties about the obvious ambivalence of his position. He wants the reader to know that he is not immoral, or amoral. The implication is that if he is conscientious in deploring the preemptive strike, there is no moral danger in his basic policy: testing, stockpiling, preparedness, and above all sharing our nuclear weapons with our allies in NATO.

We need not delay to examine the morality of Teller's program. The statement that he wants a "world community" tends to become questionable when we see he is prepared to solve this "central problem of our age" by the very means that make war inevitable: increasing the tempo, the expansion and the variety of nuclear armaments, and especially by arming West Germans with nuclear devices against the Russians. Since this is the nature of his logic, we can leave Dr. Teller to his theories about big holes, underground art museums, and the "postwar organization that must be planned now," the "teamwork" that will become necessary when a nuclear war has reduced the standard of living from the highest in the world to zero (*Legacy,* 257).

We might find it easier to accept the synthetic sunshine disseminated by Teller and Kahn if they showed some indication of realizing that they themselves seem to be the ones exerting the most decisive influence in this country to bring about the war that may reduce our vaunted affluence to zero.

There can be no question that the publication of Kahn's theories contributed a great deal to the renewal of war tensions during the Berlin Crisis of 1961. Certainly it was the shelter scare that brought home to Americans the shocking imminence of nuclear disaster. Shelters of course are the keystone in the edifice of Kahn's thought which might be summed up as follows: although no one wants to go down in history as the first man to annihilate one hundred million people, we are all arming to the teeth and it is obvious that we are not just going to stockpile H-bombs as a deterrent. Of course the main thing is to make our nuclear threats perfectly *credible*. If we say we are able to launch a first strike against Russia we must prove that we are also willing to do so, and to prove this we must give the impression that we can absorb the retaliation that would follow. We are not of course planning a war right now but if our defense posture is to be credible, we must ourselves believe that nuclear war is not only possible, but that it is a rational choice, and that we may very well get into one and win it.

Such statements from a highly respected, semiofficial spokesman of a corporation engaged in research for the Air Force can easily be interpreted to mean that the United States seriously contemplates the possibility of nuclear war and that nuclear war now enters into our policy as an accepted and important factor. Obviously in such circumstances it is not hard to see why such great tensions were generated over Berlin, fallout shelters and nuclear testing in 1961 and 1962.

Fortunately, as we have seen, not all scientists are aligned with Teller and Kahn. Leo Szilard who prompted Einstein to write the famous letter to Roosevelt which initiated the development of the A-bomb has always been the most prominent of those who have made the right use of nuclear energy their central concern. I think it can be said without exaggeration that the sanity and sagacity of Leo Szilard's moral reasoning about the ethics of nuclear war recommends his plan as one which really fulfills the basic Christian moral demands. It is a wonder and a pity that Szilard has exerted less influence than Kahn in the formation of our national conscience on nuclear war.

The following notes are taken from an important conference given at several universities in the fall of 1961 and reprinted in the *Bulletin of the Atomic Scientists* for April 1962.[27] They summarize his practical suggestions for peace here and now by means of a "council for the abolition of war."

He starts with the observation that in his opinion the nuclear powers have entered upon a policy that leads to an unlimited arms race and therefore to an all-out war within perhaps ten years. The pattern of behavior both in Russia and in the United States must be changed if this disaster is to be averted.

The issue must be faced: the United States is not ready, perhaps not even willing to disarm. Is Russia more willing? Szilard does not say. Disarmament may in fact present almost as much of a problem to both power blocs as war itself. In this dilemma disarmament negotiations are "guided mainly by the public relations aspect rather than by the substantive aspect of the issue." This means that productive political action is generally blocked and even those politicians who have real insight are unable to put their ideas to work. Indeed they often do not even dare to express their true thoughts. Others are content to maneuver for immediate political advantage. The advantage may be infinitesimally small, and it may have to be gained at the cost of immense risks.

In such a situation, while first observing without ambiguity that "the problem that the bomb poses to the world cannot be solved except by abolishing war, and nothing less will do," Szilard concentrates on the overwhelmingly urgent short-term objectives, the ones that must be pursued within the next few years in order to reduce tensions and restore perspectives that will eventually permit effective thought and negotiation for peace.

Szilard is not a unilateralist by any means. He is not proposing drastic or utopian measures, to be adopted in haste without regard for consequences. When he says that in such a crisis, either of the contestants must be willing and able to take certain limited, but positive unilateral *initiatives* he is simply saying what ought to be obvious to anyone with any experience of life: someone has to take the first step, even if the step is not a very big one.

> Some of the steps would be taken in order to reduce the present danger of war, others would be taken so that if a war breaks out, which neither America nor Russia wants, it may be possible to bring hostilities to an end before there is an all-out atomic catastrophe.

Dismissing the issue of shelters and of atomic testing as peripheral, "more symptoms of the trouble we are in than the cause of the trouble," he turns to what he considers to be more relevant matters.

First of all he condemns the whole conduct of the Cold War by both sides. There is immense danger in all the senseless and petty international harassments which exhaust the energies of Cold War politicians without achieving any useful purpose whatever. These maneuvers produce a climate of permanent meaninglessness in the world. They keep the peoples of the world under constant pathological tensions. They foment anger, desperation and confusion which may at any moment erupt into the blind fury of a totally senseless and totally destructive war.

Two crucially important policy decisions could, says Szilard, be made with immense advantage.

> *First of all, America should resolve and proclaim that she would not resort to any strategic bombing of cities or bases of Russia (either by means of atomic bombs or conventional explosives) except if American cities or bases are attacked with bombs, or if there is an unprovoked attack with bombs against one of America's allies.* (Italics in the original)

The second policy decision would be a very strict limitation of the use of tactical nuclear weapons against troops in battle. Such use would be limited to *our own side of a prewar boundary.* The implication of this is the key to Szilard's policy, that nuclear weapons, even tactical, should be used only insofar as they are necessary to *stop an invasion* or an enemy takeover of our own or allied territory. Hence it would involve a *purely defensive use* of weapons and in no sense an aggressive use sophistically rationalized as defense. Obviously while passing muster as a moral minimum, this pledge does not represent the full Christian ideal. Szilard's point is that it is at least believable and doubtless workable, provided the same restraint is observed on both sides.

The main difference between Szilard and Teller on this point of tactical weapons is that Szilard thinks chiefly in terms of preventing an invasion of an ally, Teller thinks chiefly of smashing a Communist maneuver for power. Hence Teller is not as concerned as Szilard with defense limits but rather with a stated limitation of aggression. Szilard's policy says: "once you cross this line, you will meet with tactical nuclear weapons." Teller says: "once you initiate a move to gain power we will take immediate countermeasures to smash you with nuclear weapons, but only within certain limits." The limits would remain flexible, to be defined by the policy makers at the time, thus leaving plenty of room for aggression.

Returning to Szilard: his ultimate goal is effective and total disarmament: but as long as this could not be attained, only a sufficient number of bombs and missiles should be kept to provide a minimum deterrent. And note that while these bombs would be used on enemy cities in case of attack, Szilard stipulates that *they should not be used without warning.* In other words, while he admits in principle that nuclear weapons may be used to destroy cities, *the populations must be given a genuine chance to evacuate.* As far as I can see, this is the only way in which the "massive" retaliatory use of nuclear weapons can be reconciled with the Christian conscience. Here for once we have a real and serious distinction between the physical evil of destruction of property and the moral evil of genocide.

In this event, also, the threat of nuclear bombardment would no longer be a general deterrent, to be used when we feel ourselves threatened or provoked in some ill-defined way. It would be a defensive response to a nuclear attack on our own land or on our allies.

Szilard also believes in the renunciation of a first strike policy, whether as a normal war move or as a deterrent to prevent war. He feels that there is still sufficient doubt of the value of the first strike, in Washington, for the policy to be dropped, and this would considerably reduce international tensions. There can be no question that at the time of writing what seems to be the most serious and crucial development in the policy of the United States is this indefinite but growing assumption of the necessity of a first strike.

Finally Szilard asserts, against Teller, that atomic bombs and missiles should by no means be given to the Germans.

Disarmament will be out of the question as long as the people of America cannot regard it as credible and possible, and of course it will not be credible until there is a genuine meeting of minds between America and Russia on the question of *how peace may be secured after disarmament*. This is another central issue. Szilard is not one of those who assumes that the whole idea of disarmament is purely and simply a trap proposed by the Russians in order to make us let down our guard so that we can be immediately and treacherously knocked out.

Leo Szilard has proposed concrete steps for the study of these vital questions and for the implementation of policies based on them. It seems to me that the principal argument in favor of his suggestions, at least from the Catholic point of view, is that they are in complete accordance with all the moral principles on modern war as enumerated by Popes Pius XII and John XXIII.

Szilard's proposals assume, as do the papal pronouncements, that Communism itself must be resisted. They also admit, with the popes, that even tactical nuclear weapons may be used in this resistance, but above all Leo Szilard limits all use of force to a *clearly defensive action,* and he *completely outlaws all indiscriminate massive destruction of civilian populations* as Pius XII did in the most unmistakable terms. Finally, Szilard's ultimate goal is disarmament and the abolition of war by international agreement, which Pius XII declared was a most serious obligation, binding on all, that would brook no further delay.

14

Red or Dead?
The Anatomy of a Cliché

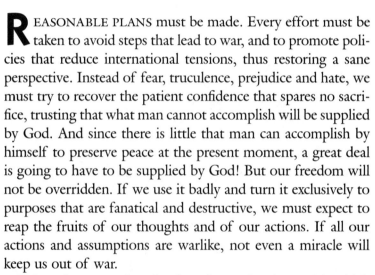

R EASONABLE PLANS must be made. Every effort must be taken to avoid steps that lead to war, and to promote policies that reduce international tensions, thus restoring a sane perspective. Instead of fear, truculence, prejudice and hate, we must try to recover the patient confidence that spares no sacrifice, trusting that what man cannot accomplish will be supplied by God. And since there is little that man can accomplish by himself to preserve peace at the present moment, a great deal is going to have to be supplied by God! But our freedom will not be overridden. If we use it badly and turn it exclusively to purposes that are fanatical and destructive, we must expect to reap the fruits of our thoughts and of our actions. If all our actions and assumptions are warlike, not even a miracle will keep us out of war.

It is unfortunate that the thoughts and actions with which we are increasingly familiar offer little serious hope for a constructive solution. The muddleheaded, frustrated, stubborn and obtuse assumptions that underlie our view of the world and its problems, produces no clarity, only darkness and desperation.

Thought becomes more and more rudimentary. We strive to soothe our madness by intoning more and more vacuous clichés. And at such times, far from being as innocuous as they are absurd, empty slogans take on a dreadful power. Their very emptiness, their total lack of seriousness, enables them to justify the raw frustration of minds exasperated by the calculated futilities of the Cold War.

Let us briefly anatomize one of the current clichés which tries to sound decisive and brave: "better dead than Red." It appears that the saying began in Germany, and began the other way around: "better Red than dead." It was deftly fielded on the first bounce by the Americans and came back in reverse, thus acquiring an air of challenge and defiance. "Better dead than Red" was a reply to effete and decadent cynicism. It was a condemnation of "appeasement." (Anything short of a nuclear attack on Russia rates as "appeasement.")

Actually, whichever way you take it, the phrase is both empty and absurd. It evades the issue. It reduces a complex and critical human problem to a choice between meaningless alternatives. Whichever way you take it, this catch phrase ends up by saying that there is no way out but one form or other of destruction and that one must either have recourse to the bomb or renounce all hope of solving the international problem. If you are foolish enough to take this seriously then, as a kind of psychological bonus, you can treat yourself to the pleasure of thinking yourself brave, either because you are willing to face death, or because you are willing to face slavery under Communism.

What the cliché ignores is of course the real bravery of patient, humble, persevering labor to effect, step by step, through honest negotiation, a gradual understanding that can eventually relieve tensions and bring about some agreement upon which serious disarmament measures can be based. The Red or dead alternative is actually a dismissal of all the patient labor and sacrifice that are required for us to build a unified and peaceful world. When one invokes the falsely momentous choice between death and Red domination, one dispenses himself from any further effort of thought and settles down to the easier business of letting hate, suspicion and fanaticism simmer along as they please, thus giving little relief to feelings of confusion and despair.

To embrace this absurd alternative as final, and to look at the international crisis in this light and no other, is to renounce all confidence in the peaceful creativity of our society which we are so proud to call free. Actually, however, it seems the "Red or dead" attitude that so many people have adopted, masks a real inner recognition of some of the inconsistencies that demand to be resolved by our own society. The petulance which accepts death or slavery so easily is perhaps an admission that the superficial optimism of the eighteenth-century ideologies, still considered fundamental to our political thinking, has perhaps worn too thin. But surely our society does not stand or fall with the naive doctrines of Adam Smith, Tom Paine or Rousseau? Or does it? Have we a philosophy at all? Have we any clear idea of what we are trying to do? One wonders if all this emotion about "Red or dead" does not really express a general confusion and aimlessness, an overall immaturity which would rather explode with petulant, suicidal rage than grow up and face the responsibilities of full maturity and leadership in a turbulent international community.

Since this kind of thinking is at once so prevalent and so obnoxious, it might be worthwhile to draw out some of the implications hidden in the Red or dead cliché.

From the moment you take dead or Red as the expression of a realistic alternative, from the moment you pretend to base serious discussion upon this alternative, you are implicitly admitting that you believe the following:

1. You are saying that you think the very survival of democracy is bound up with total nuclear war. That without recourse to the threat of total nuclear war, without the readiness to wage such a war, without the ability to annihilate the enemy by a

"first strike," the survival of democracy, freedom and western civilization are no longer conceivable.

2. In other words, you believe that it is not possible for democracy, for western civilization, perhaps even Christianity to survive by peaceful means. That we have exhausted the resources of humanity and reasonableness which would make negotiation unthinkable except on a basis of terror.

3. You are saying that if we of the west survive at all, we must expect to survive as Communists. That it is a choice between surviving and becoming a Communist, or dying in defense of the ideals of democracy, the capitalist economy, freedom, the American Way of Life. If you push this far enough you are simply implying that the American Way of Life cannot survive except by war, but that Communism can survive without recourse to total nuclear war. This is hardly a confession of faith in democracy.

4. You are saying that since for the Communists survival automatically means victory, they must be prevented at all costs from surviving. That since for the west survival without nuclear war practically means defeat, then to reject nuclear war and negotiate for peace in order to survive is purely and simply to admit defeat. This is "appeasement" and cowardice, therefore bravery demands that Communism be prevented from surviving, even at the risk of our own destruction. Gradually nuclear terror comes to look like the only reasonable, honest, upright course open to western man. Our mass media seem to have settled comfortably in this position, and of course the majority accept this verdict with passive fatalism.

5. The last assumption is at once the most horrible, the most absurd and the most revealing. It is purely and simply that if we are reduced to a choice between the survival of the Communists and the destruction of the entire human race, then the brave, noble, heroic, and even *Christian* course is to choose the destruction of the human race. This is of course not frankly

admitted, because such reasoning always leaves a kind of irrational loophole for "survival." There is always a chance that
some "fifty million on our side" might be left standing after
everyone else had been blown up. No one seems to consider
the possibility that such survival might be at once culpable,
subhuman and infernally awful.

To my mind this whole line of "reasoning" is purely and
simply insane. For all its gestures of conquest it is a mentality of
defeat. It is nothing but appeasement in reverse — it does not
grovel, but it blows everything up, assuming there is no alternative between groveling and destruction. Such an assumption
is a pure surrender to irrationality and to hysteria. Nothing
could be more directly contrary to the spirit of liberty, and of
reasonable initiative characteristic of the American tradition.

1. This kind of thinking represents a *mentality of defeat*. All
down the line it presumes that democratic values are not strong
enough to prevail by peaceful means. All down the line it accepts the very arguments which Marx long ago drew up against
the capitalist system: *that it could not survive except by recourse
to war,* and that *it would resort to any extreme in order to crush
opposition.* To admit this Marxian analysis as the last word on
western civilization is, it seems to me, a complete moral and intellectual capitulation. It means the complete justification of all
the self-righteous arguments on which the Communists base
their hostility to us.

2. It represents a mentality of despair. While claiming to believe in democratic ideals, in the creativity inherent in our way
of life, it admits in reality a *radical doubt of all these values.* It has
no practical faith in them because it cannot believe they have
retained enough power to overcome the opposition raised by
Communism. Only nuclear weapons can do the trick. This attitude is the result of the secularist, irreligious, pragmatic spirit
which [has] actually undermined the whole moral structure of
the west. It springs from the emptiness, the resentment, the

sense of futility and meaninglessness which gnaw secretly at the heart of western man.

3. It is finally nothing else than a *mentality of suicide*. It is the self-destructive, self-hating resentment that follows from accumulated petty humiliations, repeated errors, reiterated blunders and stupidities with which we have continually lost face before those whom we secretly despised. In order to release the pent-up and desperate pressures of our self-hate we are now ready to destroy ourselves and the whole world with us in one grand explosion. And we justify ourselves by claiming that we prefer death (for ourselves and everyone else) to tyranny. What right have we to choose death for everyone else? Is not that an act of supreme tyranny and injustice?

Where have we seen this kind of thinking before? We do not have to look far. Have we already forgotten Hitler? Have we already forgotten his paranoid hatreds, his love for "definitive solutions," for "finalizing" such problems as the existence of races he did not happen to like? Have we forgotten his ultimate determination to bring all Germany down with himself to destruction? Have we forgotten that for the Nazis the greatest virtue, the greatest reasonableness, was to be found in blind obedience to the destructive mania of the Führer?

Those in this country who are now seriously thinking that it would be worthwhile to risk the destruction of the whole world rather than allow it to become Communist are not only defeatists who have lost their grasp of the democratic ideal, they are thinking like Hitler. They have a Nazi mentality. And unfortunately they have much more powerful weapons of destruction than the Nazis ever knew. These errors and illusions are no small matter. Insofar as they are prepared seriously to implement their thinking by destructive action, these men are potential war criminals. And those who follow them in their line of thought are in danger of becoming criminals themselves.

15

Christian Perspectives in World Crisis

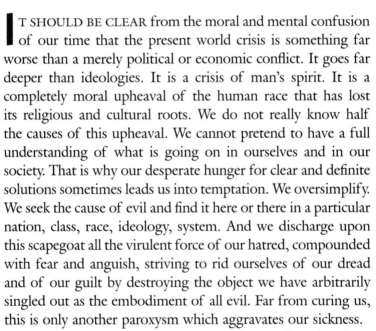

I T SHOULD BE CLEAR from the moral and mental confusion of our time that the present world crisis is something far worse than a merely political or economic conflict. It goes far deeper than ideologies. It is a crisis of man's spirit. It is a completely moral upheaval of the human race that has lost its religious and cultural roots. We do not really know half the causes of this upheaval. We cannot pretend to have a full understanding of what is going on in ourselves and in our society. That is why our desperate hunger for clear and definite solutions sometimes leads us into temptation. We oversimplify. We seek the cause of evil and find it here or there in a particular nation, class, race, ideology, system. And we discharge upon this scapegoat all the virulent force of our hatred, compounded with fear and anguish, striving to rid ourselves of our dread and of our guilt by destroying the object we have arbitrarily singled out as the embodiment of all evil. Far from curing us, this is only another paroxysm which aggravates our sickness.

The moral evil in the world is due to man's alienation from the deepest truth, from the springs of spiritual life within himself, to his alienation from God. Those who realize this try desperately to persuade and enlighten their brothers. But we are in a radically different position from the first Christians, who revolutionized an essentially religious world of paganism with the message of a new religion that had never been heard of.

We on the contrary live in an irreligious post-Christian world in which the Christian message has been repeated over and over until it has come to seem empty of all intelligible content to those whose ears close to the word of God even before it is uttered. In their minds Christian is no longer identified with newness and change, but only with the static preservation of outworn structures.

But why is this? Is it merely that the spiritual novelty of Christianity has worn off in twenty centuries? That people have heard the Gospel before and are tired of it? Or is it perhaps because for centuries the message has been belied and contradicted by the conduct of Christians themselves?

Christianity is essentially the revelation of the divine mercy in the mystery of Christ and his Church. Infinite mercy, infinite love are revealed to the world, made *evident* to the world in the sanctity of the Mystical Body of Christ, united in charity, nourished by the sacramental mystery of the Eucharist in which all participate in the divine *agape,* the sacrifice of the word made flesh. To say Christianity is the revelation of love means not simply that Christians are (or should be) nice charitable people. It means that love is the key to life itself and to the whole meaning of the cosmos and of history. If Christians, then, are without love they deprive all other men of access to the central truth that gives meaning to all existence.

"By this shall all men know that you are my disciples, if you have love for one another" (John 13:35). "That they all may be one in us, as thou Father in me and I in thee; so that the world may believe that Thou hast sent me" (John 17:21). "My peace I give unto you. . . . I do not give peace as the world gives it" (John 14:27). "The wisdom that comes from above is marked chiefly indeed by its purity but also indeed by its peacefulness. . . . It carries mercy with it and a harvest of all that is good; it is uncensorious and without affectation. Peace is the seed ground of holiness and those who make peace will win its harvest. What leads you to war, what leads to quarreling among you? . . . The appetites which infest your mortal bodies. Your desires go unfulfilled and so you fall to murdering" (James 3:17–4:2).

It must be admitted therefore that if the gospel of peace is no longer convincing on the lips of Christians, it may well be because they have ceased to give a living example of peace, unity and love. True, we have to understand that the Church was never intended to be absolutely perfect on earth, and she is a Church of sinners, laden with imperfection. Christian peace and Christian charity are based indeed on this need to "bear one another's burdens," to accept the infirmities that plague one's own life and the lives of others. Our unity is a struggle with disunity and our peace exists in the midst of conflict.

But the fact remains that a warring and warlike Christendom has never been able to preach the Gospel of charity and peace with full conviction or full success. As Cardinal Newman so rightly said, the greatest victories of the Church were all won before Constantine, in the days when there were no Christian armies and when the true Christian soldier was the martyr, whose witness to Christ was nonviolent. It was the martyrs who conquered Rome for Christ with a conquest that has been stable for twenty centuries. How long were the crusaders able to hold Jerusalem?

This should teach us that though the words of the Gospel still objectively retain all the force and freshness of their original life, it is not enough now for us to preach and explain them. It is not enough to announce the familiar message that no longer seems to be news. Not enough to teach, to prove, to convince. Now above all is the time to embody Christian truth in action even more than in words. No matter how lucid, how persuasive, how logical, how profound our theological and spiritual statements may be, they are usually wasted on anyone who does not already think as we do. That is why the serene and classic sanity of moralists exposing the traditional teaching of Christian theologians on the "just war" is almost a total loss in the general clamor and confusion of half truths, propaganda slogans, and pernicious clichés, many of which are preached and disseminated by Christians themselves, not excluding the clergy.

What is needed now is the Christian who manifests the truth of the Gospel in social action, with or without explanation. The more clearly his life manifests the teaching of Christ, the more salutary it will be. Clear and decisive Christian action explains itself, and teaches in a way that words never can.

Christians must not only assert the existence of a moral order and of natural law in the midst of a world where law and order are questioned or even completely forgotten. Christians above all must act in all things, in their work, their social relations, their political life as if justice and objective right were to them vital and essential realities, not just consoling ideas.

Pope John XXIII said in *Mater et Magistra:*

Let men make all the technical and economic progress they can, there will be no peace nor justice in the world until they return to a sense of their dignity as creatures and sons of God, who is the first and final cause of all created being. Separated from God man is but a monster, in himself and toward others, for the right ordering of human society presupposes the right ordering of man's conscience with God, who is himself the source of all justice, truth and love. (215)

And Pius XII said in his Christmas Message of 1955 that Christians have a most serious obligation to help build a society based on genuinely Christian principles:

If ever Christians were to neglect this duty of theirs by leaving inactive insofar as in them lies the guiding force of faith in public life they would be committing treason against the God-Man.[28]

What is wanted now is therefore not simply the Christian who takes an inner complacency in the words and example of Christ, but who seeks to follow Christ perfectly, not only in his own personal life, not only in prayer and penance, but also in his political commitments and in all his social responsibilities.

We have certainly no need of a pseudo-contemplative spirituality that claims to ignore the world and its problems entirely, and devotes itself supposedly to the things of God, without concern for human society. All true Christian spirituality, even that of the Christian contemplative, is and must always be deeply concerned with man, since "God became man in order that man might become God" (St. Irenaeus). The Christian spirit is one of compassion, of responsibility and of commitment. It cannot be indifferent to suffering, to injustice, error, untruth. Precisely for that reason then a genuine Christian spirituality must be profoundly concerned with all the risks and problems implied by the mere existence of nuclear stockpiles and biological weapons.

In the presence of an international politic based on nuclear deterrence and on the imminent possibility of global suicide, no Christian may remain indifferent, no Christian can allow himself a mere inert and passive acquiescence in ready-made formulas fed to him by the mass media.

Still less can a Christian conscience be content with an ethic that seeks to justify and permit as much as possible of force and terror, in international politics and in war. The Christian is formally obliged to take positive and active means to restrain force and bring into being a positive international authority which can effectively prevent war and promote peace.

The whole world faces a momentous choice. Either our frenzy of desperation will lead to destruction, or our loyalty to truth, to God and to our fellow man will enable us to perform the patient, heroic task of building a world that will eventually thrive in unity, order and peace.

In the present crisis, Christian action can be decisive. That is why it is supremely important for us to keep our heads and refuse to be carried away by the wild projects of fanatics who seek an oversimplified and immediate solution by means of ruthless violence. Power alone is not the answer.

In a world that has largely discarded moral imperatives and which indeed no longer seriously considers the violent death of one hundred million human beings as a moral issue, but only as a pragmatic exercise of power, the Christian must regard himself as the custodian of moral and human values, and *must give top priority to their clarification and defense.*

This implies first of all the duty of unremitting study, meditation, prayer and every form of spiritual and intellectual discipline that can fit him for so serious a task. Obviously this responsibility is first of all binding on the clergy and religious, and above all on those entrusted with their education and spiritual formation.

In this all-important matter we have to rediscover the sources of Christian tradition, and we must come to realize that we have to a great extent abandoned the early Christian ideal of peace and nonviolent action. Surely it is curious that in the twentieth century the one great political figure who has made a conscious and systematic use of the Gospel principles for nonviolent political action was not a Christian but a Hindu. Even more curious is the fact that so many Christians thought Gandhi was some kind of eccentric and that his nonviolence was an impractical and sensational fad.

Christians have got to speak by their actions. Their political action must not be confined to the privacy of the polling booth. It must be clear and manifest to everybody. It must speak loudly and plainly the Christian truth, and it must be prepared to defend that truth with sacrifices, accepting misunderstanding, injustice, calumny, and even imprisonment or death. It is crucially important for Christians today to adopt a genuinely Christian position and support it with everything they have got. This means an unremitting fight for justice in every sphere — in labor, in race relations, in the "third world" and above all in international affairs.

This means reducing the distance between our interior intentions and our exterior acts. Our social actions must conform to our deepest religious principles. Beliefs and politics can no longer be kept isolated from one another. It is no longer possible for us to be content with abstract and hidden acts of "purity of intention" which do nothing to make our outward actions different from those of atheists or agnostics.

Nor can we be content to make our highest ideal the preservation of a minimum of ethical rectitude prescribed by natural law. Too often the nobility and grandeur of natural law have been debased by the manipulations of theorists until natural law has become indistinguishable from the law of the jungle, which is no law at all. Hence those who complacently prescribe the duty of national defense on the basis of "natural law" often forget entirely the norms of justice and humanity without which no war can be permitted. Without these norms, natural law becomes mere jungle law, that is to say crime.

Many Christians will with complete docility accept opinions and decisions that bear the stamp of jungle law rather than that of the Gospel. They will submit without protest to such directives, and they will feel little or no uneasiness of conscience, even though someone who has lost his faith in God may be shocked by such insensitivity and scandalized by this apparent perversion of the moral sense.

It is unfortunate that a spirit of minimalist legalism has in the past distorted the Christian perspectives both of the laity and the clergy. Hence we have sometimes allowed our consciences to be content with pharisaism and spiritual trifling, "straining [at] gnats and swallowing camels." Undoubtedly one of the most important objectives of John XXIII in calling the Second Vatican Ecumenical Council is to favor and encourage the great movement of renewal that is making itself felt in the Church today. The Holy Father obviously feels there is a real hope of the Church turning the tide of secularism and violence by

> taking the perennial, vital divine power of the Gospel and injecting it into the veins of the human society of today which glories in its recent scientific and technological advances at the same time as it is suffering damage to its social order. (*Humanae Salutis,* December 25, 1961)

But at the same time this will not be possible, says Pope John, unless the grave dangers of the time "point up the need for vigilance *and make every individual aware of his own responsibilities.*" In particular the pope refers specifically to questions of social justice, international relations and the whole climate of secularism and materialism in modern thought.

Nuclear war is certainly a case in point. It is quite certain that many Catholics who are spontaneously revolted by the natural injustice involved in the threat to answer "intolerable political provocation" with the annihilation of enemy cities, may swallow their repugnance and accept the prospect with docility, believing that "the leaders know best" and that in this case, as well as in any other case, it is always more Christian to suspend judgment and leave the decision to someone else. But how can this be true if the decision is left in the hands of men without firm moral standards, or compassion, or humanity? Worse still if it really depends on men of whom we know nothing, and who determine the policies and decisions of leaders we hopefully trust?

Lloyd George said that if the churches had resolutely refused their blessing and cooperation, the First World War would never have been fought. It is quite true that the popes and other religious spokesmen have come out tirelessly with clear, uncompromising directives to avoid violence: but these directives have either been minimized or set aside as inopportune by Catholics in countries that were actually at war. One can certainly appreciate the difficult position of the churchmen, for instance in Nazi Germany during World War II. The fact remains that their cooperation with Hitler's unjust war effort is something of a scandal.*

The popes have repeatedly pleaded with Christians to show themselves in all things disciples of Christ the Prince of Peace, and to embody in their lives their faith in his teaching. "All his teaching is an invitation to peace," says Pope John XXIII in the 1961 Christmas message. Deploring the ever increasing selfishness, hardness of heart, cynicism and callousness of mankind, as war becomes once again more and more imminent, Pope John says that Christian goodness and charity must permeate all the activity, whether personal or social, of every Christian. The Pontiff quotes St. Leo the Great in a passage which contrasts natural ethics with the nonviolent ethic of the Gospel: "To commit injustice and to make reparation — this is the prudence of the world. On the contrary, *not to render evil for evil, is the virtuous expression of Christian forgiveness.*" These words, embodying the wisdom of the Church and the heart of her moral teaching, are heard without attention and complacently dismissed as if they could not seriously apply to the present international crisis.

---

*See Gordon Zahn, *German Catholics and Hitler's Wars* (New York: Sheed and Ward, 1962).

Here we come face to face with a serious ambiguity, which is very near the heart of the problem.

It is quite true that the blunt, unqualified statement that one "must not render evil for evil" seems disconcerting and hopelessly impractical when it is brought face to face with any concrete political problem, here and now. What possible relevance can such a principle have, we ask, when Khrushchev is threatening to rain down H-bombs on western Europe and America?

To say that we must not "render evil for evil" seems to mean that we must placidly fold our hands and allow ourselves to be enslaved or destroyed. But this is not the meaning of this basic Christian principle, otherwise how could such a principle ever be applied in politics? To take the principle as if it meant that alone is to understand it in an absurd sense.

It is obvious, too, that appeals to nonviolent action or even to unilateral disarmament tend to create the same false and absurd impression. It is certainly neither practical nor even sane to expect that thousands of military bureaucrats who people the Pentagon will suddenly have a change of heart and listen to the message of nonviolence one fine day, close down all their offices, cancel all the orders for new missiles, tear up all the defense contracts, and retire to *ashrams*.

Of course the "realist" who has finally discarded the thought of "not rendering evil for evil" as purely meaningless has perhaps something to be said for him. He has simplified his life. He has abolished the need to make his practical action conform to deep spiritual norms of morality. He has abolished a definitely uncomfortable and frustrating state of inner contradiction. When the enemy threatens him with a thousand megatons he can reply with a threat of ten thousand, and no nonsense about good and evil.

The sincere Christian cannot have it that easy. He is bound by his religious commitment to live with this inner conflict between seemingly irreconcilable extremes. Yet he is also bound to attempt, as far as he can with the grace of God, to reconcile them.

In reality the plea not to render evil for evil must retain some meaning even for a General in the age of nuclear war. What can that meaning be? Obviously it is not that one who has all his life lived in and for and by war and threat of war, should suddenly renounce all thought of retaliation when he is threatened. But nevertheless the principle is there, and one has to begin somewhere to observe it.

The point at which even a military strategist should consider himself bound not to render evil for evil is at least this: that an evil which takes the form of a political or military *threat* and which is most probably a bluff, is not to be met, ethically, *with the evil of actual force.* Not only that, but he should strive, if possible, to refrain from meeting it with an equally sinister or even more sinister political threat, and, while maintaining his defensive capacity, he should do all that he can to reduce tensions and to work for an eventual elimination of this evil altogether, by other than violent means.

This is certainly not unreasonable, and though it may not measure up to the perfection of the Gospel, it is at least a good start and one who can do this in our time has no reason to be ashamed.

But in actual fact politicians and military strategists in general tend to reject the uncomfortable principle of "not rendering evil for evil" altogether. They can do so quite easily by *simply refusing to take it in any other than an absurd sense.*

It is a tragic fact that one of the effects of the "Cold War mentality" is precisely this. Not only militarists but also theologians, priests and bishops have come to the point where, in the context of the Cold War crisis, they are *practically unable to take this basic principle seriously.* As Christians they will give it a formal nod of assent, but in a concrete political situation their complete obsession by Cold War phobias makes it *morally impossible for them to take the principle in any sense which is not absurd.* In a word, they cannot see it in any light that makes it worth considering, and hence they reject it from their practical judgments. It may end by having no influence whatever in the decisions of their conscience regarding nuclear war.

That is why, in practice, we tend to assume that the teaching of Christian forgiveness and meekness applies only to the individual, not to nations or collectivities. The state can go to war and exert every form of violent force, while the individual expresses his Christian meekness by shouldering his gun without resistance and obeying the command to go out and kill. The state need never forgive. The state can hate with impunity. The state can render evil for evil, and indeed even evil for good! This is not Pope John's idea at all. He utters a solemn warning to rulers of nations:

> With the authority we have received from Jesus Christ we say: *Shun all thought of force; think of the tragedy of initiating a chain reaction of acts, decisions and resentments which could erupt into rash and irreparable deeds.* You have received great powers not to destroy but to build, not to divide but to unite, not to cause tears to be shed but to provide employment and security. (Christmas Message, 1961)

On the contrary, Pope John insists that peace must be based on an

> appreciation of true brotherhood, for a resolution of sincere cooperation that stays clear of all intrigue and of those destructive factors that we will once again call by their proper names without any disguise: pride, greed, callousness, selfishness.

In this same Christmas Message the pope says that the mentality of suspicion and hatred is unfortunately encouraged and strengthened by those who possess the art of forming public opinion and have a partial monopoly over it! In very serious terms he warned these men "to fear the stern judgment of God and of history and to proceed cautiously with respect and a sense of moderation."

He added, "We say this regretfully but frankly — the press has helped to create a climate of hostility, of animosity, of sharp division."

16

Christian Conscience
and National Defense

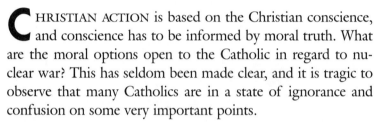

C HRISTIAN ACTION is based on the Christian conscience, and conscience has to be informed by moral truth. What are the moral options open to the Catholic in regard to nuclear war? This has seldom been made clear, and it is tragic to observe that many Catholics are in a state of ignorance and confusion on some very important points.

The vague statement that a "Catholic cannot be a pacifist" is often taken to mean that a Catholic is never under any circumstances permitted to object to war on moral grounds. It is understood to mean that as soon as a Catholic layman approaches a priest with doubts about participating in a nuclear war effort he is told to forget his doubts, and treated as if the matter had been automatically settled for him. On the contrary, it comes to be assumed that a Catholic is in duty bound to participate in *any* and *every* war effort, whatever may be the cause, whatever be the means used, whatever the possibilities that war will arrive at an equitable and rational solution of international problems. All these considerations are for the government, for the military. The only thing the Catholic has to do is to obey blindly decisions made by somebody else for reasons which he does not fully understand.

This is, of course, caricature. Yet can we deny that in fact many Catholics assume this is what the Church wants? We have to face the danger that in the greatest problem the social conscience of man has had to face in the course of its history, the consciences of many Christians are not fully functioning because they are not facing the real issue, not discussing its full implications, not considering all its aspects.

War, especially nuclear war, must always present to every Christian an *agonizing problem of conscience*. War is not, and never can be, something one accepts passively, stoically and without examination. When the pope himself deplores war, protests against it, pleads with leaders to avoid it and to seek a peaceful alternative, how is it that the Catholic conscience is not awakened to protest, to discussion, to examination of new ways of solving the problem? Where are the Catholic peace movements? What is the Catholic press saying about nuclear weapons? What is being preached about nuclear war?

Unfortunately it must be admitted that instead of protesting against the most enormous arms race ever known, instead of considering its implications and trying to forestall its effects, Catholics by and large accept this as a good thing, as a necessity, as a "lesser evil."

It is true of course that in the Christmas Message of 1956 Pope Pius XII reminded the faithful of their duty to face the "unpleasant reality . . . of an enemy determined to impose on all peoples, in one way or another, a special and intolerable way of life." Referring to violent tactics used by Communists, including atomic blackmail and the ruthless suppression of resistance in weaker nations, the pope said that these tactics would have to be resisted. Pius XII clearly had the recent Hungarian uprising in mind when he declared that Christians might have the right and the duty to resist oppression by force if no other means were available or effective.

Hence he said that in the case of extreme danger, a legitimately constituted government, "after every effort to avoid war has been expended in vain" might lawfully wage a war of *"self-defense against unjust attack."* The pope laid down many clear conditions for the legitimacy of such a war. It would have to be *strictly a war of defense, against unjust attack. All (genuine) efforts at keeping peace must have been unavailing. Legitimate means of self-defense must be used.* There must be a *genuine hope of effective self-defense* and of a favorable outcome. In view of such a situation, if the nation takes defensive precautions with legitimate instruments of internal and external policy, then the citizen would have an obligation to serve the nation in its defense effort. He could not appeal to his conscience to refuse military service imposed by law.

At the same time the pope deplored the necessity of such laws and pointed out "general disarmament" as an "effective remedy."

Without commenting in detail on this statement of Pius XII, two things must be stressed: first that the pope is not setting aside the Christian conscience in peace and war. The Christian remains obliged in conscience to weigh the matter seriously and to consider whether or not the conditions for a just war are in fact fulfilled. In the case of an all-out nuclear war, there exists a serious problem as to whether or not the "means" may be considered legitimate, either in themselves or in the manner in which they are obviously to be used. There also remains an even more serious question as to whether such a war offers any hope of a "favorable outcome." Finally, there remains the not unimportant question whether the negotiations to avoid war have been really genuine or merely gestures made for the sake of appearances and propaganda.

Far from dismissing the individual conscience in this grave matter, the pope says immediately that "there are occasions in the lives of nations when *only recourse to higher principles* can establish clearly the boundaries between right and wrong." He adds: "It is therefore consoling that in some countries amid today's debates, *men are talking about conscience and its demands*" (Christmas Message, 1956).

Let us recall once again that Pope Pius XII declared unequivocally that while nuclear weapons were not by their very nature forbidden, that nuclear, chemical and biological warfare could very well be "universal." Let us recall that his numerous pronouncements on modern war technology cast grave doubt upon the likelihood of such weapons being used in a just and ethical way in a war of serious proportions.

In 1955, Pope Pius considered three vitally important steps to be taken to reduce tensions and prevent war. First the renunciation of atomic tests, second the renunciation of all use of nuclear weapons and third, a general control of all arms.

He then declared, "The sum total of these three precautions as an object of international agreement *is an obligation of conscience of nations and their leaders.*" Note he says an obligation of conscience for *nations*. Does this not mean for the *individual citizens and voters*? Of course it does. It means that every individual Catholic citizen has a strict obligation in conscience to work *against* nuclear testing, *against* the arms race, and for general arms control. Of course he must do this in such a way that he does not put his country in danger — but he must work for peace, according to the Papal pronouncements.

Who ever hears a word said about this obligation of conscience? Where do we read about it in the Catholic press? Where do we hear it in the pulpit? If a Catholic priest got up and said it was obligatory for Catholics to deplore nuclear weapons, and did not support his statement by showing how the pope himself had said it, he would be treated as a heretic and a Communist. Indeed, even quoting the pope he could be so treated.

It must therefore be clearly stated that the measured and qualified terms in which Pius XII admitted that there could still be a just war, at least (so the context seems to suggest) with conventional weapons, it did not mean that the government purely and simply had the last word and that Christian conscience was no longer to be consulted. Pius XII was not prescribing blind obedience to any government in every situation in which the power struggle might suggest war by any methods as the expedient solution.

Note also that the obligation is not strictly *to fight and to kill* but to *serve the country* in some capacity, according to the laws. Hence the Catholic who feels that in conscience he ought to choose the more perfect way of avoiding bloodshed and serving in the ambulance corps or in some other noncombatant capacity retains the right to follow his conscience in this matter, and indeed ought to follow it. And his requests to do so ought to be respected if the law permits. In this sense there clearly can be such a thing as a "Catholic conscientious objector."

But do these distinctions apply in all-out nuclear war?

One other remark made by Pius XII in the same address is very important. He devotes several paragraphs to the problem of discerning accurately when peace is and is not really threatened, when there is and is not a serious emergency, and how the calculated threats and recriminations of power politicians are really to be interpreted. This gravely affects the whole question of deciding when there really exists an "extreme danger" which makes defensive measures urgent and obligatory.

In conclusion, we must not forget that Pope Pius XII's affirmation that a just war could still be possible and that the Christian might be bound to serve in it, must always be seen against the background of his unremitting insistence upon general disarmament and the policy of peace. He explicitly states in this message that he is not "abandoning that mission of peace which flows from our apostolic office," still less "calling Christendom to a crusade."

Clearly, we cannot assert that a Catholic is bound in conscience to cooperate with any and every form of war and violence that his government may decide to use against an enemy. According to this view, a good Christian would be one who shrinks from no work of cruel or violent destruction commanded by the state.

Such a misconception could lead to the awful conclusion that a Catholic commanded by a new Hitler to operate the furnaces of another Dachau would only be "doing his duty" if he obeyed. The noble Christian concept of duty and sacrifice must not be debased to the point where the Christian becomes the passive instrument of inhuman governments. Christian "morality" should not justify Eichmanns, still less produce them.

Succinctly: a Catholic is permitted to hold the following views of nuclear war:

a) Many sound theologians have taught that the traditional conditions of a just war will not, in practice, be fully realized when nuclear weapons are involved, and that, as Pope Pius XII himself said even before Hiroshima, "the theory of war as an apt and proportionate means of solving international conflicts is now out of date." In practice, what has been called "relative pacifism" can very certainly be held and is held by many Catholics. Without rejecting the traditional teaching that a "just war" can be fought and perhaps even should be fought under certain well-defined conditions, this view holds that nuclear war will almost inevitably violate many and perhaps all the required conditions and will be in one or in many ways a grievously unjust war. This can be supported by very clear statements of Cardinal Ottaviani and even of Pope Pius XII. Hence, even though it is not the definitive "teaching of the Church" it is certainly not only a tenable doctrine but seems to be the soundest and safest opinion. It is certainly the opinion which best fits the traditional ethical norms of the Church and the just war theory.

b) Absolute pacifism in a completely unqualified form has been reproved. A Catholic may not hold that *all* war under no matter what conditions is by its very nature unjust and evil. A Catholic may not formally deny that a community has a right to defend itself by force if other means do not avail. It is certainly true that war should never be anything but a *last resort* and that it is always to be regarded, however just it may happen to be, as a regrettable necessity.

A pacifist position, or even an imprudent or ill-considered disarmament policy which would leave a nation helpless in the presence of a ruthless and unjust aggressor, and would, we suppose, invite aggression on his part, would of course not be moral or permissible to a Christian.

But let us remember that hasty condemnations of disarmament as "imprudent" may be based on false or emotionally loaded assumptions about the enemy. This may indeed resolve itself into a question of fact rather than a question of *principle*.

A Catholic may certainly and legitimately prefer a form of service in which he is not obliged to kill others and in this he should be praised and encouraged for following the more Christian course, provided he takes this course sincerely for the sake of charity, and not in order to avoid death himself. (Note that since there is no longer any distinction between civilian and military, as regards danger, one does little or nothing to protect his life by being a noncombatant.)

A Catholic may and must oppose war in a particular case when there are very serious reasons for believing that even a limited war may be unjust, or may "escalate" to proportions which violate justice. It is to be noted that *when a war is evidently unjust* a Catholic not only *may* refuse to serve but he is *morally obliged to refuse to participate* in it.

c) Catholic tradition has always admitted the legality of a defensive war where there is just cause, right intention and use of right means. It is argued that a limited nuclear war for defensive purposes can fulfill the requirements of a just war, and that therefore it is right and just to possess stockpiles of nuclear weapons and to threaten retaliation for nuclear attack. This may be and is held by many Catholics, and it is probably the majority opinion among Catholics in the United States.

Certainly an ideal picture of "limited war with clean tactical weapons" has been painted by Edward Teller. Obviously this ideal picture fulfills all the conditions of the just war. It was printed precisely for that purpose. It was an exercise of the imagination to support his contention that tactical nuclear weapons are just what we need, and that we ought to manufacture as many as possible. How far can this ideal picture be accepted with confidence?

First of all there is no serious guarantee that a nuclear war will ever be kept "limited." Still less is there any indication that the military strategists have any intention of "limiting" a nuclear war unless it appears in some way expedient to do so.

Secondly it must be asked how a Christian can commit himself in conscience to support a ruthless policy of power the exercise of which remains largely dependent on the decisions of a military and economic elite which has discarded Christian moral principles and operates on a basis of vague pragmatism without any definite or verifiable ideology.

Moralists who admit a nuclear war are assuming there will be a highly conscious and responsible use of political power. Such moral responsibility is certainly lacking in the Soviet Union, and though it may still exist in some quarters in the United States, the pressure of Soviet ruthlessness is liable to overwhelm all the good will and good intentions of our own military leaders. War tends to reduce all to one level of morality — the lowest.

All theologians agree that the unrestricted use of nuclear weapons for the simple purpose of annihilation of civilian centers is completely immoral. It is nothing but murder and is never permitted, any more than a nuclear preemptive strike on civilian centers would be permitted by Christian ethics. Could a preemptive attack on the military installations of the enemy be admitted as a "just" defensive measure? To do so would seem very rash at least in view of the disastrous consequences of the retaliatory war that would inevitably be unleashed, and would inevitably entail the total mass destruction of great centers of population. The statement quoted above from Pope John XXIII, while not formally declaring such an action intrinsically evil, is a solemn warning not to initiate, by any form of aggression, a chain of acts of war and violence. While it may be all very well for theologians to theorize about a limited nuclear war, it is only too clear that the game of nuclear deterrence uses the civilian population of the enemy as hostages and the policies of the great power blocs include the threat of an all-out war of annihilation.

Finally of course there is the overwhelming menace of accident, miscalculation, misunderstanding, technical failure, mental breakdown. Already we are aware that there have been several false alarms, in which hundreds of bombers loaded with megatonic weapons were on the runways ready to take off for a *massive knockout blow* on Russia. Does this give any indication that there is going to be a "limited war" fought by "just means" and according to the strictest requirements of Christian ethics?

Does this permit us to continue the ever increasing arms race? Does it not indicate that we have a *most grave obligation in conscience* to do everything possible to limit and control those armaments and work for peace?

If we continue to neglect this obligation how can we convince ourselves that we are worthy of the name of Christians?

In such a situation our Christian duty is clear. Though no Catholic is formally obliged to adhere to a policy of immediate nuclear disarmament, whether multilateral or unilateral, he is certainly obliged to do everything he can, in his own situation, to work for ultimate peace. It is difficult to see how one can work for peace without ultimately seeking disarmament or at least a drastic limitation in the arms race.

It would however be insufficient to limit Christian obligation, in the present crisis, merely to a course of action that can be somehow reconciled with moral principles. The problem is deeper. What is needed is a social action that will have the power to renew society because it springs *from the inner renewal of the Christian and of his Church.*

The real problem of our time is basically spiritual. One important aspect of this problem is the fact that in many Christians, the Christian conscience seems to function only as a rudimentary vestigial faculty, robbed of its full vigor and incapable of attaining its real purpose: a life completely transformed in Christ.

The mature moral conscience is the one that derives its strength and its light not from external directives alone but above all from an inner spiritual connaturality with the deepest values of nature and grace.

Without this inner ground of connatural love of the good one cannot make really sound and perceptive judgments in applying objective moral principles. The meaning and intent of law does not fully reveal itself to a conscience that is not made delicately alert by a spirit of love. Such a conscience is rooted and grounded in human compassion and in the charity of Christ, and the most important thing for us all to do (and this is a spiritual task which is essential to Christian renewal) is to recover this hidden "ground" in which sound moral judgment and fruitful action can grow abundantly.

But the great danger of our Cold War obsessions is their dreadful capacity to sterilize that inner "ground" and make it utterly fruitless. The delicate and compassionate conscience is hardened in hate and suspicion. When this happens we tend to judge by a connaturality with violence, and not with love of peace. Constantly exposed to dread, to anguish, to an incubus of fear for the future of our affluent society with its privileges, its soothing irresponsibilities and all its comforts, we come to feel our insecurity as basic spiritual reality. Insofar as our existence is at stake, and the structure of our religious beliefs and practices is at stake along with it, we experience the threat of Communism and of war as a kind of ultimate spiritual challenge. We wrestle with this threat as Jacob wrestled with the angel, in anguish of conscience. In this inner struggle we forget there might be other, deeper and more subtle challenges for us to face. We forget the tragic and demonic complexities of our situation, and in resisting our obvious enemy we may well succumb to a fatal temptation and lose everything by our impatience. We may concentrate on a good end and then do evil, forgetting that the end does not justify the means.

There is a fateful element of irony even in the prospect that our death at the hands of a persecutor might rate as martyrdom. Are we to die as Christians or because we are prosperous and comfort-loving organization men? It does make a difference! But at any rate, the possibility of persecution by a ruthless and clever enemy, whose power and success we are never allowed to forget, begets anguish, and to a man beset by anguish, hatred can seem to be bravery.

Like the disciples who wanted to call down fire upon the city of the Samaritans, we are too naïve and too obsessed to identify the spirit by which we are inspired. In this Cold War climate our judgments grow from this ground of sterility and frustration in which the best seed can hardly thrive and in which the weeds of hatred and incipient totalitarianism grow luxuriantly.

It is therefore vitally necessary to cultivate an inner ground of deep faith and purity of conscience, which cannot exist without true sacrifice. Genuine Christian action has, in fact, to be based on a complete sacrificial offering of our self and our life, in the service of truth. Short of this, we cannot attain sufficient detachment from our own selfish interests and from the peripheral concerns of a wealthy, spiritually indolent society. Without this detachment we cannot possibly see nuclear war as it really is, and we will consequently betray Christ and his Church, in the mistaken conviction that in defending our wealth we are defending Christian truth.

There are many reasons to believe that the social action of someone like Dorothy Day, who is willing to refuse cooperation even in civil defense drills and ready to go to jail for her belief in peace, is far more significantly Christian than the rather subtle and comfy positions of certain casuists. When I consider that Dorothy Day was confined to a jail in nothing but a light wrap (her clothes having been taken from her) and that she could only get to Mass and Communion in the prison by dressing in clothes borrowed from prostitutes and thieves in the neighboring cells, then I lose all inclination to take seriously the self-complacent nonsense of those who consider her kind of pacifism sentimental.

17

The Christian Choice

L ET US BEWARE of simple and ideal solutions. The most tempting of all "simple" solutions are the ones which prescribe annihilation or submit to it without resistance. There is a grim joke underlying all our talk about "Red or dead." The inherent destructiveness of the frustrated mind distorts the whole Christian view of life and of civilization by evading the difficult and complex way of negotiation and sacrifice, in order to resort, in frustrated desperation, to "magic" power and nuclear destruction. Let us not ignore this temptation. It is one of the deepest and most radical in man. It is the primal temptation, and the root of all the others. "You shall be as gods . . . " (Gen. 3:5).

On the contrary, our Christian obligation consists in being and remaining not gods but men, believing in the Word who emptied himself and became man for our sakes. We have to look at the problem of nuclear war from the viewpoint of humanity and of God made man, from the viewpoint of the Mystical Body of Christ, and not merely from the viewpoint of abstract formulas. Here above all we need a reasoning that is informed with compassion and takes some account of flesh and blood, not a mere legalistic juggling with principles and precedents.

In the light of these deep Christian truths we will better understand the danger of fallacious justification of every recourse to violence, as well as the peril of indifference, inertia and passivity.

152

It is not a question of stating absolutely and infallibly that every Christian must renounce, under pain of mortal sin, any opinion that the use of the bomb might be legitimate. The H-bomb has not been formally and officially condemned, and doubtless it does not need to be condemned. There is no special point to condemning one weapon in order to give casuistical minds an opportunity to prove their skill in evasion by coming up with another "licit" way of attaining the same destructive end. It is not just a matter of seeing how much destruction and murder we can justify without incurring the condemnation of God and of the Church.

But I submit that at this time above all it is vitally important to avoid the "minimalist" approach. The issue of nuclear war is too grave and too general. It threatens everybody. It involves the very survival of the human race. In such a case one is not allowed to take any but strictly unavoidable risks. We are obliged to choose the more secure alternative in guiding our moral choice. Let us remember too that while a doubt of the existence of an obligation leaves us with a certain freedom of choice, the doubt of an evil fact does not permit such freedom.

We may well dispute the legitimacy of nuclear war on principle: but when we face the *actual fact* that recourse to nuclear weapons can result in the quasi-total destruction of civilization, even possibly in the suicide of the entire human race, *we are absolutely obliged to take this fact into account and to avoid this terrible danger.*

It is certainly legitimate for a Catholic moralist to hold in theory that a limited nuclear war, in defense, is permitted by traditional Christian moral principles. He may even hold that the strategic use of nuclear, bacteriological and chemical weapons is theoretically permissible for defense, provided that there is a possibility that the basic values we are presumably defending will continue to exist after they have been "defended."

But when we come face to face with the terrible doubt of fact, *dubium facti,* the absolutely real and imminent probability of massive and uncontrolled destruction, including the annihilation of civilization and even of life itself, then there is no such latitude of choice. We are most gravely and seriously bound by all the norms of Christian morality, however minimal, to choose the safer course and to try at all costs to avoid so enormous a disaster.

Let us remember that even if one were to admit the theoretical legitimacy of nuclear weapons for purposes of defense, that use would become gravely unjust as soon as the effects of nuclear destruction overflowed upon neutral or friendly nations. Even though we may feel justified in risking the destruction of our own cities and those of the enemy, we have no right whatever to bring destruction upon helpless small nations which have no interest whatever in the war and ask only to survive in peace. It is not up to us to choose that *they* should be dead rather than Red.

Pope Pius XII said in 1954 (concerning ABC warfare, described above as a sin, an offense, and an outrage against God): "Should the evil consequences of adopting this method of warfare *ever become so extensive as to pass entirely beyond the control of man, then indeed its use must be rejected as immoral.*" He adds that uncontrolled annihilation of life within a given area "*is not lawful under any title*" (Address to the World Medical Association, September 1954).

Nor is it moral to overindulge in speculation on this dangerous point of "control." A lax interpretation of this principle would lead us to decide that a twenty megaton H-bomb dropped on Leningrad is "fully under control" because all its effects are susceptible to measurement, and we know that the blast will annihilate Leningrad while the fallout will probably wipe out the population of Helsinki and Riga, depending on the wind. Obviously what the pope meant was something much more precise than that. He meant that if there was un-controlled annihilation of everybody in Leningrad, without any discrimination between combatants and noncombatants, enemies, friends, women, children, infants and old people, then the use of the bomb would be "not lawful under any title" especially in view of the "bonus" effects of fallout drifting over neutral territory, certainly without control.

Hence though nuclear warfare as such has not been entirely and formally condemned, the mind of the Church is obvi-ously that every possible means should be taken to avoid it, and John XXIII made this abundantly clear in his Christmas message of 1961 where he pleaded in most solemn terms with the rulers of all nations to "shun all thought of force" and remain at peace. The words of Pope John in this connection imply grave reservations even with regard to limited war which might possibly "escalate" and reach all-out proportions.

There can be no doubt whatever that the absence of formal condemnation cannot be twisted into a tacit official approval of all-out nuclear war. Yet it seems that this is what some are trying to do.

Our duty then is to help emphasize with all the force at our disposal that the Church earnestly seeks the abolition of war. We must underscore declarations like those of Pope John XXIII pleading with world leaders to renounce force in the settlement of international disputes and confine themselves to negotiations.

Now let us suppose that the political leaders of the world, supported by the mass media in their various countries, and carried on by a tidal wave of greater and greater war prepara-tions, see themselves swept inexorably into a war of cataclysmic proportions. Let us suppose that it becomes morally certain that these leaders are helpless to arrest the blind force of the process that has irresponsibly been set in motion. What then? Are the masses of the world, including you and me, to resign

themselves to our fate and march to global suicide without resistance, simply bowing our heads and obeying our leaders as
showing us the "will of God"? I think it should be evident to
everyone that this can no longer, in the present situation, be
accepted unequivocally as Christian obedience and civic duty.

No theologian, however broad, however lax, would insist
that one was bound in conscience to participate in a war that
was *evidently* leading to global suicide. Those who favor nuclear war can only do so by making all kinds of optimistic
suppositions concerning the political and military facts: that
it will be only a limited war or that the destructive effects of
H-bombs are not as terrible as we have been told.

Hence it is extremely disturbing to note that moral judgments are being influenced by the complacent estimates of
Herman Kahn, whose computers have told him that nuclear
war is quite reasonable even though "damage cannot be kept
to the classical levels" and "the postwar environment would
be more hostile to human life for some ten thousand years,"
and "we might no longer live in a democracy." It seems that
many theologians, accustomed to dealing with authoritative
statements, are prone to accept the statements of a Kahn with
almost as much uncritical docility as they would the declarations of Church authority. And yet even the obvious sense of
Kahn's most "optimistic" estimates leads one to the conclusion
that a nuclear war of massive proportions, even if it could be
"won," would fail to measure up to one of the basic conditions
for a just war. The destruction would be beyond all proportion
to the good achieved, and indeed there is no reasonable ground
for believing that any good would be achieved. Even by Kahn's
own estimate we would be far worse off after the "victory" than
before it. How can anyone in his right mind propose this insane
choice as one that could be dictated by Christian morality?

This brings us face to face with the greatest and most agonizing moral issue of our time. This issue is not merely nuclear

war, not merely the possible destruction of the human race by a sudden explosion of violence. It is something more subtle and more demonic. If we continue to yield to theoretically irresistible determinism and the vague "historic forces" without striving to resist and control them, if we let these forces drive us to demonic activism in the realms of politics and technology, we face something more than the material evil of universal destruction. We face *moral responsibility for the destruction of civilization or even for global suicide.* Much more than that, we are going to find ourselves gradually moving into a situation in which we are practically compelled by the "logic of circumstances" deliberately *to choose a course which leads to destruction.*

The great danger is then the savage and self-destructive commitment to a policy of nationalism and blind hate, and the refusal of all other policies more constructive and more in accordance with Christian ethical tradition. Let us realize that this is a matter of *choice,* not of pure blind determinism.

We all know the logic of temptation. We all know the confused, vague, hesitant irresponsibility which leads us into the situation where it is no longer possible to turn back, and how, arrived in that situation, we have a moment of clear-sighted desperation in which we freely commit ourselves to the course we recognize as evil. That may well be what is happening now to the whole world.

The free choice of global self-destruction, made in desperation by the world's leaders and ratified by the consent and cooperation of their citizens, would be a moral evil second only to the crucifixion. The fact that such a choice might be made with the highest motives and the most urgent purpose would do nothing whatever to mitigate it. The fact that it might be made on a gamble, in the hope that some might escape, would never excuse it. After all, the purposes of Caiaphas were, in his own eyes, perfectly noble. He thought it was necessary to let "one man die for the people."

The most urgent necessity of our time is therefore not merely to prevent the destruction of the human race by nuclear war. Even if it should happen to be no longer possible to prevent the disaster (which God forbid) there is still a greater evil that can and must be prevented. It must be possible for every free man to refuse his consent and deny his cooperation to this greatest of crimes.

In what does this effective and manifest refusal to consent consist? How does one "resist" the sin of global suicide? The ordinary man has no access to vital information. Indeed, even the politician may know relatively little about what is really going on. How would it be possible to know when and how it was necessary to refuse cooperation in a disastrous and suicidal war effort? Can we draw a line clearly, and say precisely when nuclear war becomes so dangerous that it is suicidal? If a war of missiles breaks out, we will have at the most thirty minutes to come to our momentous conclusions — even if we ever know what is happening at all. It seems to me that the time to form our conscience and to decide upon our course of action is *now.*

It is one thing to form one's conscience and another to adopt a specific policy or course of action. It is highly regrettable that this important distinction is overlooked and indeed deliberately obfuscated. To decide, in the forum of conscience, that one is obligated in every way, as a Christian, to avoid actions that would contribute to a worldwide disaster, does not mean that one is necessarily committed to absolute and unqualified pacifism. One may start from moral principle, which is repeatedly set before us by the popes and which cannot be seriously challenged, and one may then go on to seek various means to preserve peace. About these different means, there may be considerable debate.

It seems to me, however, that the enormous danger represented by nuclear weapons and the near impossibility of controlling them and limiting them to a scale that would fit the traditional ethical theory of a just war, makes it both logical and licit for a Christian to proceed, from motives of conscience, to at least a relative pacifism, and certainly to a policy of nuclear disarmament.

In so doing, however, he has a strict obligation to see that he does not take a naïve and oversimplified position which would permit him to be ruthlessly exploited by the politicians of another nuclear power. The logic of all serious efforts to preserve peace demands that our very endeavors themselves do not help the war effort of the "enemy," and thus precipitate war. There is sometimes a danger that our pacifism may be somewhat short-sighted and immature. It may consequently be more an expression of rebellion against the status quo in our country than an effective opposition to war itself.

In this event, the American pacifist, particularly if he is extremely outspoken and gives the impression of a tendency to revolt, may create a false impression in the mind of Soviet policy makers and induce them to follow a dangerous course, leading more rapidly and inexorably to war.

In a word, there are three things to be considered. (1) Christian moral principles, which by their very nature favor peace, and according to which nuclear war remains, if not absolutely forbidden, at least of exceedingly dubious morality. (2) The facts about weapons systems and defense policies. Our moral decisions and the morality of our participation in the economic and political life of a society geared for nuclear war, demand imperatively that we realize the real nature of the military policies to which we contribute by taxation and perhaps also by our work in industry. Everything in our national life is today centered on the greatest arms race in the history of man. Everything points to the fact that these frightful weapons of destruction may and will be used, most probably on the highest and most expanded scale. (3) We must finally consider factors by which these military policies are dictated.

The Christian moral principles are relatively clear. While there is still much to debate over details, no Christian moralist worthy of the name can seriously defend outright a nuclear war of unqualified aggression.

The facts about ABC warfare are also clear enough. There is no question of the immense destructiveness of the weapons available to us. There is no question that the destruction of civilization and even global suicide are both possible. There is no question that the policies of the nuclear powers are geared for an all-out war of incredible savagery and destructive power.

What remains to be explored by the Christian is the area that is least considered, which also happens to be the area that most needs to be examined and is perhaps the one place where something can be done.

By what are our policies of hatred and destructiveness dictated? What seems to drive us inexorably on the fate which we all dread and seek to avoid? This question is not hard to answer. What started the First World War? What started the Second World War? The answer is, simply, the rabid, short-sighted, irrational and stubborn forces which tend to come to a head in nationalism. Christopher Dawson has said:

> The defeat of Hitlerism does not mean that we have seen the end of such movements. In our modern democratic world, irrational forces lie very near the surface, and *their sudden eruption under the impulse of nationalist or revolutionary ideologies is the greatest of all the dangers that threaten the modern world.* . . . It is at this point that the need for a reassertion of Christian principles becomes evident. . . . Insofar as nationalism denies the principles (of higher order and divine justice for all men) and sets up the nation and the national state as the final object of man's allegiance, *it represents the most retrograde movement the world has ever seen,* since it means a denial of the great

central truth on which civilization was founded, and the return to the pagan idolatries of tribal barbarism.

Dawson then goes on to quote Pope Pius XII who distinguishes between "national life" and "nationalistic politics." National life is a combination of all the values which characterize a social group and enable it to contribute to the whole polity of nations. Nationalistic politics on the other hand are divisive, destructive, and a perversion of genuine national values. They are "a principle of dissolution within the community of peoples."

This then is the conclusion: the Christian is bound to work for peace by working against global dissolution and anarchy. Due to nationalist and revolutionary ideologies (for Communism is in fact exploiting the intense nationalism of backward peoples), a worldwide spirit of confusion and disorder is breaking up the unity and the order of civilized society.

It is true that we live in an epoch of revolution, and that the break-up and re-formation of society is inevitable. But the Christian must see that his mission is not to contribute to the blind destructive forces of annihilation which tend to destroy civilization and mankind together. He must seek to build rather than to destroy. He must orient his efforts towards world unity and not towards world division. Anyone who promotes policies of hatred and of war is working for the division and the destruction of civilized mankind.

We have to be convinced that there are certain violences which the moral law absolutely forbids to all men, such as the use of torture, the killing of hostages, genocide (or the mass extermination of racial, national or other groups for no reason than that they belong to an "undesirable" category). The destruction of civilian centers by nuclear annihilation is genocide.

We have to become aware of the poisonous effect of the mass media that keep violence, cruelty and sadism constantly present to the minds of unformed and irresponsible people. We have to recognize the danger to the whole world in the fact that today the economic life of the more highly developed nations is in large part centered on the production of weapons, missiles and other engines of destruction.

We have to consider that hate propaganda, and the consistent heckling of one government by another, has always inevitably led to violent conflict. We have to recognize the implications of voting for extremist politicians who promote policies of hate. We must consider the dire effect of fanaticism and witch-hunting within our own nation. We must never forget that our most ordinary decisions may have terrible consequences.

It is no longer reasonable or right to leave all decisions to a largely anonymous power elite that is driving us all, in our passivity, towards ruin. We have to make ourselves heard.

Every individual Christian has a grave responsibility to protest clearly and forcibly against trends that lead inevitably to crimes which the Church deplores and condemns. Ambiguity, hesitation and compromise are no longer permissible. We must find some new and constructive way of settling international disputes.

It is clearly the mind of the Church that every possible effort must be made for the abolition of war, even though the theory of the "just war" and the right of legitimate self-defense remain intact. But appeal to this right must not blind us to the much higher and more urgent duty of working with all our power for peace.

This may be extraordinarily difficult. Obviously war cannot be abolished by mere wishing.

Severe sacrifices may be demanded and the results will hardly be visible in our day.

We have still time to do something about it, but the time is rapidly running out.

Notes

1. The term ABC warfare refers to "Atomic, Biological, and Chemical" weapons (now generally categorized as "weapons of mass destruction"). Research done to complete this book for publication indicated that quotations from papal statements were common currency among peace writers in the days before the encyclical *Pacem in Terris,* and that writers generally quoted them by occasion and date as Merton has throughout the book. In a recent communication to the editor, Jim Forest wrote that "Merton and all of us used certain papal quotes over and over in talks and essays. We also used them as fillers in *The Catholic Worker.*"

2. Edward Teller, "The Feasibility of Arms Control and the Principle of Openness," *Daedalus* (Fall 1960): 792.

3. During the Cold War, Herman Kahn was famous for his argument that a nuclear war could be fought and won. He describes "the rationality of irrationality" in *On Thermonuclear War* (Princeton, N.J.: Princeton University Press, 1960), 6–7, 24–27. Ronald Powaski defines it succinctly as follows: "According to deterrence theory, the deterring state has to convince the state which is to be deterred that, if necessary, it would act irrationally — by triggering a nuclear war that was bound to result in massive destruction on both sides — in order to prevent aggression" (Ronald E. Powaski, *Thomas Merton on Nuclear Weapons* [Chicago: Loyola University Press, 1988], 23).

4. After writing *PPCE,* Merton carried on his study of Clement, and published selections and his own translations in *Clement of Alexandria: Selections from the Protreptikos* (New York: New Directions, 1963). The book is now rare, but the selections are reprinted in *The Collected Poems of Thomas Merton* (New York: New Directions, 1977), 933–42.

5. Origen, *Contra Celsum,* translated with an introduction and notes by Henry Chadwick (Cambridge [Eng.]: Cambridge University Press, 1953), III: 8, 133. Subsequent references will be cited with chapter and paragraph from *Contra Celsum* followed by pagination in the Chadwick translation.

6. Migne, *Patrologia Latina* 79.407. Merton's lecture notes for the novitiate indicate that he freely translated selections of Migne's classic edition of *Patrologia Latina* from the Latin. The *Patrologia* comprises the works of the Church Fathers from Tertullian in 200 AD to the death of Pope Innocent III in 1216.

7. John C. Ford, S.J., "The Morality of Obliteration Bombing," *Theological Studies* 5, no. 3 (1944): 261–309.

8. Niccolò Machiavelli, *The Prince,* translation by Luigi Ricci, revised by E. R. P. Vincent (London: Oxford University Press, 1960), XV.68. Subsequent references will be cited with chapter from *The Prince* followed by pagination in the Ricci-Vincent translation.

9. Merton is quoting the epigraph of the book *Nuclear Weapons and Christian Conscience* (see note 22 below).

10. Edward Teller, *The Legacy of Hiroshima* (Westport, Conn.: Greenwood Press, 1962). Subsequent references will be cited as *"Legacy."*

11. See Erich Fromm and Michael Maccoby, "The Question of Civil Defense: A Reply to Herman Kahn," in *Breakthrough to Peace* (New York: New Directions, 1962), 61–62. Merton edited *Breakthrough* and wrote an introduction and an essay for it, but was not credited as editor because of worries about censorship.

12. John Courtney Murray, S.J., "Remarks on the Moral Problem of War," *Theological Studies* 20 (1969): 40–61.

13. John Courtney Murray, S.J., *We Hold These Truths: Catholic Reflections on the American Proposition* (New York: Sheed and Ward, 1960). Subsequent references will be cited as "Murray."

14. *God and the H-bomb,* edited by Donald Keys with a foreword by Steve Allen (New York: Bellmeadows Press, 1961).

15. Bishop Fulton J. Sheen, "Is Nuclear War Justifiable?" in *God and the H-bomb,* 145.

16. Dr. Norman K. Gottwald, "Nuclear Realism or Nuclear Pacifism?" in *God and the H-bomb,* 66.

17. Samuel Dresner, "Man, God and Atomic War," in *God and the H-bomb,* 166–78.

18. Franziskus M. Stratmann, *Peace and the Clergy* (London: Sheed & Ward, 1936); *The Church and War* (New York: P. J. Kenedy and Sons, 1928).

19. Franziskus M. Stratmann, "War and Christian Conscience," in *God and the H-bomb,* 37–57.

20. *Morals and Missiles: Catholic Essays on the Problem of War Today,* with an introduction by M. De La Bedoyere, edited by Charles S. Thompson (London: J. Clarke, 1961).

21. E. I. Watkin, "Unjustifiable War," in *Morals and Missiles,* 51–62.

22. Walter Stein, "Introductory: The Defense of the West," in *Nuclear Weapons and Christian Conscience* [*NWCC*] (London: Merlin Press, 1961),

37–38. Subsequent references will be cited as "Stein." A shortened version of this essay appeared in *Breakthrough to Peace,* 139–58.

23. G. E. M. Anscombe, "War and Murder," Stein, 57.

24. R. A. Markus, "Conscience and Deterrence," Stein, 81.

25. John C. Bennett, *Nuclear Weapons and the Conflict of Conscience* (New York: Scribner, 1962), 96. Subsequent references will be cited as "Bennett."

26. Herman Kahn, "The Arms Race and Some of Its Hazards," *Daedalus* (Fall 1960): 765.

27. See *The Atomic Age: Scientists in National and World Affairs.* Articles from the *Bulletin of the Atomic Scientists* 1945–62, edited and with introductions by Morton Grodzins and Eugene Rabinowitch (New York: Basic Books, 1963). This collection of articles and documents traces the scientists' opinions in the early years after the development of nuclear weapons.

28. Pope Pius XII used the term "God-Man" to refer to Christ. The complete text of the sentence is, "If ever Christians neglect this duty of theirs by leaving inactive the guiding forces of the faith in public life, to the extent that they are responsible, they would be committing treason against the God-Man Who appeared in visible form among us in the cradle of Bethlehem." See Vincent A. Yzermans, ed., *The Major Addresses of Pope Pius XII,* vol. 2: *Christmas Messages* (St. Paul: Northern Central Publishing Co., 1961), 205. This is a slightly different translation than Merton was using.

Of Related Interest

Seeking Paradise
The Spirit of the Shakers
Thomas Merton
ISBN 1-57075-501-9

"Through this beautiful and inspiring volume the American soul is laid bare . . ."
—*M. Basil Pennington, OCSO*

Thomas Merton
Essential Writings
Selected with an Introduction by Christine M. Bochen
ISBN 157075-331-8

"May well become the standard anthology for Merton courses and study groups."
—*William H. Shannon*

Living With Wisdom
A Life of Thomas Merton
Jim Forest
ISBN 0-88344-755-X

"If you have to read one book about Thomas Merton, this is the one to read. It is concise, insightful, complete."
–*Paul Wilkes*

Please support your local bookstore, or call 1-800-258-5838.

For a free catalog, please write us at

Orbis Books, Box 308
Maryknoll NY 10545-0308

or visit our website at www.orbisbooks.com

Thank you for reading *Peace in the Post-Christian Era*.
We hope you enjoyed it.

Chapter 3.

BACKUP COPIES OF PROGRAMS

When working with a computer it is essential that you learn how to make backup copies of individual files, or of complete disks. This is necessary both to guard against accidental damage or corruption of a disk (which could arise through operator error, equipment malfunction, or mains failure), and also the effects of old age and wear. Remember that disks will eventually wear out.

Throughout this book it is assumed that you are running WordStar under the CP/M operating system. WordStar will also run under several other CP/M like operating systems. If you are using one of these, some of the operating system commands will be different, but the WordStar commands will be exactly the same.

If you have only one copy of the system disk which contains CP/M, or of programs which you have purchased such as WordStar, or a BASIC interpreter, then if something unfortunate happens to this disk you will have the expense and inconvenience of buying another. To ensure that this does not happen users are advised to make at least one, or perhaps two working copies of the system disk, and other important programs, and to store the factory master in a safe place. The working copies should be used as needed, but the factory master should be used only for making backup copies. (Remember that these programs are copyrighted, and you are only allowed to make copies for your own use, but not for sale or distribution to others).

The steps in copying the appropriate disks and files are probably too complicated and technical for absolute beginners. They should get a friend who has some experience of using a microcomputer or their dealer to copy the disks for them, as specified below:

1. It is essential that you backup (that is duplicate) your master copy of the CP/M disk. For those who have to do this for themselves, the steps involved in copying an entire CP/M system disk are set out in Appendix 1.

2. The master copy of your WordStar disk must also be duplicated in a similar way, and in addition the un-installed version of the WordStar program, which is generally called WSU.COM must be installed, that is changed to work with the particular vdu and printer in your system. The installed version of WordStar is called WS.COM, and this installing must be carried out before you try to use WordStar. This may be a difficult job, and requires some understanding, and is best carried out by someone with experience of microcomputers. Some notes on how to install WordStar are given in Appendix 2.

3. In addition you should produce a working disk containing the CP/M operating system, the CP/M transient programs PIP and STAT, and the WordStar programs WS.COM, WSMSGS.OVR and WSOVLY1.OVR. The steps to do this are given in Appendix 3.

4. Format a blank disk if this is necessary on your computer, ready for use to store the WordStar data files which you will produce.

Chapter 4.

GETTING STARTED

This chapter is designed to take a beginner through the essential steps of loading the operating system, calling up WordStar, typing a very simple document, saving it on disk and finally printing it out. WordStar is so easy to use that it is possible to do all this in a single session of less than one hour. Master these essentials before trying the clever features in subsequent chapters.

Switching on and loading CP/M

First switch on the mains to the computer and the vdu, and then insert a floppy disk which contains the operating system (CP/M) and also the word processing program (WordStar) into disk drive A:. **Do NOT insert a disk before switching on.** If your computer has a second disk drive, either insert a new blank disk (which has previously been formatted), or insert a disk which already contains WordStar data files in to drive B:. Consult the manual for your particular machine to find out how to make it start. (To do this, most computers have a special button called the Boot-strap switch which must be pushed). The disk light on drive A: will then come on, indicating that something is being read from the disk, - in this case CP/M itself. A sign-on message will then appear on the vdu screen. The message varies slightly depending on the computer used: TRS-80, RML 380Z, Superbrain, Cromemco etc. and for example with a North Star Horizon it may appear as shown in Figure 4.1:

FIGURE 4.1   The sign-on message

```
CP/M on North Star
56K Version 2.22 DQ
(C) 1981 Lifeboat Associates

A>
```

This message shows which computer this version of CP/M has been written for, the memory size it is set up for, and who holds the copyright for this version. The prompt A> indicates that disk drive A: is currently logged-in, that is the computer expects to read or write information from or to drive A: at present. At this stage CP/M is loaded, and any of the CP/M utilities may be used. The most common of these are DIR (which lists the directory, that is lists the names of files on the disk), STAT (which finds the size of files and the free space left on a disk), PIP (for copying files either on the same disk, or from one disk to another), REN (to rename an existing file) and ERA (to erase a file from the disk). These are described in chapters 41 - 45 on CP/M commands at the end of the book.

Loading WordStar

The next step is to load the word processing program WordStar from the disk, (where it is stored as a file called WS.COM), into the computer's memory, so that the program may be run. To do this simply type in **WS** and press the **RETURN** key. The disk lights again come on while the computer reads the file from the disk, and a screen of information is displayed, which gives the serial number of this particular copy of the WordStar program, a copyright notice, and information detailing exactly which vdu and printer this version of WordStar has been customised for. (If the version being used has been customised for a different vdu or printer, refer to the WordStar manual on how to run the program INSTALL).

After a few seconds this screenful of information disappears, and is replaced by the "No-File" menu. This is shown in Figure 4.2 and comprises a list of commands from which you must choose the one you wish to operate. This menu is so called because you have not yet picked a file to work on. In addition, the directory is displayed on the screen. This is simply a list of the names of all the files present on the disk which is currently logged-in - in this case on disk drive A:.

FIGURE 4.2   The "No-File" menu - WordStar version 3.0

```
            < < <  N O - F I L E   M E N U  > > >
    ——Preliminary Commands——  | --File  Commands--  | -System Commands-
L  Change logged disk drive    | P  Print  a file    | R  Run  a  program
F  File directory     off (ON) | E  RENAME a file    | X EXIT to system
H  Set Help level              | O  COPY   a file    |
    ——Commands to open a file——| Y  DELETE a file    | -WordStar Options-
    D  Open a document file     |                     | M Run MailMerge
    N  Open a non-document file |                     | S Run SpellStar


DIRECTORY of disk A:
WS.COM        WSMSGS.OVR    WSOVLY1.OVR  MAILMRGE.OVR
```

Changing the logged-in disk drive

An explanation of the various options given in the "No-File" menu is given later in chapter 6, but for the moment you should change the logged-in disk drive. The logged-in drive is simply the drive which is in current use. At the moment, this is drive A:, which is the drive containing the disk with CP/M and WordStar. Because of this, the directory which is displayed at the bottom of the "No-File" menu is the directory of files present on drive A:. If there are two disk drives in your computer, they will be called drives A: and B: respectively. **It is highly desirable that the programs are kept on drive A:, and the WordStar data files containing the letters, documents, notices and other text you may want to save are kept on drive B:.** Unless the logged-in drive is changed, then when text typed in under WordStar is saved onto disk, the text file will be stored on drive A: together with the programs. To change the logged-in drive simply type **L.** A new menu appears on the screen, and this is shown in Figure 4.3.

FIGURE 4.3   The L command menu

```
    L          editing no file

        The LOGGED DISK (or Current Disk or Default Disk) is the
        disk drive used for files except those files for which
        you enter a disk drive name as part of the file name.
        WordStar displays the File Directory of the Logged Disk.

        THE LOGGED DISK DRIVE IS NOW A:

        NEW LOGGED DISK DRIVE (letter, colon, RETURN)?

        DIRECTORY of disk A:
        WS.COM        WSMSGS.OVR    WSOVLY1.OVR  MAILMRGE.OVR
```

The most important part of this menu is the question:

NEW LOGGED DISK DRIVE (letter, colon, RETURN)?

To make drive B: the currently logged-in drive, insert a disk, type B: and press **RETURN.** The "No-File" menu is displayed again, but it now shows the directory for files on drive B:. (If the computer only has one disk drive, then plainly this step must be omitted, but since the WordStar program is already stored on the disk in drive A:, it follows that the amount of space that may be used for data files will be correspondingly reduced).

Opening a file for editing

The next step is to type **D** to open a document file, that is a file which contains text such as a letter, a notice or a book. The menu on the screen changes as shown in Figure 4.4. (Should you wish to edit a non-document file such as a computer program you should type **N** instead).

FIGURE 4.4 The D command menu

```
    D           editing no file

        Use this command to create a new document file,
        or to initiate alteration of an existing document file.

        A file name is 1 to 8 letters/digits, a period,
        and an optional 1-3 character type.
        File name may be preceded by a disk drive letter A-D
        and a colon, otherwise current logged disk is used.

      ^S=delete character    ^Y=delete entry    ^F=File directory
      ^D=restore character   ^R=Restore entry   ^U=cancel command

        NAME OF FILE TO EDIT?

    DIRECTORY of disk B:
```

The directory is blank, that is no files exist on disk B:. This is what would be expected, since you put a new (empty) disk in this drive. Had the disk already contained files, their names would appear in the directory.

The most important part of this menu is that WordStar is asking for the name of the file you wish to edit. If you have previously stored a text file on this disk, then you could type its name, and you could then alter the contents of the file or add to it as required. In this case you should start a new file, and you must choose a suitable filename.

CP/M filenames

CP/M filenames comprise two parts - the **primary filename**, which may be up to eight letters or numbers, optionally followed by a **file extension** of a full stop and up to three more letters. These last three characters indicate the file type. Under CP/M certain endings have special meanings. For example the ending .COM is reserved for machine code programs, .OVR is used for overlay files, .BAS is commonly used for BASIC programs, and it is recommended that the ending .TXT is used for text files.

WordStar will accept either upper-case (CAPITAL letters) or lower case (small letters) typed in filenames, but lower case letters are converted to upper case, and the file name is always stored in capitals.

The example given illustrates how to type a few sentences from a well known song on the word processor, and the name STAR.TXT has been chosen for the filename. To proceed you merely have to type **STAR.TXT** and press **RETURN**. As the filename is typed, it appears on the screen in the line:

NAME OF FILE TO EDIT? **STAR.TXT**

After the filename has been typed the **RETURN** key must be pressed. The program detects that there is no existing file called STAR.TXT on the logged-in disc drive, and so the message **NEW FILE** is displayed. After a few seconds, the screen clears and the Main Menu is displayed. This is shown in Figure 4.5. It lists commands for moving the cursor, scrolling through a document to display different parts on the screen, how to delete text, a few miscellaneous commands, and a list of the menus which may be called up to explain particular WordStar features. The main menu serves as a reminder, particularly for beginners, but for the moment you can ignore its contents and get on with typing the text.

FIGURE 4.5

```
      B:STAR.TXT    PAGE 1 LINE 1  COL 01              INSERT ON
                  < < <    M A I N   M E N U    > > >
    --Cursor Movement--  | -Delete- |  -Miscellaneous-  | -Other  Menus-
^S char left ^D char right |^G  char  | ^I Tab   ^B Reform | (from Main only)
^A word left ^F word right |DEL chr lf| ^V INSERT ON/OFF  |^J Help  ^K Block
^E line  up  ^X line down  |^T word rt|^L Find/Replce again|^Q Quick ^P Print
     --Scrolling--        |^Y  line  |RETURN End paragraph|^O Onscreen
^Z line up   ^W line down  |          | ^N Insert a RETURN |
^C screen up ^R screen down|          | ^U Stop a command  |
L----!----!----!----!----!----!----!----!----!----!----!--------R
```

Typing the text

Type the verse given in Figure 4.6 just as if you were using a typewriter. Use the shift key to get upper and lower case letters, and the space bar to get a space inbetween words. You must use carriage returns to force WordStar to end each line, in the same way as on a typewriter, and also to get a blank line. These places have been marked **(RETURN)**. (In later exercises you will type in a whole paragraph, and let WordStar's word-wrap feature sort out the ends of lines automatically).

If you make a typing mistake, press the **DELETE** key, which is sometimes labelled **RUBOUT** or **BS** - (press once to delete the last character typed, or several times to delete several letters). Then type the correct letter(s). In cases of desperation, type **^Y** (that is hold the CONTROL key down and press Y) to delete the entire line marked by the cursor. Several alternative methods of correcting mistakes are explained in chapter 10 - Basic Editing, and chapter 16 - the Find and Replace Commands.

FIGURE 4.6 A children's song

Twinkle, twinkle, little star,**(RETURN)**
How I wonder where you are;**(RETURN)**
Up above the world so high,**(RETURN)**
Like a diamond in the sky.**(RETURN)**
(RETURN)

Saving the file on disk

The document just typed is not permanently stored, and cannot be printed, until it has been "saved" on disk. There are several ways of storing files, which are explained later on in chapter 12 - Saving Files. For the moment you should save the letter in a disk file called STAR.TXT by typing ^KD. The disk drives will make clicking noises, and the disk lights will come on as the document is written on the disk. While this is happening, the status line at the top of the screen displays a message **WAIT**, and beneath this appears a message **SAVING FILE B:STAR.TXT**. Once the file has been written to the disk, the WAIT message disappears, and the "No-File" menu is displayed once again. Note that the directory of the logged-in disk drive is also displayed, in this case B:, and this shows that the disk now contains one file, called STAR.TXT.

Printing the verse

First make sure that the printer is plugged in to the computer, that the mains are switched on to the printer, and that paper is loaded and correctly positioned in the printer. The "No-File" menu is currently displayed on the screen. The next step is to select the Print option by typing **P.** The screen display changes, as shown in Figure 4.7.

FIGURE 4.7 The P command menu

```
P       editing no file

 ^S=delete character    ^Y=delete entry    ^F=File directory
 ^D=restore character   ^R=Restore entry   ^U=cancel command

   NAME OF FILE TO PRINT? STAR.TXT


 DIRECTORY of disk B:
 STAR.TXT
```

Near the top there are two lines of instructions explaining how the Print command may be cancelled if you have got into this by accident, and how to delete the last letter typed should you spell the file name incorrectly. At the bottom the directory is displayed, showing the files present on the logged-in disk. The most important part of this menu is the question which asks which file you wish to print. The filename STAR.TXT must be typed, and this is displayed on the screen. **The simplest way of printing the document, is to press ESCAPE rather than RETURN.** Printing should start at once. The "No-File" menu is displayed on the screen, and while printing is in progress the message **printing B:STAR.TXT** will be displayed on the top line of the screen.

If you have some special reason for doing so, you may press **RETURN** after typing the file name. A whole series of questions will appear on the screen one after another. These are shown in Figure 4.8.

FIGURE 4.8 Questions when printing a document

```
For default press RETURN after each question:
    DISK FILE OUTPUT (Y/N):
    START AT PAGE NUMBER(RETURN for beginning)?
    STOP AFTER PAGE NUMBER (RETURN for end)?
    USE FORM FEEDS (Y/N):
    SUPPRESS PAGE FORMATTING (Y/N):
    PAUSE FOR PAPER CHANGES BETWEEN PAGES (Y/N):
Ready printer, press RETURN:
```

The simplest way is to press **RETURN** in answer to each question, which usually gives acceptable answers by default. The meanings of the questions are considered in detail in chapter 13 - Printing a Document.

Finishing the session

After the printing is completed, the "No-File" menu is again displayed. This time, choose the option to Exit to the operating system by typing **X.** When the CP/M prompt B> appears on the screen, and the disk lights have gone off, remove both floppy disks. Put the disks in their paper envelopes at once. Then switch the mains off on the computer, vdu and printer. It is essential that you do NOT try to remove disks while the disk lights are on, and also essential that you do NOT switch the mains off while the disks are in the disk drives. (If you cannot make the printer work, seek help from a friend, or your dealer, since there are numerous simple things which might be wrong).

Chapter 5.

PRACTICE WRITING A LETTER

This chapter is designed to consolidate what you have learned in the previous chapter. It will give you further practice in typing, saving and printing a letter. The layout of a letter is more complicated than the example in the previous chapter. The file that you produce should be saved on disk, and will be used for another exercise later in the book.

Typing a letter

1. Follow the instructions given in the last chapter to switch the computer ON, to load CP/M, and then WordStar. Make sure that you have the disk you have prepared for WordStar data files in disk drive B:.

2. At the "No-File" menu change the logged-in drive to B: by typing first **L**, and then **B**, and pressing **RETURN.**

3. From the "No-File" menu type **D** to open a document file for editing, and type the filename **LETTER.TXT** as the name of this new file, and then press **RETURN.**

4. Type the letter given in Figure 5.1. The following points may be helpful:

   (a) Use the shift key to get upper and lower case letters.

   (b) You must use either the space bar or ^I (or the tab key if present) to indent the lines with the date, Yours sincerely, and Headmaster. (Remember that the cursor moving keys will only move the cursor within existing text, and will not move the cursor along a blank line).

   There are a few small differences from a typewriter:

   (c) You must not use carriage returns at the end of each line when you are typing text. The word-wrap feature in WordStar does this for you automatically. You must press **RETURN** in a few places, at the end of paragraphs and to get a blank line. These places have been marked **(RETURN).**

   (d) If you make a typing mistake, press the **DELETE** key, (sometimes labelled **RUBOUT** or **BS**) - one or more times to delete the appropriate number of characters. Then type the correct letter(s). If you make an awful mess of one line, you can delete the whole line by typing ^Y (that is hold the CONTROL key down and press Y) to delete the entire line marked by the cursor. Several alternative methods of correcting mistakes are explained in chapter 10 - Basic Editing, and chapter 16 - Editing - The Find and Replace Commands.

5. When you have finished typing, save the file on to disk with a ^KD command.

6. Switch the printer on, and make sure that paper is loaded and correctly positioned. Print the file by typing **P** to select the Print option from the "No-File" menu, and then type the name of the file to print as **LETTER.TXT.** If possible avoid the detailed questions about printing by pressing **ESCAPE** in a similar manner to that described in the last chapter, otherwise press **RETURN** and answer the questions one by one. These questions are explained in chapter 13 - Printing a Document.

FIGURE 5.1. A sample letter

1st. June 1984**(RETURN)**
(RETURN)
(RETURN)
(RETURN)
Dear Mr. Smith,**(RETURN)**
(RETURN)
The school will be holding the annual Prize-giving ceremony on
Friday 5th. July, at 7.30 pm. in the School hall. Since your son
William is amongst the prize winners, I am pleased to be able to
invite you to join the special guests, who will be seated at the
front of the hall. Since seating is strictly limited, a reply
would be appreciated before 10th. June, stating how many seats
you require.**(RETURN)**
(RETURN)
You will no doubt have heard of the appeal launched by the
Governors, to put stained glass window in the library, as a
lasting tribute to our late chemistry master Mr. Kipps, who
died so tragically following an accident in the laboratory
earlier this year. I would be pleased to receive your donation
to the appeal. Cheques should be made payable to the Headmaster.**(RETURN)**
(RETURN)
(RETURN)
(RETURN)

Yours sincerely,**(RETURN)**

(RETURN)
(RETURN)
(RETURN)
(RETURN)

Headmaster.**(RETURN)**

Chapter 6.

THE "NO-FILE" MENU

The "No-File" menu is displayed automatically when WordStar is loaded, and also when a particular job has been finished. In many ways this is the central point of the program. From here you choose the next task to be performed, and when completed this is where you come back to. This chapter briefly describes the function of the commands available from this menu.

FIGURE 6.1 The "No-File" menu

```
            < < <  N O - F I L E   M E N U  > > >
    ---Preliminary Commands---  | --File  Commands--  | -System Commands-
L  Change logged disk drive     | P  Print  a file    | R Run a  program
F  File directory      off (ON) | E  RENAME a file     | X EXIT to system
H  Set Help level               | O  COPY   a file     |
  ---Commands to open a file---  | Y  DELETE a file     | -WordStar Options-
   D  Open a  document file      |                      | M Run MailMerge
   N  Open a non-document file   |                      | S Run SpellStar

DIRECTORY of disk A:
WS.COM        WSMSGS.OVR   WSOVLY1.OVR  MAILMRGE.OVR
```

The recommended arrangement of disks

To start the computer in the first place, (to "boot" it), CP/M must be present on the disk in drive A:. Thus at the start drive A: is the logged-in drive, that is the one which is active, and communicates with the computer. On all computers with two floppy disk drives it is recommended that the disk in drive A: contains CP/M and the necessary CP/M utility programs (STAT.COM is essential for finding the size of files, and the amount of free space, and PIP.COM is very useful for copying files). In addition it is recommended that the WordStar programs are also stored on this disk. Thus when WordStar is loaded, the logged-in drive is still A:. It is recommended that drive B: is used for WordStar data files. This arrangement allows the entire space on the disk in drive B: to be used for storing data files, and since no programs are stored on it, there is much more room for data. This disk arrangement is used throughout the book. The logged-in drive is still A:, and before data files on drive B: can be used, it is necessary to change the logged-in drive to B:.

Users with only one disk drive plainly have to use drive A: throughout. Since each disk will have to hold CP/M, any utility programs and WordStar, there will be only a limited space for data files. Users with a hard disk have the advantage of a vast amount of storage space, and very quick access to files. In this case, CP/M, the utility programs, WordStar and the data files should all be stored on the hard disk.

The preliminary commands

L may be typed to log-in to a different disk drive. This is usually done to allow you to work on a different drive, (for example when WordStar is loaded you are logged-in to drive A: and want to use data files stored on the disk mounted in drive B:). The command may also be used to see what files are present on the disk in another drive, or to see which drive is currently logged -in. If the disk in the working drive has been replaced by another disk, the command L may be used to log-in the new disk. (See chapter 19 - When it is Safe to Change Disks). When L is pressed, the screen changes as shown in Figure 6.2.

FIGURE 6.2 The L command display

```
L              editing no file

   The LOGGED DISK (or Current Disk or Default Disk) is the
   disk drive used for files except those files for which
   you enter a disk drive name as part of the file name.
   WordStar displays the File Directory of the Logged Disk.

   THE LOGGED DISK DRIVE IS NOW A:

   NEW LOGGED DISK DRIVE (letter, colon, RETURN)?

   DIRECTORY of disk A:
   WS.COM        WSMSGS.OVR   WSOVLY1.OVR  MAILMRGE.OVR
```

The important part of this menu is that it displays the drive which is logged-in, and asks which drive you wish to log-in. Typing **B:** and **RETURN**, or just **B** and pressing **RETURN** will log-in drive B:. Alternatively pressing **RETURN** or **ESCAPE** will leave the logged-in drive unchanged. Note that the logged-in drive may be changed during editing with a **^KL** command.

By default the file directory is displayed under the "No-File" menu. It shows the names of the files on the logged-in disk. The directory display may be turned OFF by typing **F**, and typing **F** again turns the directory ON again.

The command **H** may be used to set the Help level, to change the number and the length of messages displayed on the screen, from 3 for maximum help, to 0 for no help. The Help level may also be changed while you are editing, using the **^JH** command. This has exactly the same effect as **H**, and is fully described in chapter 22 - Changing the Help Level.

Commands to open a file

There are two commands which may be used to open files. These are **D** to open a document file, and **N** to open a non-document file. Text documents are best entered using the **D** command. This is fully described in chapter 4 - Getting Started.

Non-document files

Non-document files produced by the **N** command are used (a) to make command files for MailMerge, (b) when using WordStar as an editor to alter programs written in BASIC, PASCAL, FORTRAN, machine code etc., and (c) for files which must be compatible with programs other than WordStar. The main differences between document and non-document file are:

1. The display of page breaks on the screen is permanently disabled.

2. The status line shows the number of lines and characters up to the cursor rather than the page, line and column occupied by the cursor.

3. The word-wrap feature, (which automatically moves a word down on to the next line if it will not fit on the current line), is turned on for document files. With non-document files it is turned OFF, but may be turned ON again with a **^OW** command.

4. With document files the right margin is justified unless you switch justification OFF. This means that extra spaces are automatically added to lines of text to make all of the lines end at the same point, so that the right margin is straight. With non-document files, justification is turned OFF, but may be switched ON with a **^OJ** command.

5. When editing document files, the ruler line is normally displayed, and the
    variable tabs in the ruler all work as tab stops. With non-document
    files both the ruler display and the variable tabs are switched OFF, but
    they may be turned ON with a ^OT and ^OV commands respectively.

6. Dot commands are not checked by the editor when in non-document mode.
    (When editing in Document mode invalid dot commands are shown with a ?
    flag at the right of the screen).

File commands to print, rename, copy and delete

Printing files

The P command is used to print a file, and this is covered in chapter 13 -
Printing a Document.

Renaming files

The commands E to rename a file, O to copy a file and Y to delete a file
are all rather similar. They perform the same functions as CP/M does with REN
for renaming files, PIP for copying files and ERA for erasing files. The
WordStar commands are much easier to use than the equivalent CP/M commands.
The CP/M commands work provided that you get the syntax of the commands exactly
correct, but they do not provide any help. In contrast, WordStar prompts with
a message in English which asks for the name of the file you wish to rename,
copy or erase, and then asks for the new filename where appropriate. WordStar
tells you if you type a filename which does not exist. However, the "wild
card" characters ? and * cannot be used in filenames.

When the command E is typed to rename a file, the screen changes as shown
in Figure 6.3:

FIGURE 6.3 The E command display

```
E           editing no file

   ^S=delete character   ^Y=delete entry    ^F=File directory
   ^D=restore character  ^R=Restore entry   ^U=cancel command

      NAME OF FILE TO RENAME? LETTER.TXT


DIRECTORY of disk B:
  LETTER.TXT
```

If the name of the file to be renamed is typed, in this case **LETTER.TXT**, and
RETURN is pressed, WordStar asks:

NEW NAME?

The new file name must be typed in, followed by **RETURN**, and the file is renamed. Files may also be renamed during editing by using the ^KE command.

Copying files

The command O is used to copy a file, and when this is typed the screen
changes as shown in Figure 6.4.

FIGURE 6.4 The O command menu

```
O            editing no file

   ^S=delete character    ^Y=delete entry    ^F=File directory
   ^D=restore character   ^R=Restore entry   ^U=cancel command

      NAME OF FILE TO COPY FROM?


   DIRECTORY of disk B:
   LETTER.TXT
```

The name of the file you wish to copy must be typed, followed by **RETURN**. WordStar then asks another question:

NAME OF FILE TO COPY TO?

You then type the name that you would like the copy to be called, and press **RETURN** and the task is completed. Remember that the drive letter and a colon may be included at the beginning of the filename, thus allowing you to copy a file from one drive to another. If the new file name that you have chosen already exists on that disk, a message will appear:

FILE (filename you used) EXISTS - overwrite? (Y/N):

WordStar is being rather clever. The instructions you have given will destroy the original file stored on disk. This question is to check that this is what you intended, and it gives you the opportunity to change your mind. If you wish to overwrite, that is destroy the existing file, type **Y**. If you have made a mistake type **N**, or any character other than Y or y, and the question will be repeated: **NAME OF FILE TO COPY TO?**. You may now choose a different filename. A file may be copied in the same way while you are editing a file, by using the command **^KO.**

Deleting files

If **Y** is typed to delete a file, the screen changes as shown in Figure 6.5.

FIGURE 6.5 The Y command menu

```
Y            editing no file

   ^S=delete character    ^Y=delete entry    ^F=File directory
   ^D=restore character   ^R=Restore entry   ^U=cancel command

      NAME OF FILE TO DELETE?


   DIRECTORY of disk B:
   LETTER.TXT
```

To delete a file, type the file name and press **RETURN**. If a drive letter is specified at the beginning of the filename, then the file will be deleted from the drive which was specified. Otherwise, the logged-in drive is taken by default. A file may also be deleted when you are editing a file by using the command **^KJ.**

System commands

The command **R** is used to run some other program without having to exit from WordStar. A common example of its use is to run the CP/M program STAT to

find the file sizes and the amount of free space on the disk. When **R** is typed, a new menu is displayed, as shown in Figure 6.6.

FIGURE 6.6 **The R command menu**

```
  R           editing no file

  Enter name of program you wish to Run,
  optionally followed by appropriate arguments.
    Example (shows disk space):    STAT

  ^S=delete character    ^Y=delete entry    ^F=File directory
  ^D=restore character   ^R=Restore entry   ^U=cancel command

     COMMAND?


  DIRECTORY of disk B:
  LETTER.TXT
```

The question **COMMAND?** is asking you to type the name of the program you wish to run. In this case, typing **STAT** and pressing **RETURN** will run the program STAT, and the free space on the logged-in disk will be shown on the screen. Arguments are extra information which is specified together with the program. Thus the command **STAT LETTER.TXT** has the argument LETTER.TXT. When this is run, the size of the file LETTER.TXT is displayed, and also the free space on the disk. Other variations are **STAT *.BAK** which will list the names and sizes of all files with the ending .BAK, and **STAT *.*** which will give the file sizes of all the files on the disk. (See chapter 43).

Any other program with the ending .COM may be run in a similar way. Make sure that you only try to run programs which are executable, or you may obtain an error message (if you are lucky), or crash the system with a locked keyboard. The only way out of this is to reboot the system. Note that **R** will not run any of the intrinsic CP/M commands DIR, ERA, REN, TYPE and SAVE. (These are described in chapter 42 - CP/M Intrinsic Commands). WordStar has alternative commands for these, shown in Figure 6.7.

FIGURE 6.7

CP/M command	Function	from "No-File" menu	while Editing
		------WordStar commands------	
DIR	Display file directory	F	^KF
ERA	Erase a file from the disk	Y	^KJ
REN	Rename a file	E	^KE
SAVE	Save a file from memory to disk		^KD, ^KS, ^KX
TYPE	Display the file	D or N	
TYPE ^P	Print the file	P or M	^KP

The last system command is **X**, which transfers control from WordStar back to the CP/M operating system. This is similar to the command **^KX** which may be used during editing. This saves the file that is currently being edited on disk, and then returns you from WordStar back to the CP/M operating system.

WordStar options

There are two WordStar options. The command **M** runs MailMerge, the program to merge files, print chain letters, and books. This is described in chapters 33 - 39. The command **S** runs Spellstar, which finds spelling mistakes, and is described in chapter 40.

Chapter 7.
PRACTICE IN USING SOME OF THE "NO-FILE" COMMANDS

The "No-File" menu is displayed automatically when WordStar is loaded, and is described in some detail in the previous chapter. In this chapter you will actually use the commands in a practical session on your computer. The files you produce will be used in examples later in the book.

A practice session

1. Load CP/M and then WordStar. (Refer to chapter 4 - Getting Started if you need help with this).

2. At the "No-File" menu type **L, B** and **RETURN** to change the logged-in drive to B: if you are using the recommended arrangement of two disk drives.

3. From the "No-File" menu type **D** to open a document file, and when asked for **NAME OF FILE TO EDIT?** type **CUBS.TXT** and press **RETURN.**

4. Now type the Cub Scout Promise and Law given in Figure 7.1. The places where you must press **RETURN** are marked **(RETURN).**

   Very simple typing mistakes such as pressing a wrong letter may be corrected by using the **DEL** key to delete the last letter typed, and you may then type the correct letter. It does not matter if you leave a few typing mistakes, since these can be corrected later, when you have learned more about editing.

FIGURE 7.1

> Cub Scout Promise**(RETURN)**
> **(RETURN)**
> I promise that I will do my best**(RETURN)**
> to do my duty to God and the Queen,**(RETURN)**
> to help other people**(RETURN)**
> and to keep the Cub Scout Law.**(RETURN)**
> **(RETURN)**
> Cub Scout Law**(RETURN)**
> **(RETURN)**
> A Cub Scout always does his best,**(RETURN)**
> thinks of others before himself**(RETURN)**
> and does a good turn every day.**(RETURN)**

5. Next type ^**KD** to save the file on the disk in the logged-in drive B:. The "No-File" menu will be displayed on the screen, and if you examine the directory displayed beneath this, you will see the entry **CUBS.TXT** for the new file you have just typed.

6. Now you can make a copy of this file on the same disk (B:). CP/M will not allow you to have two files with exactly the same filename on the same disk, so you should call the copy CUBSCOPY.TXT. To do this, type the command **O.** In reply to the question **NAME OF FILE TO COPY FROM?** type **CUBS.TXT** and press **RETURN.** The next question is **NAME OF FILE TO COPY TO?,** and you should type **CUBSCOPY.TXT** and press **RETURN.**

7. The "No-File" menu is again displayed on the screen, and if you examine the directory, you will see entries for both the original file **CUBS.TXT** and for the new copy of the file that you have just produced called **CUBSCOPY.TXT.**

8. You should now now run the CP/M program called STAT to find the size of the new file **CUBS.TXT**, and to see how much free space exists on the disk. The steps to do this are outlined below. The "No-File" menu is displayed on the screen, and you must type **R** to run a program, followed by **STAT CUBS.TXT** and **RETURN**. STAT is the name of the program you wish to run, and the filename CUBS.TXT is an optional parameter. Remember that there must be a space inbetween STAT and the filename CUBS.TXT. (See chapter 43 - The STAT Command for further details). A message will be displayed on the screen giving the size of the file **CUBS.TXT** as either 1K bytes or 2K bytes depending on your version of CP/M, and will also give the free space left on the disk (also in K bytes).

9. Next you should change the logged-in disk drive from **B:** to **A:**, and then copy the file **CUBS.TXT** present on drive **B:** to give a copy on drive **A:**. The steps are:
   (a) Type **L** followed by **A** and **RETURN** to change the logged-in drive from **B:** to **A:**. Note that the directory now displayed is that for drive **A:**.
   (b) Before copying the file from drive **B:** to drive **A:** make sure that there is space for the new file on drive **A:** by repeating the commands in paragraph 8, except that instead of typing **STAT CUBS.TXT** simply type **STAT**. This will give the free space on drive **A:**.
   (c) Make sure that a write-protect tab is **not** present on the disk in drive **A:** if you are using 5.25 inch floppies, or that a tab **is** present if you are using 8 inch floppies, or you will be unable to write on the disk.
   (d) The "No-File" menu is displayed, and you should follow the instructions in paragraph 6 to copy the file. The only difference is that the **NAME OF FILE TO COPY FROM?** should include the disk drive letter, that is **B:CUBS.TXT**. Since you are logged-in to drive **A:** the new file will be written to this drive automatically, so in reply to the question **NAME OF FILE TO COPY TO?** it does not matter whether you type **CUBS.TXT**, or whether you include the drive letter **A:CUBS.TXT**. When this has been done, the file directory for drive **A:** will include the new filename.

10. Since the disk in drive **A:** is really used for the CP/M and WordStar programs, you do not really want to clutter it up with data files. The steps for deleting (that is erasing) this file are outlined below. The "No-File" menu is displayed, together with the directory for drive **A:**. You must type **Y** to delete a file, and in reply to the message **NAME OF FILE TO DELETE?** you must type **CUBS.TXT** and press **RETURN**. It is worth pointing out that a file of this name exists on both drive **A:** and on drive **B:**. Since you did not specify the drive letter as part of the filename, it is assumed that you are referring to the logged-in drive, which in this case is **A:**. Check the directory to verify that this filename has now disappeared from the directory of drive **A:**.

11. Next change the logged-in drive back to **B:** by typing **L** and **B** then **RETURN** at the "No-File" menu, and then rename the existing file **CUBSCOPY.TXT** with the new name **SCOUTS.TXT**. To do this type **E**. Reply to the question **NAME OF FILE TO RENAME?** with **CUBSCOPY.TXT** and press **RETURN**, and reply to the question **NEW NAME?** with **SCOUTS.TXT** and **RETURN**. Examine the directory, and verify that CUBSCOPY.TXT has disappeared, and SCOUTS.TXT is now present.

Two new files CUBS.TXT and SCOUTS.TXT are now present on the disk in drive B, and these will be used later in the book in further practice sessions. You should now type **X** to exit from WordStar, remove the disks from both drives, and and only when this has been done is it safe for you to switch the mains off.

Summary

In this chapter you have practised saving a file, changing the logged-in drive, copying a file both on to the same disk and on to another drive, deleting a file, renaming a file, and running a program from WordStar.

Chapter 8.

SIMPLE CURSOR MOVEMENT

The cursor is a small block of light on the screen, which indicates the position where the next character typed will appear. As new text is typed, the cursor moves along. When a document which has already been typed is being edited, to make corrections, additions or deletions, the cursor must be moved to the appropriate point in the document. The basic commands for moving the cursor are displayed in the Main Menu at Help level 3, and are described in this chapter. Other ways of moving the cursor are described later in chapter 15 - Advanced Cursor Movements and Scrolling Text.

It is only possible to move the cursor while you are editing a document, and then it can only move within existing text. This means that when you start to edit a new file, it contains no text, and if you press the keys to move the cursor then nothing happens, and the cursor does not move. Similarly the cursor moving keys will not move the cursor into empty space at the end of a document, nor will it move along a blank line. However, in all of these situations, text may be typed, and if you want to type text indented several spaces rather than starting at the left margin then you must either type some spaces with the space bar, or press ^I to indent the text to the next tab stop.

WordStar must first be loaded, and when the "No-File" menu is obtained D must be typed to open a Document file, which is the sort of file used to store WordStar text. (Alternatively N could be typed to open a Non-document file, which might be a MailMerge command file, or a computer program). After typing the name of the file to be edited, the Main Menu (Figure 8.1) will appear on the screen provided that the Help level is set to 3. (This is the default setting for Help and corresponds to maximum help).

FIGURE 8.1 The Main Menu

```
            < < <    M A I N    M E N U    > > >
   —Cursor Movement—   | -Delete- |  -Miscellaneous-    |  -Other Menus-
 ^S char left ^D char right |^G  char |  ^I Tab   ^B Reform | (from Main only)
 ^A word left ^F word right |DEL chr lf| ^V INSERT ON/OFF   |^J Help  ^K Block
 ^E line up  ^X line down   |^T word rt|^L Find/Replce again|^Q Quick ^P Print
   --Scrolling--           |^Y  line |RETURN End paragraph|^O Onscreen
 ^Z line up   ^W line down  |         | ^N Insert a RETURN |
 ^C screen up ^R screen down|         | ^U Stop a command  |

Moving the cursor one place left ^S, right ^D, up ^E or down ^X
```

Many keyboards have special function keys marked with arrows pointing left, right, up and down. Provided that WordStar has been configured to use these, pressing these keys will move the cursor one character to the left or right, or one line up or down. It is much easier to use these special keys if they are present, but for those without them, the general cursor moving commands are given below.

The commands for moving the cursor all use control characters, that is the control key must be held down while another key is pressed. For example, holding the control key down and pressing the letter D is called control D, and in this book it is printed as ^D. This command moves the cursor one place to the right. Pressing ^D twice moves the cursor two places, pressing it three times moves three places. In a similar way, ^S moves the cursor one place to the left, ^E moves the cursor up one line, and ^X moves the cursor down one line. The arrangement of the four keys E, S, D and X, which are used for cursor movements makes a diamond shape on the keyboard (Figure 8.2). It is easier to remember the 'diamond' positions rather than the letters, since the top of the diamond ^E moves up a line, the bottom of the diamond ^X moves down a line, the right of the diamond ^D moves one character right, and the left of the diamond moves one character left. Beginners may find it helpful to mark the keys on these keyboard using sticky labels.

FIGURE 8.2 The diamond of keys for cursor movements

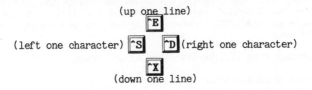

(up one line)
^E
(left one character) ^S   ^D (right one character)
^X
(down one line)

Moving the cursor one word left ^F, and one word right ^A

The idea of a 'diamond' of four control characters for moving the cursor is now extended. The character ^D moves the cursor one place to the right, and the character to the right of this namely ^F moves the cursor one word to the right. It is much quicker to move along a line jumping a whole word at a time, and moving in single spaces when you get near to the correction you wish to make. In much the same way, ^S moves the cursor one place to the left, and the character to the left of this, namely ^A moves the cursor one whole word to the left. (Figure 8.3).

FIGURE 8.3 Moving the cursor a whole word

(left one word) ^A   ^S   ^D   ^F (right one word)

Scrolling

In ancient times documents were written on scrolls. A scroll was a roll of leather, parchment or paper. To read such a document, it must be unrolled at one end and rolled up at the other end. The modern meaning of scrolling is the up or down movement on the screen of a piece of text too long to be viewed in its entirety, until the desired line(s) appear. Much confusion arises from the use of the words up and down. Scrolling upwards means that the text moves upwards, and consequently you read text lower down the document. Similarly scrolling downwards means that text moves down, hence you read text nearer the beginning, (nearer the top) of the document.

Scrolling up or down one line

The command ^W scrolls the text down one line, so that one line disappears off the bottom of the screen, and one line from nearer the beginning of the document becomes visible on the screen. Pressing ^W several times moves several lines. In a similar way, the command ^Z scrolls the text up one line, so that one line nearer the bottom of the file shows on the screen.

Chapter 9.

PRACTICE MOVING THE CURSOR

In this chapter you will get some practice moving the cursor to the appropriate place in a document, and making minor changes.

1. Start the computer, load CP/M and WordStar, and change the logged-in drive to B:. From the "No-File" menu type **D** to edit a file, and then specify the filename as **STAR.TXT**, which you typed and stored in chapter 4 - Getting Started.

2. The text in this file will be displayed on the screen:

> Twinkle, twinkle, little star,
> How I wonder where you are;
> Up above the world so high,
> Like a diamond in the sky.

The cursor will appear over the letter T of "Twinkle" at the beginning of the document.

(a) The first change is to alter the word "star" at the end of the first line into "bat". To do this you must move the cursor along the top line until it is over the letter "s" of "star". This may be done by pressing ^D repeatedly to move the cursor one place to the right each time, or better by pressing ^F to move the cursor one word to the right each time the key is pressed. When you have positioned the cursor correctly, press the ^G key to delete the letter under the cursor. The letter "s" disappears, and if you press the key three times more, the letters "tar" will also disappear. Now type the word "bat", and you will see this inserted at the end of the line.

(b) Next alter the words "where you are" in the second line to "what you're at". To do this, move the cursor down one line by pressing ^X. Then move the cursor to the right, in jumps of a whole word, by pressing ^F, until it is over the "w" of "where". Press ^G repeatedly until you have deleted the letters required, and then type in the new words.

(c) The third line should be altered in a similar way, changing the words "so high" into "you fly".

(d) Change the word "diamond" in the fourth line in to "Teatray". You could do this by exactly the same method as described in paragraph (b), but try this slightly different procedure. Move the cursor down on to the fourth line with ^X, then move the cursor to the right in whole words with ^F until the cursor is over the "i" of "in". This is past the word "diamond" which you want to delete. Press the **DELETE** key (this may be labelled **DEL** or **RUBOUT**), and the space between "diamond" and "in" disappears. By pressing this key again, the letters d n o m a i and d will disappear in turn. Pressing DELETE removes the character to the left of the cursor. Type the word "Teatray" and a space to complete the change.

(e) Finally alter the comma at the end of the first line, and the semi-colon at the end of the second line to exclamation marks. To do this, move the cursor up on-to the top line by pressing ^E three times. Press ^F to move right along the line, in whole words, until the cursor is one space past the comma. Press **DELETE** to delete the comma to the left of the cursor, and then type the exclamation mark! Move the cursor down a line with ^X, and repeat the procedure to replace the semi-colon by an exclamation mark.

(f) Save the file with a ^KD command, and then print it out. You have now created a verse from "Alice in Wonderland"!

Chapter 10.

BASIC EDITING

One of the most important advantages of a word processor over a typewriter is the ease with which the original document may be altered, updated and improved. Altering a document is called Editing. This chapter describes some of the most simple and commonly used editing features, namely the deletion and addition of text, followed by tidying up or reforming the altered paragraph. Also discussed are how to obtain a document with a ragged right edge instead of right justified, (or vice versa), how to split a large paragraph into two, and how to join paragraphs together. In the next chapter you will get some practice of these operations and of changing the line spacing and the margins. Later on, chapter 16 describes the more advanced editing features Find, and Find and Replace.

File changes that occur during editing

Suppose that you are editing an existing document called LETTER.TXT which is stored as a disk file. First this is copied from the disk file into RAM (memory), to give a working document. The working document may be displayed on the screen, or parts of it may be changed by adding text to it or deleting parts of it. The changes are made to the working document, not to the original disk file. The working document is of a transitory nature, and is not permanently stored on disk until it is Saved. A mishap such as a power failure, a computer malfunction, or terminating the edit without saving the working document will totally destroy the working document. The various ways of saving files on disk are described in chapter 12 – Saving Files. WordStar has a Save and Re-edit command ^KS which saves the working document on disk, and returns to edit the file just saved. This command should be used every 15 minutes during editing, to prevent accidental loss of work. The command ^KD should be used at the end of editing, and ^KQ may be used should you want to abandon the changes you have made to the current file and keep the original unchanged disk file.

When a new document is typed, it goes straight into the working document, and is only recorded permanently on disk with a Save command.

When the working document containing all the changes is saved on disk, it is given the original filename LETTER.TXT, and the old version is renamed LETTER.BAK. If a file called LETTER.BAK already exists on the disk, it will be deleted.

If the original disk file is too large to fit in RAM, part of it will be stored in RAM and part will be stored in temporary disk files, which will be created and deleted automatically. Since this all happens without the user being aware of it, is is said to be transparent to the user. WordStar works much better with files small enough to be held in RAM, since this avoids wasting time handling temporary files. This is discussed in chapter 32 – Problems With Large Files & Disk Full Errors.

<u>Summary</u>

1. Disk files are not changed until a Save command is used.

2. Any work not Saved will be lost.

3. When Saved, the working document is filed under the original filename.

4. When an existing file is edited and Saved, the original file is renamed with the original file name, but the file-type .BAK. Only one backup file is kept.

28

Insert mode

WordStar can operate in two different modes when editing a document. These are with INSERT ON, and with INSERT OFF. If you do nothing about it then the default is INSERT ON, and you can tell that this is so because a message will be displayed in the status line (the top line of the screen) which says INSERT ON.

It does not matter when a new document is typed whether INSERT is ON or OFF. Each time another letter is pressed on the keyboard, it is shown on the screen and the cursor moves on one place.

It matters a great deal which mode you are in when an existing document is being edited. For example if INSERT is ON, then when the cursor is moved into the middle of some text, anything typed will be added to the document at this point. If some extra text is added, it will upset the neat arrangement of the lines after the change, and it will be necessary to reform the paragraph involved after the changes have been made. (Reforming is discussed later in this chapter). When INSERT is switched OFF, the status line does not show a message about INSERT, and if the cursor is moved into the middle of some text, then anything which is typed will overwrite and consequently replace what was already there.

For most purposes you are advised to keep INSERT switched ON, and to turn it OFF for special jobs like filling tables. By default INSERT is ON, but it may be switched OFF by pressing ^V, and switched on again by pressing ^V again.

Adding and deleting text

When a document is first being typed, the most common error is hitting a wrong key, and thus getting the wrong letter. Generally this sort of mistake is detected straight away, and the simplest way of correcting it is to press the **DELETE** key, (which may also be marked DEL, RUB or RUBOUT). This deletes the last character typed and moves the cursor back one place. The correct character may then be typed. Pressing **DEL** several times removes the appropriate number of characters, and typing may now proceed as if no mistake had occurred.

Suppose that a wrongly typed letter is spotted some distance from where typing is currently in progress. The cursor must be moved till it is over the incorrect letter. (Moving the cursor is described earlier in chapter 8 - Simple Cursor Movement). Pressing ^G deletes the character actually under the cursor, and provided that INSERT is switched ON, the correct character may be typed and inserted in the document at this point. Alternatively if INSERT is OFF, the cursor should be positioned over the mistake, and the correct letter typed - thus overwriting the incorrect letter.

The alterations may be more extensive than changing one letter, perhaps replacing a word by another word, several words, or several sentences. This is easy. Move the cursor over the first letter of the word to be deleted, and press ^T. The character under the cursor together with the rest of the word which lies to the right of the cursor will disappear from the screen. WordStar is rather clever - if you delete a whole word with ^T, it deletes both the word and the following space. If you delete part of a word it leaves the space. (If ^T is pressed again, the space before the next word, or the next word itself will be deleted, and so on). Check that the message INSERT ON is displayed in the status line, and if it is not displayed press ^V to turn INSERT ON. The replacement word(s) or sentences to be added to the document should now be typed. The alterations will have spoilt the tidy layout of the text on the screen. To tidy the paragraph up, move the cursor to the beginning of the changed paragraph, or to the first line which was altered, or to any line between these two points. Then reform the paragraph by pressing ^B.

Sometimes deletions may be more extensive, and rather than pressing ^T repeatedly to delete many words, three other commands may be useful. Pressing ^Y deletes the entire line in which the cursor lies, and the command ^QY deletes the rest of the line to the right of the cursor. To delete large amounts of text, perhaps several pages, it may be better to mark the block of text to be deleted, and then delete the block. To mark the block the cursor must be moved onto the first character to be deleted and ^KB pressed. Then the cursor must be moved one character past the last character to be deleted and ^KK pressed. If the vdu supports highlighting the marked block will appear highlighted, (that is, displayed in inverse video or in half intensity). Otherwise the block will be marked with <B> at the beginning and <K> at the end. This marked block can be deleted by typing ^KY.

Reforming a paragraph

After making alterations to a paragraph, it is necessary to reform it to tidy up irregularities in line lengths. Pressing ^B makes reforming start by tidying the line containing the cursor, and continues up to the end of the paragraph. The text is rearranged and respaced, so that it looks the same as it would if it had been typed in correctly the first time. Each line is filled, and text which will not fit on the line moved down onto the next line.

When a paragraph is reformed by pressing ^B with hyphen help switched on, (by default it is switched on), then WordStar may stop reforming before the end of the paragraph. This is because WordStar has found a long word containing more than one syllable, which does not quite fit on a line. Moving the whole word onto the next line would leave a lot of gaps in the current line, and so WordStar stops and asks if you wish to hyphenate the word. Instructions are displayed on the screen, and are shown in Figure 10.1.

FIGURE 10.1

```
        TO HYPHENATE, PRESS - Before pressing -, you may
           move cursor: ^S=cursor left, ^D=cursor right.
        If hyphenation not desired, type ^B.
```

These instructions are straightforward. If you accept a hyphen at the place in the word where WordStar has displayed one, type -. Reforming will then continue either to the end of the paragraph, or until WordStar finds another word which may need hyphenating. If you can choose a better place to put the hyphen, move the cursor to the left or right, and press - when the cursor is where you want the hyphen. Reforming will then continue. (If the cursor is moved too far, that is outside the word, or to the right of the margin, or if any other character is typed, then the message on the screen disappears, reforming stops, and the paragraph is left looking untidy). If you do not want this word hyphenated, type ^B again. Should you want to stop WordStar trying to hyphenate words at all, type the command ^OH to turn hyphen-help off.

Normally there is no text to the left of the left margin, but it is possible that sections have been numbered, and the whole paragraph has been indented to give a hanging paragraph, by using the command ^OG. The left margin can also be reset with the ^OL command. (See chapter 23 - Special Print Effects). The command ^B starts reforming on the cursor line, at the left margin or at the cursor position, whichever is furthest to the left. Thus if the left margin has been reset in this way, it is possible to reform the paragraph and allow section numbers to remain to the left of the margin.

Three screenfuls of helpful information about reforming paragraphs, and hyphen help may be displayed on the screen at any time when a document is being edited, simply by pressing ^JB.

Obtaining a document with a ragged right margin

If you are about to type a document, and you would like a ragged right margin rather than a straight right justified margin, this can be done as follows. First at the "No-File" menu type **D** and the filename to edit the document. Then change the justification toggle by typing **^OJ.** (If you type **^O** and pause, the **^O** On-screen menu will be displayed, and at the top of the third column you will see **J Justify off (ON).** This shows that justification, that is producing a straight right edge, is switched ON. Typing **J** turns it OFF. If **^O** is now typed again, the message now displayed says **J Justify on (OFF)).** Press the space bar to return from the menu without changing anything else. If you now type the document, it will have a ragged right margin. The document must be saved with a **^KD** command, and then printed.

Suppose that an existing document has a right justified (straight) margin, and you would like to print it out with a ragged margin, so that it looks like normal typing. The procedure is simple. First edit the document. Then change the justification toggle by typing **^OJ.** Press the space bar to return from the menu without changing anything else. Next put the cursor at the beginning of the first paragraph, and reform it by pressing **^B.** Reform each paragraph in turn. Finally save the edited file by typing **^KD,** and then print it out.

Splitting a paragraph into two

Move the cursor to the point where you would like to divide the paragraph, check that INSERT is ON, and press **RETURN.** The letter that was under the cursor together with text to the right of the cursor are moved down a line, and the cursor moves to the beginning of the second paragraph. Alternatively you may press **^N** which splits the paragraph, but does not move the cursor down.

The last line of the first paragraph may contain "soft" spaces which were used to right justify the line when it was part of the larger paragraph. These can be removed by moving the cursor up onto this line if necessary, and reforming it by typing **^B.** If blank lines are required between paragraphs then RETURN should be pressed once or twice as needed. Next the cursor must be moved onto the first letter of the second paragraph. This line will probably be incompletely filled, and will not be properly indented. Spaces to the left of the first word should all be removed by pressing the **DEL**ete key the necessary number of times, because we are not sure whether these are "hard" or "soft" spaces. The paragraph may then be indented either by typing **^I** or by pressing the space bar the required number of times to add spaces before the first word in the paragraph. Finally type **^B** to reform the paragraph.

Joining two paragraphs together

Position the cursor one character after the full stop at the end of the first paragraph. Press **^T** to delete a word, and repeat this until the first letter of the second paragraph is under the cursor. (Alternatively you may use **^G** to delete one character at a time to join the paragraphs, rather than **^T,** but this will take more key-strokes). All of the spaces between the paragraphs must be deleted. Use the space bar to insert one or two spaces after the full stop, and then press **^B** to reform the paragraph and tidy up the rather long line produced through joining the paragraphs.

You must remove all spaces between the two paragraphs, and then insert the required number because with WordStar there are two kinds of spaces. "Hard" spaces are ones which have been typed, and will always remain there. "Soft" spaces are inserted by WordStar to justify the right margin, and may disappear when the paragraph is reformed. If you leave the required number of spaces between the paragraphs, it is possible that you have left "soft" ones. For the present this does not matter, but if at a later date you reform the paragraph, these "soft" spaces could disappear and spoil the spacing you intended.

Chapter 11.

PRACTICE IN BASIC EDITING

This chapter gives you some practice in making simple changes to the letter typed in chapter 5 - Practice Writing a Letter, which was saved on disk under the filename LETTER.TXT, and is shown in Figure 11.1.

FIGURE 11.1 A sample letter

1st. June 1984

Dear Mr. Smith,

The school will be holding the annual Prize-giving ceremony on Friday 5th. July, at 7.30 pm. in the School hall. Since your son William is amongst the prize winners, I am pleased to be able to invite you to join the special guests, who will be seated at the front of the hall. Since seating is strictly limited, a reply would be appreciated before 10th. June, stating how many seats you require.

You will no doubt have heard of the appeal launched by the Governors, to put stained glass window in the library, as a lasting tribute to our late chemistry master Mr. Kipps, who died so tragically following an accident in the laboratory earlier this year. I would be pleased to receive your donation to the appeal. Cheques should be made payable to the Headmaster.

Yours sincerely,

Headmaster.

Suggested alterations:

1. Add the command **.OP** as the first line in the file to omit page numbers.

2. Change the name "Smith" to "Evans".

3. Indent the paragraph "The school ... ". Make sure that INSERT is switched ON, place the cursor on the letter T (the first letter of the paragraph), and either press **^I**, or type five spaces.

4. Change the date and time from "Friday 5th. July at 7.30 pm." to "Saturday 6th. July at 2.30 pm."

5. Change "son William" to "daughter Elizabeth".

6. Reform the altered paragraph.

7. Delete the whole of the second paragraph about the appeal.

8. Save the edited letter by typing **^KD**. (The directory now contains the new letter stored as LETTER.TXT, and the original letter stored as LETTER.BAK)

9. Print the new letter. It should look like Figure 11.2 if you have chosen not to hyphenate any words.

FIGURE 11.2 The edited letter

1st. June 1984

Dear Mr. Evans,

The school will be holding the annual Prize-giving ceremony on Saturday 6th. July, at 2.30 pm. in the School hall. Since your daughter Elizabeth is amongst the prize winners, I am pleased to be able to invite you to join the special guests, who will be seated at the front of the hall. Since seating is strictly limited, a reply would be appreciated before 10th. June, stating how many seats you require.

Yours sincerely,

Headmaster.

Changing the line spacing

The command ^OS is used to set the line spacing. When this is typed, a message appears on the screen:

ENTER space OR NEW LINE SPACING (1-9):

If for example double spacing is required, type 2. A message **LINE SPACING 2** will appear and will remain in the status line as long as double spacing is in effect. Normally you would set the spacing before typing a document, so it would automatically be double spaced. Suppose that having typed a letter in single spacing, it is apparent that it would fill the page better if it was double spaced. To do this the letter must be edited, the line spacing set to 2, and then ^B pressed to reform the first paragraph to give double spacing, followed by ^B to reform each subsequent paragraph in turn.

(Better ways of producing double spacing are described later in the section on line height in chapter 26 - Dot Commands, and the section line spacing in chapter 39 - Special Dot Commands for MailMerge).

Suggested changes to letter:

1. Edit the file LETTER.TXT.

2. Type ^OS then 2 to set the line spacing to double.

3. Move the cursor onto the first line of the first paragraph, which begins "The school will ... ", and press ^B to reform the paragraph.

4. Since there are no other paragraphs to reform, type ^KD to save the new letter on disk.

5. Print the letter. It should look like Figure 11.3 if you have chosen not to hyphenate words.

FIGURE 11.3 The double spaced letter

1st. June 1984

Dear Mr. Evans,

The school will be holding the annual Prize-giving ceremony

on Saturday 6th. July, at 2.30 pm. in the School hall. Since

your daughter Elizabeth is amongst the prize winners, I am

pleased to be able to invite you to join the special guests, who

will be seated at the front of the hall. Since seating is

strictly limited, a reply would be appreciated before 10th. June,

stating how many seats you require.

Yours sincerely,

Headmaster.

Changing the margins

Suppose that having typed the above letter set out for A4 paper, you decide that it would look better on a smaller piece of paper, for example A5 size, which is approximately 5.7 inches wide, and 8.7 inches long. The procedure is as follows:

1. Edit the document (in this case LETTER.TXT).

2. The present ruler is set for 65 characters in one line. This must be reduced for the narrower A5 paper. Suppose that the printer is printing 10 characters per inch. The paper width is 5.7 inches, that is 57 characters. However, there must be a margin at both the left and right hand side. Suppose that you leave a margin of 0.8 inches (8 characters) at either side, the maximum amount of useful text on a line will be:

$$57 - 8 - 8 = 41 \text{ characters}$$

The easiest way to reset the ruler is to type ^OR followed by 41 then **RETURN** to set the right margin to column 41, and leaving the left margin set on 1. (Alternatively you could reset both the left and right margins, for example with ^OL 10 and ^OR 51. The line length is still 41 characters, but the left margin has been increased by 10 spaces, hence printing is further to the right).

3. Since this document is double spaced, and you want it to be single spaced, you must type ^OS followed by a 1 to set single spacing.

4. The cursor must be moved to the first line of the first paragraph, and ^B pressed to reform the paragraph. This must be repeated on each subsequent paragraph in turn. This reforming is doing two jobs at once, changing to single spacing, and also changing to narrower margins.

Suggested changes to the letter

Change the letter stored in the file LETTER.TXT from double spacing to single spacing, and set the line length for 41 characters, so that it can be printed on A5 paper. Three lines in the letter have been positioned to make them print in exactly the right position. These are the line with the date, and the lines "Yours sincerely", and "Headmaster". These should be repositioned in a sensible place under the new ruler, by placing the cursor on a blank in one of these lines, and pressing ^G an appropriate number of times to delete spaces until the text is correctly positioned. The main paragraph can be changed by reforming with ^B. Then save the edited file, and print it out. If you have rejected any offers to hyphenate words, the result should look like Figure 11.4.

FIGURE 11.4 Letter reformed for A5 paper

1st. June 1984

Dear Mr. Evans,

The school will be holding the annual Prize-giving ceremony on Saturday 6th. July, at 2.30 pm. in the School hall. Since your daughter Elizabeth is amongst the prize winners, I am pleased to be able to invite you to join the special guests, who will be seated at the front of the hall. Since seating is strictly limited, a reply would be appreciated before 10th. June, stating how many seats you require.

Yours sincerely,

Headmaster.

Making sure that the ruler fits text already in the document

If the text in an existing document is altered, then inevitably one or more paragraphs will need to be reformed to tidy up at the end. The page width is indicated by the ruler, and the ruler used when you reform the paragraph must be the same as the ruler used when the text was originally typed. For example, in the above letter, the right margin was set to column 41 so that it would fit on A5 paper. Should you subsequently edit the letter, you will obtain the default ruler with the right margin set at column 65. Plainly if you reform text from the letter above, you will finish with some paragraphs 41 characters wide, and others 65 characters wide! This will not look very good. It is necessary to reset the ruler to match the original text before you reform any of the paragraphs. While the left and right margins can be set with ^OL and ^OR commands (see chapter 28 - On-screen Formatting - Margins Tabs and Ruler), the simplest way is to move the cursor onto a full line in the text, and to press ^OF. This sets the margins on the ruler to match those in the line of text. It is always wise to do this before editing an existing document.

Practice in splitting paragraphs

For practice, edit the letter stored in LETTER.TXT, and break the paragraph into three. Make the second and third paragraphs begin with the word "Since". Details of how to split paragraphs in given in the last chapter on Basic Editing. Remember to set the margins by moving the cursor on to a full line, and typing ^OF before you start. The finished document should look like Figure 11.5.

FIGURE 11.5 Letter with paragraphs split

1st. June 1984

Dear Mr. Evans,

The school will be holding the annual Prize-giving ceremony on Saturday 6th. July, at 2.30 pm. in the School hall.

Since your daughter Elizabeth is amongst the prize winners, I am pleased to be able to invite you to join the special guests, who will be seated at the front of the hall.

Since seating is strictly limited, a reply would be appreciated before 10th. June, stating how many seats you require.

Yours sincerely,

Headmaster.

Chapter 12.

SAVING FILES

After a file has been typed in for the first time, or after an existing file has been edited, it is necessary to save it on disk. It is at first surprising that there are four different save commands. These are all shown on the ^K Block menu, (Figure 12.1), which can be displayed at any time when a file is being edited simply by typing ^K. The different ways of saving a file are described in this chapter.

FIGURE 12.1 The ^K Block Menu

```
^K      B:EXAMPLE  PAGE 1 LINE 1  COL 1                INSERT ON
                  < < <   B L O C K   M E N U    > > >
-Saving Files- | -Block Operations- | -File  Operations- |  -Other Menus-
S Save & resume | B  Begin  K  End   | R Read    P  Print | (from Main only)
D Save--done    | H  Hide / Display  | O Copy    E Rename | ^J Help  ^K Block
X Save & exit   | C  Copy   Y Delete | J Delete           | ^Q Quick ^P Print
Q Abandon file  | V  Move   W Write  | -Disk Operations-  | ^O Onscreen
-Place Markers- | N  Column off (ON) |L Change logged disk| Space bar returns
0-9 Set/hide 0-9|                     |F Directory on (OFF)| you to Main Menu.
```

Save and resume ^KS

Typing the command **^KS** copies the file which you are currently typing or editing from memory onto the disk, and leaves you running WordStar editing the same file. It is advisable to use this command every 15 minutes if you are working for any length of time on a WordStar file. In the event of a mishap, such as the disk becoming full, accidentally deleting most of the text, or a computer crash, there will be a fairly recent copy of the file on disk to fall back on, so that you will only lose the work done since the last ^KS command. After using ^KS to save the file, but before work on it is resumed, a message appears on the screen which explains the ^QP command. This is the **Q**uick way of moving to the **P**revious position, that is to the point in the file where you were working immediately before saving the file.

> TO RETURN CURSOR TO POSITION BEFORE SAVE,
> TYPE ^QP BEFORE TYPING ANYTHING ELSE.

Alternatively you may wish to move straight to the bottom of the file, which can be done most simply by typing **^QC.**

Save--Done ^KD

When the typing or editing of a document is finished, typing **^KD** saves the file on disk, and returns you to the WordStar "No-File" menu. You can now choose whether to print the document, check its spelling, edit another file, or exit to CP/M.

Save and Exit ^KX

Typing the command **^KX** saves the file you are currently working on on the disk, and returns you to the CP/M operating system. The screen will show the CP/M prompt **B>** or **A>** depending on whether drive B: or A: is logged-in. Under CP/M the logged-in drive may be changed, for example to A:, by typing **A:** and pressing **RETURN.** Any of the CP/M utility programs such as PIP, STAT, or FORMAT may be run, or any other software such as BASIC, PASCAL, FORTRAN or a Database, or you may remove the disks and switch off.

Abandon the Edit ^KQ

It may be that you have used WordStar to have a look at a file, but you have not altered it, and would like to abandon it rather than save it. Alternatively you may get into such a mess when editing a file that the best action is to throw away the edited version of the file, and keep the old original version on the disk. This can be done by typing ^KQ. Since this is a destructive command, you will be given a chance to change your mind in case you typed the command by mistake. A message appears on the screen:

ABANDONING EDITED VERSION OF FILE B:LETTER.TXT ? (Y/N):

You must type either **Y** to abandon the file or **N** if you have changed your mind, and press **RETURN**. Should you try to abandon a file which has not had any changes made to it, WordStar is clever enough to detect this, and instead of asking you the above question, it abandons the file in memory and displays the message on the screen:

ABANDONING UNCHANGED FILE B:LETTER.TXT

After a ^KQ command, you will be returned to the WordStar "No-File" menu, where you can choose whether to print a file, check its spelling, edit another file etc.

Chapter 13.

PRINTING A DOCUMENT

This chapter describes exactly what the operator has to do to print a document under WordStar. The options available are explained, together with some of the differences between daisy wheel and expensive dot matrix printers which support microspacing, and the cheaper teletype-like and dot matrix printers which do not.

Any WordStar text file can be printed provided that it has previously been stored on disk. If the margins at the top, bottom, left, and right have been specified by dot commands, or if headings or footings have been specified, then these will be used, (see chapter 26 - Dot Commands), otherwise the default values will be used. The print control characters described in chapter 23 - Special Print Effects will be interpreted during printout, and will produce the required effects such as bold, underlined, subscripts, changes in character pitch and line spacing if your printer is capable of doing this.

The WordStar Print function is primarily designed for printing its own text files, but it may also be used to print program listings, or output files produced by other programs, provided that they are in ASCII code. There may be differences in the way these are formatted, and they may need editing with WordStar before they can be printed properly.

Microspacing

Printers capable of microspacing can print characters at variable positions in both the horizontal and vertical directions. With microspacing, a character may usually be positioned in increments of 1/120th of an inch in the horizontal direction, and 1/40th inch in the vertical direction. Most daisy wheel printers and a few expensive dot matrix printers support microspacing. In contrast to this, teletype printers and many cheaper dot matrix printers are not capable of microspacing, and print characters in fixed positions. These may be 1/10th inch or 1/12th inch apart horizontally, and 1/6th inch apart vertically.

When WordStar justifies the right margin, it inserts "soft-spaces" into the line to make the line the correct length. On the screen it can be seen that some words have an extra space between them. Printers which are not capable of microspacing will print a line spaced exactly as it appears on the screen. If the printer supports microspacing, and WordStar has been configured correctly for this printer, then microspace justification will occur during printing. This simply means that the "soft-spaces" inserted by WordStar into a line to justify the right margin are removed, and are replaced by an equivalent number of very small spaces or micro-spaces of 1/120th inch. These very small spaces are inserted between words, and possibly between characters as well. This produces an evenly spaced line, without large gaps between words, which greatly improves the appearance of the text. An additional improvement in appearance is obtained by slightly reducing the space used for full stops and commas, and increasing the space for certain wide letters such as M and W.

Simultaneous printing and editing

Printing a document may take some time, and provided the computer has sufficient memory, WordStar will allow the simultaneous printing of one document while another document is being edited. (The amount of memory needed is not well defined, but in the author's experience, 48K of memory was sufficient to run WordStar on its own, but insufficient for printing and editing at the same time. With 56K or 64K of memory, WordStar ran much faster on its own, because it made far fewer disk accesses, and 56K was sufficient for printing and editing at the same time). The keyboard response is slower than usual when concurrent printing and editing are being carried out, and you are advised to look for the message DISK WAIT in the status line, or listen for clicks from the disk drive, and to stop typing until the disk activity is over. (Some machines have a keyboard buffer, which allows you to type ahead of the computer. This feature reduces interference due to disk activity). Reviewing a document or making minor corrections can be carried out without much interference, but major editing may be slow or very slow.

The response from WordStar, during simultaneous printing and editing depends critically on the method by which the printer is interfaced. This is covered in the WordStar Installation manual, and uses a program called INSTALL. Under INSTALL, the simplest way of interfacing the printer is as the CP/M list device. Though this works, the keyboard response when simultaneously printing and editing is very poor, whereas if the printer can be driven by direct-port access, the keyboard response is much better. You will need expert help from your dealer to install WordStar for direct port access.

Errors during printing

Because editing is allowed at the same time as printing, there are no menus for printing, and either the "No-File" menu, or the document being edited is displayed on the screen. There are no error messages during printing. If a control character is encountered which has no meaning, then it is printed as ^ and the letter. Invalid dot commands are ignored, and the line is not printed. Though with normal text it is impossible to have a line beginning with a full stop, it could occur when printing non-WordStar files, which need not be normal text. Beware, any line beginning with a full stop will not be printed. Note that if a file is printed using MailMerge rather than WordStar, then unrecognised dot commands are reported as errors. (See chapter 34 - Producing Multiple Copies of a Document).

Printing out a file

There are three ways printing may be initiated:

1. When the "No-File" menu is obtained from WordStar, the P command may be selected to print the document. This is described in detail below.

2. When editing a file, the command ^KP may be used to invoke printing.

3. Alternatively, when the "No-File" menu is obtained from WordStar, the M command may be selected to merge-print the document. This is described in detail in chapter 34 - Producing Multiple Copies of a Document.

Suppose that CP/M has been loaded, WordStar called up, and the logged-in disk drive changed to B:. The disk in drive B: contains the file to be printed. WordStar displays the "No-File" menu on the screen, as shown in Figure 13.1:

FIGURE 13.1 The "No-File" menu

```
            < < < N O - F I L E  M E N U  > > >
   ----Preliminary Commands----  | --File Commands-- | -System Commands-
L  Change logged disk drive      |  P  Print a file  | R Run a  program
F  File directory      off (ON)  |  E  RENAME a file |  X EXIT to system
H  Set Help level                |  O  COPY   a file |
   ---Commands to open a file---  |  Y  DELETE a file | -WordStar Options-
   D  Open a  document  file      |                   | M Run MailMerge
   N  Open a non-document file    |         .         | S Run SpellStar

DIRECTORY of disk B:
LETTER.TXT
```

The command **P** must be typed to print a file. As soon as this is typed, the screen changes as shown in Figure 13.2.

FIGURE 13.2 The P command display

```
P     editing no file

 ^S=delete character    ^Y=delete entry    ^F=File directory
 ^D=restore character   ^R=Restore entry   ^U=cancel command

 NAME OF FILE TO PRINT?


DIRECTORY of disk B:
 LETTER.TXT
```

The important part of this display is the question asking for the name of the file to print. The filename in this case is called LETTER.TXT, and as the name is typed in, it is displayed immediately after the question. Should the filename be typed incorrectly, the two line menu explains how to delete the last letter, or the whole filename, or how to cancel the print command. There are two choices when the file name has been typed. These are either to press **ESCAPE** and skip a whole series of questions, or to press **RETURN** and be asked a number of questions about the printout.

If the **ESCAPE** option is selected, it is absolutely essential that you make sure that the printer is switched on, that the paper is correctly positioned, and if more than one page is to be printed that continuous paper is loaded (either a roll or fan folded paper), because printing will start as soon as **ESCAPE** is pressed. If you have not used the printer previously, a few trials may be necessary to find where to put the paper so that printing occurs in the correct vertical and horizontal position.

If the **RETURN** key is pressed after the filename has been typed, a series of questions are displayed on the screen one by one, allowing various choices to be made. In many cases the default value is an acceptable reply to each question and you press **RETURN**. The whole menu with the list of questions is shown in Figure 13.3.

FIGURE 13.3 Questions when printing

```
P     editing no file
 ^S=delete character    ^Y=delete entry    ^F=File directory
 ^D=restore character   ^R=Restore entry   ^U=cancel command

 NAME OF FILE TO PRINT? LETTER.TXT

 For default press RETURN after each question:
     DISK FILE OUTPUT (Y/N):
     START AT PAGE NUMBER(RETURN for beginning)?
     STOP AFTER PAGE NUMBER (RETURN for end)?
     USE FORM FEEDS (Y/N):
     SUPPRESS PAGE FORMATTING (Y/N):
     PAUSE FOR PAPER CHANGES BETWEEN PAGES (Y/N):
 Ready printer, press RETURN:

DIRECTORY of disk B:
 LETTER.TXT
```

It is possible to press **RETURN** to obtain the default answer for each question. These defaults are:

No disk file output ie. print on paper and not to a disk file
Start at page number 1, ie. at the beginning
Stop after page number - stop at end of document
Use form feeds to start a new page - default is No
Suppress page formatting ie. ignore dot and print commands - default No
Pause for paper changes between pages - default No

Replies to these questions

1. **DISK FILE OUTPUT (Y/N)**
If the file is to be printed on paper in the usual way, the reply to this question should be **N**, **n** or **^N**, followed by **RETURN**, or more simply pressing **RETURN** gives the default answer of 'no'.
If the reply is **Y**, **y**, or **^Y**, followed by **RETURN**, then the "printout" is sent to a disk file instead of being printed on paper. WordStar asks for the **OUTPUT FILE NAME** to be typed. The text written to the disk file is exactly the same as would have appeared on paper. Dot commands have disappeared, but have been executed. Thus .HE commands disappear, but headings are printed at the top of pages. Similarly, .PA and .CP commands disappear, but new pages start where required. In addition, page numbers are printed. This file of the "printed" version can then be examined on the screen for typing and layout errors, which can be edited if necessary. This is a good way of checking when a printer is not available, and is a faster alternative to using a slow printer. This "printed" file may be printed on paper at a later date (see following section 5 on Page Formatting).

2. **START AT PAGE NUMBER?**
Normally a file is printed starting at the beginning. To do this, the reply should be **1** (for page one) followed by **RETURN**, or more simply press **RETURN** for the default answer of the beginning of the file.
Perhaps the end part of a document may need reprinting, either because a mistake in the original has been corrected, or because of some difficulty with the printer, (for example it might have run out of paper, jammed, or the ribbon may have come off part way through the previous job). The first page to be printed may be specified. For example, typing **5** results in page five and subsequent pages being printed.

3. **STOP AFTER PAGE NUMBER?**
Generally the whole of a file will be printed, that is right up to the end of the document, and to do this you press **RETURN**. This question allows the last page printed to be specified. Should it be necessary to print only the first four pages, then typing **4** will stop the printing at the end of page four. Sometimes only one page needs re-printing. If for example you specify START AT PAGE NUMBER **3**, and STOP AFTER PAGE NUMBER **3**, then only page three will be printed.

4. **USE FORM FEEDS (Y/N)**
On some printers the length of the paper used is defined by means of switch settings, and a form feed signal is required to make them start a new page. Answering **Y** or **y** followed by **RETURN** makes WordStar transmit a form-feed character to the printer at the end of a printed page. Make sure that the switches have been set appropriately for the required page length, and also remember to set the top of the first page. Advantages of this are that the pagelength set in WordStar with a .PL command, need not match the size of paper used, and the printer may move much faster to the beginning of a new page with a form-feed than with a series of several line feeds. If the printer cannot do this, the reply is **N** or **n** followed by **RETURN**, or just **RETURN**, and the pagelength must be set exactly in WordStar. (Remember top and bottom margins are set with .MT and .MB commands, so WordStar must start a new page after PL - MT - MB lines of text have been printed).

5. **SUPPRESS PAGE FORMATTING (Y/N)?**

    If page formatting is carried out, dot commands are executed, and headings and footings, top and bottom margins, page length, page offset, line height, character width and page numbering are all carried out. (Other features such as the print enhancements bold ^PB, underline ^PS, overprinting ^PH, subscript ^PV and superscript ^PT are also implemented).

    The usual answer to the question is **N**, **n** and **RETURN**, or simply **RETURN**, in which case page formatting is not suppressed.

    With **Y** or **y** followed by **RETURN**, then page formatting is suppressed. Dot commands are then printed as commands, rather than being executed, but the print enhancements are carried out as usual. This option has two uses. First, it may be useful to print out and then proof-read the dot commands in a file, particularly with command files used with MailMerge. Second, it is useful to print files which have already been formatted. Examples of this are: printing a file which has been "printed" to disk with the DISK FILE option in section 1 above, or printing a file produced by some program other than WordStar.

6. **PAUSE FOR PAPER CHANGE BETWEEN PAGES (Y/N)?**

    A reply of **N** or **n** followed by pressing **RETURN**, or **RETURN** will make WordStar print continuously. In this case, it is essential that a roll of paper, or continuous fan folded paper are used in the printer, or that an automatic single sheet feeder is fitted.

    A reply of **Y** or **y**, followed by pressing **RETURN** makes the printer pause at the end of each page, so that a new sheet of paper may be manually inserted into the printer. This is useful when printing on letterheads, forms, or single sheets of A4 paper. When the printer pauses at the end of a page, the message **PRINT PAUSED** appears on the top (status) line of the screen. After changing the paper, the printer may be restarted by typing **P** and pressing **RETURN**.

7. Ready Printer, press RETURN

    This is a warning message, to remind you to check that the printer is switched on, that paper is correctly loaded and positioned, and if appropriate that the printer is switched to "on-line" operation, rather than "off-line", or "local". Pressing **RETURN** (or any other key), will cause printing to start.

Interrupting the printout

    It is easy to stop the printer in the middle of a printout, by typing P. A message is then displayed on the screen:

        TYPE "Y" to ABANDON PRINT, "N" TO RESUME, ^U TO HOLD:

To abandon printing, that is to stop printing altogether, type **Y**. To resume printing from exactly the point where it was suspended then type **N**. There will be nothing in the printout to show that there has been an interruption. It is possible to hold (suspend) printing by typing ^U. You may then return to the "No-File" menu and do other things, such as editing another file, checking the name of a file from the directory, or running STAT to find the size of a file or the space left on a disk. The printer will remain in a paused state until **P** is typed, which makes printing resume as if there had been no interruption.

Answering some but not all of the questions

    With early versions of WordStar you must choose either to skip the questions about printing, or to answer them all. WordStar version 3.0 introduced an enhancement allowing you to answer one or more of the questions at the beginning of the list, and to take the default answers for later question(s). Suppose for example that the default answers are acceptable to all the questions, except that you would like printing to stop after page five has been printed. Questions 1 (Disk file output) and 2 (Start page number) may each be answered by pressing **RETURN.** Question 3 (Stop after page number) must be answered by typing 5 to stop after page five, but instead of pressing RETURN, press **ESCAPE.** With WordStar version 3.0 and later, this stops you from being asked any more of the questions, and provides the default answers to those questions which have been missed. Printing starts without any further warning, so it is essential that the printer has previously been made ready.

Delays in printing

Should the starting page for printing be some way into the document, for example, start at page 20, then there will be some delay after the questions before printing actually begins. This is because WordStar has to read page by page through the document, starting from the beginning, so that it can find where page 20 begins.

It is possible that printing may pause of its own accord. The most likely reason for this is that the printer is waiting for you to change the paper, because you answered **YES** to the question **PAUSE FOR PAPER CHANGE BETWEEN PAGES.** Alternatively the printer may have sensed that it is out of paper, or that the ribbon has run out. Another possible reason is that a ^C character has been typed in the text. This is usually done to allow you to change the daisy wheel or print thimble, (see chapter 23 - Special Print Effects). If you are "printing" to disk, it is possible that the disk is full, in which case a DISK **FULL** error message will have appeared on the screen.

Chapter 14.

THE SCREEN DISPLAY

The information that is displayed on the screen during editing is described in this chapter. This may comprise of some or all of the following: the status line, a menu, the file directory, the ruler, and the file display area. The latter contains the text from the file which is being edited, and in addition the "flag" characters at the right of the screen.

The status line

The top line of the screen is called the status line, and during editing it is used by WordStar to display information. Typing ^JS makes WordStar display information about the status line on the screen. The following information is usually present, arranged from left to right:

1. The command being executed (if any). If for example the command ^JS is typed to obtain help about the status line, ^JS will show at the left of the status line. The single key commands such as moving the cursor do not show, and when text is being entered there is no command to show.

2. The name of the file being edited is always shown, preceded by the disk drive letter.

3. The page number, line number and column number occupied by the cursor are normally shown. These are continually changed as the cursor is moved. The page number assumes that the document will be printed with the first page numbered 1. If a .PN command has been used to start page numbering with a different number then this is NOT taken into account in the status line. The page display goes wrong if a .PL command is used to change the page length in the middle of a document. Note that the line and column refer to what will be printed out rather than what appears on the screen. Thus dot commands are not counted as lines, and commands such as ^PB for bold, or ^PS for underlining appear on the screen as ^B and ^S, but do not count as printing characters. (If a file is being edited in Non-Document mode, or alternatively if a normal Document file is being edited but the command ^OP has been typed, then page breaks are not shown, and instead of displaying page and line numbers, the status line gives FC= and FL=, where FC is the number of characters and FL the number of lines. Note that FL counts a dot command as a line).

A number of other messages are displayed when applicable:

4. The message INSERT ON is displayed if insert is ON. This is explained fully in chapter 10 - Basic Editing. Briefly when Insert is ON, text typed will be added to the document at the cursor position, even if this is in the middle of a document. If Insert is OFF, no message is displayed in the status line, and any text typed in the middle of a document will overwrite what is already there. Typing ^V turns Insert OFF, and typing ^V again turns Insert ON again.

5. WAIT - is displayed when information is being written to or read from the disk. Since the computer is busy with this disk activity, it is advisable to stop typing, or type very slowly, otherwise some of the characters typed may be lost. WordStar has a keyboard buffer to try to prevent such loss of input data, but disk activity is slow, and overfilling the buffer will result in loss of data.

6. PRINT PAUSED - may occur when a full page has been printed because you have answered YES to the question PAUSE BETWEEN PAGES. The message also occurs when P is typed to suspend printing, or when ^C is read from the

file, to allow the daisy wheel to be changed.

7. REPLACE (Y/N): - occurs when the replace command ^QA has found the specified character string, and you are being asked whether to replace it or not. (See chapter 16 - Editing - the Find and Replace Commands).

8. LINE SPACING 2 - this indicates that double spacing has been specified with a ^OS command. Triple spacing would have the number 3, and so on. No message is displayed for single spacing. (See chapter 23 - Special Print Effects).

9. MAR REL - is displayed when the margins have been released with a ^OX command. (See chapter 23 - Special Print Effects).

10. decimal - this shows after tabbing to a decimal tab stop. (See chapter 28 - On-Screen Formatting - Margins, Tabs and Ruler).

The menu

The menu usually displayed during editing is the Main menu, which is shown in Figure 14.1.

FIGURE 14.1

```
      B:LETTER.TXT   PAGE 1 LINE 1   COL 01              INSERT ON
                 < < <      M A I N   M E N U    > > >
      --Cursor Movement--    | -Delete- |   -Miscellaneous-  |  -Other Menus-
 ^S char left ^D char right |^G  char  | ^I Tab   ^B Reform  | (from Main only)
 ^A word left ^F word right |DEL chr lf| ^V INSERT ON/OFF    |^J Help  ^K Block
 ^E line  up  ^X line down  |^T word rt|^L Find/Replce again!^Q Quick ^P Print
       --Scrolling--        |^Y  line  |RETURN End paragraph!^O Onscreen
 ^Z line up  ^W line down   |          | ^N Insert a RETURN  |
 ^C screen up ^R screen down!          | ^U Stop a command   |
L----!----!----!----!----!----!----!----!----!----!----!--------R
```

This gives the simple single control character commands for moving the cursor to the required place in a document, and the commands for scrolling through a document to display the required part on the screen. These are fully described in chapters 8 - Simple Cursor Movement, and 15 - Advanced Cursor Movements & Scrolling Text. The commands for deleting text, and some miscellaneous commands are also given. A list of other menus which may be called up if required is also given. These are described in chapter 21 - The Control Character Menus. Once these basic commands have become familiar, it is a good idea to change the Help level from its present value of 3 to 2 or 1, so that this menu is not displayed, thus leaving more room to show the text in the document being edited. This is explained in chapter 22 - Changing the Help Level. Other explanatory, warning or error messages are displayed above or below this menu when appropriate, and these usually disappear when the next key is pressed.

The file directory

This is a list of the files present on the logged-in disk drive. However, the directory is not normally displayed during editing, so as to leave more space to display text. The file directory display may be switched ON by typing the command ^KF at any time during editing, and may be switched OFF by typing ^KF again. If the directory is not displayed at the "No-File" menu, it can be turned ON by typing F, or at any time when you are asked to type a filename, the directory can be temporarily turned ON to check the filename by typing ^F.

When displayed, the directory appears between the menu and the ruler. If there are many files in the directory, a partial directory may be displayed, showing one or two lines of filenames, rather than all of them. A message explains the commands ^Z and ^W which scroll the directory up or down to allow inspection of all the filenames.

Provided that the file directory is not very long, the filenames of the text files are displayed in alphabetical order, with .BAK files after the current version of the corresponding file. Non-text files with endings .COM and .OVR are shown at the end of the directory, as are any temporary files with the ending .$$$.

The ruler

The ruler is displayed beneath the menu and the directory if these are present.

L----!----!----!----!----!----!----!----!----!----!----!--------R

It shows the current left and right margins, thus indicating the width, (that is the maximum number of characters which may appear on a line). The ! marks are called variable tabs. Pressing the TAB key will normally make the cursor jump to the next tab. The left and right margins, and the position of these TABS may be changed, and this is explained in chapter 28 - On-Screen Formatting - Margins, Ruler and Tabs. A brief explanation of the Ruler may be obtained by typing the command ^JR. It is possible to set decimal tabs, which are shown by a # sign in the ruler, and these are useful for typing columns of numbers, since they right justify the numbers.

The left margin may temporarily be changed for a paragraph by typing ^OG. This has been done for this paragraph. A "hanging paragraph" may be produced by typing the paragraph number at the beginning of a line, and then typing ^OG, which indents the rest of the paragraph as it is typed. The first page of this chapter illustrates this. When ^OG is typed, the part of the ruler outside the temporary margin is displayed but not high-lighted on terminals which support the highlighting of text, or the --- signs are omitted on terminals which have no highlighting.

It is possible to release the margins, to allow typing outside these limits, by typing the ^OX command.

The file display area

The rest of the screen is used to display lines of text from the document being edited. Most screens display 80 columns, and text may occupy up to 79 columns. The rightmost column (column 80) is either blank, or displays a "flag" character, which indicates the type of line. Some explanation of the "flag" characters may be obtained by typing the command ^JF. These are explained further below:

A number of "flag" characters may appear in the last column on the screen. These are shown in Figure 14.2.

FIGURE 14.2 "Flag" characters

<   This indicates that **RETURN** has been pressed, to force the end-of-the line. Normally **RETURN** is used to indicate the end of a paragraph, or to obtain a blank line. This is called a "hard carriage return", and a line break will always occur here, even if the text is changed and the paragraph is subsequently reformed.

space This indicates a "soft carriage return", that is an end of line break which has been put in by WordStar. If the text is changed, and the paragraph is reformed, then the break at the end of the line may occur in a different place.

+ If a line of text is too long to display on one line on the screen, that is more than 79 characters on an 80 column screen, then WordStar displays as much as possible on one line, and puts a **+** at the right hand edge of the line. Early versions of WordStar displayed the continuation of the line on the line below. WordStar version 3.0 and later continue the line out of sight, beyond the right of the screen. The text beyond column 80 may be displayed on the screen by moving the cursor past column 79. Since the window of text being viewed has moved to the right, this means that text at the extreme left of the line is no longer visible. The column number displayed in the cursor line still shows the correct print column. When the cursor is moved back far enough to the left, the window of text displayed changes again, to show the left part of the line again. Thus WordStar version 3.0 allows users to work more easily with lines longer than will fit on the screen display.

P Page breaks are normally displayed on the screen as a row of ----- signs, with a **P** in the right hand column.

? If a dot command is incorrect, that is not understood, it will be marked with the flag ? at the right of the screen. If the file containing this invalid command is printed by WordStar, the invalid command is treated as a comment, and the whole line is ignored. If the file is printed by MailMerge, then the error is reported on the screen, and again the line is ignored.

– It is possible to get one line overprinted by the next line, to produce a special effect. (See chapter 23 - Special Print Effects). To do this, ^P and **RETURN** are typed at the end of a line. Such a line has a – flag at the right of the screen, and this line will be overprinted by the next line.

. When the document ends before the bottom of the screen, any blank lines are marked by a . at the right of the screen.

: If the text is moved down so that the beginning of the file is below the top of the screen display area, then any lines on the screen before (above) the file are marked with a : at the right of the screen.

M There are some special dot commands which apply only to MailMerge. These are described in chapter 39 - Special Dot Commands For MailMerge. Any lines containing these commands are marked with a **M** at the right of the screen.

Chapter 15.
ADVANCED CURSOR MOVEMENTS AND SCROLLING TEXT

The basic commands for moving the cursor are described in chapter 8 - Simple Cursor Movement. More advanced commands for moving the cursor and for scrolling, are described in this chapter. Scrolling commands are particularly useful. They enable you to move the lines of text up or down on the screen, so that you may examine the appropriate portion of text.

Scrolling text up or down one screen

The command ^R scrolls a screenful of text downwards off the bottom of the screen, so that text nearer the beginning of the document can now be read. Actually it only moves about 3/4 of the lines on a screen, so that there is some overlap from one screenful to the next. The position of the cursor does not necessarily change during scrolling. A similar command ^C scrolls the text upwards, again by 3/4 of a screenful, hence text lower down, that is nearer the end of the document can then be read.

The position of the keys used for scrolling are shown in Figure 15.1 in relation to the 'diamond' of keys described earlier.

FIGURE 15.1 Some keys used for scrolling

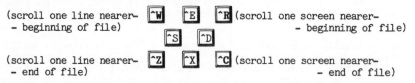

(scroll one line nearer- [^W]   [^E]   [^R] (scroll one screen nearer-
 - beginning of file)   - beginning of file)
                                [^S] [^D]
(scroll one line nearer- [^Z]   [^X]   [^C] (scroll one screen nearer-
 - end of file)   - end of file)

It is essential that the six cursor movements and the four scrolling commands described above are mastered. There are a number of additional cursor moving and scrolling commands which may be regarded as optional extras, and these are described in the remainder of this chapter.

Moving the cursor to the left, right, top and bottom of the screen

A second set of commands exist utilizing the diamond of keys already described, but each command is preceded by a ^Q. These commands provide a quick way of moving the cursor to the edges of the line or screen, and are shown in Figure 15.2. Pressing ^QD moves the cursor to the end of the line, or more strictly to a position one character past the last character displayed on that line. (This is not usually the extreme right of the screen, unless you have set the right margin to column 80). Pressing ^QS moves the cursor to the extreme left of the present line. The command ^QE moves the cursor to the top line of text shown on the screen. (This is not the same as moving to the top of the screen, since the top line is the status line, and there may be the Main Menu on the screen if the Help level is 3, and the ruler line will also be showing unless you have typed ^OT to turn it off). **The cursor can only move within the text area of the screen, not into the menus, and not into empty spaces.** Similarly pressing ^QX moves the cursor to the next to bottom line of the screen. The arrangement of the diamond of keys, and the similarity in the movements left, right, top and bottom makes these commands easy to remember.

FIGURE 15.2 The diamond of keys for Quick cursor movements

(cursor to top of text area of screen)
`^QE`

(cursor to left side) `^QS`   `^QD` (cursor to right side)

`^QX`
(cursor to bottom of screen)

Moving the cursor to the top or bottom of the file

The command ^QR moves the cursor to the beginning of the file. To do this, WordStar may have to write a temporary file on the disk. Though this involves no work by the user, with a large file it may be slow, and it needs quite a lot of space on the disk. With a large file it is quicker and safer (less likely to produce a disk full error) to type ^KS to save the file and re-edit it. The command ^QC moves the cursor to the end of the file. This is discussed in chapter 32 - Problems With Large Files and Disk Full Errors.

Moving the cursor to Block Markers

If block markers are present, then typing ^QB moves the cursor to the <B> marker at the beginning of the block, and the command ^QK moves the cursor to the <K> marker at the end of the block. Full details on setting block markers, and the uses of blocks are given in chapter 30 - Manipulating Blocks of Text.

Setting Place Markers, and moving the cursor to them

It may be useful to insert place markers at particular points in the file. These will not print anything, but provide an easy way of jumping to a particular point in the file. Suppose that you are editing something in the middle of a file, and you want to have a look at text somewhere else in the file, and then jump back to finish this correction. At the place where you are editing, you can put a place marker by typing ^K followed by a number 0 to 9. If ^K2 is typed, the extra characters <2> appear on the screen at this point, (highlighted if the terminal supports highlighting). You may now move anywhere in the file to look at something, or to edit something. When you want to jump back to this marker, type ^Q2. You may set up to 10 markers at different places in the file if you so wish, by typing ^K0, ^K1, ^K2 ... ^K9. To jump to the appropriate marker you must type ^Q and the marker number 0 - 9. These markers disappear when the file is saved on disk.

Continuous scrolling commands

In addition to the scrolling commands described earlier and shown in Figure 15.1, there are two commands which cause continuous scrolling through the document.

The command ^QZ causes continuous scrolling in an upwards direction. Scrolling begins at once, and one line after another disappears off the top of the screen. The area of text displayed moves nearer and nearer the end of the file. A message appears on the screen:

TYPE 1-9 TO VARY SPEED, SPACE TO STOP

Any appropriate number in this range may be typed to change the scrolling speed from its default value of 3. The value of 1 gives the fastest scrolling, and this is still at a speed which can be read. A value of 9 gives the slowest speed, which hardly moves. The scrolling speed may be changed as often as desired by typing a new number in the range 1-9. Text will continue to scroll, either until any key other than a number is pressed to stop it, or when the bottom of the file is reached.

The command ^QW causes continuous scrolling in a downwards direction. Lines of text disappear off the bottom of the screen, and the window of text displayed on the screen moves nearer the beginning of the file. The scrolling speed may be varied in exactly the same way as for scrolling downwards continuously. Scrolling will continue until the top of the file is reached, or any key other than a number is pressed.

Chapter 16.

EDITING - THE FIND AND REPLACE COMMANDS

In addition to the basic editing described in the last chapter,
WordStar provides some very powerful editing commands which can search
through a document to Find a specified character string, or
alternatively to find it and Replace it by another string. These
provide a convenient way of moving the cursor to a given point in the
file, both quickly and easily. The right place can be found without
the need to inspect the entire contents of the file on the screen.
These commands can be made to work once, or repeatedly throughout the
entire document. The string searched for may be located either as
part of a word or optionally only as a whole word. Similarly the
string may be matched exactly as typed, or optionally may contain a
mixture of upper and lower case letters. The editing commands to make
WordStar search through a file to find and/or replace parts of the
text are covered in this chapter. Block movements are described in
chapter 30 - Manipulating Blocks of Text.

Finding a specified character string ^QF

When a document is printed, it may be found to contain errors. These
should be edited out and the document reprinted. It is usually easiest to use
the WordStar Find function to locate the error automatically, rather than
manually scanning through the document, especially if the document is fairly
long. The cursor is automatically moved to the required place in the file, and
the correction may now be made. If you do not locate the right place first
time, or if the same word is mis-spelled more than once, you may wish to repeat
the Last Find or Replace command. This can be done by typing ^L, when the next
occurrence of this string in the file, will be located.

Suppose for example that the word 'star' had been mistyped as 'stat', then
WordStar should be asked to Find the character string 'stat', so that it can
then be corrected. To initiate the Find function type ^QF. A small menu is
displayed (Figure 16.1):

FIGURE 16.1

```
     ^S=delete character    ^Y=delete entry    ^F=File directory
     ^D=restore character    ^R=Restore entry    ^U=cancel command

        FIND?
```

The menu gives instructions for cancelling the command if you decide you do not
want to continue with Find, and also how to make corrections to your reply
should you make a mistake. The most important part is the question:

                    FIND?   - type stat and press **RETURN**
WordStar then asks **OPTIONS? (? FOR INFO)** -   press **RETURN**

By pressing **RETURN** in answer to the last question, the options question has
been ignored, and no options have been selected. The options will be described
later. WordStar starts searching through the file from the current position of
the cursor, towards the end of the file. It stops when it finds the character
string 'stat'. A screenful of text near this point is displayed, with the
cursor positioned immediately after the string. If this is the place where the
word 'star' should have been typed, then the required correction may now be
made.

It is possible that the character string 'stat' has been matched as part
of a word such as 'state', 'statics', 'station', 'statistics', 'statue',

'stature', 'statute', 'devastating' ... and so on. If such a word has been found, you should leave it alone, and search for the next occurrence of the string 'stat'. To do this the command to repeat the Last command should be used by typing ^L. The search continues until the next occurrence of the string is found, and a screenful of text is displayed with the cursor positioned immediately after the string. The process may be repeated again if necessary.

If the end of the file is reached and the specified string has not been found, an error message appears on the screen:

> **FIND?** stat   **OPTIONS?(? FOR INFO)**
>
> ***** NOT FOUND *** "stat" *** Press ESC Key *****

This means that the string does not exist. This may have occurred because the string to search for has been typed incorrectly, which would explain why it cannot be found. There is no option but to press the **ESCAPE** key. The cursor is now at the bottom of the file. It may be moved to the top (beginning) of the file by typing ^QR, or back to the position before the last Find command by typing ^QV. The search may be started again if necessary.

Next the meaning and use of the options which were ignored earlier will be examined. The Find command ^QF is again used to search for the string 'stat'.

```
                                  - type ^QF
WordStar replies  FIND?           - type stat and press  RETURN
WordStar then asks OPTIONS? (? FOR INFO) - type ?  and press  RETURN
```

This reply is to ask for information. WordStar displays a message on the screen:

> **Normally press RETURN only, or enter one or more of:**
> number=repeat count, B=search Backwards, W=whole Words only,
> U=ignore case, N=replace w/o asking, G=replace in entire file.

If none of the options is required, **RETURN** should be pressed, and WordStar will search for a match of the characters 'stat', starting from the current cursor position and moving towards the end of the file, exactly as before.

If the string you wish to find is before the cursor position, then typing **B** and pressing **RETURN** will search for the string in the reverse direction, that is starting from the cursor position and moving towards the beginning of the file. This is probably easier than moving the cursor to the beginning of the file with a ^QR command followed by a Find ^QF in the usual direction. (You are warned, however, that moving backwards through a large file requires a lot of disk space for scratch files, and if used without care you may obtain a disk full error).

The **W** option is useful to make WordStar look only for whole words. Thus if asked to find the word 'stat' and the option **W** has been selected, the Find function would not find 'state', 'statics' or 'station' since 'stat' is part of the word, not the complete word.

Since you are trying to match the string 'stat', which is in lower case letters, the Find command would not find the word 'Station', since this begins with a capital letter. The option **U** is useful when it is not known whether the word begins with a capital letter, or has any capital letters in it. With **U** selected, the letters in the string are matched, but no account is taken of whether they are capitals or small letters. Thus 'stat' would be matched as well as 'Stat', 'STAT' and so on. The **U** option is useful when repeated searches are being made, since it allows for the possibility of a word starting with a capital letter because it is used to start a sentence.

The 'number count' may be used as an Option, for example by typing 3. If the command is Find, it will find the third occurrence of the string. If the command is Replace, it will find the first match, stop and offer the choice of replacing the string (Y/N), and do the same for the second and third match, and then stop searching.

Any combination of the options may be used, so for example to find whole words, ignoring differences between upper and lower case, and searching in the backwards direction (towards the beginning of the file), type **WUB** for the options, and press **RETURN**.

Note that the string which you are searching the document for may be any combination of up to thirty letters, numbers or control characters.

The commands **N** and **G** have no real meaning here but are explained below in the Replace section.

The Replace command ^QA

The Replace command **^QA** provides a convenient way of finding a specified string, which may be one word, a phrase, or any other string of characters, and replacing it by another word, phrase or string. This avoids the effort of finding the word(s) to be changed, positioning the cursor correctly, deleting the unwanted word(s), and inserting the new word(s). The options already described for the Find command may also be used with the Replace command. There are two extra options. Global or G finds all occurrences of the specified string in turn, and asks one by one whether you want to make the substitution. This allows you to be selective. In contrast, the N option makes the substitution without stopping to ask.

Consider how the Replace command could be used to replace the string 'stat' by the string 'star'. To initiate the Replace command **^QA** is typed:

	– type **^QA**
WordStar replies **FIND?**	– type **stat** and press **RETURN**
WordStar replies **REPLACE WITH?**	– type **star** and press **RETURN**
WordStar then asks **OPTIONS? (? FOR INFO)** –	press **RETURN**

Note that by pressing RETURN in answer to the last question, none of the possible options has been selected. If the string is not found, then an error message NOT-FOUND is displayed, exactly as described for the Find command. If the string is matched, the screen shows the text adjacent to the string. The cursor flashes alternately over the first letter of the string, and over a message displayed in the top right corner of the status line which says:

REPLACE (Y/N):

To make the substitution, type **Y**, or **y**, or **^Y**. If you do not want the substitution, type **N**, or any other character. This makes sure that you do not get any changes made by mistake. In this particular case, the string substituted is the same length as the original string, so substitution will not affect the justification of the text. If the two string lengths are different, it will be necessary to reform the paragraph by typing **^B**. The command to repeat the Last command **^L** may be used, with all three parts (original string, final string, and options) exactly the same as before.

The Replace command **^QA** is often used for making systematic changes in conjunction with the Global **G** Option. Global really does mean everywhere in the file, rather than from the cursor position onwards. After a Replace command with the **G** option, regardless of where the cursor is positioned, Word-Star moves the cursor to the beginning of the file, and starts searching from there. The whole file is then searched for the first string, and each time it is found the user is asked whether to replace or not (by typing **Y** or **N**). If **Y** is typed then the exchange is made, otherwise no change is made. The **G** option may give a DISK-FULL error if the file is large, and the cursor is not near the beginning. (This is because **G** moves the cursor to the beginning of the file before starting the search. To do this it must write a scratch file on the disk). The solution is to avoid large files, to make sure that there is plenty of space on the disk, or to save and re-edit the file by typing `^KS`, which results in the cursor being at the beginning of the file, rather than writing a scratch file through moving backwards.

If you want to do a mass substitution, are sure that there are no undesired matches, and all occurrences of the string are to be changed, then the fastest method is to select the **N** Option as well as **G**. The order in which the options are typed is unimportant, and both **GN** and **NG** have the same effect. With this combination of options, WordStar makes all the changes very rapidly without asking whether to do each exchange. Even so, WordStar is slowed down by displaying each change it makes on the screen. The process may be further speeded by pressing any harmless key once, such as one to move the cursor, while this command is executing. WordStar will then make the substitutions without displaying the change on the screen, and will work much faster. If you see that a global change with the **N** option is creating unexpected havoc with the file, then pressing the space bar or any other key will only make things worse, but the command can be aborted part way through the file by typing `^U`.

The command `^L` can be used at any time to repeat either the last Find, or the last Replace command issued. This saves a lot of tedious retyping of the string(s) and the options. Repeated use of `^L` is slower, but has some advantages over the **G** option for making a global change throughout a document. If you use the `^L` command, you may make other changes (such as reforming the paragraph with `^B`) to tidy up before using `^L` for the next change. If you use the **G** option instead, then all the exchanges are done one after another, and no other alterations can be made until all the exchanges are done.

After a Replace `^QA` command, or after the command `^L` to repeat the Last command, `^QV` may be used to move the cursor back to where it was before the command was issued. This is particularly useful after Replace has failed to find the string requested, because the user has typed it incorrectly.

When performing global searches or replacements, the last Find or Replace command may be repeated with slightly different options, or a slightly different string, using the `^R` Repeat command. Suppose that you have just used a Find command. To repeat the command with different parameters first type the Find command `^QF`. A message asks **FIND?** Instead of typing the string to be found, press `^R` and the string used last time appears. The string can be modified if you wish, using the editing commands displayed on the screen (see Figure 16.1). When the string is correct, press **RETURN**. The next question is **OPTIONS?** You may either type them in, or press `^R` to get the same options as last time. The command is executed as soon as **RETURN** is pressed. A Replace command may be repeated in a similar way by typing `^R` to obtain the same answer to a question as in the last command.

The Replace command can be used in a novel way to insert the same phrase in a number of different places in the file. First type the Replace command `^QA`. In reply to the question **FIND?**, press **RETURN** to give a null string. Answer the question **REPLACE WITH?** by typing the phrase or string to be inserted. Then select the **N** option, and move the cursor to the place where the string is to be inserted, and press `^L`. The string is inserted. Move the cursor to the next place, and type `^L` again, and so on.

The Replace command can also be used for mass deletions. Type the Replace command ^QA, then type the string you wish to FIND, but when asked REPLACE? press RETURN to give a null string. Thus WordStar will find the string, and replace it with nothing, which effectively deletes the string. The G or GN options may be used to do this repeatedly. This may be very useful in special circumstances.

Handling non-WordStar text files

Suppose that a text file that was not created under WordStar is to be adapted to run under WordStar. A common problem with such files is that each line ends with a hard carriage RETURN. Because of this, WordStar treats each line as a paragraph, hence reforming the lines into a paragraph is impossible. The way to remedy this is as follows:

1. Type the Replace command ^QA
2. In reply to FIND? type ^N, which is the command for a hard carriage RETURN
3. In reply to REPLACE WITH? press RETURN to give a null string.
4. In reply to OPTIONS? type N and press RETURN.
5. WordStar will Find the first carriage RETURN, and replace it by nothing, that is it will be removed.
6. Type ^L to go on to the next RETURN, which is also removed, ^L again and so on until the end of the paragraph is reached. Leave the last RETURN in the paragraph, or if you remove it, put one back by pressing RETURN.
7. Move the cursor to the first line in the paragraph, and reform it by pressing ^B.
8. The cursor will now be at the end of the paragraph which has just been reformed. Move the cursor past the RETURN at the end of the paragraph, to the beginning of the next paragraph, and repeat the process with more ^L commands.

Alternatively the ^QA command may be used to Replace the string ^N by a blank space, using the options G and N. This deletes all RETURNs from the file. The cursor should then be moved to the top of the file with a ^QR command, and you must scan through the file and press RETURN at the end of each paragraph. The cursor should again be moved to the top of the file with ^QR, and each paragraph should be reformed by pressing ^B for each in turn.

FIGURE 16.2   Summary of options for Find and Replace commands

Use in both Find and Replace commands

U   Ignore any distinction between upper and lower case letters when trying to match a string.

B   Search in a backwards direction.

W   Match on whole words only. (This command will not find a match on a word at the very beginning, or the very end of a file).

3   Find the third occurrence of the string, or find and offer to Replace the next three occurrences of the string. Numbers up to 65,535 may be used.

Use in Replace command only

G   Global replacement - finds each occurrence of the specified string in turn throughout the file, stops and asks each time whether to change it.

N   Replaces the specified string by a new string without asking. When used with the G option exchanges are made throughout the file without asking.

The Find question which is part of both the Find command and the Replace command may contain special characters as part of the string to search for. These are shown in Figure 16.3.

FIGURE 16.3   Special characters which may be used in a Find string

^A   This may be used as a "wild card" in a string. It matches against any single character in the same way that ? may be used to match any character in a CP/M file name. Note that the ^A command is interpreted by the editor as move the cursor one word to the left. To enter ^A you must type ^P^A. For example if the reply to **FIND?** was **screen^P^Afull,** it would show on the screen as **screen^Afull,** and this would match the string **screen full** and also the string **screen-full** in the document.

^S   This matches against any single character that is not a letter or a digit. This is a "wild card" for characters such as commas, full stops, brackets, control characters etc. Note that ^S is interpreted by the editor as move the cursor one space to the left. To enter ^S you must type ^P^S.

^Ox   This may be used to match against any single character other than **x,** the character typed immediately after the ^O. Note that the command ^O is used to display the On-screen menu. To enter ^Ox you must type ^P^Ox.

^N   This is used to match the "carriage RETURN and line feed" which occur at the end of a line, and may cause a problem when non-WordStar files are used under WordStar.

Chapter 17.

MANAGING DISK SPACE

The four different commands to save files are described earlier in chapter 12 - Saving Files, and are shown on the ^K Block menu, (Figure 17.1), which can be displayed by typing ^K when a file is being edited. This chapter describes how blocks of information may be saved as files, and gives some insight into the management of file space. This describes which files are retained on disk, how to use a WordStar backup file, how to backup files onto another disk and how to find out how much free space remains on a disk.

FIGURE 17.1 The ^K Block Menu

```
^K      B:EXAMPLE  PAGE 1 LINE 1  COL 1              INSERT ON
                 < < <   B L O C K   M E N U   > > >
-Saving Files- | -Block Operations- | -File  Operations- | -Other  Menus-
S Save & resume | B  Begin  K  End  | R Read    P  Print | (from Main only)
D Save--done    | H  Hide / Display | O Copy    E Rename | ^J Help  ^K Block
X Save & exit   | C  Copy   Y  Delete| J Delete           | ^Q Quick ^P Print
Q Abandon file  | V  Move   W  Write | -Disk Operations- | ^O Onscreen
-Place Markers- | N  Column  off (ON)|L Change logged disk| Space bar returns
0-9 Set/hide 0-9|                    |F Directory on (OFF)| you to Main Menu.
```

Writing a block to a disk file ^KW

This is described fully in chapter 30 - Manipulating Blocks of Text. However, it is worth a brief mention here. If a block of information is marked with ^KB at the beginning, and ^KK at the end, the marked block can be written to a disk file by typing ^KW . WordStar then asks for the name of the file you wish to write to, and you type a suitable name of up to eight letters, optionally followed by a full stop and a three letter extension, and then press **RETURN**. The block of text is then copied into a disk file, which may be accessed later and included in other documents using the Read file from disk command ^KR which is described in chapter 30 - Manipulating Blocks of Text. It is important to realise that the the marked block of text now appears both in its original position in the document, as well as in the disk file just created. The text in the original document is still highlighted, and to remove the markers <B> and <K> and switch the highlighting off you should type ^KH.

Which files are retained on the disk

Suppose that you type in a new file called CHAPTER1.TXT. When you save this with a ^KS (save and resume), ^KD (save and done) or ^KX (save and exit) command, then the file will be stored on disk and called CHAPTER1.TXT.

If you subsequently edit the file CHAPTER1.TXT, you may type the command **^KS** part of the way through the editing session. This will save the changes made so far, and allow you to continue editing the file. The most up-to-date version of the file with the changes you have just made will be stored on the disk under the name CHAPTER1.TXT, and the original file of that name on the disk will be renamed CHAPTER1.BAK. Alternatively at the end of editing the most up to date version is stored as CHAPTER1.TXT and the earlier version is renamed with the file extension .BAK.

Should you now edit the file again, the disk starts off containing two files: CHAPTER1.TXT and CHAPTER1.BAK. At the end of the edit, the most up to date information is taken from memory and is stored on disk as a file called CHAPTER1.$$$. The suffix .$$$ is the usual CP/M ending for a temporary file). When the new version has been completely written to disk, the original .BAK file is erased, the original .TXT file is renamed .BAK, and the .$$$ file is renamed with the suffix .TXT. This procedure ensures that the original .TXT file is not altered until WordStar is sure that the .$$$ file containing the new information is intact. If the disk becomes completely full, then the .BAK file will be erased in an attempt to make enough space for the .$$$ file. A warning message is displayed on the screen if this occurs. If there is still insufficient space, you will get a **DISK FULL** error. If a write error occurs on the disk, the .$$$ file will not be renamed and will be left on the disk, containing some but not all of the most up to date information, but the original .TXT file will remain unchanged.

How to use a WordStar .BAK (backup) file

WordStar automatically keeps a backup copy of the file (which is probably slightly out of date) in addition to the most recent version. This gives some protection against the possibility that the disk file may not read properly the next time you use it, and more important you may have second thoughts about the changes you made. If you wish to use the .BAK file instead of the most up to date version, you must first rename the file, since WordStar will not edit or print a .BAK file. Renaming can be done from the "No-File" menu under WordStar, by typing the command **E**, and when prompted giving the old filename CHAPTER1.BAK and the new filename for example NEWCHAP.TXT. Alternatively the file may be renamed under CP/M. Suppose that the logged-in drive is A: and the file CHAPTER1.BAK is on a disk in drive B: First change the logged-in drive by typing B: and pressing **RETURN.** Then rename the file by typing:

REN NEWCHAP.TXT=CHAPTER1.BAK

Finally, check that you have renamed the file correctly by typing **DIR** to display the directory of filenames.

Backing up of files onto another disk

Despite the fact that WordStar keeps a backup copy of each file on the disk, it is also essential to keep a copy of the file on at least one other disk. This is described fully in chapter 19 - Backing up Data Files, but because it is so important it is mentioned briefly here. First type ^KX to save the file on disk, to leave WordStar and to return to CP/M. It is assumed that the CP/M file copying program called PIP.COM is present on the same disk as the WordStar data file CHAPTER1.TXT which you wish to back up onto a separate disk. First place the disk with these files in drive A:, and the disk to be used for the back up copies in drive B:. Since the disks present in the drives have been changed, ^C must be typed so that CP/M reads in the header tables for the new disks. If you want to copy one file called CHAPTER1.TXT from disk drive A: to drive B: you should type:

PIP B:=A:CHAPTER1.TXT   and press **RETURN**

Should you wish to copy all the files on drive A: onto B: you should type:

PIP B:=A:*.*   and press **RETURN**

To copy all the files on drive A: which end .TXT onto B: type

PIP B:=A:*.TXT   and press **RETURN**

Remember that if a file already exists on drive B: with the same filename as one being copied from drive A: then the original file on drive B: will be overwritten without any warning.

Checking that you have enough disk space

It is important to keep at least twice as much empty space on a disk as the WordStar data file you are editing. If you fail to do this then under some circumstances it may be impossible to save the file that you have been editing. It is therefore prudent to check how full the disk is, both when you start at the beginning of a day, and at intervals during the session.

It is possible to check how much disk space is free under CP/M, before WordStar has been loaded. The procedure is first to boot the system, and type **DIR** to make sure that the CP/M utilty program called STAT.COM is present on the disk. Provided that it is present, you should type **STAT** and press **RETURN**. The amount of free disk space will then be reported, for example:

        A: R/W, Space: 30k
        B: R/W, Space: 338k

If you would like details of the names and sizes of the individual files present on the disk, in addition to the total amount of free space, then you should type **STAT *.*** and press **RETURN** when information about files on drive A: will be displayed. If you have CP/M, the CP/M utility programs, and WordStar stored on the disk in drive A: and the WordStar data files on the disk in drive B: then you are really interested in the sizes of files on drive B:. To obtain this, information type **STAT B:*.*** and press **RETURN**. If there is insufficient space, you must either erase some unwanted file(s), or use another disk.

Once WordStar has been loaded, you can check on the free disk space, or the file sizes in a slightly different way. First you must get to the "No-File" menu, by saving or abandoning the editing which was in hand, or waiting till printing is finished, or abandoning the printout. If the command **R** is then selected you may now run another program from WordStar itself. You may type **STAT**, or **STAT *.***, and will get exactly the same information as if you had run the STAT program under CP/M, except that when you have done this you will still have WordStar loaded, and will be at the "No-File" menu. Perhaps after seeing the amount of free disk space you decide to erase some unwanted files. This can be done by selecting the **Y** option from the "No-File" menu, when you will be asked to type the full file name for the file to be erased. Remember that it is quite easy to save the file you are editing, and get the "No-File" menu, and Run the program STAT at intervals during a session. In this way you will see problems of insufficient free disk space <u>before</u> they cause you trouble. It is always difficult, and sometimes impossible to escape without losing your data if you get the disks full. Prevention is better than attempting a cure, but the problems of large files, and full disks are considered further in chapter 32 - Problems With Large Files & Disk Full Errors.

When running CP/M programs such as STAT under WordStar, you may notice that the environment is more friendly than when running directly under CP/M. First the file directory of the logged-in drive may be displayed. Furthermore if disk drive B: is logged-in then when running under WordStar drive B: is examined first for a program of the given name, but if it is not found then drive A: will be searched for the program. Under CP/M only the logged-in drive is looked at, unless the drive is specified as part of the program name, in which case only the specified drive is looked at. This means that if CP/M, the CP/M utilities such as STAT, WordStar and MailMerge are all kept on one disk in drive A:, then the whole of the disk in drive B: can be used for WordStar data files. This gives much more space on disk B: for data files, and it is strongly recommended that on any system with two disk drives this arrangement is adopted. (You may choose to keep PIP on the disk in B: to facilitate making backup copies). Should you have a hard disk as drive A:, then it will obviously be preferable to have all the programs and the data files together on it. If your computer has only one floppy disk drive then you have no choice but to put both the programs and the data files on one disk, but the presence of the programs reduces the space available for data files, as shown from the program sizes given in Figure 17.2. Note that WordStar only searches the logged-in drive for ordinary text files.

FIGURE 17.2 Some program sizes

WS.COM	16k	Main WordStar program
WSMSGS.OVR	28k	WordStar messages file
WSOVLY1.OVR	34k	WordStar overlay file
MAILMRGE.OVR	8k	MailMerge program (optional)
SPELSTAR.OVR	18k	SpellStar spelling checking program (optional)
SPELSTAR.DCT	98k	SpellStar dictionary (minimum size)
STAT.COM	6k	CP/M file size utility program (optional)
PIP.COM	8k	CP/M file copying program (optional)

It is worth working out approximately how much text can be stored on a floppy disk. Taking the WordStar default values for page length (66), top margin (3) and bottom margin (8), the number of "useful" lines of text on a page is 66 - 3 - 8 = 55 lines per page. The default ruler gives 65 characters on a line. A page may therefore contain a maximum of 55 x 65 = 3575 characters. Since one character occupies one byte, a full page of text would occupy 3575/1024 = 3.5K bytes. In practice a page is never completely filled, for example there is usually a blank line between paragraphs, and some incompletely filled lines. An average A4 sheet usually contains between 2K and 2.25K of characters. Some typical floppy disks are listed in Figure 17.3, together with their storage capacity in K bytes of storage, and the approximate number of pages of text they will hold.

FIGURE 17.3 Some typical floppy disk capacities

Type (Size, recording density, and sides)	Capacity in K	Capacity in pages of text (approx)
5.25 inch single sided single density	90	40
5.25 inch double sided double density	350	155
8 inch IBM format single sided single density	250	110
8 inch single sided double density	500	220

Should you obtain a **DISK FULL** error message, then you have exceeded the capacity of your disks. The remedy is to type ^KF to display the file directory, and then ^KJ to delete an unwanted file to make some space. This is explained fully in chapter 32 - Problems with Large Files & Disk Full Errors.

Chapter 18.

PRACTICE USING FILES

This chapter will give you practice reading from files.

1. Load CP/M and WordStar, with your disk containing WordStar data files in drive B:. Type **L** and then **B** to change the logged-in drive to B:, and type **D** to open a new file called **VERSE1.TXT**. Then type the text given in Figure 18.1, and save the file with **^KD**.

FIGURE 18.1

> If you can keep your head when all about you
> Are losing theirs and blaming it on you,
> If you can trust yourself when all men doubt you
> But make allowance for their doubting too;
> If you can wait and not be tired of waiting
> Or being lied about, don't deal in lies,
> Or being hated, don't give way to hating,
> And yet don't look too good, nor talk too wise.

2. Open a new file called **VERSE2.TXT**. Then type the text given in Figure 18.2, and save the file with **^KD**.

FIGURE 18.2

> If you can dream - and not make dreams your master,
> If you can think - and not make thoughts your aim,
> If you can meet with Triumph and Disaster,
> And treat those two imposters just the same;
> If you can bear to hear the truth you've spoken
> Twisted by knaves to make a trap for fools,
> Or watch the things you gave your life to broken,
> And stoop to build 'em up with worn out tools.

3. Open a new file called **VERSE3.TXT**. Then type the text given in Figure 18.3, and save the file with **^KD**.

FIGURE 18.3

> If you can make one heap of all your winnings
> And risk it on one turn of pitch-and-toss,
> And lose, and start again at your beginnings
> And never breathe a word about your loss;
> If you can force your heart and nerve and sinew
> To serve your turn long after they are gone,
> And so hold on when there is nothing in you
> Except the Will which says to them "Hold on!"

4. Open a new file called **VERSE4.TXT**. Then type the text given in Figure 18.4, and save the file with **^KD**.

FIGURE 18.4

> If you can talk with crowds and keep your virtue,
> Or walk with Kings - nor lose the common touch,
> If neither foes nor loving friends can hurt you,
> If all men count with you, but none too much;
> If you can fill the unforgiving minute,
> With sixty seconds worth of distance run,
> Yours is the earth and everything thats in it,
> And - which is more - you'll be a Man my son!

5. These four verses make up the well known poem called "If", which was written by Rudyard Kipling. You can now assemble the whole poem in to a single file. The steps are outlined below:

    (a) Open a new file for editing called **IF.TXT**.

    (b) Read the first verse from the file VERSE1.TXT, and include it in the file IF.TXT which you are currently editing. (The command to do this is discussed briefly in chapter 17 - Managing Disk Space, and more fully in chapter 30 - Manipulating Blocks of Text). You must first type the command to read a file **^KR**, and when asked **NAME OF FILE TO READ?** you must type **VERSE1.TXT** and press **RETURN**. After some disk activity you will find that the first verse is now present in the file you are editing, just as if you had typed it in. (Note that the original file called VERSE1.TXT still exists on the disk unchanged). You will find that the cursor is at the beginning of the first verse, and you should move it to the end of the file by typing **^QC**. Press **RETURN** once or twice to make a gap between paragraphs, and to start a new line.

    (c) Repeat the steps in paragraph (b) to read in verses 2, 3 and 4 from their files VERSE2.TXT, VERSE3.TXT and VERSE4.TXT respectively.

    (d) Add the author's name (Rudyard Kipling) at the bottom, move the cursor to the top of the file with a **^QR** command, and type in the title "IF".

    (e) Save the file with a **^KD** command, and print the new file IF.TXT.

6. The "No-File" menu will show on the screen, and beneath this you will see the directory of files present on disk B:. This will include entries for IF.TXT, VERSE1.TXT, VERSE2.TXT, VERSE3.TXT VERSE4.TXT, and any other files you have stored on this disk.

7. Next type **Y** to delete a file, and in reply to the question **NAME OF FILE TO DELETE?** type **IF.TXT** and press **RETURN**. The file containing the whole poem will disappear. Check the directory to make sure that this is so. Keep the four files containing the individual verses, since these will be used later in the book.

8. Finally type **X** to exit from WordStar to CP/M, remove the floppy disks, and switch the mains OFF.

Summary

In this chapter you have practised the following:

1. Typing and saving new files

2. Reading existing files and incorporating them in to a new document

3. Printing a document

4. Deleting a file from the disk

Chapter 19.

BACKING UP OF DATA FILES

Every time that you use data files stored on a disk, there is a small but finite risk that something disastrous might happen, such as accidentally erasing a file, a power transient, mains failure, or machine failure, in which case the time and effort invested in generating the data would be wasted. The file could be a large Word-Star data file, a database, or a firm's accounts, and there would be no option but to start again at the beginning. Obviously it is essential to keep backup copies to insure against this. The way to do this is examined in this chapter.

Experience both on large mainframe computers as well as on microcomputers suggests that a backup system of data files which keeps three generations of the file provides the best insurance against data loss. Suppose that the first day's work is stored on a disk labelled "Disk A". At the end of the day the original data on "Disk A" is copied onto a second blank disk which is labelled "Disk B". On the second day, "Disk B" is used to make all the additions or changes, and at the end of the day the most up to date information on "Disk B" is copied onto another blank disk which is labelled "Disc C". The next day, you work on "Disk C", and at the end of the day this is copied onto "Disk A". This cycle is continued, (see Figure 19.1), updating each disk in turn.

FIGURE 19.1 Backup of data disks

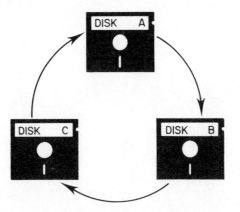

The three generations of disk differ both in their age, and how up to date they are, and they are sometimes likened to grandparent, parent and child. There is a major advantage to keeping three disks with some version of the same data. In the worst possible case of a power transient, or a failure of either the mains or the computer occurring while backing up is taking place at the end of a day, then it is possible to corrupt two disks at the same time. With three generations of disks, it is always possible to recover the data from the one remaining disk, and though this disk is not quite up to date, you will only lose the alterations made in the last day.

The copying of a whole disk is best done under CP/M. Suppose that you are logged-in to drive A:, which contains the files you want to back up and also the program PIP.COM. All of the files present on this disk (but not the system tracks), may be copied onto the disk present in drive B: by typing:

PIP B:=A:*.*[V]

Alternatively suppose that you are logged-in to drive B: and the files you want to back-up and the program PIP.COM are present on the disk in drive B:. All of the files present on this disk (but not the system tracks), may be copied onto the disk present in drive A: by typing

PIP A:=B:*.*[V]

The operating system, which is stored on the system tracks of the disk, may be copied using the CP/M utility program called SYSGEN.COM, as described in Appendix 1 and Chapter 45. Since the system tracks cannot be used to store any of your own files, there is no good reason why all of your disks should not have the operating system stored on them, and this may be useful.

Some computer systems are provided with a system command such as CD, or a program with a name such as COPY or COPYDISK, that makes a copy of the entire diskette, and in addition verifies it to make sure that it has been copied correctly. It is worth the effort of finding out if these utilities are provided for your machine, since they generally copy much faster than PIP, and have the advantage of automatic verification. In particular you should check whether it copies track by track from the disk, in which case both the files and the system tracks containing CP/M will be automatically copied, or whether copying is file by file, in which case files will be copied but not CP/M.

Chapter 20.

WHEN IT IS SAFE TO CHANGE DISKS

Changing disks in the middle of a computing session may in some circumstances result in valuable information on the disk being destroyed. The times when it is safe to change disks when running either under the CP/M operating system or WordStar are discussed.

A disk should never be removed from the disk drive except when the CP/M prompt **A>** or **B>** is displayed on the last line of the screen. When the prompt is displayed the computer is waiting for you to type something, and so it cannot be using the disks. Removing the disk when it is in use may result in new information not being written to the disk, information already written on the disk being corrupted, the surface of the disk being damaged, and it might upset the alignment of the disk heads - necessitating an expensive repair.

Under CP/M

When the computer is under the control of the operating system CP/M, it is safe to change disks at any time when the prompt **A>** or **B>** is displayed on the screen. After changing disks, it is important to press ^C, to warm boot the system _immediately after the change_. (With some CP/M-like operating systems, for example CDOS on the Cromemco computer, warm booting is unnecessary, but it does no harm). When first CP/M looks at a disk, it reads and stores a header table showing the names and locations of files stored on the disk. Warm booting makes the computer re-read this information. If the disks are changed and you do not warm boot, then information can usually be read from the newly inserted disk without any problem, but if you write anything to the disk then you may get an error message, or you may destroy existing files on the disk.

Under WordStar

1. It is always safe to change disks when the "No-File" menu is displayed on the screen provided that the computer is not simultaneously printing a disk file. The new disk must then be logged-in. This is not done by pressing ^C as when running under CP/M, but instead it is done using the command **L** to change the logged-in drive. If for example the disk containing the WordStar data files in drive B: was changed, then typing **L** to change the logged-in drive, followed by typing **B:** or just **B** and pressing **RETURN** will log the new disk in. You can see that this has happened, because the file directory from the new file will be displayed. Note that the command to change the logged-in drive is normally used to change from drive B: to A:, or vice versa, and here it is being used to log in a new disk on the same drive. (If the new disk is not logged-in then files from the new disk may be read or printed provided that you know the filename. The directory displayed will be for the disk which was removed - which is confusing. Problems occur if you try to write to the disk. This procedure is dangerous, and it is recommended that when a disk is changed it is always logged-in).

2. A disk may be changed when you are editing, provided that it is only to read data. (For example to allow you to use a ^KR command to read a file from the disk, and insert it into the working document). Make sure that you do not try to write on the changed disk unless it has been logged-in.

3. If a drive has not been used in any way since the computer was switched on, then if there has been no disk in that drive one may be inserted, and if a disk is present it may be changed. This is because until the computer accesses the drive, it does not look at it, and does not store anything from the directory.

4. Disks may be changed when a message on the screen instructs you to do so, because of a CHANGE command used in MailMerge, of when using SpellStar.

Chapter 21.

THE CONTROL CHARACTER MENUS

One of the powerful features of WordStar in the amount of helpful information which can be displayed on the screen, in the form of Menus. The menus encountered so far are the "No-File" menu, and the Main menu. These are displayed automatically and describe commands which are one character long. These commands perform the basic features of opening a file for editing, printing, or the simple cursor movements. In addition to these, there are five control character menus, ^J, ^K, ^O, ^P, and ^Q. These differ from the earlier menus described in two main ways. First they are only displayed when the user requests help or information by typing the appropriate control character, and second they explain much more sophisticated and powerful commands. These commands are all two characters long, made up of the control character which produced the menu, followed by a second letter.

Suppose for example that you typed ^Q to display the Quick menu, but when you examined it you either found that it was the wrong menu, or decided not to use any of the commands listed. Hitting the **ESCAPE** key, the **space bar**, or any key which is not a command will return you to the file you were editing. If having looked at the menu you decide to use one of the commands described, for example ^QX is the command to move the cursor to the bottom of the screen, then since you have already typed in ^Q it only remains to type **X** to complete the command. If however you can remember the command, you can type **^QX** without a pause, and the command will be implemented without the delay caused by having to find and display the menu. The same principle applies to all of the commands on each of the five control character menus. The five menus are given in this chapter for reference, but the commands are described more fully in separate chapters and appendices.

The ^J Help menu

At any time when a file is being edited, the Help menu can be displayed on the screen by typing ^J. This menu is shown in Figure 21.1, Changing the Help Level is described in chapter 22, and the other commands are described in Appendix 4.

FIGURE 21.1 The ^J HELP Menu

```
^J     B:EXAMPLE  PAGE 1 LINE 1  COL 1              INSERT ON
             < < <    H E L P   M E N U    > > >
                                         !       ! --Other  Menus--
  H  Display & set the help level ! S  Status line  ! (from Main only)
  B  Paragraph reform (CONTROL-B) ! R  Ruler line   ! ^J Help    ^K Block
  F  Flags in right-most column   ! M  Margins & Tabs! ^Q Quick   ^P Print
  D  Dot commands, print controls ! P  Place markers ! ^O Onscreen
                                  ! V  Moving text   ! Space bar returns
                                  !                 ! you to Main Menu.
  L----!----!----!----!----!----!----!----!----!----!--------R
```

The ^K Block menu

The ^K menu can be displayed by typing ^K when a file is being edited. The menu is shown in Figure 21.2, and the commands it contains are described in Appendix 5. Further details are given in chapter 12 - Saving Files, chapter 17 - Managing Disk Space, and chapter 30 - Manipulating Blocks of Text.

FIGURE 21.2   The ^K Block Menu

```
^K       B:EXAMPLE  PAGE 1 LINE 1  COL 1                  INSERT ON
                   < < <   B L O C K   M E N U   > > >
 -Saving Files- | -Block Operations- | -File  Operations- |  -Other  Menus-
S Save & resume | B  Begin  K  End   | R Read    P  Print |  (from Main only)
D Save--done    | H  Hide / Display  | O Copy    E Rename | ^J Help  ^K Block
X Save & exit   | C  Copy  Y  Delete| J Delete           | ^Q Quick ^P Print
Q Abandon file  | V  Move  W  Write | -Disk Operations-  | ^O Onscreen
 -Place Markers-| N  Column  off (ON)|L Change logged disk| Space bar returns
0-9 Set/hide 0-9|                    |F Directory on (OFF)| you to Main Menu.
L----!----!----!----!----!----!----!----!----!----!----!--------R
```

The ^O On-screen menu

The on-screen formatting commands are all given in the ^O menu, which may be displayed simply by typing ^O at any time when you are editing a file. The commands are described in Appendix 6, and the menu is shown in Figure 21.3. Further details are given in chapters 28 - On-screen Formatting - Margin, Tabs and Ruler, and 29 - More On-screen Formatting - Line Functions and Toggles.

FIGURE 21.3   The ^O On-screen Menu

```
^O       B:LETTER.TXT  PAGE 1 LINE 1 COL 01              INSERT ON
                   < < < O N S C R E E N   M E N U  > > >
-Margins & Tabs-  | -Line Functions- |  --More Toggles-- |  -Other Menus-
L Set left margin |C Centre text     |J Justify   off (ON)|  (from Main only)
R Set right margin|S Set line spacing|V Vari-tabs off (ON)|^J Help  ^K Block
X Release margins |                  |H Hyph-help off (ON)|^Q Quick ^P Print
I Set  N Clear tab|   ---Toggles---  |E Soft hyph on (OFF)|^O Onscreen
G Paragraph tab   |W Wrd wrap off (ON)|D Prnt disp off (ON)|Space Bar returns
F Ruler from line |T Rlr line off (ON)|P Pge break off (ON)|you to Main Menu.
L----!----!----!----!----!----!----!----!----!----!----!--------R
```

The ^P Print menu

The Print menu can be displayed on the screen any time that a document is being edited by typing ^P. The menu is shown in Figure 21.4. The commands are described in Appendix 7, and in chapter 23 - Special Print Effects.

FIGURE 21.4   The ^P Print menu

```
^P       B:LETTER.TXT  PAGE 1 LINE 1 COL 01              INSERT ON
                   < < <   P R I N T   M E N U   > > >
 ------ Special  Effects -------- | -Printing Changes- |  -Other  Menus-
(begin and end) | (one time each) | A Alternate pitch  |  (from Main only)
B Bold D Double | H Overprint char | N Standard pitch  |^J Help  ^K Block
S Underscore    | O Non-break space | C printing pause  |^Q Quick ^P Print
X Strikeout     | F Phantom space  | Y Other ribbon color|^O Onscreen
V Subscript     | G Phantom rubout | --User  Patches--  |Space Bar returns
T Superscript   | RET Overprint line | Q(1) W(2) E(3) R(4) |you to Main Menu.
L----!----!----!----!----!----!----!----!----!----!----!--------R
```

The ^Q Quick menu

The Quick menu, which is shown in Figure 21.5, may be displayed any time editing is in progress by typing ^Q. It contains powerful commands for moving the cursor, which are quicker than those given in the Main menu. In addition, it contains commands for deleting text and finding or substituting text. These commands are described in Appendix 8. The cursor moving commands are fully explained in chapter 15 - Advanced Cursor Movements, and Scrolling Text, and finding and replacing text are described in chapter 16 - Editing - The Find and Replace Commands.

FIGURE 21.5 The ^Q Quick Menu

```
^Q      B:EXAMPLE  PAGE 1 LINE 1  COL 1              INSERT ON
                  < < <     Q U I C K   M E N U     > > >
      ---Cursor Movement---  | -Delete- |  ---Miscellaneous--- | -Other  Menus-
   S left side  D right side |Y line  rt|F Find text in file | (from Main only)
   E top scrn   X bottom scrn|DEL lin lf|A Find & Replace    |^J Help  ^K Block
   R top file   C end file   |L Find Misspelling |^Q Quick ^P Print
   B top block  K end block  |Q Repeat command or |^O Onscreen
   0-9 marker   Z up   W down|  key  until space  |Space bar returns
   P previous   V last Find or Block | bar  or other key |you to Main Menu.
   L----!----!----!----!----!----!----!----!----!----!----!-------R
```

Chapter 22.

CHANGING THE HELP LEVEL

WordStar provides help in the form of messages on the screen which prompt the user automatically. An absolute beginner will require a large amount of help, but an experienced user needs much less. Being given more help than you require makes WordStar run more slowly, may partly fill the screen with information you can do without, and causes irritation. To cater for all levels of expertise, you may set the help level for yourself, from the value of 3 for maximum help to 0 for no help. In addition a large amount of helpful information is stored on a series of menus. The most important of these are the No-File menu, the Main menu, the ^J Help menu, the ^K Block menu, the ^O On-screen menu, the ^P Print menu and the ^Q Quick menu. The last five of these can be displayed at any time when you are editing a file and need assistance, by typing ^J, ^K, ^O, ^P or ^Q and pressing **RETURN**. After you have obtained the required information, you can continue editing the document as if there had been no interruption. The fact that these menus can be accessed so easily solves most problems, and makes reference to the WordStar manual a rare event. The Help levels and Menus are described in this chapter.

Setting the Help level

When the WordStar program is first loaded, it briefly displays a sign-on message on the screen, as described in chapter 4 - Getting Started. Then the No-File menu is displayed (Figure 22.1).

FIGURE 22.1 The No-File Menu

```
           < < < N O - F I L E   M E N U  > > >
    ——Preliminary Commands———  | ——File  Commands—— | -System Commands-
L  Change logged disk drive    | P  Print  a file   |  R Run a  program
F  File directory     off (ON) | E  RENAME a file   |  X EXIT to system
H  Set Help level              | O  COPY   a file   |
   ——Commands to open a file——— | Y  DELETE a file   | -WordStar Options-
   D  Open a  document  file    |                    |  M Run MailMerge
   N  Open a non-document file  |                    |  S Run SpellStar
```

Typing the command **H** allows the Help level to be reset, and a menu about Help levels is displayed (Figure 22.2).

FIGURE 22.2 Help levels

```
H       editing no file

HELP LEVELS
   3  all menus and explanations displayed
   2  main editing menu (1-control-char commands suppressed)
   1  prefix menus (2-character commands) also suppressed
   0  command explanations (including this) also suppressed

CURRENT HELP LEVEL IS 3

ENTER Space OR NEW HELP LEVEL (0, 1, 2, OR 3):
```

When WordStar is first loaded, the default value for Help is 3, that is maximum help. Typing a digit 0,1,2 or 3 will set the help level appropriately. Typing anything else will leave the help level unchanged. If a digit is typed before this menu has been displayed, the explanation will be omitted, and when you are confident you may type **H2** quickly, rather than typing **H**, waiting for the menu then typing 2, to set the Help to level 2.

The differences between the help levels may be summarized as follows. Level 3 gives the maximum help, all possible messages and menus are shown on the screen, (and this is the level set by default). Level 2 does not display the Main Menu, except for the status line. This menu occupies 10 lines of the screen, and suppressing it allows much more of the document being edited to show on the screen. The information in the Main Menu is shown in Figure 22.3, and it concerns the basic information on how to move the cursor, scrolling, deleting and a few miscellaneous commands. Most users become familiar with these functions after two or three sessions with WordStar, and it is recommended that users move to this level of help as soon as possible.

FIGURE 22.3 The Main Menu

```
     B:LETTER.TXT  PAGE 1 LINE 1  COL 01           INSERT ON
                   < < <    M A I N   M E N U    > > >
     --Cursor Movement--   | -Delete- |   -Miscellaneous-  | -Other Menus-
 ^S char left ^D char right |^G  char  | ^I Tab   ^B Reform | (from Main only)
 ^A word left ^F word right |DEL chr lf| ^V INSERT ON/OFF   |^J Help ^K Block
 ^E line  up  ^X line down  |^T word rt|^L Find/Replce again|^Q Quick ^P Print
     --Scrolling--         |^Y  line  |RETURN End paragraph|^O Onscreen
 ^Z line up  ^W line down   |          | ^N Insert a RETURN |
 ^C screen up ^R screen down|          | ^U Stop a command  |
```

In addition to the above, level 1 also suppresses the ^J (Help), ^K (Block), ^P (Print), ^O (On-screen) and ^Q (Quick) menus except for the status line. Level 1 also suppresses the two lines which give you a reminder of the control characters which you may use when answering any question which ends in a question mark. These are shown in Figure 22.4.

FIGURE 22.4

```
     ^S=delete character   ^Y=delete entry   ^F=File directory
     ^D=restore character   ^R=Restore entry   ^U=cancel command
```

Level 0 suppresses the "No-File" menu commands in addition.

However, the ^J sub menus listed below in Figure 22.5 will still be displayed even at help levels 1 or 0, provided that you can remember the full command.

FIGURE 22.5 The ^J sub-menus

```
    ^JB details of paragraph reforming and hyphenation
    ^JD explains print features, dot commands, headers and footers
    ^JF gives the meaning of flags at the right of the screen
    ^JH displays a menu and allows you to change the help level
    ^JI gives information on editing commands, but is NOT listed in the menu
    ^JM explains margins, justification and tabs
    ^JP describes the use of place markers
    ^JR explains the ruler
    ^JS explains the status line
    ^JV describes how to move a block of text
```

Users are recommended to try changing the help level, and moving around from one menu to another, to see how the help level affects the explanations and the on-screen displays. There is no need to be apprehensive, since typing ^**JH** will always get the sub-menu allowing you to reset the help level. This ^JH sub-menu is shown in Figure 22.2, and even at the help level 0 it displays as in Figure 22.6. Equally you can always type **^JH3** to set the help back to level 3.

FIGURE 22.6

^JH   B:LETTER.TXT PAGE 2 LINE 4 COL 16

CURRENT HELP LEVEL IS 0

ENTER Space OR NEW HELP LEVEL (0, 1, 2, OR 3):

Chapter 23.

SPECIAL PRINT EFFECTS

WordStar can produce a variety of special print effects, the most commonly used being **bold-faced text**, underlined text, subscripts$_3$ and superscripts^4. In addition a number of printing changes are possible, such as changing the colour of the ribbon from black to red and back again, or the pitch (number of characters per inch). These are all listed on the Print Menu, which can be displayed on the screen by typing ^P, (shown in Figure 23.1). This chapter describes all these features, and how to use them.

FIGURE 23.1 The ^P Print menu

```
^P      B:LETTER.TXT   PAGE 1 LINE 1 COL 01              INSERT ON
                    < < <    P R I N T   M E N U    > > >
    ------ Special  Effects -------  | -Printing  Changes- | -Other  Menus-
  (begin and end) | (one time each)  | A Alternate pitch   | (from Main only)
  B Bold D Double | H Overprint char | N Standard pitch     |^J Help  ^K Block
  S Underscore    | O Non-break space| C printing pause     |^Q Quick ^P Print
  X Strikeout     | F Phantom space  | Y Other ribbon color |^O Onscreen
  V Subscript     | G Phantom rubout | --User  Patches--    |Space Bar returns
  T Superscript   | RET Overprint line| Q(1) W(2) E(3) R(4) |you to Main Menu.
  L----!----!----!----!----!----!----!----!----!----!----!--------R
```

Bold type ^PB

Most daisy-wheel printers, and some of the more expensive matrix printers are capable of incremental spacing, which is more commonly called microspacing. This simply means that they can move in very small increments, often 1/120th. of an inch horizontally and 1/48th. of an inch vertically. Bold type has characters which are thicker than the usual type. Even though the letters are the same size, they appear blacker, and heavier, and such type is commonly used for headings or parts which require emphasis. WordStar produces bold type on printers capable of microspacing, by printing a letter normally, moving 1/120th. of an inch and printing the same letter a second time, moving another 1/120th. of an inch and printing the letter a third time. Note that all printers are not capable of microspacing, and therefore cannot produce bold type.

The command ^PB is used to produce bold type. ^P indicates that it is a print feature, and B indicates Bold. To produce bold type, ^PB must be typed immediately before and after the words to be boldfaced. The symbol ^B appears on the screen either side of the text to be boldfaced, but these extra control characters do not count as characters in the line. However, they make the line longer than usual and slightly spoil the on-screen layout. (If required, the display of control characters may be hidden by typing ^OD, so that the layout can be checked. It is recommended that ^OD is typed again when the checking is finished, so that the print display toggle is switched ON again. Otherwise you may inadvertently delete "hidden" control characters during editing). Figure 23.2 illustrates the use of bold type, showing what must be typed, what appears on the screen, and what will be printed.

FIGURE 23.2

Type this	^PBthis is an example of bold type^PB
Screen display	^Bthis is an example of bold type^B
Printout	**this is an example of bold type**

Because bold text is effectively typed three times, the time taken to print the document will be increased. Remember also that failure to put ^PB at the end of the text to be enhanced will result in the rest of the document being printed in bold type, which will be both slow and heavy on the ribbon.

Double strike ^PD

Double strike means that the printer hits the same letter twice. First the text is printed normally, and then the printer goes back and types the same letters on top of the original ones. This produces a blacker image than typing just once. All printers can produce double strike. On those which cannot do microspacing, bold and double strike look exactly the same. On printers which can do microspacing, doublestrike and bold are different, and complement each other. Double strike produces text which stands out more than ordinary text, but not as well as bold, hence bold and double can be used to give headings of differing importance. If a carbon ribbon is not available, a whole document may be printed in double strike mode to produce an extremely black document. Double strike helps to improve the readability if multiple forms are used. Remember that typing text twice increases the time taken to print the document, and that failure to put ^PD at the end of the enhanced text will cause the rest of the document to be printed in double strike.

The command for double strike is ^PD. ^P indicates that it is a print function and D stands for Double strike. To produce double strike, ^PD must be typed before and after the text to be enhanced. The screen will show ^D markers either side of the text to be printed in double strike mode. This is illustrated in Figure 23.3.

FIGURE 23.3

Type this	^PDthis is an example of double strike^PD
Screen display	^Dthis is an example of double strike^D
Printout	this is an example of double strike

Underlining text ^PS

Any amount of text may be underlined using WordStar, but spaces are not underlined. (Underlining is sometimes called underscoring, and this word is used in the Menu and the WordStar manual. This also explains the choice of the symbol ^PS for underlining. ^P indicates that it is a print function, and S indicates Score from underScore). To underline text simply type ^PS before and after the text to be underlined. The control characters ^S appear on the screen at either side of the text to be underlined. This is illustrated in Figure 23.4. A method of underlining both characters and spaces is described later in this chapter in the paragraph on Overprinting Whole Lines.

FIGURE 23.4

Type this	^PSthis is an example of underlining^PS
Screen display	^Sthis is an example of underlining^S
Printout	this is an example of underlining

Strikeout ^PX

Certain applications, such as legal documents, may require text to be printed, and then crossed out with hyphens. To do this the command ^PX must be typed on either side of the text you wish to strike out, and the markers ^X show on the screen. This is illustrated in Figure 23.5.

FIGURE 23.5

Type this	^PXthis is an example of strikeout^PX
Screen display	^Xthis is an example of strikeout^X
Printout	this is an example of strikeout

Subscripts ^PV and superscripts ^PT

Subscripts are parts of the text which are printed below the line, for example in chemical formulae such as water H_2O or glucose $C_6H_{12}O_6$. Superscripts are parts which are printed above the line, such as indices or powers in mathematical expressions like $E = mc^2$, or references to footnotes.

Printers which are not capable of microspacing will print subscripts on the line below, and superscripts on the line above - if it is blank. Otherwise they appear on the same line - that is not sub or superscripted. With such printers, it is wise to use double spacing if the text contains subscripts and superscripts. Even so, it is possible to get a conflict between a subscript from one line and a superscript from the line below, though the chance of this happening is slight except in highly technical literature.

On printers capable of microspacing, the subscripted numbers are moved down a fraction of a line. WordStar sets a default value of 3/48th of an inch for the amount of roll (that is movement down or up) with subscripts/superscripts. With the usual spacing of 6 lines to an inch, this means that the subscripts are printed 3/8 of a line lower down, and of course superscripts are printed 3/8 of a line higher. This default value can be changed for example to 4/48ths of an inch by typing the dot command .SR 4 (starting in column 1 on a new line in the document). Since sub/superscripts are only moved a fraction of a line, it is quite possible that they do not interfere with the lines below and above, with the line spacing set at the usual 6 lines per inch. If there is a problem, then double spacing can be selected with a ^OS command, or the line spacing may be increased slightly using a dot command such as .LH9 (giving a line spacing of 48/9 = 5.3 lines per inch), or .LH 10 (giving 48/10 = 4.8 lines per inch). This is discussed in chapter 26 - Dot commands.

Subscripted text is produced by typing ^PV before and after the parts to be printed lower down, and on the screen the markers ^V are displayed before and after. In a similar way, superscripted text is produced by typing ^PT before and after, and this is indicated on the screen by ^T markers. This is illustrated in Figure 23.6.

FIGURE 23.6

Type this	Glucose has the formula C^PV6^PVH^PV12^PVO^PV6^PV
Screen display	Glucose has the formula C^V6^VH^V12^VO^V6^V
Printout	Glucose has the formula $C_6H_{12}O_6$

Type this	E = mc^PT2^PT
Screen display	E = mc^T2^T
Printout	$E = mc^2$

The control symbols ^V and ^T which appear on the screen either side of the text to be subscripted/superscripted do not count as characters in the line, but they make the line longer than usual and ruin the on-screen layout. It is absolutely essential when checking the layout on the screen to hide these control characters by typing ^OD. Note that it is not possible to display subscripts and superscripts below or above the line on the screen, even though they will print correctly. It is recommended that ^OD is typed again when the checking is finished, to switch the print display toggle ON again, or you may inadvertently delete "hidden" control characters during editing.

Overprinting characters ^PH

Overprinting (called strikeover in the WordStar manual) occurs when the next character to be printed is printed on top of the preceding character in the line. It is useful for generating new characters, for example accent, umlaut or tilde symbols which are printed over a letter in certain foreign languages. Overprinting may also be useful to cross a letter out, perhaps with an X, or with a / to produce the Scandinavian letter ø.

Overprinting applies to just one character, hence it is only necessary to mark where it begins. This is done by typing ^PH after the first letter, and before the second letter which will overprint the first. The symbol ^H will show on the screen. Superscripts may be used in conjunction with overprinting to get an accent mark printed above the letter, as illustrated in Figure 23.7.

FIGURE 23.7

Type this	ku^PH"hl	me^PH^PT/^PTre	fene^PH^tre
Screen display	ku^H"hl	me^H^T/^Tre	fene^H^tre
Printout	kühl	mére	fenêtre

Non-break spaces ^PO

Sometimes there is a space between two words, but it would not look right if the two words were separated with one at the end of a line and the other at the beginning of the next line. For example, if Queen Elizabeth II is typed, it would look wrong if Elizabeth was on one line, and II on the next line. This could easily occur if the word-wrap feature of WordStar decided that the best place to end a line was after Elizabeth, either when the text was first typed, or subsequently if the paragraph is edited and then reformed with ^B. WordStar provides a special non-break character ^PO which can be typed instead of a space, and will print as a space, but will not be treated as a space for line breaks. Thus it makes the two words behave as if they were a single word. To solve the problem mentioned above, you should type Elizabeth^POII, which would show as Elizabeth^OII on the screen, and the two words will then always be printed on the same line.

Printing special characters - phantom space ^PF and phantom rubout ^PG

Many daisy wheel printers provide the option of printing two special characters, in addition to the usual character set. The first of these is usually called phantom space, (20 hex), which is obtained by typing ^PF. The screen displays ^F, but exactly what is printed depends on the particular daisy wheel or thimble on the printer. The British pound symbol £, or the American cent symbol ¢ may often be obtained. The second special symbol is called phantom rubout (7F hex), and is obtained by typing ^PG. This appears on the screen as ^G, and may print as a double underline or a graphics character.

Overprinting whole lines ^P RETURN

Sometimes overprinting is used to produce special effects, for example a whole paragraph of text might be crossed out with slashes /// or X's. (Two other commands have already been described which produce overprinting. These are ^PH for overprinting the last character, and the strikeout command ^PX for crossing out a whole block of text with hyphens). To overprint a whole line, type ^P at the end of the line you want overprinting, and press **RETURN**. This line will have a - flag showing at the extreme right of the screen, in contrast to the < sign for lines with a normal carriage return as at the end of a paragraph, or a blank if word-wrap has terminated the line. (These flags are described in chapter 14 - The Screen Display). The next line typed will overprint the line, for example a whole line of slashes, ending with RETURN. Should you require a third line to overprint the last two, then line two should also end with ^P and RETURN.

This overprinting feature is sometimes used to produce underlined text, where both characters and spaces are underlined, in contrast to the ^PS feature which only underlines text and not spaces. For example the text in the well known quotation by Adelaide Stevenson:

76

Eggheads of the world unite, you have nothing to lose but your yolks.

is produced by typing:

Eggheads of the world unite, you have nothing to lose but your yolks.^P RETURN
_____RETURN

Overprinting a whole line may also be useful for setting out mathematical equations. For example:

$$\frac{P_1.V_1}{T_1} = \frac{P_2.V_2}{T_2}$$

could be printed by typing:

```
^PTP^PT1^PT.V^PT1  =  ^PTP^PT2^PT.V^PT2   ^P RETURN
_____        _____                    RETURN
  T^PV1^PV        T^PV2^PV                 RETURN
```

(^PT is for superscripting, ^PV is for subscripting and ^P RETURN is for overprinting). The layout of this equation can be checked on the screen by typing ^OD, which has the effect of switching OFF the display of control characters. The normal characters will appear lined up exactly as they will be printed, except that because the line of underline characters is overprinting the first line, the equation will only occupy two lines on paper, though it uses three lines on the screen. Remember to type ^OD again to turn the display of control characters on again.

Changing pitch - alternate pitch ^PA and normal pitch ^PN

Some printers such as teletypes and very cheap dot matrix printers can only print characters at one fixed spacing, such as 10 characters per inch. The commands ^PA and ^PN have no effect on such printers. However, many matrix printers provide two different character spacings, usually 10 or 12 characters per inch. If WordStar has been correctly installed, then the commands ^PA and ^PN may be used to change from one spacing or pitch to another. These commands will also work on printers capable of microspacing (most daisy wheel printers and some expensive dot matrix printers), but a dot command such as .CW 11 is often preferred on a printer capable of microspacing. This is described in chapter 26 - Dot Commands.

The default value for the normal pitch used by WordStar is 10 characters per inch along a line (for example Pica or Courier type). The default value for the alternative pitch is 12 characters per inch (for example Elite type).

If you are printing at the standard 10 characters per inch, you can change to the alternate pitch of 12 characters per inch by typing ^PA. If required, you can change back to the normal pitch after typing the required word, line, or paragraph by typing ^PN. The screen displays ^A and ^N at the appropriate place in the text to indicate where the change will be made.

If you are changing the pitch on a daisy wheel printer, you will probably want the printer to stop, so that you can change the daisy wheel to one of different pitch. The next section describes how to stop the printer for this purpose. It is worth experimenting with your own particular printer. A daisy wheel which gives 12 characters per inch can be made to print at 10 characters per inch, and this spreading out of the letters may look attractive for headings. Alternatively, printing 11 characters per inch using a 10 character per inch daisy wheel gives compact text which some people find attractive. These default values may be changed permanently by installing your copy of WordStar with different values.

Stopping the printer to change daisy wheels ^PC

If you would like to change the daisy wheel at some point in the middle of a document, then ^PC should be typed at the exact point in the file where you want to stop. This is useful if you would like to change the daisy wheel to one of a different pitch, or one with Greek or mathematical symbols, or one with italics. After printing a word, a line or a whole section, you will probably want to change back to the original daisy wheel. Another ^PC must be placed at the end of the special section to stop the printer at this point to allow you to replace the original daisy wheel. The message **PRINT PAUSED** appears in the status line on the screen when the printer stops, and printing can be resumed by typing **P**.

Changing the ribbon colour ^PY

If the printer is fitted with a two colour ribbon, for example red/black, then it is easy to change from one colour to the other. Since black is normally used, you only have to type ^PY before and after the section you require in red. On the screen the section in red is marked at both ends by the symbols ^Y. Since the more heavily used black part of the ribbon on a two colour ribbon will only last half as long as an all black ribbon, a two colour ribbon should only be fitted if the alternate colour feature will be used extensively. A switch under the ribbon cartridge of the printer should be checked to make sure that it is set for red/black. Remember to switch it back if you fit a multi-strike carbon film ribbon.

If an all black ribbon is fitted, some printers have a twist in the ribbon (to make a moibus band), so that both the upper and lower halves are used automatically. Other printers do not do this, and **^PY** may be typed to use the other half of the ribbon, rather like changing to red on two colour ribbons.

User defined features ^PQ, ^PW, ^PE and ^PR

Despite the large number of print features which already exist, WordStar has four so far undefined printer functions, ^PQ, ^PW, ^PE and ^PR. Until they are installed, they will do nothing. The WordStar INSTALL program will automatically install a number of different printers, and this may activate one or more of them. For example ^PQ is used to obtain the other font, and ^PW to change back to the main font on printers with a print thimble with 128 characters. The WordStar installation manual explains how you may define these functions for yourself, for example to obtain WIDE characters on some matrix printers, to activate a single sheet feeder, or to change the typeface or font on certain special very high density dot matrix printers, or some ink-spray printers.

Chapter 24.

<u>PRACTISING</u> <u>SOME</u> <u>PRINT</u> <u>ENHANCEMENTS</u>

1. Load CP/M and WordStar, open a document file called USA.TXT and type in the text given in Figure 24.1.

FIGURE 24.1 Unlucky for some!

PARTS OF THE AMERICAN DECLARATION OF INDEPENDENCE

In Congress, July 4, 1776

The unanimous Declaration of the thirteen united States of America,

When in the course of human events, it becomes necessary for one people to dissolve the political bands which have connected them with another, and to assume among the powers of the earth, the separate and equal station to which the Laws of Nature and of Nature's God entitle them, a decent respect to the opinions of mankind requires that they declare the causes which impel them to the separation. We hold these truths to be self evident, that all men are created equal, that they are endowed by their Creator with certain unalienable Rights, that among these are Life, Liberty and the pursuit of Happiness. That to secure these rights, Governments are instituted among Men, deriving their just powers from the consent of the governed. That whenever any form of Government becomes destructive of these ends, it is the Right of the People to alter or abolish it, and to institute new Government, laying its foundation on such principles and organising its powers in such form, as to them shall seem most likely to effect their Safety and Happiness. ...

We therefore, the representatives of the united States of America, in General Congress, assembled, appealing to the Supreme Judge of the world for the rectitude of our intentions, do, in the Name, and by the Authority of the good People of these Colonies, solemnly publish and declare that these United Colonies are, and of Right ought to be Free and Independent States.

2. Change the page width to 70 characters, by changing the right margin with a ^OR **70** command. The text is still formatted for the default page width of 65 characters, and you must press ^B to reformat each paragraph in turn. (This is fully explained in the next chapter 25 - Page Layout).

3. Enhance the title by making it print in bold text, underlined, and with the heading centred. To do this move the cursor to the top of the file with a ^QR command, and the cursor should be on to the P of "PARTS". Now type ^PB to start bold type, type ^PS to start underlining, then move the cursor one space past "INDEPENDENCE" and type ^PS and ^PB to stop underlining and bold. Finally centre the line by typing ^OC. (Centering text is described later in chapter 29 - More On-Screen Formatting, Line Functions and Toggles.

4. Now centre the line "In Congress, July 4, 1776". To do this move the cursor on to this line and type ^OC.

5. Next make the line "The unanimous Declaration of the thirteen united States of America," print in double strike, and centre the line. To do this type ^PD at the beginning and end of the line to start and stop double strike, then type ^OC to centre the line.

6. Indent the first line of each paragraph. To do this move the cursor over the W of "When". Check that **INSERT ON** is showing in the cursor line at the top of the screen, (if it is not then press ^V to turn INSERT ON), and press ^I to indent the line. This spoils the right justified margin, and you must press ^G to reform the paragraph. Repeat this procedure on the second paragraph which begins "We therefore,".

7. Add the following phrase at the end: "that they are absolved from all Allegiance to the British Crown, and that all political connection between them and the State of Great Britain is and ought to be totally dissolved".

8. Next make the words "all men are created equal" print in bold type. You may do this by manually moving the cursor to the appropriate points and adding ^PB. A better way is to use the editing command ^QF to Find the string, or ^QA to Find and Replace the string. These are explained in chapter 16 - Editing - the Find and Replace Commands. (When searching for a long string of several words it is important to remember that in document files the editing commands will not find a string which is split on to two lines. This is because an invisible carriage return character is inserted in the file at the end of the line, hence the string of characters in the file will not exactly match the string you are searching for. It is therefore safer to use the editor to search for a single word, or even a part of a word).

9. Save the document with a ^KD command, and then print it out with a **P** command from the "No-File" menu. The printout should appear the same as in Figure 24.2.

FIGURE 24.2

PARTS OF THE AMERICAN DECLARATION OF INDEPENDENCE

In Congress, July 4, 1776

The unanimous Declaration of the thirteen united States of America,

When in the course of human events, it becomes necessary for one people to dissolve the political bands which have connected them with another, and to assume among the powers of the earth, the separate and equal station to which the Laws of Nature and of Nature's God entitle them, a decent respect to the opinions of mankind requires that they declare the causes which impel them to the separation. We hold these truths to be self evident, that **all men are created equal**, that they are endowed by their Creator with certain unalienable Rights, that among these are Life, Liberty and the pursuit of Happiness. That to secure these rights, Governments are instituted among Men, deriving their just powers from the consent of the governed. That whenever any form of Government becomes destructive of these ends, it is the Right of the People to alter or abolish it, and to institute new Government, laying its foundation on such principles and organising its powers in such form, as to them shall seem most likely to effect their Safety and Happiness. ...

We therefore, the representatives of the united States of America, in General Congress, assembled, appealing to the Supreme Judge of the world for the rectitude of our intentions, do, in the Name, and by the Authority of the good People of these Colonies, solemnly publish and declare that these United Colonies are, and of Right ought to be Free and Independent States, that they are absolved from all Allegiance to the British Crown, and that all political connection between them and the State of Great Britain is and ought to be totally dissolved.

10 You may have noticed that the word United States is spelt throughout as
united States. This is not a printing error, but is faithfully copied
from the American Declaration of Independence. If you feel that you would
like to teach the Americans some English, or simply to practice the find
and replace command, try the following:

Edit the file USA.TXT and type the command ^QA to find and replace a
string. In reply to the question **FIND?** type **united**, and in reply to the
question **REPLACE BY?** type **United.** Answer the question **OPTIONS?** with **G** for
global replacement. At two places where the string "united" is found, the
program will stop and ask **REPLACE (Y/N).** Type **Y** each time, and the string
will be replaced. Finally, save the file. You have now re-written
history!

Some printers are not capable of micro-spacing, and so cannot implement
bold type. On these you will not see any difference between bold and double
strike. All printers should be able to implement double strike, but the way in
which they do so may vary. Some will print the letter, backspace, and print
the letter again on top of the first, while others will print the whole line
and then come back and print the line again just typing the double strike
letters. Underlining works properly on micro-spacing printers. Most matrix
printers now have descenders (letters which go below the line), and they can
usually underline. Some very cheap matrix printers do not have descenders, and
if they underline at all, they do so by overprinting the bottom line of each
"underlined" character. This type of underlining may print through the
letters, and so make the text nearly illegible. If this happens then you
should either avoid using the underline feature, or alternatively use the
following crude method of underlining. This may always be achieved by pressing
RETURN at the end of the line of text, and then typing spaces and minus signs
where appropriate on the next line to "underline" the text in the line above.

Summary

In this chapter you have practised the following:

1. Opening a document file for editing

2. Changing the right margin

3. Producing bold underlined text

4. Producing bold text

5. Producing double strike text

6. Centring headings and other lines of text

7. Indenting the first line of a paragraph and then reforming it.

8. Using the Find command and the Find and Replace command

9. Saving a file and printing it

Chapter 25.

PAGE LAYOUT

The page layout which is produced automatically by WordStar may fit your requirements, in which case there is no need to change anything. A brief review of some of the basics of page layout is given in this chapter, explaining exactly what this layout is, the default values which are used, and some of the Dot commands which may be used to control or change this layout. All Dot commands must begin with a dot (or full stop) in column one. Further information on these commands is given in chapter 26 - Dot Commands.

Vertical page layout

In the United States, the most commonly used paper size is 8.5 inches wide by 11 inches long. Most typewriters and printers print six lines to the inch in the vertical direction, hence an 11 inch page is equivalent to 66 lines. The paper length is set by default to 66 lines, equivalent to including a .PL 66 command in the file. You can specify a different paper length by including a dot command in the file with .PL followed by the appropriate number. The dot must be in column one. Plainly a margin is needed at both the top and bottom of the page, and by default WordStar has a top margin of three lines (equivalent to a .MT 3 command), and a bottom margin of eight lines (equivalent to a .MB 8 command). The number of lines of text printed on a page is thus:

pagelength - margin at top - margin at bottom

in this case   66   -   3   -   8   =   55 lines.

In Britain the most commonly used paper size is A4, which measures 297 mm. long by 210 mm. wide, or approximately 11.7 inches long by 8.2 inches wide. The paper length should be changed by including a .PL 70 command in the file, corresponding to a paper length of 70 lines. If nothing else is changed then a page will contain 70 - 3 - 8 = 59 lines of text. If the margins at the top or bottom are changed by including appropriate .MT or .MB commands in the file, then the number of lines of text per page will change accordingly.

It is worth examining the bottom margin. The total length of this is eight lines, equivalent to a .MB 8 command. This is made up of two blank lines after the text, a footer which by default includes the page number and occupies one line, followed by 8 - 2 - 1 = 5 more blank lines. If a smaller margin at the bottom is required, the inclusion of a .MB 5 command for example would make the total bottom margin five lines, and would allow 70 - 3 - 5 = 62 lines of text on an A4 page. At the end of the text there would be two blank lines, the page number, followed by 5 - 2 - 1 = 2 more blank lines.

The gap between the text and the page number is called the footer margin, and it is set by default to two lines, equivalent to a .FM 2 command. This gap may be changed to one line with .FM 1, or three lines with .FM 3. Note that changing this command does not affect the number of lines of text per page, it merely affects how the bottom margin is arranged.

In much the same way the top margin is subdivided. The top margin includes a header, and a header margin. A header is a title or heading which is printed at the top of each page. By default this is set to a blank line, but by using a .HM command a one line message can be printed in this line. By default the header margin, that is the space between the header and the first line of text is set to two lines, equivalent to a .HM 2 command. Thus the top margin of three lines is made up of one line of header plus two lines of header margin. Changing the header margin does not change the number of lines of text which will fit on a page, it merely changes the arrangement of the lines in the top margin.

Some printers print at eight lines per inch, and many daisy-wheel printers support micro-spacing, and can vary the vertical spacing of lines in intervals of 1/48th. of an inch. The line height is set by default to 8/48 = 1/6 inch, and this is equivalent to a .LH 8 command. The command .LH 7 sets the spacing to 7/48 = 0.146 inch for one line, or 6.8 lines per inch. Similarly .LH 6 corresponds to 6/48 = 1/8th. inch per line = 8 lines per inch. If the line height is changed, the exact position of the command in relation to other dot commands is important. If first of all the paper length is set to 70 lines, the default line height of 1/6 inch is assumed, and 70 x 1/6 = 11.66 inches. If the line height is then set to .LH 6, that is eight lines per inch, the number of lines on a page becomes 11.66 x 8 = 93. From this the top and bottom margins must be subtracted. This method ensures that the A4 page is filled with as many lines as possible. If instead the line height is set to eight lines per inch before the page length is set to 70 lines, then the page will contain 70 lines at 1/8th. of an inch spacing. This only occupies 8.8 inches, so the A4 page is not filled.

Horizontal page layout

The maximum length of a line is shown by the ruler line while editing is in progress, and this is set by default to 65 characters. Many typewriters and printers print ten characters per inch along a line, so 65 characters occupy 6.5 inches. With the American paper 8.5 inches wide, this leaves one inch margin at the both the left and the right hand sides. If the ruler is not changed, then using A4 paper which is 8.2 inches wide, the total for both margins is 1.7 inches, perhaps eight spaces on the left and seven on the right. To retain a one inch margin at both left and right, the ruler must be reduced in length to 62 characters. This may be done by changing the right margin using a ^OR 62 command before the document is typed. If the document is subsequently edited, and requires the reforming of one or more paragraphs, then the right margin must again be reset to 62 before reforming a paragraph, or some text will have lines 62 characters wide, and others the default width of 65. The ruler may be reset either by using the ^OR 62 command as before, or a very simple way is to put the cursor on any full line in the original document, and pressing ^OF, which resets the ruler to match the text.

Some typewriters and printers print twelve characters per inch, and many daisy-wheel printers support micro-spacing, and allow the horizontal spacing to be varied in intervals of 1/120th. of an inch. The WordStar default of ten characters per inch is equivalent to including a .CW 12 command to set the character width to 12/120 inch = 1/10th. inch per character. Including the command .CW 10 sets the character width to 10/120 inch = 1/12th. inch per character, or twelve characters per inch. Other possibilities are discussed in chapter 26 - Dot Commands. When printing at twelve characters to the inch, a line of 65 characters occupies only 65/12 = 5.42 inches, which on A4 paper leaves 8.2 - 5.4 = 2.8 inches for the margins. These margins are probably too wide, and to obtain one inch margins at both sides, the length of lines should be increased to 8.2 - 1 - 1 = 6.2 inches, or 6.2 x 12 = 74.4 characters. The ruler should therefore be reset with a ^OR 74 command before the document is typed, or before paragraphs are reformed.

Similar calculations should be done for A5 paper, which measures approximately 8.2 inches long by 5.8 inches wide. At the usual six lines per inch, the page length is 8.2 x 6 = 49.2 lines, and a .PL 49 command is needed. The page width is 5.8 inches, and allowing a margin of 0.9 inch at either side, this leaves 4 inches for text. Printing at 10 characters per inch, the length of a line should be set to 4 x 10 = 40 characters using a ^OR 40 command before typing the document. To print at 12 characters per inch, the length of the line should be set to 4 x 12 = 48 characters, using a ^OR 48 command.

The position where characters are actually printed on the paper may need moving sideways. This can be done most easily by changing the page offset, but the same effect can be achieved by changing the left margin. The page offset can be changed at any time, but the margin must be set before the text is typed. The page offset is the number of columns that text is moved across from the left side of the printer. The default value for the page offset is eight columns, equivalent to having a **.PO 8** command in the file. This may be changed to any suitable value. This offset is in addition to any which may be caused if the left margin of the ruler has been reset from its original value of column one.

FIGURE 25.1 Page layout

Default values

.PL	paper length	66 lines
.MT	margin at top	3 lines
.MB	margin at bottom	8 lines
.HM	header margin	2 lines
.FM	footer margin	2 lines
.PO	page offset	8 characters
	left margin	column 1
	right margin	column 65
.CW	character width	12 = 10 characters per inch
.LH	line height	8 = 6 lines per inch

Chapter 26.

DOT COMMANDS

A number of special print features have already been described in chapter 23. In addition to these, WordStar provides a large number of dot commands, which will allow you to modify the layout of a document to your exact requirements. They are called dot commands because they must begin with a full stop in column 1. These commands are all optional. An entire document can be typed and printed without using any of them, provided that the layout and features provided by default are acceptable. Dot commands are embedded in the text of the document, and they should occupy a whole line, since any text on the command line other than the command itself will be ignored. Though they show on the vdu screen, they are not printed. Most of the commands may occur anywhere in the text, though a few must appear at the beginning of a file. A summary of the dot commands can be obtained by typing ^J to get the help menu, and then typing ^D to select information on dot commands. If ^JD is typed without a pause, then the help menu is not displayed, but information about the dot commands is given straight away. Typing an incorrect or non-existent dot command will cause a question mark to be displayed at the extreme right of the screen, but erroneous commands are ignored, and are not printed.

Comments or remarks .. or .CO

It is easy to add a comment or remark in a file, simply by typing .. or .CO starting in column one. Anything typed on this line will be ignored, and will not be printed. It is useful to add such comments to document the file, giving the date when the file was last altered, who it was typed for, or a reminder of parts which are missing, or need correcting. If a line that starts with a dot in column one is not a valid dot command, it is treated as a comment.

Paper Length .PL

This defines the physical length of a page of paper as the maximum number of lines which it can hold. The default value for paper length is 66, which has the same effect as including a .PL 66 command. The actual number of lines of text printed on the page is less than this because some space is needed for margins at both the top and bottom of the page. The number of text lines on a page is calculated as the paper length PL, minus the top margin MT, minus the bottom margin MB. Unless the default values for any of these three terms are changed, the number of lines of text printed on a page will be 66 - 3 - 8 = 55. Should you wish to get as much text as possible on A4 paper, use .PL 70 for a paper length of 70 lines, giving 70 - 3 - 8 = 59 lines of text per page.

If this command is used, it is important that it is placed right at the beginning of a file, before any text, and preferably before any other dot commands, or page breaks will be displayed in the wrong place on the screen.

Margin at the Top .MT

This sets the top margin, that is the number of blank lines at the top of the page before text is printed. The default value is 3, which is equivalent to including a .MT 3 command. This may be changed, and for example .MT 4 will increase the top margin to 4 lines, but at the same time it will decrease the number of lines of text printed on the page. If however the top margin is increased by 1 and the bottom margin is reduced by 1, then the number of lines of text on a page will remain the same - but they will appear lower down the page. WordStar has a feature which will print a running heading (that is a page heading) at the top of every page. The heading, and the heading margin if used, will appear in the top margin. If a .MT command is used, then it must appear at the beginning of the file, before any text, otherwise the page breaks will be incorrectly displayed on the screen.

Margin at the Bottom .MB

This is the number of lines at the bottom of the page which are not used for text. The page number is usually printed in this space, and if the Word-Star option to print a footing (a message at the bottom of every page), is used then this too will appear in this space. The default value is 8 lines, equivalent to a .MB 8 command. If it is required to get the maximum number of lines on a page, and footings are not used, then the bottom margin can be reduced to 5 lines with a .MB 5 command. If at the same time a .PL 70 command is used (for A4 paper), then the number of lines of text per page is:

$$PL - MT - MB \quad = \quad 70 - 3 - 5 \quad = \quad 62$$

If a .MB command is used, it must appear at the beginning of the file before any text, otherwise page breaks will be incorrectly displayed on the screen.

Page Offset .PO

The page offset command .PO followed by a number is used to control where printing will occur on the paper in a lateral direction. The number indicates how many columns the entire text will be indented, that is moved from the left margin of the printer, or the left-hand edge of the paper. If the ruler has not been changed then this is the total amount of indentation. The default value is to indent all text by 8 columns, equivalent to a .PO 8 command. If the left margin of the ruler has been reset with an ^OL command, then text is indented this additional amount as well. The page offset may be changed to to provide a wider space at the left so that sheets may be bound in a book or file. The command is also useful if a single sheet paper feeder is used on the printer, since these are fitted in the middle of the carriage, rather than at the left-hand side.

Page breaks .PA and conditional page breaks .CP

At any point in a document you may decide that you would like to start a new page. This can be achieved by typing .PA followed by **RETURN**, starting in column 1 on a new line, and text following this will start on a new page. These unconditional page breaks are often used either at the end of a chapter or at the end of a section, and may also be used where a full page is required for a drawing, graph or photograph on the next page.

There are other occasions where a conditional page break is required. For example, when typing a table it is generally better to get the whole table on the same page, rather than having part at the bottom of one page and part at the top of the next page. Suppose that there are 10 lines in the table, including the table heading, then a .CP 10 command starting in column 1 of the line immediately preceding the table heading will ensure that if there are less than 10 lines left on the current page, then a new page will be started before printing the table.

This command is also useful just before headings. Suppose that after the heading there is a blank line, followed by the lines of text, similar to the layout of this page. It would look badly arranged if the heading came at the bottom of a page, and the text on the next page. If a .CP 3 command is typed on the line before the heading, you can ensure that there is room for three lines on the current page, that is the heading, the blank line, and one line of text. If there are not three blank lines left on the current page, then heading, blank and text will start on the next page. It may be that you would like to ensure that there is room to print the heading, blank line and at least two or even three lines of text. In this case, a .CP 4 or a .CP 5 command should be used, but it should be remembered that this will increase the chance of leaving a noticeable amount of unfilled space at the bottom of a page.

Omit Pagenumbers .OP, Page Numbers .PN and Page number Column .PC

By default WordStar numbers pages at the bottom when they are printed, starting with page 1, 2, 3 ... and so on. These page numbers are not displayed at the bottom of the page on the screen, but they are displayed in the status line of the screen. For some purposes it would be better if page numbers are not printed, for example on a letter which only occupies one page. The .OP command (starting in column 1) suppresses the printing of page numbers. The command may also be used to suppress printing page numbers at the bottom of a page when special steps have been taken to print the page number as part of the heading or footing.

It is possible that a page number was not required on the first page (title page) of a document, but that the subsequent pages should be numbered. If a .PN command is inserted after the first page, this will switch page numbering on, and subsequent pages will be numbered starting from 1.

Sometimes you might like page numbering to start with a page number other than 1, for example page 15. This is simply achieved by typing .PN 15. (The maximum page number which WordStar can handle is 65,533 - a limit which is unlikely to affect many users, though some word-processors cannot handle page numbers bigger than 255). The .PN feature may be useful if a large document is stored as more than one file. If the appropriate command, for example .PN 15 is inserted at the beginning of the second file, then it can be printed with the pages correctly numbered (starting 15, 16, ...), so that they follow on sequentially from pages in the first file. It must be noted that though this command affects the page numbers printed out, it does not affect the page numbers displayed in the status line on the screen. Thus the first page of the second file mentioned above will show in the status line on the screen as page 1, but will be printed out numbered page 15.

By default page numbers are printed at the bottom centre of a page. The default position is set as column 33, corresponding to the centre of a page containing 65 characters per line (the default page width). If the page width has been changed for example to 50 characters wide with a .OR 50 command, then a .PC 25 command should be used to print the page number centrally.

Micro-justification on or off .UJ

By default micro-justification is switched ON. This means that any "soft" spaces added to a line to justify the right margin are printed on daisy wheel printers as many small or micro-spaces of 1/120th of an inch, which are evenly distributed along the line. This improves the look of the text. There are occasions, particularly with tables, when you would like text printing out exactly as it was lined up on the screen. If inadvertently some "soft" spaces have got into the table through word wrap, or reforming with ^B, then even though the table looks correctly lined up on the screen, micro-justification will spoil the table when it is printed. This can be avoided by turning micro-justification off before the table with a .UJ 0 command (beginning in column 1), and turning it on again with a .UJ 1 command after the table. (Some versions of WordStar use slightly different commands .UJ OFF and .UJ ON instead).

Headings .HE and Heading Margins .HM

The initial (default) heading is a blank, so by default no heading is printed. If the command .HE is typed starting in column 1, then any further text on that line will be used as the heading, and will be printed on each of the following pages, or until another .HE command is encountered. For example the command:

.HE Part 1.

would print Part 1. at the top of each page, until another .HE command is encountered:

.HE Part 2.

This would print the heading Part 2. at the top of each page, and so on.

To obtain a heading on the first page, the .HE command must come before all the text. Apart from this, heading commands may appear anywhere in the text (provided that the . falls in column 1). Headings may be changed as often as required, and they may contain bold type, underlined text, or any other print enhancement. If after using a heading for one section of a document, a later section is required without a heading, then this is accomplished by inserting a blank heading with .HE and no text. It is essential to leave a space between the .HE command and the heading. Thus when composing a heading, and working out where it will appear, it is important to remember that since the .HE and a space will not print, the heading itself will be printed four columns to the left of where it is displayed on the screen.

It may be required to print the page numbers at the top of the page, rather than at the bottom. This is easily accomplished by giving a .HE command with a # symbol at the position where the page number is to be printed. At the same time an .OP command must be included to suppress the printing of page numbers at the bottom of the page. If the pages are only printed on one side, they will all be right-hand pages. Assuming that the number of characters in a line is set at 65, the page number should be printed in column 65. Since there are four "wasted" characters for .HE and a space, sufficient spaces should be typed to make the # sign (for printing the page number) appear in column 4 + 65 = 69.

```
      .HE                                                                      #
col.  123456789012345678901234567890123456789012345678901234567890123456789 0
```

Including page numbers in the heading is a little more complicated when the pages are printed on both sides as in a proper book. Pages are normally numbered at the side furthest away from the binding. There are now both right-hand and left-hand pages. The first page is always a right-hand page, and this should be numbered at the right. The second page is a left-hand page, which should be numbered at the left. In general, all odd numbered pages should be numbered at the right, and all even numbered pages numbered at the left. A special command ^P^K may be included in the heading. When this is typed in a heading (or a footing - see later) the characters ^K appear on the screen, and if the page number is even this command suppresses the printing of spaces after the command right up to the next printing character. The printing of spaces in the heading is not affected when the page number is odd. Extending the example above, with 65 characters per line, the page number should appear starting in column 65 on odd numbered pages, and starting in column 1 on even numbered pages. There are now six "wasted" characters on the screen, .HE space ^ and K. The # sign (for printing the page number) should appear in column 65 + 6 = 71.

```
      .HE ^K                                                                   #
col.  1234567890123456789012345678901234567890123456789012345678901234567890 12
```

The example above prints page numbers in left and right headings with spaces suppressed where necessary. This can be extended from just printing the page number to printing a heading line which contains text, or text and the page number, and the command ^P^K will work equally well.

If you would like to print a # symbol as part of a heading, it will be confused with the symbol to print the page number. To overcome this, the backslash symbol \ may be used before the # to print the next character literally, without interpreting it as a control symbol. This feature allows the printing of characters which normally do not appear. To print a \, it is necessary to type \\.

It is possible to control the number of blank lines between the heading and the first line of text, using the header margin .HM command. The heading is printed in the margin at the top .MT. This has the default value of three lines. The header margin .HM has a default of two lines. Thus the heading will be printed on the top line of the page, followed by two blank lines, and then followed by the text. If instead .MT was set for six, and .HM for three, then there will be two blank lines before the header, and three after it.

Footings .FO and Footing Margins .FM

Footings are very similar to headings, except that they are printed at the bottom of the page rather than the top. They begin .FO followed by a space, and then optionally by a message, or spaces and a # symbol to print the page number. They differ in that if a footer is not specified, then the default is a line with the page number printed in the middle (actually in column 33, unless you have reset the column with a .PC command, or unless the printing of page numbers at the bottom has been suppressed with an .OP command). If a footer is included, the text in the .FO command will be printed on every page until it is cancelled by another .FO command, and the page numbers are not automatically printed. This may be what is required if page numbers are printed as part of the heading, but alternatively the page number can be printed as part of your footer, by including a # at the appropriate column. If alternating page numbers are required at the bottom right of right- handed pages, and the bottom left of left-hand pages, this can be handled using the ^P^K command in the same way as for headings.

The footer is printed within the bottom margin. The margin at the bottom .MB is set by default to 8 lines, and how this space is used is explained below. The footer margin .FM has a default value of two lines, and is used to give two blank lines after the last line of text at the bottom of the page. The footer is printed on the next line. Thus with these default settings, the last line of text is followed by two blank lines (from .FM), then the footer, and then five more blank lines, which adds up to the eight lines set by .MB. The values of .MB and .FM may be changed as required.

Line Height .LH

The command ^OS, (described in chapter 23 - Special Print Effects), provides a means of producing double or triple spacing on all types of printer. It has two disadvantages: first it results in fewer lines being displayed on the screen, and second it does not permit small changes in vertical spacing.

The .LH command provides a more sophisticated way of changing the vertical spacing of lines on printers capable of micro-spacing. These can move vertically in intervals of 1/48th inch, hence the line spacing may be adjusted in intervals of 1/48th of an inch, rather than in whole lines. Furthermore, the use of an .LH command does not reduce the number of lines displayed on the screen. The default line height is set at 8, equivalent to a .LH 8 command. This corresponds to a spacing of 8/48 = 1/6th of an inch per line, that is 6 lines per inch. The effect of various .LH commands is shown in Figure 26.1.

FIGURE 26.1 Line heights

Command	lines/inch	Command	lines/inch	Command	lines/inch
.LH 1	48.0	.LH 8	6.0 (single)	.LH 16	3.0 (double)
.LH 4	12.0	.LH 9	5.3	.LH 18	2.6
.LH 6	8.0	.LH 10	4.8	.LH 20	2.4
.LH 7	6.8	.LH 12	4.0	.LH 24	2.0 (triple)

When the line height is changed, any previously specified commands about the vertical format, such as the paper length and margins remain unaffected. However, any subsequent commands such as .PL, .MT, .MB, .HM and .FM will be interpreted in terms of the new line height. Thus it is essential to consider the order of .LH and the other commands. For example if the paper length is set to 70 with .PL 70 (by default single spaced lines are assumed), then the line height is set to 3 lines per inch (double spacing) with .LH 16, then ignoring the margins at the top and bottom there would be room for 35 double spaced lines on a page. If however the commands were in the other order, that is .LH 16 first and then .PL 70, the page would be set for 70 double spaced lines - rather a long page!

The line height may be changed as many times as you wish throughout the document, and it will be printed exactly as specified. However, this confuses the page break display on the screen, and page breaks will be displayed in the wrong place. If you wish to change line spacing in mid document it is a good idea to turn the page break display off by typing ^OP, which will avoid confusion. If the page breaks are to be displayed correctly then the line height may only be set at the beginning of the file, and may not be changed later.

It is possible to obtain varying line heights without interfering with the correct display of page breaks. Suppose that you really require some of the document in single spacing, and some in one and a half spacing. At the very beginning of the document, or immediately after the paper length has been set, the line height is set to 4 with a .LH 4 command. (This corresponds to 12 lines per inch, or 1/12th inch per line, which is half the normal spacing). The command ^OS 2 described in chapter 23 - Special Print Effects will produce double spacing, but since you have set the line height to half its usual value, in reality this will be printed at 2/12 = 1/6th inch per line which is normal single spacing. In the same way ^OS 3 will give triple spacing, which in this case will print at 3/12th of an inch per line which is normal one and a half spacing. Similarly ^OS 4 would result in text being printed at 4/12 = 1/3rd inch per line which is normal double spacing. A disadvantage of the ^OS command is that it reduces the number of lines of text displayed on the screen.

Character Width .CW

Chapter 23 - Special Print Effects describes how the commands ^PA and ^PN can be used to select the alternate pitch (which is set by default to 12 characters per inch), or the normal character pitch (which has the default of 10 characters per inch). These commands will only work if WordStar has been properly installed (using the program INSTALL), for the particular printer being used. The advantage of these commands is that they will work on many of the cheaper dot matrix printers which do not support micro-spacing, as well as daisy wheel printers capable of micro-spacing. However, the micro-spacing printers can produce more subtle changes in spacing with the .CW command, but these have no effect on non-micro-spacing printers.

The character width is measured as the number of 1/120ths of an inch allocated to each character. This unit of distance is chosen because this is the smallest horizontal distance which printers with micro-spacing can move. The default for standard pitch is 12, equivalent to a command .CW 12. This corresponds to 12/120 = 1/10th of an inch per character, or a pitch of 10 characters per inch, which is the spacing used for Pica or Courier type. The alternative pitch has a default of 10, equivalent to .CW 10, giving a spacing of 10/120 = 1/12th of an inch per character, or a pitch of 12 characters per inch which is the spacing used for Elite type. To print at 15 characters per inch, a .CW 8 command must be included in the file, with the dot in column one, since 8/120 = 1/15th of an inch per character. The spacings which can be produced by various .CW commands are given in Figure 26.2.

FIGURE 26.2 Dot commands and spacings

Dot command	Characters/inch	Dot command	Characters/inch
.CW 6	20	.CW 13	9.2
.CW 7	17.1	.CW 14	8.6
.CW 8	15	.CW 15	8
.CW 9	13.3	.CW 16	7.5
.CW 10	12 (alternative-pitch)	.CW 17	7
.CW 11	10.9	.CW 20	6
.CW 12	10 (normal pitch)	.CW 24	5

A further use for the .CW command is to change the pitch, so that the letters are spread out more than usual. This can be used to emphasize headings, as illustrated in Figure 26.3. It can equally well be used to print characters slightly closer together to give a compact look, and get more text on a page. These features are illustrated using a print wheel which is designed for use at 12 characters per inch, but where the spacing is deliberately being altered.

FIGURE 26.3 Use of .CW commands

The line below shows the printout produced by a 12 character per inch daisy wheel that was set to print at 13.3 characters per inch by a .CW 9 command.
WORDPROCESSING USING WORDSTAR MAILMERGE AND SPELLSTAR

Now it is set to print at 12 characters per inch by a .CW 10 command.
WORDPROCESSING USING WORDSTAR MAILMERGE AND SPELLSTAR

Now it is set to print at 10 characters per inch by a .CW 12 command.
WORDPROCESSING USING WORDSTAR MAILMERGE AND SPELLSTAR

Now it is set to print at 9.2 characters per inch by a .CW 13 command.
WORDPROCESSING USING WORDSTAR MAILMERGE AND SPELLSTAR

Now it is set to print at 8.6 characters per inch by a .CW 14 command.
WORDPROCESSING USING WORDSTAR MAILMERGE AND SPELLS

Now it is set to print at 8 characters per inch by a .CW 15 command.
WORDPROCESSING USING WORDSTAR MAILMERGE AND SPE

Subscript Roll and Superscript Roll .SR

Daisy wheel printers roll the paper down to print a superscript, and roll the paper up to produce a subscript. The amount of roll is measured in 1/48ths of an inch. The default value is 3, equivalent to a command of .SR 3, and this rolls the paper 3/48ths of an inch. Some of the modern matrix printers can do this too. If the line spacing is the default of 6 lines per inch, one line occupies 1/6th of an inch (that is 8/48ths of an inch) so the amount of roll is 3/8ths of a line. If the line spacing is different, the amount of roll may need changing. Alternatively it may be useful to change the amount of roll to half a line with a .SR 4 command, so that mathematical equations may be typed with the top line superscripted and the bottom line subscripted as illustrated below.

$$I = \frac{E}{R}$$

this was typed as
.SR 4

I = ---^PH^PH^PTE^PT^PH^PVR^PV

Chapter 27.

PRACTICE IN CHANGING THE PAGE LAYOUT

1. Load WordStar and open a document file called HHGG.TXT. By default the left margin is set to column 1, and the right margin to column 65. Change the right margin to column 79 by typing ^OR79 and pressing **RETURN**. Then type in the information given in Figure 27.1. Save the file on the disk with a ^KD command.

FIGURE 27.1

Extracts from The Hitch Hiker's guide to the Galaxy

The Hitch Hiker's guide to the Galaxy is a wholly remarkable book. It has been compiled and recompiled many times over many years and under many different editorships. It contains contributions from countless numbers of travellers and researchers.

The Hitch Hiker's guide to the Galaxy says that if you hold a lungful of air you can survive in the total vacuum of space for about thirty seconds. However it does go on to say that what with space being the mind boggling size it is the chances of getting picked up by another ship within those thirty seconds are two to the power of two hundred and sixty-seven thousand seven hundred and nine to one against.

The Hitch Hiker's guide to the Galaxy also mentions alcohol. It says that the best drink in existence is the Pan Galactic Gargle Blaster. It says that the effect of drinking a Pan Galactic Gargle Blaster is like having your brains smashed out by a slice of lemon wrapped round a large gold brick.

The fabulously beautiful planet Bethselamin is now so worried about the cumulative erosion by ten billion visiting tourists a year that any net imbalance between the amount you eat and the amount you excrete whilst on the planet is surgically removed from your bodyweight when you leave: so every time you go to the lavatory there it is vitally important to get a receipt.

"The Babel fish" said the Hitch Hiker's Guide to the Galaxy quietly, "is small, yellow and leech like, and probably the oddest thing in the Universe. It feeds on brainwave energy received not from its own carrier but from those around it. It absorbs all unconscious mental frequencies from this brainwave energy to nourish itself with. It then excretes into the mind of its carrier a telepathic matrix formed by combining the conscious thought frequencies with nerve signals picked up from the speech centres of the brain which has supplied them. The practical upshot of this is that if you stick a Babel fish in your ear you can instantly understand anything said to you in any form of language. ... Meanwhile, the poor Babel fish, by effectively removing all barriers to communication between different races and cultures, has caused more and bloodier wars than anything else in the history of creation.

2. Print the file, and if your printer prints 10 characters per inch you will find that the length of each line is 79 characters multiplied by the character width of 1/10th. inch, which equals 7.9 inches. There are incidentally 36 lines printed including the heading.

3. Note that the page number 1 is printed at the bottom of the page in column 33. This would be at the bottom centre of the page if you were using the default page width of 65 characters, but since you have reset the right margin, the page number column must also be reset with a .PC40 command. Edit the file, insert this command at the beginning, save the file, and print it again.

4. Next change the page width to 51 characters. This can be done by opening the file for editing with a D command from the "No-File" menu, and

changing the right margin with a ^OR51 command. Before reforming to the new size, switch hyphen-help OFF with a ^OH command. This will stop WordStar attempting to hyphenate words which do not quite fit on a line. Each paragraph must then be reformed in turn with a ^B command. Move the cursor to the beginning of the file with a ^QR command, delete the .PC40 line with a ^Y command, and insert a .OP command at the beginning to omit page numbers. Save the file, and print it. You will find that there are now 54 lines including the heading, lines are 5.1 inches wide (if your printer prints 10 characters per inch), and that the page is not numbered.

5. Now you can alter the document to fit on to A5 paper. This measures approximately 5.7 inches wide by 8.7 inches in length. Often to get the maximum text on a page you may set a margin of 0.8 inches at the left and right, leaving 4.1 inches for text. At 10 characters per inch, this is 41 characters, which can be set with a ^OR41 command. Instead of this leave 1 inch margins, giving 3.7 inches for text. Edit the file, and type ^OR37 to reset the page width to 37 characters. Each paragraph will have to be reformed, but before doing this you should reset the page length. By default this is set to 66 lines, and the default setting for the top margin is 3 lines, and the bottom margin is 8 lines. Thus a page normally has 66 - 3 - 8 = 55 lines of text. Here the paper is 8.7 inches long, and printing at 6 lines per inch this gives a paper length of 8.7 multiplied by 6 = 52 lines. At the beginning of the file you should type a .PL52 command to reset the paper length. Now reform each paragraph with ^B. You will find that the heading is now split on to two lines, and is not centred. Tidy this up by placing the cursor on each of these two lines in turn, and centring them with ^OC commands. The document now occupies two pages, and you will see the page break of a line of dashes showing where this occurs. The first page is completely full and holds 41 lines, whilst the second page is partly full with 30 lines. The 41 lines arises from the paper length (52) less the top margin (3), less the bottom margin (8). Save the file with a ^KD command, print it, and check that the layout is as described.

6. Next you should try the effect of changing the margin at the top of the page, and the margin at the bottom of the page using .MT and .MB commands. The default settings are .MT3 and .MB8, giving a margin of 3 lines at the top, and 8 lines at the bottom. First open the document file HHGG.TXT and one line below the existing command .PL52 insert the command .MT6 on one line, and .MB5 on the next line. Save the file with a ^KD command, print it, and compare it with the previous printout. You will find that increasing the top margin by three lines, and decreasing the bottom margin by three lines results in exactly the same number of lines being printed on each page, but the text is printed three lines lower down the page. A change of this sort is therefore useful to alter the vertical position of printing on the page.

7. Now edit the file again and change the .MT and .MB commands by different amounts, or only change one of them. Change the commands to .MT2 and .MB3. Save the file, and print it. You will find that the number of lines printed on a page has changed, as well as the position on the page. The maximum number of lines printed on a page is PL - MT - MB, which in this case is 52 - 2 - 3 = 47.

8. Next you can practise the use of the .CP conditional page break, and the .PA unconditional page break. In the printout obtained from the exercise in paragraph 7, you will observe that the page break occurs where indicated by the line of dashes:

> "The Babel fish" said the Hitch
> --
> Hiker's Guide to the Galaxy quietly,

Since "The Babel fish" ... starts a new paragraph, and only one line of this paragraph is printed at the bottom of the page, you may prefer to change the layout to make the paragraph start on a new page. This may be achieved in two ways. First move the cursor over the quotation mark " which precedes The Babel fish, check that INSERT is ON, and type **.PA** and press **RETURN**. Instantly the effect of putting a page break in the file is displayed on the screen. Thus there is no need to print the file to see where the page break occurs:

```
------------------------------------------------
"The Babel fish" said the Hitch
Hiker's Guide to the Galaxy quietly,
```

Now replace the **.PA** command by a **.CP3** command. This forces a page break unless there is room for at least three lines on the present page. Since there is in fact only room for one line, a page break will occur exactly as described for the **.PA** command. The advantage of the **.CP** command is that if you subsequently add text, change margins, or reform the text differently, it will cause a page break only if there is not room for the specified number of lines. Save the file with **^KD**.

9. Next practise numbering the pages at the top right hand corner of the page, rather than at the bottom and in the centre. To do this you must have a **.OP** command to suppress page numbering at the bottom, and a **.HE** command with a hash symbol # in the column where you want the page number to be printed. Open the file HHGG.TXT for editing. The file already contains a **.OP** command, so you only need to add the **.HE** command. The file has been formatted with the right margin set at column 37. You would like to print the page number in column 37 to line up with the right margin. Insert the line given below, before any text in the file, with the dot in column 1, and starting on a new line:

```
.HE                                      #
```

The command begins with **.HE** and one space, which occupies 4 columns. You want the page number in column 37, so you must type spaces after the .HE and put the # in column 4 + 37 = column 41. (The column occupied by the cursor is shown in the status line at the top of the screen). The file will be displayed on the screen as shown in Figure 27.2.

FIGURE 27.2

```
.PL 52
.MT 2
.MB 3
.HE                                      #
        ^BExtracts from The Hitch
    Hiker's guide to the Galaxy^B

The Hitch Hiker's guide to the Galaxy
is a wholly remarkable book.  It has
```

Save the file, and then print it. It will look like Figure 27.3.

94

FIGURE 27.3

1

**Extracts from The Hitch
Hiker's guide to the Galaxy**

The Hitch Hiker's guide to the Galaxy
is a wholly remarkable book. It has

It should be noted that if you try to include page numbers at the top of the page as just described, and you have not altered the margins, the right margin is set by default to column 65. The **.HE** command should therefore have the # symbol in column 4 + 65 = column 69. **Since the right margin is set to column 65, you will not be allowed to type up to column 69, and after column 65, you will start on a new line!** To overcome this, you should use the margin release command **^OX** before you try to type the **.HE** command.

10. Now alter the file to make it print odd page numbers at the top right of the page, and even page numbers at the top left of the page. This arrangement is needed when you are producing a book with printing on both sides of the paper. Edit the file HHGG.TXT and move the cursor to column 5 of the **.HE** command line, that is after **.HE** and a space. Type **^PK** and save the file. Print it to check that the page numbers do alternate.

11. Lastly, alter the file so that it will print a heading at the top of each page. Edit the file HHGG.TXT and replace the existing **.HE** command which printed the page numbers by the following line:

  .HE Hitch Hiker's Guide

Save the document, and print it.

Summary

In this chapter you have practised the following:

1. Changing the right margin, and hence the page width.

2. Switching the hyphen-help toggle OFF so that WordStar does not try to hyphenate words.

3. Changing the column where the page number is printed at the bottom of the page.

4. Omitting page numbers at the bottom of the page.

5. Centring a line of text.

6. Changing the page length, and the margins at the top and bottom of a page.

7. Using conditional and unconditional page breaks.

8. Printing page numbers at the top of the page, both for one sided and two sided printing.

9. Printing a heading at the top of every page.

Chapter 28.
ON-SCREEN FORMATTING - MARGIN, TABS AND RULER

One of the most outstanding features of WordStar, which makes it superior to most other word-processing programs, is that it implements on-screen formatting. This means that as text is typed in it is displayed on the screen, laid out as it will appear when printed. If the layout is unsatisfactory, then this is immediately obvious, and it is easy to change it and re-examine it repeatedly until it is acceptable. (Other word-processing programs must have the formatting and layout commands embedded in the text. Since these commands are only carried out when the file is printed on paper, you have the slow and possibly wasted task of printing the file to check the layout).

WordStar initially assigns default values to set the width of the page, the number of lines per page, the spacing, and the tab settings. These values have been chosen to be useful when typing on A4 paper, and this chapter explains how they can be altered to fit other sizes. Other features such as word-wrap, micro-justification, and automatic hyphenation are initially set switched ON by their default values. Any of these default values may be changed if required, using simple commands which are described in the next chapter. When any of the default values are changed, then WordStar will reformat the text on the screen showing how it will appear when printed.

The on-screen formatting commands are all given in the ^O menu, which may be displayed simply by typing ^O. The menu is shown in Figure 28.1, and the features described in this chapter are shown in bold type. All of the commands comprise two characters, ^O and another letter. If the two letters are typed in quick succession, then the command is implemented without delay. If however there is a pause after the ^O, then provided you are at Help levels 3 or 2 the On-Screen menu will be displayed. This causes a time delay, but is useful if you have forgotten what letter to type next. When the required letter is typed, then the On-Screen menu disappears, and the command is implemented.

FIGURE 28.1 The ^O Menu

```
^O      B:LETTER.TXT  PAGE 1 LINE 1 COL 01            INSERT ON
                      < < < O N S C R E E N   M E N U  > > >
 -Margins & Tabs-  | -Line Functions- |  --More Toggles--  |  -Other Menus-
L Set left margin  |C Centre text     |J Justify   off (ON)|  (from Main only)
R Set right margin |S Set line spacing|V Vari-tabs off (ON)|^J Help  ^K Block
X Release margins  |                  |H Hyph-help off (ON)|^Q Quick ^P Print
I Set N Clear tab  |    ---Toggles--- |E Soft hyph on (OFF)|^O Onscreen
G Paragraph tab    |W Wrd wrap off (ON)|D Prnt disp off (ON)|Space Bar returns
F Ruler from line  |T Rlr line off (ON)|P Pge break off (ON)|you to Main Menu.
L----!----!----!----!----!----!----!----!----!----!----!--------R
```

The ruler line

The ruler line is displayed on the screen, and is shown in Figure 28.2. This indicates the width of a line of text, (that is the maximum number of characters on a line), and also the extreme positions where the cursor may move, and hence the position where typing may occur on a page.

FIGURE 28.2 The ruler line

L----!----!----!----!----!----!----!----!----!----!----!--------R

This line is set to a default size of 65 letters, beginning with a letter L in column 1, and a letter R in column 65. The - signs indicate spaces, and the ! signs are tab settings, which occur after 5 spaces (in columns 6,11,16,21,26,31,36,41,46,51 and 56). The length of the ruler controls the line length, and may be altered by changing either the left margin, the right margin, or both. The tabs may be used exactly as they are, or alternatively some or all of these tabs may be removed, and additional tabs inserted in different positions if required.

Altering the margin settings ^OF, ^OL and ^OR

There is a particularly easy way of setting both left and right margins simultaneously, to match the margins used in some text which has previously been typed. To do this, simply move the cursor to any position on the line to be matched, and type ^OF. There are no messages and no delays, and this is a very valuable command for the experienced user.

The command ^OL is used to set the left margin. When this is typed, a message appears on the screen:

LEFT MARGIN COLUMN NUMBER (ESCAPE for cursor column)?

If for example you would like your typing to start in column 6, giving a wider left margin, then you should type 6 and press RETURN. The ruler line will change as shown in Figure 28.3.

FIGURE 28.3   Original and changed ruler lines

Original
```
L----!----!----!----!----!----!----!----!----!----!----!--------R
1234567890123456789012345678901234567890123456789012345678901234 5
```

Changed
```
     !----!----!----!----!----!----!----!----!----!----!--------R
```

Any text which is typed now will start at the first position on the ruler, that is in column 6. The letter A of Any (at the beginning of this paragraph) appears under the ! in column 6. In much the same way the last letter on a line falls under the letter R at the right hand edge of the ruler.

Suppose that you would like to edit an existing WordStar document which had been typed with the left margin reset in this way. Rather than count how many columns the margin had been moved, and reset the margin manually as just described, WordStar will do the counting for you. The procedure is to move the cursor on top of the first character in a line. For example in the paragraph above you could choose the A of Any (in the first line), the o of on (in the second line), the (at the start of the third line and so on. The number of the column occupied by the cursor is indicated in the top (status) line of the screen. Then type ^OL to set the left margin, followed by the column number just obtained from the status line. An even simpler way is to position the cursor as above, and then to type ^OL and press **ESCAPE** which makes WordStar set the margin to the column in which the cursor is positioned.

If you are not quite sure how to reset the margin, and you type ^O and wait a few seconds, then provided that you are at Help level 3 or 2 the on screen menu will be read from the disk and displayed on the screen. When you type L and either a number or **ESCAPE** there will be a further time delay while the On-Screen menu is replaced by text. If however you are confident, and type ^OL quickly, then WordStar will not bother to display the On-Screen menu, and the ruler is changed in much the same way as previously, except that the change is much more rapid.

The command ^OR is used to reset the right margin. When this is typed, a message appears on the screen:

RIGHT MARGIN COLUMN NUMBER (ESCAPE for cursor column)?

A number must now be typed to indicate the column number for the right hand margin. Suppose you would like to set the right margin to column 53, you should type 53 and press **RETURN.** The original ruler, the one with the left margin changed, and the latest one with both the left and right margins changed are shown in Figure 28.4.

FIGURE 28.4

Original ruler
L——!——!——!——!——!——!——!——!——!——!——!————————R

Left margin set
!——!——!——!——!——!——!——!——!——!——!——!————————R

Left and right margins set
!——!——!——!——!——!——!——!——!——!——!——!-R

In exactly the same way as described for setting the left margin, if there is an appreciable delay in between typing ^O and R then the On-Screen menu will be displayed, provided that the Help level is set to 3 or 2. If ^OR is typed quickly the delay of finding and displaying the On-Screen menu is avoided. If the cursor is positioned at the right hand edge of an existing piece of text before the command ^OR, then pressing **ESCAPE** will set the margin to the column indicated by the cursor.

Margin release ^OX

The command ^OX is used to release the margins. This allows the cursor to be moved outside the limits shown by the ruler, so that text may be inserted beyond the margins. This is often useful for putting headings, or comments at the side of paragraphs, as illustrated in the paragraph below. The margin settings used are shown by the ruler:

!——!——!——!——!——!——!——!——!————————R
On typing the command ^OX, a message **MAR REL** (short for margin release) appears in the status line of the screen, and the ruler changes to show all the tabs which have been set:

!   !   !   !——!——!——!——!——!——!————————R
The cursor may now be moved beyond the margin, and the appropriate text added - in this

USE OF THE MARGIN RELEASE KEY.

case the heading "USE OF THE MARGIN RELEASE KEY". On moving the cursor back within the margins, the margin release is turned OFF, and no further text can be typed outside the margin without typing ^OX again. Should you change your mind after typing ^OX to release the margin, the command can be cancelled by typing ^OX again. Thus ^OX acts as an ON/OFF toggle switch. (A word of warning: it is difficult to reform this paragraph without destroying the layout).

To reform the hanging paragraph above, you must first set the margins to match the paragraph. This may be done by moving the cursor to a line below the ones with the hanging heading, and typing ^OF. (Alternatively you may set the left and right margins with ^OL and ^OR commands). The text in the paragraph may then be altered and reformed without altering the hanging heading.

If the hanging heading is to the right of the paragraph, alterations to the paragraph below the hanging part can be carried out in the same way. However, if you attempt alterations and reforming at or above the level of the hanging part, the hanging part will become incorporated in the paragraph. The only way to handle this is first to delete the hanging part, alter and reform the paragraph, then use the margin release ^OX again and re-type the hanging part.

Hiding the ruler ^OT

It is possible that you may wish to hide the ruler, so that it is not displayed on the screen. If you type ^OT the ruler will disappear, and typing ^OT a second time will switch the ruler display ON again. The ruler is still in operation, limiting the margins and fixing the tab positions, regardless of whether it is displayed or not. The usual reason for switching the ruler OFF is to make room on the screen for one more line of useful text from the document being edited.

Using tab settings ^I

Often when typing you want to indent some text, such as the first line of a paragraph, or you may wish to line up information typed in a table. This could be done by typing the appropriate number of spaces before typing the text or numbers. This method is not recommended because it is slow. A much better way of indenting the first line of a paragraph is to use the tab settings by pressing ^I. (A number of keyboards have a key marked TAB, which has exactly the same effect). This moves the cursor to the next tab stop, (that is to the next ! mark in the ruler line).

If INSERT is switched ON, spaces are inserted to move the cursor to the next tab stop. This pushes all text to the right of the cursor forward the appropriate number of spaces, so existing text can be indented. If there is no text to the right of the cursor, then any text now typed will be indented. (If INSERT is switched ON, the message **INSERT ON** will show in the status line on the screen. If INSERT is not switched ON, pressing ^V will switch it ON).

If INSERT is switched OFF, the cursor will move over any existing text to the next tab stop, but without inserting any spaces. This would normally be used only for such jobs as moving the cursor to a particular point in a table, to correct a wrong entry.

If the ^I key is pressed more than once, then the cursor will move more than one tab position. When typing a table, one value may be typed, then ^I typed to move to the next column, then type the next value, then ^I ... and so on. If there are no more tab stops on the line, pressing ^I will move the cursor to the first tab stop on the next line.

Using paragraph tab settings ^OG

You may wish to indent all the lines in a paragraph. One way to do this is to reset the left margin using an ^OL command. However, when you would like to return to the original margin setting - perhaps after this one paragraph, it will be necessary to use another ^OL command. WordStar makes it very easy to change the left margin setting temporarily with "paragraph tabbing". Typing ^OG makes all the lines in the paragraph start at the first tab stop, rather than at the left margin. Typing ^OG a second time will indent the paragraph to the second tab stop ... and so on. On terminals which have highlighting, the fact that ^OG has been pressed is shown by not highlighting the ruler up to the appropriate tab stop. The effect of the ^OG key is temporary, and is cancelled by:

1.   Pressing the RETURN key, which will happen at the end of a paragraph.

2.   Changing the margins.

3.   Moving the cursor before the point where ^OG was typed, that is nearer the beginning of the file.

Alternatively you may want to produce a "hanging paragraph", that is one where a paragraph number or heading sticks out at the side, but every line in the paragraph is indented, as for example the three paragraphs above.   To do this, type the paragraph number, and then press ^OG to temporarily indent the paragraph.   Type the paragraph, and it will be indented.   When you press **RETURN** at the end of the paragraph you will go back to the normal margin.

Setting and removing tabs and decimal tabs ^OI and ^ON

The original ruler line displayed by WordStar may not have tabs set in the positions required for a particular job, and might be easier to use with some extra tabs added, or existing tabs removed.   The command ^OI is used to set tabs.   (On terminals which have a TAB key, pressing ^O followed by **TAB** has the same effect).   When ^OI is typed, a message is displayed on the screen:

SET TAB AT COLUMN (ESCAPE for cursor column)?

If a column number is typed, for example 61, followed by pressing **RETURN,** then a tab is set at column 61, and a ! appears in the ruler line at the appropriate place, as shown in Figure 28.5.   If **ESCAPE** is pressed instead of typing a number, then a tab is set at the column occupied by the cursor.

FIGURE 28.5

Original ruler
L————!————!————!————!————!————!————!————!————!————!————!————!————————R

Ruler with extra tab set at column 61
L————!————!————!————!————!————!————!————!————!————!————!————!————!———R
1234567890123456789012345678901234567890123456789012345678901

In addition to the "normal" sort of tabs described above, WordStar has "decimal" tabs.   These are invaluable when typing columns of numbers, and provides a quick and easy way of lining up the decimal points in columns of figures, or of producing other tables of text with right alignment, rather than the left alignment produced with normal tabs.   When the set tab command ^OI is typed, two lines of message appear on the screen:

For decimal tab stop enter # and decimal point column
SET TAB AT COLUMN (ESCAPE for cursor column)?

To set a decimal tab, first type # and then the required column number, and press **RETURN.**   A # symbol appears at the appropriate place in the ruler line. If a decimal tab is required at the column occupied by the cursor, the command ^OI followed by # and **ESCAPE** may be used instead.

When the ^I key (or the TAB key) is pressed, the cursor jumps to the next tab stop, regardless of whether in is a "normal tab" marked in the ruler by !, or a "decimal tab" marked by a #.   After tabbing to a decimal tab position, WordStar displays the word "decimal" in the status line on the screen.   The cursor is at the tab position, and it remains there even when text or numbers are typed.   The characters typed are moved to the left of the cursor in order to maintain right alignment.   Right alignment continues until one of the following occurs:

1. A decimal point, or full stop is typed. Thus decimal numbers will all have their decimal points aligned at the decimal tab position.

2. The **RETURN** key is pressed, indicating the end of a paragraph.

3. The space bar is pressed, indicating the end of the number or word.

4. Another tab operation is performed by pressing either ^I or **TAB**.

It may be necessary to remove tab stops from the ruler line. This is performed by typing the command ^ON and pressing **RETURN**. A message then appears on the screen:

CLEAR TAB AT COL (ESCAPE for cursor col; A for all)?

There are three possible replies:

1. If a column number is typed and **RETURN** pressed, then provided that a tab has previously been set at that column, it will disappear from the ruler line.

2. If the cursor has previously been positioned at a tab stop, then pressing **ESCAPE** will remove that tab setting.

3. Typing **A** and pressing **RETURN** will remove all the tab stops from the ruler line.

Substituting your own ruler line ^OF

It is possible to create a ruler line and to store it in the file with the text. This ruler may be substituted for the default ruler line, simply by placing the cursor on the special ruler and typing the command ^OF. This allows both margins and all the tabs to be reset with a single command, once the original substitute ruler has been created. This facility is particularly useful for laying out tables, or if a special format is required for some text. It is a considerable time-saver if it is needed more than once, either for producing other tables or other text in the same format. Steps must be taken to prevent the special ruler being printed as a line of text. When an overprint line follows a dot command, WordStar takes the overprint line as part of the dot command, and does not print it. This feature is exploited to store a "non printing ruler" in the file, as shown below.

A substitute ruler line may be produced in the following way:

1. Move the cursor to the place in the text where you would like the new format to apply. This could be the beginning of a document, if you want the whole document formatting in this way, or alternatively it could be immediately before a table, or a special piece of text.

2. First type ^N to start working on a new line. Next type two full stops in columns 1 and 2 so that WordStar will treat this line as a "comment", and will not print it out as a normal line of text. (For further details see chapter 26 - Dot Commands). Then type ^P and press **RETURN**. (The overprinting sequence ^P and RETURN enters a carriage return into the file, but no line feed). This makes WordStar overprint the whole of this line with the next line. Lines which will be overprinted by the next line on the screen show a - flag at the right hand edge of the screen.

3. Type ^O to display the onscreen menu, and check in the third column that the line **E Soft hyph on (OFF)** really does say OFF. If it does, press **RETURN**, but if it says ON then you must press **E** to turn it OFF.

4.   The cursor is now in column 1, and if you would like the new ruler to start at column 1, start typing hyphens. If the left margin is to be set at some other column, for example column 6, then type 5 spaces and then type as many hyphens as are required to indicate the width of the text across the paper. Normal tab stops may be included where required by typing ! marks, and decimal tab stops obtained with # marks. At the end of the ruler, where you would like the right margin to appear, press **RETURN.**

5.   Now that the special ruler has been produced, it can be used very easily. Move the cursor any place on the new ruler line, and press **^OF.** This causes WordStar to discard the old ruler together with the old tabs and old margins. The ruler line from the file, with its new margins and tab settings now become the currently effective ruler line, which will remain in effect until one of the following occurs:

a) Another ruler line is read from the file with another **^OF** command. If it is intended to use this format more than once, it will be worth making a second ruler line in the text which contains the normal parameters for text. Then you can toggle back and forth between "text ruler" and "table ruler" as often as necessary.

b) The left margin or the right margin may be changed with ^OL or ^OR commands, or tabs are inserted or removed using ^OI or ^ON commands.

c) On leaving WordStar, the special ruler which you had stored in the computer's memory is lost. On starting WordStar up again, the default ruler is always displayed. Provided that the special ruler has been stored in the file, it can be made effective again by moving the cursor onto the ruler and pressing **^OF.**

Chapter 29.
MORE ON-SCREEN FORMATTING - LINE FUNCTIONS AND TOGGLES

WordStar utilizes on-screen formatting, that is it displays text on the screen laid out as it will be printed. This almost unique feature makes it superior to other word-processing programs. In addition to setting margins and tabs and altering the ruler, which were described in the last chapter, many other on-screen formatting facilities exist, including centring text, setting the line spacing, and a set of toggles for word-wrap, justification, automatic hyphenation, and displaying the ruler, page breaks and control characters. The full set of on-screen formatting commands are given in the On-Screen menu, which may be displayed simply by typing ^O. The menu is shown in Figure 29.1, and the features described in this chapter are shown in bold type. All of the commands comprise two characters, ^O and another letter. If the two letters are typed in quick succession, then the command is implemented without delay. If however there is a pause after the ^O, at Help levels 3 and 2 the On-Screen menu will be displayed. This causes a time delay, but is useful if you have forgotten what letter to type next. When the required letter is typed, then the On-Screen menu disappears, and the command is implemented.

FIGURE 29.1 The ^O On-screen Menu

```
^O      B:LETTER.TXT   PAGE 1 LINE 1 COL 01              INSERT ON
                    < < < O N S C R E E N   M E N U  > > >
 -Margins & Tabs-  ¦  -Line Functions-  ¦  --More Toggles--  ¦  -Other Menus-
 L Set left margin ¦C Centre text       ¦J Justify    off (ON)¦ (from Main only)
 R Set right margin¦S Set line spacing  ¦V Vari-tabs off (ON)¦^J Help  ^K Block
 X Release margins ¦                    ¦H Hyph-help off (ON)¦^Q Quick ^P Print
 I Set  N Clear tab¦    ---Toggles---   ¦E Soft hyph on (OFF)¦^O Onscreen
 G Paragraph tab   ¦W Wrd wrap off (ON)¦D Prnt disp off (ON)¦Space Bar returns
 F Ruler from line ¦T Rlr line off (ON)¦P Pge break off (ON)¦you to Main Menu.
```

Centring lines of text ^OC

Sometimes it is necessary to centre a line of text, so that a page heading appears exactly in the middle of the page, or to make the layout of a notice or a menu look more professional. When using a typewriter, the number of letters in the line must be counted, and then the number of spaces to insert before the text must be calculated. WordStar makes it easy to centre a line between the margins which are currently in operation. Simply type the line, or if it has already been typed move the cursor to any point on the line, and press ^OC. WordStar ignores any spaces at either end of the line, and centres the text.

Setting the line spacing ^OS

WordStar uses single spacing by default, and if typing is required on every line then there is no need to make any change. If double spacing is required (typing on alternate lines), or triple spacing (typing on one line, then two blank lines), or even wider spacing then type ^OS. A message is displayed on the screen:

ENTER space OR NEW LINE SPACING(1-9):

Typing 2 gives double spacing, and as long as this spacing is in operation, the

message **LINE SPACING 2** will be displayed at the right of the top line (status

line) of the screen. (The effect of this command can be seen from the spacing

of the lines in this paragraph).

Remember that double spacing affects both what is printed on paper and also the display on the screen. Only half the usual number of lines of text are shown on the screen, which makes reading and checking the document from the screen more difficult. It may be preferable to type and correct the document using single spacing, and only when this has been done to change the document into double spacing. To do this, you must move the cursor to the beginning of the document, or the place where double spacing is required, and then type ^OS2. Though the message **LINE SPACING** 2 appears in the status line, the text which has already been typed single spaced remains unchanged. The first paragraph of text may be reformed by typing ^B, when it is transformed into double spacing. Each subsequent paragraph must then be reformed in a similar manner.

A better way of obtaining a double spaced document is to type it single spaced, (with the full number of lines displayed on the screen), and to print it double spaced using MergePrint. This is done using .PF and a .LS command to change the spacing. (See chapter 39 - Special Dot Commands for MailMerge).

It is possible to select triple spacing by typing 3 in reply to the message ENTER space OR **NEW LINE SPACING(1-9):**, and the status line will show the message **LINE SPACING** 3. If required, any spacing up to 9 (that is one line of typing followed by 8 blank lines) may be chosen. If a space is typed as the reply rather than a number, then the spacing remains unchanged. The line spacing may be changed any number of times in a single document, should different spacings be required in different places.

This form of line spacing can be used on any printer, teletype, converted electric typewriter, dot matrix printer, or daisy wheel printer. However, most daisy wheel printers are capable of spacing lines in much smaller intervals, usually 1/48 inch. This allows intermediate spacings to be used, such as 1.5 spacing. These are described in chapter 26 - Dot Commands.

Word wrap toggle ^OW

When WordStar is first loaded, the "word wrap" toggle is switched ON. This is the normal way of working in WordStar, and removes the need to type RETURN at the end of each line - in fact you must not do so, except at the end of a paragraph. You simply keep on typing, and when a word will not fit on the current line, the word wrap feature of WordStar moves the entire word down onto the next line, thus starting a new line automatically. This feature is excellent for beginners at typing, who can concentrate on reading the document and hitting the right keys, and for experienced typists who are trying to get a job done at great speed, because it saves them the effort of laying the text out. The toggle may be turned OFF by typing ^OW, and then you must decide for yourself where to end a line by pressing RETURN. Turning word wrap OFF may be useful where you wish to format text exactly for yourself, perhaps in a table. Pressing ^OW again will switch word wrap ON again. At any time you may check the state of the ^OW toggle by typing ^O and examining the menu.

Ruler display toggle ^OT

By default, WordStar displays the ruler line on the screen, showing the margins currently in force, and the position of tabs. Typing ^OT turns the ruler display OFF, but the margin settings and tabs still operate even though the ruler is invisible. Pressing ^OT again will switch the ruler display ON again. At any time you may check the state of the ^OT toggle by typing ^O and examining the menu. Switching the ruler display OFF may be useful if you would like to display one extra line of text on the screen.

Right margin justification toggle ^OJ

Justification of the right margin is switched ON by default, and each line of text is padded out with spaces to make the last letter of the last word on each line finish exactly at the right margin. This gives a straight right hand edge, like that usually found in typeset books. Spaces inserted by WordStar are called "soft-spaces", in contrast to "hard-spaces" which are spaces you actually typed. WordStar will always leave "hard-spaces" exactly as they were typed, but WordStar may remove "soft-spaces" if a paragraph is reformed after words have been added or deleted, or after changing the margins. On the screen, "soft-spaces" appear as extra spaces between words. In much the same way, most cheaper printers can only print characters in fixed positions along the line, so "soft-spaces" are printed as extra spaces between words. In contrast, most daisy wheel printers can print characters at almost any position, because they can move in small intervals (such as 1/60th. or 1/120th. of an inch). Such printers insert very small extra spaces between letters in words as well as between words, during printout. This is called micro-justification, and the white space is shared out all over the line, giving a more pleasing appearance.

Typing ^OJ turns the justification toggle OFF, and stops the addition of "soft-spaces". The text therefore has a ragged right hand margin, which is typical of normal typing, and is illustrated by this paragraph. Pressing ^OJ again will switch justification ON again. At any time you may check the state of the ^OJ toggle by typing ^O and examining the menu.

Variable tabs toggle ^OV

The tab stops in the ruler line are called variable tabs because they can be changed by the user, as described in the previous chapter. The variable tabs toggle is switched ON by default, which means that the tabs set in the ruler really function.

The variable tabs toggle may be switched OFF by typing ^OV. The variable tabs displayed in the ruler line now have no effect, and instead fixed tabs operate every 8 spaces, that is at columns 9, 17, 25, 33, 41, 49, 57, 65 ... and so on. The width of the page is still defined by the ruler. If for example the left and right margins are set to the usual values of 1 and 65 then all the tabs listed above will operate. However, if the left and right margins were set at 20 and 50 respectively, then pressing the TAB key the first time would move the cursor to column 25, and subsequent tabs would move to columns 33, 41, 49, and then to column 25 on the next line.

When variable tabs are switched OFF, (that is we are in fixed tabbing mode), the information stored in the file actually contained the tab control character ^I rather than the appropriate number of spaces. The tab control characters are expanded into spaces when the file is printed. This compression of tabs always happens when editing a file in Non Document mode, and is useful when typing assembly code, since the file produced is appreciably smaller.

It is simple to check if this toggle is ON or OFF, either by typing ^O and seeing from the On-Screen menu whether it is switched ON or OFF, or by pressing the TAB key and seeing where the cursor moves to.

Hyphenation toggle ^OH

A very special WordStar feature called hyphen-help is normally switched ON when the program is first loaded. The hyphen-help feature works in the following manner. When a paragraph is reformed by typing ^B, WordStar tidies up the text in that particular paragraph. If there is a big word which is just too long to fit at the end of a line, then moving it down onto the next line would leave a large gap. If hyphen-help is switched ON, then WordStar examines the last word to see if it contains more than one syllable, and if so it displays a message on the screen (Figure 29.2), which offers the option of putting a hyphen in the word at a suitable place.

FIGURE 29.2

> TO HYPHENATE, PRESS -. Before pressing -, you may
> move cursor: ^S=cursor left, ^D=cursor right.
> If hyphenation not desired, type ^B.

The suggested position for the hyphen is indicated by the cursor, and the
computer stops reforming the paragraph, and waits until you have decided which
of the following three options you wish to choose:

1. To place a hyphen where the computer suggests, type -.

2. If you think you can place the hyphen in a better place, move the
cursor to the correct place, and then type -.

3. If you do not want a hyphen in this word, press ^B again.

When the appropriate reply has been typed, reforming the paragraph continues,
either till WordStar finds another word at the end of a line which might be
better hyphenated, or up to the end of the paragraph.

It should be noted if the cursor is moved too far under option 2, then
the message offering the chance to insert a hyphen disappears from the screen.
Paragraph reforming is abandoned leaving the paragraph looking untidy, and you
may continue to edit the document or insert text.

The hyphens inserted in this way are called "soft-hyphens". On screens
which support highlighting, "soft-hyphens" are usually displayed in half
intensity or in inverse video, and they will print normally. If the paragraph
is subsequently altered and reformed, then "soft-hyphens" may now fall in the
middle of a line. They still show on the screen, but they only print if they
appear at the end of a line. On non-enhanced screens, "soft-hyphens" cannot be
distinguished from "hard-hyphens" which you have typed, and they spoil the
right justification of text on the screen. It is recommended that ^OD is used
to hide "soft-hyphens" when examining the layout.

It is important to distinguish between hyphens, (which are the same as the
minus sign), and print slightly above the bottom of the line, and the underline
character which prints slightly below the line. The distinction between "hard"
and "soft" hyphens is also important. A hyphen which is actually typed in the
text is called a "hard-hyphen". This will always be displayed on the screen
and print exactly as it was typed. "Soft-hyphens" are inserted by WordStar
when you choose options 1 or 2. These are normally displayed enhanced if the
terminal allows this. Clearly these "soft" hyphens occur at the end of a line,
but if the paragraph is subsequently altered and reformed then they may occur
anywhere in the line. Though "soft" hyphens are displayed on the screen, they
are only printed if they occur at the end of a line. If you need to examine
the layout of some text critically, it will be found that "soft-hyphens" spoil
the screen layout. The display of "soft-hyphens" can be turned OFF quite
simply by typing ^OD.

Typing ^OH will switch the hyphen-help feature OFF, and typing it again
will switch it ON again. At any time you may check the state of the ^OH
toggle by typing ^O and examining the menu. If the hyphen help feature is
switched OFF, then a word which will not fit at the end of a line will automatically be dragged down onto the next line, without offering the opportunity to
hyphenate words. The resulting text may look rather "open", that is have a lot
of white spaces showing on a line, unless the justification toggle ^OJ is also
OFF - giving a ragged right edge.

Inserting "soft-hyphens" ^OE

The "soft-hyphen" toggle ^OE is the only toggle which is switched OFF when WordStar is loaded. This means that if a hyphen is typed, it is treated a a "hard-hyphen", which will always be displayed and printed, exactly as typed. If ^OE is typed to switch the "soft-hyphen" toggle ON, then any hyphens typed will be treated as "soft-hyphens". This means that they will be displayed on the screen, (highlighted if the screen supports it), but they will only be printed when they occur at the end of a line. Thus this feature may be used to indicate where it is reasonable to break long words should this be necessary. A human being should hopefully be able to make a better and more sophisticated choice than a computer program over whether to and where to hyphenate words.

If the "soft-hyphen" toggle ^OE is ON, it is possible to type "hard-hyphens" by typing ^P followed by the hyphen, or alternatively if you have finished with "soft-hyphens" you can press ^OE again and turn the toggle OFF. Note that early versions of WordStar will not print files with "soft-hyphens" correctly, but all versions from 2.0 and later work properly.

Hiding control characters – Print display toggle ^OD

Even though WordStar has the very superior feature of "on-screen formatting", and displays text on the screen in the same format as it will be printed, there are some occasions where it is necessary to type control characters in the bulk of the text in order to produce some special effect. Some examples of this are:

1. To produce underlined text, ^PS must be typed immediately before and immediately after the part to be underlined. The characters ^S actually show on the screen before and after the text to be underlined.

2. In much the same way, ^PB is typed before and after text to appear in bold type. The characters ^B actually show on the screen.

3. The control characters ^PV are typed either side of text to be subscripted, and the characters ^V show on the screen.

4. The control characters ^PT are typed either side of text to be superscripted, and the characters ^T show on the screen.

5. "Soft-hyphens" will also be displayed. Those at the ends of lines should show, since they will be printed, but those which appear in the middle of a line are not necessary and spoil the layout.

The command ^OD is used to turn OFF the display of control characters for print enhancements and soft hyphens on the screen. When this is typed, the lines of text will all appear the same length on the screen as they will when printed out on paper. You cannot get underlining, bold, sub and superscripts displayed on the screen, but the removal of the extra characters ^S, ^B, ^V, ^T and "soft-hyphens" makes it much easier to check the layout.

It is strongly recommended that the layout of a document is checked on the screen with the control characters hidden, (that is with ^OD OFF), before printing. However, the control character display should be switched ON by typing ^OD again as soon as the checking is complete, and before editing the document. This is essential, otherwise you may delete control characters which are not displayed, and thus wreck the layout of the document. At any time you may check the state of the ^OD toggle by typing ^O and examining the menu.

Page break toggle ^OP

When a file is edited in the usual Document mode, the page break display is switched ON. The place where the end of a page occurs is automatically shown on the screen:

```
-------------------------------------------------------------------------P
```

It is most useful to see where a page ends, so that simple layout faults like having a table split on two pages, or a paragraph heading on the last line of a page, can be avoided. Chapter 26 - Dot commands describes how to force the start of a new page with a .PA command, or a conditional page throw .CP if there are less than a given number of lines left on the page, or how to set the paper length (number of lines on a page) with a .PL command. While the page break toggle is ON, the status line on the screen displays the page number, line number and column number of the cursor.

Typing ^OP turns the page break display OFF, so the ends of pages are not indicated on the screen. The status line on the screen now displays **FC=** and **FL=** rather than page number, line number and column number. FC is the file character count, which is the total number of characters in the file from the beginning up to and including the cursor position. This includes everything, letters, numbers, punctuation marks, spaces, carriage return and linefeed characters and control characters. If the cursor is at the end of the file, then the number displayed is the number of characters plus one, since the space occupied by the cursor is counted. FL is the file line count, which gives the number of lines from the start of the file to the cursor. Again, if the cursor is at the end of the file, the number displayed is the number of lines plus one.

To find the number of characters or lines in a file, type ^OP to turn the page break toggle OFF, type ^QC to move the cursor to the bottom of the file, read FC and FL from the status line and subtract one from each. The page break toggle can be switched ON again by typing ^OP again. At any time you may check the state of the ^OP toggle by typing ^O and examining the menu.

When editing in Non-Document mode, the page break display is turned OFF, and cannot be switched ON. The status line always shows FC= and FL=.

Chapter 30.

MANIPULATING BLOCKS OF TEXT

When preparing a lengthy document, it is quite common to produce a draft, which is then cut up and pasted together with the pieces in a different order. With a word processor, this sort of rearrangement can be performed very quickly and easily by electronic means, without the need to type the original draft, and without scissors and glue. The text which is to be moved is called a block, and may be a few words, a paragraph, or many pages. The WordStar commands for handling blocks are shown on the ^K menu. This chapter describes how to mark a block, how to move a block from one place to another, how to copy (duplicate) a block of text, how to delete a block and how to hide or remove the block markers.

The ^K Block Menu and the Block commands

Provided that WordStar has been loaded, and that you have typed D to edit a file, and have given the filename, then typing the command ^K will produce the menu shown in Figure 30.1 on the screen. The parts which are of special interest are the second and third columns.

FIGURE 30.1 The ^K Block Menu

```
^K       A:EXAMPLE  PAGE 1 LINE 1  COL 1                INSERT ON
                      < < <     B L O C K   M E N U     > > >
    -Saving  Files- | -Block Operations- | -File  Operations- | -Other  Menus-
                    |B  Begin   K  End  |R Read             |
                    |H  Hide / Display  |                   |
                    |C  Copy    Y  Delete|                  |
                    |V  Move    W  Write |                  |
                    |N  Column    off (ON)|                 |
```

Marking a block of text ^KB and ^KK

Before a block of text can be moved to another place, copied, written to a file, or deleted, it must be marked at the beginning and end with the markers ^KB and ^KK. It is easy to remember these commands. Block commands all begin with ^K, and the word BlocK begins with a B and ends with a K, hence the command ^KB is for the beginning, and ^KK is for the end.

First the cursor is positioned over the first letter in the block of text to be marked, and ^KB is typed to mark the beginning of the block. The characters <B> appear on the screen, and the text is moved three places to the right. The cursor is then moved one character past the last character to be included in the block and ^KK is typed. The characters <K> appear on the screen to the right of the last character in the block. Many visual display units support highlighting, and on these the text in between the block markers will be highlighted, that is displayed in half intensity, or inverse video (black characters on a white background). If the last line of the block to be marked is a complete line, then it is recommended that the end of block marker should be placed at the beginning of the next line. This ensures that the invisible carriage return character which indicates the end of a line is also copied as part of the block.

Moving a block of text ^KV

First the cursor must be moved to the precise position in the file where the block is to be inserted. When the command ^KV is typed, the block of text previously marked will be deleted from its original place and inserted at this point. At this stage, the text immediately before and after the block should be examined, to see if minor corrections such as the addition or deletion of an extra space is required. The cursor may be moved back to its position previous to the block move by the command ^QP. After tidying up there, the command ^QB may be used to move the cursor to the marker at the beginning of the block, or ^QK to move the cursor to the marker at the end of the block. Once these minor corrections have been made, the cursor is moved to a point in the paragraph before the added block, and the paragraph reformed by pressing ^B. In the same way the text adjacent to where the block was removed from may need minor editing to tidy it up, followed by a ^B to reform the paragraph. The block which was moved will still appear "highlighted", and ^KH should be typed to hide it - that is to remove the <B> and <K> marks and switch the highlighting off to make it look like normal text, or alternatively the block markers may be removed altogether.

Removing block markers

Block markers can be removed in the following way. First move the cursor to the beginning of the block. This may be marked by <B>, or may be highlighted. Typing ^KB destroys the beginning of block marker. Move the cursor to the end of block marker <K>, and type ^KK to remove the end of block marker.

Copying a block of text ^KC

This procedure is almost the same as that for moving a block described above. The difference is that though the block of text is inserted, the original block is not deleted, and remains unchanged. The details are as follows. The beginning and end of the block are marked with ^KB and ^KK respectively. The cursor is moved to the precise position in the file where the block is to be inserted. When the command to copy a block ^KC is typed, the block of text previously marked will be copied and inserted at this point. At this stage, it is worth examining the text immediately before and after the block, to see if any minor corrections are required. For example an extra space might need to be added, or a space deleted. Once these minor corrections have been made, move the cursor to a point before the added block, and reform the paragraph by pressing ^B. The block originally marked will no longer appear highlighted, but the block which has been added is still highlighted. Type ^KH to hide the block - that is to remove the <B> and <K> markers and switch the highlighting off to make it look like normal text.

Writing a block to a disk file ^KW

Suppose a paragraph or a section of a document is to be used more than once, either in the same document, or used in other documents. After typing the text for the first time, the beginning of the block should be marked ^KB and the end with ^KK as before. If the command ^KW is then typed, this block will be written to a disk file. WordStar displays the message

NAME OF FILE TO WRITE MARKED TEXT ON?

on the screen. You must then type a suitable filename of up to eight characters, optionally followed by a dot and a three character extension, and then press RETURN. The block of text is then copied into a disk file, which may be accessed later and included in documents using the Read file from disk command ^KR which is described later. It is important to realise that the the marked block of text now appears both in its original position in the document, as well as in the disk file just created. The text in the original document is still highlighted, and to remove the markers <B> and <K> and switch off the highlighting you must press ^KH. The choice of filename is also important - it should normally be a new filename. If an existing filename is used then WordStar will replace the contents of the existing file with the new block of text - thus overwriting, that is destroying the original text in that file. If the filename is preceded by the disk drive, for example A: or B:, then the file will be written to the disk drive specified. If the drive is not specified then the file will be written to the currently logged-in disk drive. It is often convenient to store standard paragraphs as disk files, and to include them in letters or documents when appropriate.

Reading a block from a disk file ^KR

If a block of text has previously been stored on disk using a ^KW command, it can readily be included into the document currently being edited by typing ^KR. WordStar then displays the question

NAME OF FILE TO READ?

Type the filename and press RETURN. The text in the disk file is inserted in the file being edited at the cursor position. It is therefore important that the cursor is correctly positioned before using a ^KR command. The filename may be preceded by the drive name A: or B: if you wish to specify disk drive where it will be found, but if it is not specified, the file will be read from the currently logged-in drive. The contents of the disk file are unchanged by this operation, so the disk file may be inserted into any number of different documents. This may be useful for including standard paragraphs, conditions of business, or legal clauses into business letters or legal documents.

Deleting a block ^KY

There are several ways of deleting text when editing a document:

```
^G    to delete the character under the cursor
DEL   to delete the character to the left of the cursor
^T    to delete the word to the right of the cursor
^Y    to delete the entire line
^QY   to delete the character under the cursor, and the rest of the line to
      the right of the cursor
^Q DEL to delete the part of the line to the left of the cursor
```

These commands are laborious if a lot of text needs deleting. A better method is to mark the beginning of the block to be deleted with ^KB, and the end of the block with ^KK, and then type ^KY to delete the entire block.

Moving the cursor to the markers at the beginning or end of a block ^QB & ^QK

If a block of text has been marked with the markers ^KB and ^KK, and you then move to another part of the file to look at something else, typing ^QB will move the cursor back to the beginning of block marker, and typing ^QK will move the cursor back to the end of block marker. This use of the ^Q Quick commands is very similar to the use of place markers ^K0 to ^K9, and moving to these with ^Q0 to ^Q9 which is described in chapter 15 - Advanced Cursor Movements and Scrolling Text.

Errors during block operations

If you try to perform a block operation when a block is not marked at all, or only marked at the beginning, or only marked at the end, or marked correctly but hidden, then an error message will be displayed on the screen:

    ### ERROR E6: BLOCK BEGINNING NOT MARKED
           (OR MARKER IS UNDISPLAYED)^G^G ### Press ESCAPE Key

or

    ### ERROR E6: BLOCK END NOT MARKED
           (OR MARKER IS UNDISPLAYED)^G^G ### Press ESCAPE Key

You must press ESCAPE before trying to do anything else.

Using column block operations ^KN

WordStar version 3.0 provides a feature not present in earlier versions, where in addition to being able to mark a block of text as one or more horizontal lines of text, it is also possible to mark a vertical column. It is then possible to delete, copy or move a vertical column of text or figures. This feature is valuable for rearranging columns of figures in a table.

Suppose that you want to rearrange the columns in the following table:

```
        original                        rearranged
    ZZZ  XXX  YYY                    XXX  YYY  ZZZ
    ZZZ  XXX  YYY                    XXX  YYY  ZZZ
    ZZZ  XXX  YYY                    XXX  YYY  ZZZ
    ZZZ  XXX  YYY                    XXX  YYY  ZZZ
```

Type **^KN** to change from normal block mode to column block mode. Then mark the ZZZ block as follows: Move the cursor over the first Z on the top line, and press **^KB** to mark the beginning of the block. The marker <B> appears:

```
    <B>ZZZ  XXX  YYY
    ZZZ  XXX  YYY
    ZZZ  XXX  YYY
    ZZZ  XXX  YYY
```

Now move the cursor to the space immediately after the ZZZ on the bottom line, and press **^KK** to mark the end of the block. On terminals which support highlighting, the column of ZZZ's will appear in half intensity or inverse video. On all other terminals the end of block marker <K> will appear:

```
    <B>ZZZ  XXX  YYY
    ZZZ  XXX  YYY
    ZZZ  XXX  YYY
    ZZZ<K>  XXX  YYY
```

Now you must move the cursor to a position three spaces past the YYY on the top line, and press **^KV** to move the marked block to its new position. Then type **^KH** to hide the marked block, and **^KN** to return from column block to normal block mode. A close examination of the final table will show that moving the block of ZZZ's, which is three characters wide, has moved the remaining columns three places to the left. Often when moving a column, for example the ZZZ column, the marked block should include the ZZZ's and the spaces between it and the XXX column, so that you do not change the spacing between columns, or sideways position of columns in the final table.

You may copy the marked column block in a similar way with a **^KC** command, or delete it with a **^KV** command. It is not possible to write a column block to a file, or to read one from a file. If you attempt either of these you will get an error message:

*** ERROR E13 COLUMN READ / WRITE NOT ALLOWED *** Press ESCAPE Key

A way round this is to copy the column to the end of the file with **^KN** and **^KC**, and pick this data up later when required. When you have finished the column block operation, it is a good idea to type **^KN** again, to return to normal block operation.

112

Chapter 31.
<u>PRACTICE</u> <u>IN</u> <u>USING</u> <u>SOME</u> <u>OF</u> <u>THE</u> <u>BLOCK</u> <u>COMMANDS</u>

Exercise 1.

(a) Load CP/M and WordStar, then edit a file called ADDRESS.TXT and type in the data given in Figure 31.1.

FIGURE 31.1

Smith John, 12 Mesnes Street, Wigan. Tel 52461
Williams David, 56 Arkwright Terrace, Wigan.
Brown Alan, 25 Throgmorton Street, Wigan. Tel 61565
Jones Bill, 3 King Street, Wigan.

(b) Rearrange the list of names in alphabetical order, as shown below:

Brown Alan, 25 Throgmorton Street, Wigan. Tel 61565
Jones Bill, 3 King Street, Wigan.
Smith John, 12 Mesnes Street, Wigan. Tel 52461
Williams David, 56 Arkwright Terrace, Wigan.

It is worth considering the easiest way to rearrange the list. Both Smith and Williams need moving beneath Jones.   One way is to place the cursor over the S of Smith and mark the beginning of a block with **^KB**. Then move the cursor just past the last character you wish to move, that is over the B of Brown and mark the end of a block with **^KK**, then move the cursor to the bottom of the list, and move the marked block to this position with a **^KV** command. Finally hide the marked block with a **^KH** command.

(c) Save the file with a **^KD** command, and then print it out.

Exercise 2.

(a) First you should correct the file SCOUTS.TXT which you typed and saved in chapter 7 - Practice Using Some of the "No-File" Commands. The present contents of the file are shown in Figure 31.2 below:

FIGURE 31.2

Cub Scout Promise

I promise that I will do my best
to do my duty to God and the Queen,
to help other people
and to keep the Cub Scout Law.

Cub Scout Law

A Cub Scout always does his best,
thinks of others before himself
and does a good turn every day.

(b) The first correction is to change the heading Cub Scout Promise into the Scout Promise. Move the cursor over the letter C of Cub, and press ^T to delete the word Cub. Then move the cursor over the letter I of "I promise", and having checked that INSERT ON is displayed in the cursor line, add the words **"On my honour, "**. Delete the word Cub in line four, and also from the heading Cub Scout Law.

(c) The three lines of text which make up the Cub Scout Law must be deleted.

While this could be done using ^Y three times to delete each of the three lines, we will practise marking this as a block, and deleting the block. (If the amount of text is substantial, this method of deleting a block is quicker than deleting single lines). Move the cursor over the A of "A Cub Scout always does his best", and press ^KB to mark the beginning of the block. Now move the cursor onto the line after "and does a good turn every day." and press ^KK to mark the end of the block. Lastly type ^KY to delete the marked block.

(d) Now type the Scout Law which is shown in Figure 31.3:

FIGURE 31.3

1. A Scout is to be trusted.
2. A Scout is loyal.
3. A Scout is friendly and considerate.
4. A Scout is a brother to all Scouts.
5. A Scout has courage in all difficulties.
6. A Scout makes good use of his time and is careful of possessions and property.
7. A Scout has respect for himself and for others.

(e) Now save the file with a ^KD command. Print the file, and it should look like Figure 31.4.

FIGURE 31.4

Scout Promise

On my honour, I promise that I will do my best
to do my duty to God and the Queen,
to help other people
and to keep the Scout Law.

Scout Law

1. A Scout is to be trusted.
2. A Scout is loyal.
3. A Scout is friendly and considerate.
4. A Scout is a brother to all Scouts.
5. A Scout has courage in all difficulties.
6. A Scout makes good use of his time and is careful of possessions and property.
7. A Scout has respect for himself and for others.

(f) Now you can combine the text about Cubs with that about Scouts in a single document. To do this, type D at the "No-File" menu to edit the file CUBS.TXT. Move the cursor to the bottom of the file with a ^QC. Then type ^KR to read a file and insert it at this point. In reply to the question **NAME OF FILE TO READ?** type **SCOUTS.TXT** and press **RETURN**. The contents of the SCOUTS file are copied on to the end of the CUBS file. Save this file with a ^KD command, and then print it out. Note that the SCOUTS file remains unchanged.

Summary

In this chapter you have practised:
1. marking a block of text
2. moving a block from one place in a document to another
3. hiding a marked block
4. deleting a marked block
5. reading and inserting text from a file into the document currently being edited

Chapter 32.
PROBLEMS WITH LARGE FILES & DISK FULL ERRORS

Users are strongly advised to avoid using large files if possible, because they make WordStar run slowly, and are more likely to cause disk full errors. Several small files can be printed together if you have MailMerge, and this is described in chapter 37 - Printing Several Files To Make a Book. Full disks can create a lot of problems, and may result in your being unable to save the work you have done. In this chapter the ways of avoiding disk full problems are examined, and a number of possible ways of recovering after a disk full error are described. There is no guaranteed method of recovery, and prevention is better than cure.

Finding the size of a file and the free space on a disk

It is both prudent and good practice to examine the contents of the floppy disk which holds WordStar data files at frequent intervals. The purpose is to see what files are present, how big they are, and to find how much free space remains on the disk. You may then tidy up by erasing any unwanted files. Assuming that CP/M is loaded, that CP/M and its associated utility programs are on drive A: and the disk with WordStar data files is on drive B:, this may be carried out by typing the command:

A:STAT B:*.*

The files on drive B: will be listed alphabetically giving the file size of each in K bytes, and the total amount of free space on the disk. An unwanted file may be erased from the disk in drive B: by typing the command:

ERA B:filename

To erase all the backup files (with the extension .BAK) type:

ERA B:*.BAK

Suppose that WordStar has been loaded, and the logged-in drive has been changed to B:. The file sizes and the free space on the disk may be found by selecting the **R** option from the "No-File" menu, which allows you to run a program. STAT may now be run by typing:

STAT *.*

Note that there is no need to specify which disk drive contains the program STAT.COM, since WordStar looks for it first on the logged-in drive, (B: in this case) and then if necessary on drive A:. The size of the file being edited can be found by typing ^QC to move the cursor to the end of the document, then ^OP to turn off the display of page breaks. This also changes the status line, which now displays the number of characters or bytes in the file as **FC=nnn**. This value must be divided by 1024 to give the size of the file in K.

Reasons for having large files

If you have WordStar but not MailMerge, then working with one big file rather than several small ones has the following advantages:

1. Automatic page numbering works only within one file. If you are printing several files, you will have to specify the starting page number for the second and subsequent files printed with a .PN command.

2. A page break is mandatory between files. If the files are separate

chapters or sections, then this is fine, but if the file contains a paragraph then starting a new page will look strange.

3. Printing is more tedious since each file must be printed individually, and this becomes very tedious if multiple copies are required.

The only good reason for having very large files, rather than dividing them into several smaller files is that you do not have MailMerge.

Invisible files

It is advisable to leave twice as much free space on a disk as the size of the WordStar data file you are working on. This is because WordStar produces temporary scratch files as part of its normal operation. These normally remain invisible to the user, but unless there is room for them on the disk, WordStar will produce a Disk Full error message when you try to save a file after editing, or when WordStar tries to save some text.

ERROR E12: DISK FULL Press ESCAPE Key

During editing, the working document or workfile is held in RAM provided that the file is small enough. WordStar works much faster if the file can be held in RAM. An indirect indication of whether the file will fit in RAM can be obtained by moving the cursor to the end of the file with ^QC. Then move the cursor back to the beginning of the file with ^QR, and note the time taken. If the time taken is one or two seconds, then the file is still small enough to be held in RAM. If the disk lights come on, and the disk whirrs and clicks, and the process takes half a minute or more, the file is too large to hold in RAM.

When editing an existing file which is too big to hold in RAM, WordStar reads the first part of the original disk file into RAM. This RAM copy is now the working document, and it may be displayed, or altered. On moving through the document, more text is read in from the original disk file when required. When the workspace in RAM is completely filled, some of the text from the beginning of RAM is automatically written to a temporary output file (sometimes called a scratch file) on the disk. As you continue to move down through the document, this process will be repeated. If the cursor is moved backwards (towards the beginning of the file), over more text than is held in RAM, then text from the end of RAM is written to a second temporary output file on the disk, and some text is read into RAM from the first temporary file. On saving the working document at the end of editing, text is copied from RAM and from temporary files if necessary to produce a disk file containing a complete copy of the edited file.

The temporary files are created and deleted automatically. The moving of portions of the workfile backwards and forwards between temporary work files and RAM is also automatic. Because of this, it is possible to work with very big files if necessary. If you can limit the size of files to what will fit in RAM, then there is no need to produce these temporary files, hence WordStar will work much faster.

At the end of an edit, the working document must be saved as a permanent disk file. Suppose the document being edited was the letter previously typed and saved as a file called LETTER.TXT. On saving this, the working document is first written onto disk as a temporary file called LETTER.$$$. If the file is written to disk without problems, then if a backup file LETTER.BAK exists on the disk it is erased, the original file LETTER.TXT is renamed LETTER.BAK, and the temporary file LETTER.$$$ is renamed LETTER.TXT. If the disk is nearly full, WordStar may delete the .BAK file while writing the working document to disk. A warning message will be displayed if this occurs. If there still is insufficient room on the disk to copy the working document into the .$$$ file, a Disk Full error occurs. The .$$$ file is incomplete and so is not renamed.

Unless you delete something from the current file to reduce its size, or alternatively delete an unwanted file from the disk to make some space available, and then save the current file successfully, then you will lose all your work!

Ways of avoiding disk full problems

There are two fundamentally different ways of obtaining Disk Full errors:
(a) there is insufficient room for temporary files
(b) there is insufficient room to store the working document
Problems due to temporary disk files may be minimised or avoided in the following ways:

1. If possible, work with small files (which can be held in RAM).

2. Organise the editing changes that you wish to perform so that changes can be made from the beginning to the end of a large file.

3. If the file is large, avoid using commands which move the cursor a long way backwards, that is towards the beginning of the file. In these cases save and re-edit the file with a ^KS command so that you may start at the beginning of the file without having to move backwards. In this way you can avoid creating an extra temporary file. Commands which could move the cursor backwards in this way are:

    ^QR moves the cursor to the beginning of the file
    ^QB moves the cursor to the beginning of a block, marked <B>
    ^QK moves the cursor to the end of a block, marked <K>
    ^Q1, ^Q2, ... ^Q9 move the cursor to a marker <1>, <2>, ... <9>
    ^QP moves the cursor to the previous position
    ^QV moves the cursor to the position of the last Find
    ^QW scrolls text downwards continuously, so the text you see is nearer the beginning of the file
    Using the backwards option in ^QF Find and ^QV Replace commands
    Using the Global option in the ^QV Replace command

4. Avoid using Block move (^KV) and Block copy (^KC) commands when the source and destination are a long way apart. It is safer to write the block to a file with ^KW, and then to read it in at the required place with a ^KR command.

Ways of recovering from Disk Full errors

If a Disk Full error message is obtained, keep cool, and think clearly. You need to make room on the disk for the working document. There are four choices which are:

1. To abandon the working file, (which is the simplest option if only a few changes have been made since last it was saved on disk).

2. To delete some files from the logged-in disk. (This makes space for the working file).

3. To use some space on the other disk drive.

4. To save just the part of the file which has been altered.

First, if you are not running at Help level 3, type ^JH3 to obtain the maximum help. The Main Menu will be displayed. If the directory is not displayed, type ^KF to turn the directory display ON. Examine the files present on the logged-in drive, and see if any can be deleted.

1.   Abandon the working file

The working file may be abandoned by typing ^KQ. A message appears on the screen:

ABANDON EDITED VERSION OF FILE B:filename ? (Y/N):

The reply to this is **Y**, and the working file then disappears, and the "No-File" menu is displayed.

2.   Delete unwanted files to make space

If any backup files are present, with the ending .BAK, these could be deleted using a ^KJ command. The screen changes, as shown in Figure 32.1. In this case a .BAK file exists, and by typing **CHAPTER4.BAK** and pressing **RETURN**, this file will be deleted. Alternatively, any files may be deleted which you know that you can replace later from a backup copy on another disk. This might apply to files like CHAPTER1.TXT or CHAPTER2.TXT, or if WordStar was stored on the same disk WS.COM or WSMSGS.OVR could be deleted. Several files may be deleted one after another if necessary. If space can be made in this way, the working document can be saved on disk with a ^KD command.

FIGURE 32.1

```
^KJ  B:CHAPTER4.TXT   PAGE 55 LINE 9 COL 01              INSERT ON

^S=delete character    ^Y=delete entry    ^F=File directory
^D=restore character   ^R=Restore entry   ^U=cancel command

  NAME OF FILE TO DELETE?CHAPTER4.BAK

DIRECTORY of disk B:
  CHAPTER1.TXT   CHAPTER2.TXT   CHAPTER3.TXT   CHAPTER4.TXT   CHAPTER4.BAK
  INDEX.TXT      BOOK
```

3.   Try to use space on the other disk drive

Assuming that the currently logged-in disk drive which contains the WordStar data files is B:, you may try to use space on the other disk in drive A:. There are several ways of doing this. One way is to type ^KO to copy a file. The screen changes, and is shown in Figure 32.2. The replies to copy the file INDEX.TXT from disk B: to disk A: are shown. Note that **RETURN** must be pressed after typing each filename.

FIGURE 32.2

```
^KO  B:CHAPTER4.TXT   PAGE 55 LINE 9 COL 01              INSERT ON

  ^S=delete character    ^Y=delete entry    ^F=File directory
  ^D=restore character   ^R=Restore entry   ^U=cancel command

  NAME OF FILE TO COPY FROM?INDEX.TXT
  NAME OF FILE TO COPY  TO ?A:INDEX.TXT

DIRECTORY of disk B:
  CHAPTER1.TXT   CHAPTER2.TXT   CHAPTER3.TXT   CHAPTER4.TXT   CHAPTER4.BAK
  INDEX.TXT      BOOK
```

The next step is to delete the file INDEX.TXT from the logged-in drive B:, which is described in paragraph 1. There may now be enough space to save the working file on drive B: with a ^KD command.

Another way is to mark the beginning and the end of the working file with the block markers ^KB and ^KK respectively. Type the command ^KW to write the block to a disk file, and in reply to the question NAME OF FILE TO WRITE TO? include the drive letter A: as part of the filename, for example A:TEMP. The file TEMP will be saved on drive A:, and the "No-File" menu will appear.

4. Save part of the working file

If you cannot find any files to delete, or having deleted what you can there still is not enough room on the disk, and you get Disk Full again, the best plan is to save just the part of the working file which has the changes or additions. (Later the original file, and the file containing the block with the changes can be copied onto another disk, where there is more space, and the two files can be combined into one). One way of doing this is to mark the beginning and end of a block in the file using ^KB and ^KK, and then write the block to disk with a ^KW command as in paragraph 3, and then quit the edit by typing ^KQ. Another way is to delete parts of the working file until it is small enough to save on the disk with a ^KD command.

The last resort

If none of the above techniques works, the file originally read from disk at the start of the present editing session may be deleted. This should be done with care, and only if a large amount of work done in the present editing session will be lost if you are unable to save the working document. First of all, type ^QC which will move the cursor to the end of the working file. Make sure that all the file is still there. If it is not, you have lost your work. If it is complete, type ^KJ to delete the original copy of the file and then save the working file with a ^KD command. NOTE THAT THIS PROCEDURE IS DANGEROUS. If this fails to save the file, you have lost both the original file, and the working file.

Fatal Error

WordStar may crash with **FATAL ERROR 29.** This terminates the WordStar run in one of several ways. The keyboard may go dead, you may return unexpectedly to CP/M, or the screen may display repetitive patterns or other garbage. The work done since the last Save has gone. Despite the name, this need not necessarily be fatal. The system should be returned to running order, if necessary by re-booting, and loading WordStar again. If the directory is examined, it will probably contain a file with the ending .$$$. This should be renamed, by selecting the E option from the "No-File" menu. (Renaming is necessary since WordStar will not edit or print a file with the ending .$$$). A different name is necessary to distinguish between this file and the original file stored on the disk. Make some space on the disk by deleting something before trying to edit the file. If this is not possible, copy the file you have just rescued onto a new disk, and then examine it carefully under Word-Star. Any attempt to to edit the renamed file straight away using WordStar, will almost certainly crash again with either a Disk Full or Fatal error.

Splitting a large file into two or more smaller files

It is worth stating once again that WordStar works much better with files of moderate size, (that is, small enough to fit into RAM). If a file becomes too large, it can easily be split. To do this, decide how much you would like to move and insert a beginning of block marker ^KB at the beginning of the part to be moved, and an end of block marker at the end of the part to be moved by typing ^KB. Then write the marked block to a disk file by typing ^KW. When you have typed the new file name for this block, and it has been stored on disk, the block can be deleted from the present file with a ^KY command.

If you wish to split the remaining file still further, the process can be repeated. (The handling of blocks is described more fully in chapter 30 - Manipulating Blocks of Text).

Alternating disk drives with very large files

When editing an existing file, WordStar must have sufficient disk space for the original file, room to Save the edited copy, plus some for scratch files. A file may become so big that there is not enough room on one disk for two copies of the file. If there is no other way to do a job but to have a massive disk file, WordStar can be made to read the original file from one drive, and write the updated file to the other drive, by adding a space, the drive letter and a colon after the filename. Suppose that CP/M, WordStar and the original file which is called BOOK.TXT are present on drive A:. First load WordStar, and in reply to the "No-File" menu type **D** to edit a document file. Then reply to the question as shown:

NAME OF FILE TO EDIT? **BOOK.TXT B:**

Alternatively after the CP/M prompt A> WordStar may be loaded and the file BOOK.TXT be set up for editing with a single command by typing:

A>**WS BOOK.TXT B:**   and pressing **RETURN**

Whichever way you do this, it is absolutely essential that nothing - not even a space is typed after B:. When the edited file is Saved with ^KD, WordStar will write the working (updated) file on drive B: and call it BOOK.TXT, and the original file on drive A: will be renamed BOOK.BAK. If the Save and Re-edit command ^KS is used, then each time the file is saved the old .BAK file is overwritten by the new file, so the drive which contains the most up to date file alternates automatically.

The maximum size of file which may be handled in this way is in principle the capacity of the disk, minus the space for the WordStar program files, less some for scratch files. With WordStar version 3.0 these sizes are WS.COM = 16K, WSMSGS.OVR = 28K and WSOVLY1.OVR = 34K, which amount to 78K plus some for scratch files.

Summary

1.   Avoid using large files if possible.

2.   If a file becomes too large, split it into smaller ones if possible.

3.   Check both the size of the file being edited, and the amount of free space on the disk frequently. Leave plenty of free space on the disk.

4.   Save your work at regular intervals of 15 minutes with ^KS Save and Re-edit, so that a file does not suddenly double or treble in size, and if anything should go wrong there will be a fairly recent version of the file stored on disk.

5.   Use the ^KS command to Save and Re-edit a file rather than moving the cursor a long way backwards in a large file.

Chapter 32.

OVERVIEW OF MAILMERGE

MailMerge is a separate program marketed by MicroPro Inc. to work in conjunction with WordStar versions 2.0 and later. It greatly enhances both the file handling and the print capability of WordStar. The Merge-print command **M** using MailMerge is similar to the WordStar print command **P** in that they are both options from the "No-File" menu, and they both print a file.

MailMerge has three main advantages:

1. Multiple copies of a document may be requested from MailMerge. Thus two or more copies of a letter, document or book may be printed without any intervention.

2. The second use is in the production of letters, in which variable information is inserted into the document before printing. (For example a standard letter can be printed to each person on a mailing list, but the letters are personalised by including a different persons name on each). To achieve this, one letter is prepared using the editor in the usual way, but instead of typing the person's name in the actual letter, the directive &name& is included at the appropriate place. This directive obtains the name of a person, and when the document is printed with MailMerge the name of the person is printed instead of &name&. (The name to be printed may either be typed from the keyboard or read from a data file). The next time the document is printed, the directive &name& obtains the next person's name, inserts that in the letter, - and so on.

    Several items of variable information may be included, such as the street name, town name, postcode, the name of goods ordered, or the amount of money outstanding, and you might choose directives for these &street&, &Town& and so on. The directive always has an ampersand & at the beginning and at the end.

    The variable information that is included in the letter need not always be the same length. After the insertion, the paragraph is automatically reformed to match the format of the original text, with either a right justified or a ragged right hand edge as appropriate. Thus the same letter may be used to produce letters to many different people. If the variable information is read from a data file, then the letter will be reprinted automatically with each new name and address until the data file is exhausted. Data files may be produced to hold information such as mailing lists, lists of club members, or customer's accounts. This can save a lot of time if the list is re-used a number of times. Data files may be produced using the WordStar editor (in the Non-document mode), or special data entry programs such as DataStar are very helpful for large amounts of data. Alternatively a data file may be produced as the output from a program written in a high level language such as BASIC or FORTRAN.

3. Another use is the "boiler plating", or assembly of a number of standard paragraphs - each stored as a separate file, into a complete document. The printout appears as if the several separate files had really been incorporated into one document. In a similar way, a set of chapters which are stored as separate files, may be assembled and printed as a complete book.

    For some purposes it is convenient to produce a command file. This is made up wholly or mainly of commands - to insert files, to stop and ask you to type in the variable information from the keyboard, to read the variable information from a data file, and to arrange the layout of the text. This is useful for printing letters and envelopes alternately, using the same data from a mailing list, or for printing the chapters of a book in sequence.

It is possible to include commands which will stop the printout, and display a message requesting that the disk inserted in a particular disk drive is changed. When this command is reached, a message is displayed on the screen, and printing stops until the requested change has been made. This allows paragraphs or chapters stored as files on different disks to be included in the document, and has the practical effect that a single document may be larger than the amount of text which can be stored on a single disk.

Commands may be included which display messages on the screen during printing. Many of these uses of MailMerge mean that printing is going on for a long time, producing enormous numbers of letters, or large books. Thus displaying the name of the person to whom the letter is addressed, or the name of the file which has just been included, will give some indication of the progress of the job. Messages may also be included to give instructions to the operator, for example to explain which disk to load after a change disk message, or a reminder to insert an envelope into the printer. MailMerge also displays some error messages. An invalid dot command is ignored by the Word-Star print function, but MailMerge reports this on the screen. If by some misadventure a line begins with a full stop, then it will not be printed, and it is better to be warned that it has been ignored and omitted.

The layout of a document is normally set up under the editor when the document is originally typed. If features such as the margins, the line spacing, or whether the right margin is justified or ragged, require changing, then this could be done by re-editing the document. However, MailMerge can make these changes automatically at print time if required. This saves the time and effort of editing the original file(s), but loses the advantage of seeing how the text is laid out on the screen before printing.

There is one drawback with MailMerge. Merge-printing of one file while editing another file is not permitted. With the normal WordStar print function P, editing of one file whilst simultaneously printing another is allowed, provided that the computer has sufficient memory, though this makes WordStar run more slowly than usual.

Chapter 34.

PRODUCING MULTIPLE COPIES OF A DOCUMENT

It is sometimes necessary to produce several absolutely identical copies of a document. In this chapter a crude way of doing this is described using WordStar on its own, and a better method is given using MailMerge in conjunction with WordStar. In the following two chapters, methods are given whereby several slightly different copies of a letter or document may be produced, where most of the letter remains the same - but each contains some variable information, which is either typed in or read from a data file.

Producing multiple copies of a document using WordStar alone

Suppose that the document has been stored on disk in a file called LETTER.TXT. It may be printed under WordStar in the usual way by selecting the P option from the "No-File" menu, and giving the filename. This is fully explained in chapter 13 - Printing a Document. When the printout is completed, the "No-File" menu is displayed again, and the P option may be selected again to give another copy of the document.

Producing multiple copies of a document using MailMerge and WordStar

If the MailMerge option is available on the WordStar disk (as a separate file called MAILMRGE.OVR), then there is a much easier and more elegant way to produce multiple copies of the document. When the "No-File" menu is obtained from WordStar, select the M command to Merge-print the document. The display on the screen changes, and is shown in Figure 34.1.

FIGURE 34.1 The M command display

```
M      editing no file
   ^S=delete character    ^Y=delete entry      ^F=File directory
   ^D=restore character   ^R=Restore entry     ^U=cancel command


   NAME OF FILE TO MERGE-PRINT?



   DIRECTORY of disk B:
   LETTER.TXT
```

The important part of this display is the question asking for the name of the file to Merge-print. The filename in this case is called LETTER.TXT, and as the name is typed in it is displayed immediately after the question. Next, the RETURN key is pressed, and a series of questions are displayed on the screen one by one, as shown in Figure 34.2.

FIGURE 34.2 Questions when Merge-printing

```
   NAME OF FILE TO MERGE-PRINT?LETTER.TXT

   For default press RETURN after each question:
      DISK FILE OUTPUT (Y/N):
      START AT PAGE NUMBER(RETURN for beginning)?
      STOP AFTER PAGE NUMBER (RETURN for end)?
      NUMBER OF COPIES (RETURN for 1)?
      USE FORM FEEDS (Y/N):
      SUPPRESS PAGE FORMATTING (Y/N):
      PAUSE FOR PAPER CHANGES BETWEEN PAGES (Y/N):
   Ready printer, press RETURN:
```

These questions allow various choices to be made, and are the same as those asked by WordStar with the normal **P** Print function, except that there is one additional question about the number of copies required. A brief explanation of the meaning of the questions is included here, but a fuller explanation is given in chapter 13 - Printing a Document. In many cases the default value is an acceptable reply, and is obtained by pressing RETURN.

1. **DISK FILE OUTPUT (Y/N)**

    If the file is to be printed on paper type **N** or **n**, followed by **RETURN**, or just press **RETURN** for the default. If the "printout" is to be sent to a new disk file type **Y**, **y** or **^Y** followed by **RETURN**.

2. **START AT PAGE NUMBER?**

    To start printing from the beginning of the file the reply should be **1** (for page one) followed by **RETURN**, or just pressing **RETURN** defaults to the beginning of the file. Typing any other number, for example **5**, will result in page five and subsequent pages being printed.

3. **STOP AFTER PAGE NUMBER?**

    To print right up to the end of the document just press **RETURN**. If the last page to be printed is specified for example as **4**, then printing will stop at the end of page four.

4. **NUMBER OF COPIES?**

    One of the advantages of MailMerge is that the number of copies of the document which are to be printed may be specified. Pressing **RETURN** in answer to the question gives the default of just one copy, but typing a number - for example **3** will give that number of copies. It should be noted that a complete document is printed out with the pages in order. If more than one copy is requested, then after printing one copy, WordStar automatically goes back to the beginning of the document, starts on a new page, and prints each page again - and so on. It does not print three copies of page one, then three copies of page two, ... etc.

5. **USE FORM FEEDS (Y/N)**

    On some printers the paper length is defined by means of switch settings, and a form feed signal is required to make them start a new page. Answering **Y** or **y** followed by **RETURN** makes WordStar transmit a form-feed character to the printer at the end of a printed page. Advantages of this are that the paper length set in WordStar need not exactly match the size of paper used, and the printer may move much faster to the beginning of a new page with a form-feed than with a series of several line feeds. If the printer cannot do this, the reply is **N** or **n** followed by **RETURN**, or just **RETURN**, and the paper length must be set exactly in WordStar.

6. **SUPPRESS PAGE FORMATTING (Y/N)?**

    The usual answer is **N**, or **n** and **RETURN**, or just **RETURN**, in which case page formatting is carried out, dot commands are executed, and the print enhancements are also implemented. If the question is answered **Y** or **y** followed by **RETURN**, then page formatting will be suppressed, and dot commands are then printed as commands, rather than being executed, but the print enhancements are carried out as usual.

7. **PAUSE FOR PAPER CHANGE BETWEEN PAGES (Y/N)?**

    A reply of **N** or **n** followed by pressing **RETURN**, or just **RETURN** will make WordStar print continuously. The printer must have a roll of paper, or continuous fan folded paper or an automatic single sheet feeder must be fitted. A reply of **Y** or **y**, followed by pressing **RETURN** is used to make the printer pause at the end of each page, so that a new sheet of paper may be manually inserted into the printer.

8. **Ready Printer, press RETURN**
   This is just a warning message, to remind you to check that the printer is switched on, that paper is correctly loaded and positioned, and if appropriate that the printer is switched to "on-line" operation, rather than "off-line", or "local". Pressing **RETURN** (or any other key), will cause printing to start.

Interrupting the printout

It is easy to stop the printer in the middle of a printout, by typing **P**. A message is then displayed on the screen:

TYPE "Y" to ABANDON PRINT, "N" TO RESUME, ^U TO HOLD:

To abandon printing, that is to stop printing altogether, just type **Y**. To resume printing from exactly the point where it was suspended then type **N**. There will be nothing in the printout to show that there has been an interruption. It is possible to hold (suspend) printing by typing **^U**. You may then go back to the "No-File" menu and do other things, such as editing another file, or checking the name of a file from the directory. The printer will remain in this paused state until **P** is typed, then printing will be resumed as if there had been no interruption.

Answering only some of the questions

It may not be necessary to go through all of the questions each time. Suppose that the default answers are acceptable to all of the questions, except that three copies are required. Questions 1 (Disk file output), 2 (Start page number), 3 (Stop after page number) may each be answered by pressing RETURN. Question 4 (Number of copies) must be answered by typing 3 to get three copies, but instead of pressing RETURN, press ESCAPE instead. This stops WordStar asking any more of the questions, and provides the default answers to those questions which have been missed. Printing starts without any further warning, so it is essential that the printer has previously been made ready.

Delays in printing

Should the starting page for printing be some way into the document, for example page 20, then there will be an appreciable delay after the questions before printing actually begins. This is because WordStar has to read page by page through the document, starting from the beginning, so that it can find where page 20 begins.

It is possible that printing starts, but pauses of its own accord before the end of the job. The most likely reasons for this are:
1.   The printer may be waiting for you to change the paper, because you answered **YES** to the question **PAUSE FOR PAPER CHANGE BETWEEN PAGES**.
2.   The computer may be waiting for you to change the floppy disk, because you have used a .FI command with .CHANGE after the filename. An explanatory message will be displayed on the screen if this has happened. (See chapter 37 - Printing Several Files as a Book, and chapter 39 - Special Dot Commands for MailMerge).
3.   The printer may have sensed that it is out of paper, or that the ribbon has run out.
4.   Another possible reason is that a **^C** character has been encountered in the text. You may have done this so that you may change the daisy wheel or print thimble, at this point. (See chapter 23 - Special Print Effects).
5.   If you are "printing" to disk, it is possible that the disk is full, in which case a **DISK FULL** error message will have appeared on the screen.

Chapter 35.

PRODUCING STANDARD LETTERS

Sometimes a number of similar copies of a letter are required, where
most of the letter remains the same - but each contains some variable
information, perhaps just a different name and address. Two methods
of doing this are described in this chapter, and a third method is
explained in the next chapter. In the first method the letters are
produced by repeatedly editing and re-printing using WordStar alone.
The second method uses MailMerge in conjunction with WordStar, and the
variable information is actually typed in when requested during the
printout. The next chapter 36 - Letters Envelopes and Labels Using
Data Files, describes a third method which also uses MailMerge, where
the variable information is read from a data file. It is also
possible to type some variable information and read some from a data
file.

Suppose that the letter shown in Figure 35.1, addressed to Mr. John Smith,
has been typed in under WordStar, and that the document has been stored on disk
in a file called LETTER.TXT. It may be printed under WordStar in the usual way
by selecting the P option from the "No-File Menu", and typing the filename. If
ESCAPE is then pressed, the printout will begin at once using the default
answers, but if RETURN is pressed then a series of questions must first be
answered. This is described fully in chapter 34.

FIGURE 35.1 Straightforward letter

```
.. letter to guests
.op omit page numbers
```

Super Computers PLC,
1 Pudding Lane,
LONDON, WC2.

29th Feb 1983

Mr. John Smith,
1 Buckingham Palace Road,
LONDON SW1 30D.

Dear Mr. Smith,

   I have pleasure in inviting you to the launch of
the 1666 range of new British microcomputers. The computer which
is truly state of the art, performs calculations faster than the
speed of light, taking full advantage of the new memory chips
developed from silica from Blackpool beach. Instead of using
power from the mains, these are fitted with the very latest solar
panels imported from Blarney to provide electrical power. These
are claimed to be so efficient that they will operate in total
darkness using stored moonshine.

   The launch will be attended by the Minister
without Technology, The Right Honourable Ned Ludd, and will be
preceded by a champagne buffet, caviare, smoked salmon and
silicon chips with everything. The event will be strictly black
tie, and will be held at Buckingham Palace on April 1st.

   Yours sincerely,

When the printout is completed, the "No-File" menu is displayed on the screen, and the **D** option is selected to edit the file LETTER.TXT. The name John Smith must be found, and changed for example to Bill Brown, the address must be changed, and a few lines further down Smith must be changed to Brown. There are several possible ways of doing this:

1. The cursor may be moved down the screen one line at a time, by pressing **^X** repeatedly, until the line is reached which contains the name Mr. John Smith. The cursor is then moved one word to the right by pressing **^F** until it lies on top of the letter J of the word John. Next the words John and Smith are deleted by pressing **^T** twice, and the words Bill Brown are typed. Next the cursor is moved down a line, (to the street name), by typing **^X**, and this whole line of the address is deleted by typing **^Y**. The new address may then be typed in, followed by pressing **RETURN**. This automatically moves the cursor down one line to the town. This whole line is deleted with **^Y**, and the new town is typed in, followed by **RETURN**. Finally the cursor is moved down again with **^X**, and sideways using **^S** or **^D** until it is over the letter S of Smith. This word is deleted with **^T**, and the new name Brown typed in. The changes are now complete, and the letter addressed to Mr. Brown must be saved on disk by typing **^KD**. When this has been done, the "No-File Menu" is displayed on the screen, and the **P** print option may be selected to print another copy of the letter – this time addressed to Mr. Brown. The entire process must be repeated to produce a letter addressed to Mr. Jones. At the best this method is tedious.

2. Another way of editing the letter under WordStar is to use the find function by typing **^QF**, which is described in chapter 16.

If the MailMerge option is available on the WordStar disk (as a separate file called MAILMRGE.OVR), then there are two much easier and more elegant ways of producing a series of standard letters from the document, using the .AV command to ask for a value, or the .RV command to read a value from a file.

How to use the .AV command

This is one of a number of special dot commands which are exclusive to MailMerge. These are described in chapter 39 – Special Dot Commands for MailMerge. The .AV command, with the dot in column one, makes the computer stop and ask for a value to be typed in from the keyboard. The command line must also contain a single word. (This word is used as a variable by WordStar, to store the information you type in, and when the computer stops, the word is displayed on the screen followed by a question mark, to remind you what information is being requested. This word may be from 1-40 characters long, must begin with a letter, and may contain letters, numbers, or hyphens but no other characters or spaces). Suppose that we put the following command in a file:

.AV Name

When the file is printed using MailMerge option M from the "No-File" menu it stops at the .AV command, and displays a message on the screen:

Name?

When the appropriate name has been typed followed by RETURN, MailMerge continues to print. The name typed is stored for later use, and is not printed at this time. At the point in the file where the variable information Name should be printed, we must insert the variable reference &Name&. The name typed in will be printed instead of &Name&.

Great care must be taken to ensure that the variable name in the .AV command matches exactly the variable reference used in the &...& command, or this process will not work, and you will obtain a useless letter with &...&

printed in it. It is usual to have several different .AV commands in one letter, to read in several different pieces of variable information, for example Name, Street, Town and County. Each .AV command uses a different variable, Name, Street etc. and must be typed on a separate line.

The variable name followed by a question mark may not be the most useful prompt to display on the screen. Suppose that we required the Full name (Mr. John Smith) in one variable and the short name (John, or Mr. Smith) to be stored in another variable. While variable names such as Name1 and Name2 could be used, these are not particularly informative, and we can use a hyphen to join two words into one in order to get a more helpful message displayed on the screen. Thus the command .AV Full-name works in conjunction with a variable reference &Full-name&. It may be that you would like to put a whole phrase or sentence as the prompt on the screen. This can be done using a .AV command with the message to be used for the prompt enclosed inside single or double quotation marks, followed by a comma, and then by the variable name. For example the command:

.AV "Type Mr. or Mrs. then the full name, & press RETURN ", NAME1

would cause the following message to be displayed on the screen:

Type Mr. or Mrs. then the full name, & press RETURN

and the information typed in would be stored in the variable NAME1, which would be printed where required by the variable reference **&NAME1&**.

Some variable information, such as the County, may be either present or absent in an address. Adding /O after the variable name in the variable reference shows that the information is optional. Thus the command .AV County will stop the computer and display the message **County** on the screen. If the County is typed, then it will be printed out as usual by the variable reference **&County&**. Alternatively if **RETURN** is pressed in reply to the .AV prompt thus leaving the County blank, then **&County&** will produce a space, or a blank line if the rest of the line is blank. If the variable reference **&County/O&** is used instead, the county will be printed if it is provided, but a blank line will not appear if **RETURN** is typed when the county is asked for.

The number of characters accepted in reply to a .AV command is limited to the number which will fit on the screen to the right of the prompt. A smaller limit may be imposed by adding a comma and the maximum number of characters at the end of the .AV command. This might be used to limit the length of a post code, and the following command could be used for a six digit telephone number:

.AV "TEL-NO ", Tel, 6

or

.AV "Type the 6 digit telephone number ", Tel, 6

Comparison of the original letter in Figure 35.1 with the form letter shown in Figure 35.2, shows that several .AV commands and variable references &...& have been included to make it run under MailMerge. The command .AV Full-name will stop the computer, and prompts with the message **Full-name?** When you have typed **Mr. John Smith** and pressed **RETURN**, the computer will continue. The other .AV commands prompt in a similar way with the following messages:

> **Type number and the street name and press RETURN**
> **Type town name and post code and press RETURN**
> **Type CITY & press RETURN, or just press RETURN**
> **Short-name**

The information typed in is stored in the variables Full-name, STREET, Town, City, and Short-name, and are printed at the appropriate places in the letter

128

with the variable references &Full-name&, &STREET&, &Town&, &City& and '&Short-name&. Note that the city name is optional.

FIGURE 35.2 Form letter using .AV Ask for Value commands

```
.. letter to guests
.op  omit page numbers
.AV Full-name
.AV "Type number and the street name and press RETURN ", STREET
.AV 'Type town name and post code and press RETURN ', Town
.AV "Type CITY & press RETURN , or just press RETURN ", City
.AV Short-name
```

Super Computers PLC,
1 Pudding Lane,
LONDON, WC2.

29th Feb 1983

&Full-name&,
&STREET&,
&Town&
&City/O&

Dear &Short-name&,

I have pleasure in inviting you to the launch of the 1666 range of new British microcomputers. The computer which is truly state of the art, performs calculations faster than the speed of light, taking full advantage of the new memory chips developed from silica from Blackpool beach. Instead of using power from the mains, these are fitted with the very latest solar panels imported from Blarney to provide electrical power. These are claimed to be so efficient that they will operate in total darkness using stored moonshine.

The launch will be attended by the Minister without Technology, The Right Honourable Ned Ludd, and will be preceded by a champagne buffet, caviare, smoked salmon and silicon chips with everything. The event will be strictly black tie, and will be held at Buckingham Palace on April 1st.

Yours sincerely,

```
.CS (clear the screen - optional)
.PA (start a new page unconditionally)
.FI LETTER.TXT
```

Printing multiple copies using .AV commands and MailMerge

To print the letter shown in Figure 35.2, the MailMerge option **M** must be selected from the "No-File" menu. Full details of the messages displayed, the questions and answers are detailed in the preceding chapter 34 - Producing several identical copies of a document. Briefly, the name of the file you wish to print with MailMerge must be typed, and if the printer is ready and only one copy is required, then the rest of the questions can be skipped by pressing

Escape. If the questions are answered individually, one of them allows you to specify the exact number of letters to be printed. If you are not sure how many copies are required, type any large number and stop the printing when you have done them all. Normally typing **P** will make printing stop, and then typing **Y** will abandon printing. There is a problem that when you type P, MailMerge might take it as the reply to a .AV command. This problem can be overcome by hitting **RETURN** followed very quickly by P, so that RETURN is taken as the reply to the .AV question, and P stops the printer.

A second way of starting an endless loop for printing out letters is to include a **File Insert** command .FI (filename) , followed by **RETURN** as the last line of the letter. In this case the letter is stored in a file called LETTER.TXT, so the command would be:

.FI LETTER.TXT

Every time MailMerge reaches this line at the bottom of the letter, the .FI command will take it back to the beginning of the same file. Printing can be stopped by pressing **RETURN** followed very quickly by P as discussed above.

It is quite possible that the answer to one or more of the .AV questions is the same as for the previous letter. For example, the city may be the same for quite a few letters. Rather than have to retype the city each time, typing **^R** and **RETURN** copies the information used for that question previously.

Obviously each letter should start on a new page, so it may be worth including a **.PA** command at the end of the letter to force unconditionally the start of a new page. This command is not needed if you have answered all the questions about Merge-printing, and have answered **YES** to the PAUSE FOR PAPER CHANGE BETWEEN PAGES question and are manually loading a new sheet of paper into the printer for each letter. However, with continuous stationery (either a roll, or fan folded paper), or with an automatic single sheet paper feeder it is essential to include this command.

In the examples so far, the letters have only occupied one page, and a .OP command has been used to prevent page number 1 appearing at the bottom of the page. If the letter is more than one page long, you may well want the pages numbered, which WordStar will do automatically by default. (Some versions of MergePrint used with WordStar version 2.X require a .PN 1 command at the beginning of the file, otherwise the page numbers in the second letter continue on sequentially from the first letter, rather than starting again at page 1. This has been cured in WordStar 3.X and the associated MailMerge program).

Perhaps you would like to clear the screen from the names and addresses used in the previous letter before starting on the details of the next letter. This can be done very simply by including a .CS command at the end of the letter. If any other text is present on this command line, it will be displayed on the screen when the screen has been cleared. Thus the command:

.CS Screen cleared, ready for the next letter

would clear the screen and display the message:

Screen cleared, ready for the next letter

It is also possible to use .AV commands to obtain information which we wish to include in the body of the text. Suppose that we wished to write to a number of Universities and Polytechnics to enquire about the courses they offered. The letter in Figure 35.3 would provide a flexible and useful form letter. MailMerge was run to print this letter, and the questions asked by the .AV commands, together with the replies given are shown in Figure 35.4.

130

FIGURE 35.3 Another form letter using .AV commands

```
.. Letter of enquiry to Universities and Polytechnics
.OP omit page numbers
.AV "Type name of University/Poly, & press RETURN ", Poly
.AV "Type Street if known & press RETURN ", Street
.AV "Type town and postcode if known, & RETURN ", Town
.AV "Type County if known & press RETURN ", County
.AV "Type career & press RETURN ", Career
.AV "Type the date & press RETURN ", Date
```

1 Valley Road,
Nottingham.
&Date&

```
The Registrar,
&Poly&
&Street/O&
&Town&
&County/O&
```

Dear Sir,

      I would be most grateful if you could send me details of Degree courses you run which would lead to a career in &Career&. I would also like some information on the "A-level" requirements for entry to these courses, and the availability of student accommodation.

               Yours faithfully,

```
.cs
.pa
```

FIGURE 35.4 Questions and replies

Type name of University/Poly, & press RETURN	**Leeds Polytechnic,**
Type Street if known & press RETURN	**Calverley Street,**
Type town and postcode if known, & RETURN	**LEEDS, LS1 3HE.**
Type County if known & press RETURN	
Type career & press RETURN	**Business studies and Accountancy**
Type the date & press RETURN	**29 Feb. 83**

The letter this produced is shown in Figure 35.5. The insertion of the date and the address are much the same as in the previous example. The interesting feature is the insertion of the words **Business studies and Accountancy** in place of the variable **&Career&** in the body of the text. It can be seen that the words have wrapped round from one line to the next, and also that the paragraph has been tidied up and reformed, in much the same way as ^B does under the editor. MailMerge does this automatically, by inspecting the paragraph before inserting the variable data, to establish the left and right margins, the spacing, and whether text is right justified or has a ragged right edge. It can then reform the paragraph to match the existing text. Since the inserted data is often longer than the variable reference, automatic reforming may make a paragraph one or more lines longer than it was previously. If this occurs then page breaks will not be printed exactly where they were shown on the screen during editing. It is recommended that conditional page breaks .CP are used generously to ensure attractive pagination.

FIGURE 35.5 Letter produced by MailMerge from the form letter in Figure 35.3 with the replies shown in Figure 35.4

                                              1 Valley Road,
                                              Nottingham.
                                              29 Feb. 83

The Registrar,
Leeds Polytechnic,
Calverley Street,
LEEDS, LS1 3HE.

Dear Sir,

        I would be most grateful if you could send me details of Degree courses you run which would lead to a career in **Business studies and Accountancy.** I would also like some information on the "A-level" requirements for entry to these courses, and the availability of student accommodation.

                Yours faithfully,

Chapter 36.
LETTERS, ENVELOPES & LABELS USING DATA FILES

For some purposes fairly standard letters will be sent to the same people at intervals. These could be letters to members of a club or professional association, a firm writing to give particulars of new products, or a Building Society writing to clients to say the interest rate on their loan had changed. It is worth preparing a mailing list, where details of the names and addresses of members or clients, and perhaps other information too, are stored in a data file. A form letter can be prepared, where the variable bits of information are replaced by variable names, which are enclosed by ampersand symbols. A line of variable information is read from the data-file,and the relevant parts inserted into the letter at the appropriate point. The same data file may be used to produce envelopes, or sticky labels. This method fully automates the production of letters and/or addressed envelopes, and requires MailMerge as well as WordStar.

Suppose that you would like to send a letter, like that shown in Figure 36.1, to all of the members of a Golf Club. Each recipient would get a similar letter, except that the names and addresses, and the membership subscriptions would differ.

FIGURE 36.1 Letter to Golf Club members

Royal Gotham Golf Club,
Links Road,
Gotham.
1st Dec. 1984

Mr. A. Palmer,
19 High Street,
Upper Missenden.

Dear Arnold,

I would like to remind you that your annual subscription as a full member of the Golf Club of two hundred guineas becomes due on 1st January 1985, and I should be pleased to receive your cheque at your earliest convenience.

I enclose formal notice of the Annual General Meeting on January 10th, and request your attendance. May I extend the compliments of the season.

Yours sincerely,

Major J. Nicklaus (Hon. Sec.)

Printing multiple copies of the letter, reading data values from a file

Figure 36.2 shows a form letter which will print a letter like that in Figure 36.1. The parts which have either been changed or added are shown in bold type. First, a number of pieces of information in the original letter have been replaced by variable references in the letter itself, and are enclosed by ampersand signs. The information required for these variables will either be set with a .SV command, or read from a data file with a .RV command.

These variable references will be replaced by the actual contents of the
variables when the document is printed by MailMerge. These dot commands are
explained later in this chapter, and also in chapter 38 - Special Dot Commands
for MailMerge.

FIGURE 36.2 Form letter to produce letters to Golf Club members

```
..Letter reminding members of annual subscriptions and AGM
.OP (omit page numbers)
.SV Date,1st Dec. 1984
.SV Secretary,Major J. Nicklaus
.SV AGM-date,January 10th
.DF MEMBERS
.RV Number, Title, Full-name, Street, Town, First-name, Class, Subscription
.DM Letter &Number& to &Title& &Full-name& now being typed
```

Royal Gotham Golf Club,
Links Road,
Gotham.
&Date&

&Title& &Full-name&,
&Street&,
&Town&,

Dear &First-name&,

          I would like to remind you that your annual
subscription as a &Class& member of the Golf Club of
&Subscription& guineas becomes due on 1st January 1985, and I
should be pleased to receive your cheque at your earliest
convenience.

          I enclose formal notice of the Annual General Meeting
on &AGM-date&, and request your attendance. May I extend the
compliments of the season.

          Yours sincerely,

          &Secretary& (Hon. Sec.)

```
.CS (clear screen )
.PA (start new page unconditionally)
..file ends here
```

The variables which have been used are:

&Date&	stores the current date
&Title&	Lord, Rev., Major, Captain, Wing Commander, Mr., Mrs., Miss,
&Full-name&	eg. A. Palmer
&Street&	eg. 19 High Street
&Town&	eg. Upper Missenden
&First-name&	eg. Arnold
&Class&	type of member eg. Full, Country, Junior, Non-playing
&Subscription&	amount in guineas
&AGM-date&	date when Annual General meeting will be held
&Secretary&	name of this year's club secretary
&Number&	the record number - discussed later under Data files

Use of the Set Variable .SV command

Several of these variables will stay the same for all the letters. These are the **Date** of the letter, the **AGM-date**, and **Secretary**, the name of this year's club secretary. These variables may conveniently be set using a .SV command. The general form of this command is:

.SV variable,value assigned to the variable

for example   **.SV Date,1st Dec. 1984**
or   **.SV Secretary,Major J. Nicklaus**
or   **.SV AGM-date,January 10th**

The first example of the set value command sets the value of the variable Date to 1st Dec. 1984. It is important to remember that the dot must be in column one, and there must be a comma between the name of the variable and the value assigned to it. Should you need to store a comma as part of the data in a variable, then the variable information must be enclosed by quotation marks.

Use of the Data File .DF command

The remainder of the variables will be read from a data file which has been prepared previously, and is stored on a floppy disk. These are the information about the first member: Title, Full-name, Street, Town, First-name, Class of member and Subscription. When the first letter has been printed, the information about the second member will be read from a data file, that letter printed, then the third member, and so on. It is essential that you specify the name of the data file you wish to use. This is done with a .DF command, which has the general form:

.DF data-file-name (CHANGE)

for example   **.DF MEMBERS**

or   **.DF NEWMEMB**

In the example, the data file is called MEMBERS, and this file must be present on the logged-in disk drive. The optional parameter CHANGE may be used should you want to stop the computer and change disks. This is described in chapter 38 - Special Dot Commands for MailMerge. An explanation of how to produce the data-file is given later in this chapter.

Use of the Read Variables .RV command

This command will read the values of variables from a previously named disk file. The general form of the command is:

.RV variable1, variable2, ...

One or more variables may be read with a single .RV command. The variables are read from the file in the order given, and if more than one is present on the line, they must be separated by a comma. The spaces which precede the variable name are optional, but spaces must not occur in the middle of the name. For example the command:

.RV Number, Title, Full-name, Street, Town, First-name, Class, Subscription

will read the eight variables Number, Title, Full-name ... etc. from the data-file. It is most important that the number and order of the data values specified in this command matches exactly with what has been stored in the data-file.

The .RV command makes the computer read a set of variables, and print the corresponding letter, read the next set of variables, and print, in a continuous manner until the data file is exhausted. If when starting MailMerge you choose to answer all the questions, and specify more than one copy, for example two copies, then letters for the entire mailing list will be printed, and MailMerge will then return to the beginning of the data-file and print the whole lot of letters a second time.

Other commands used in the letter

The first line, which begins .. is a remark, and serves to remind us of the contents of the file. It will not be printed.

The .OP command instructs WordStar to omit page numbers. Since the letter is only one page long, you do not really want a number 1 printing at the bottom of the page.

The .DM command is used to display a message on the screen under Mail-Merge. The general form of this command is:

.DM message

for example   **.DM Letter &Number& to &Title& &Full-name& now being typed**

This message is rather clever, since the values of the variables &Number& &Title& and &Full-name& have been read from the data file, they will be displayed on the screen as part of the message. Thus while the first letter is being typed, the screen displays the following message:

Letter 1 to Mr. A. Palmer now being typed

When this letter is finished, the information will be read from the data-file for the next member, and a new message containing his name will then appear on the screen. Thus the screen will show a list of messages, each corresponding to a letter which has been typed.

The .CS command is used to clear the screen at the end of the letter. Any other text on the command line will also be displayed on the screen. In this way only one message shows on the screen, giving the latest letter being typed.

Finally, the .PA command causes an unconditional page break, and is used to make the next letter start on a new page.

Data Files

A MailMerge data-file consists of a large number of records (lines). A suitable data file can be created and subsequently edited using WordStar, but if you are likely to do a lot of this kind of work it may be better to buy a special data entry program such as MicroPro's program DataStar which is specifically designed to do this. The method using WordStar is described here. From the "No-File" menu the command **N** must be selected to edit a Non-document file, rather than the usual command of **D** to edit text in a normal WordStar document. The main difference is that in Non-document mode word-wrap is switched OFF, so no soft spaces will be inserted to justify lines, and no carriage RETURNS will be inserted except those deliberately entered by you. After you have specified the name of the data file, you should type in the variable data.

A very simple and crude way of producing the data file is to type one variable piece of information on each line and then press **RETURN**. In the example of a letter to the Golf club members , the .RV command used shows that eight variables are read from the file for each member:

.RV Number, Title, Full-name, Street, Town, First-name, Class, Subscription

These could be entered in the file:

1 **RETURN**
Mr. **RETURN**
A. Palmer **RETURN**
1 High Street **RETURN**
Upper Missenden **RETURN**
Arnold **RETURN**
Full **RETURN**
two hundred guineas **RETURN**

Following this there would be a similar set of entries for the second and each of the subsequent members. Since the .RV command specifies in this case that eight items will be read from the file, there must be exactly eight items for each member. If one item of information is not known, it must be entered as two sets of quotation marks "" followed by **RETURN**, to keep the information in order. The quotation marks will not be printed. If an item contains a comma, then quotation marks must be put before and after the item, since a comma is taken to mean the end of the item.

A more convenient and better structure for the data-file is to have one record or line of information for each person. Each record contains the variable values to be used to print one letter or other document, with a RETURN after the last item in the record. The next record (line) contains all of the information for the next letter to the next person. Within one line, the variable values are separated by commas, and should a comma occur as part of the data then that variable must be enclosed in quotation marks so that Mail-Merge does not take it to be a separator. The quotation marks are not printed.

In the letter to Golf Club members, eight variables are read from the file with the .RV statement. These should be typed on one line, with a comma separating items, but no comma after the last item, and a RETURN at the end of the line. The .RV statement may have any number of variables to suit the particular job provided that the variables match what is written in the data-file.

It is strongly recommended that each record begins with a serial number, since it makes it much easier to check and edit the data. The Golf club data typed in to the MEMBERS file might appear as shown in Figure 36.3.

FIGURE 36.3 Data entered into MEMBERS file

1,Mr.,A. Palmer,1 High Street,Upper Missenden,Arnold,Full,two hundred
2,Wing Commander,J. Wilks,10 Castle Road,Winchester,WingCo,Country,one hundred
3,Miss,Felicity Anne Winstanley,"Abercromby Manor, Palace Road",Salisbury,Anne,
Non-Playing,fifty

A record may be too long to fit on one line on the screen, and the data may appear on to two or more lines on the screen. This does not matter, and provided that you keep typing the variables, with a comma between each, and press RETURN at the end of the record, the file will be correct. If the value of a variable item it is not known, or you wish to leave it blank, it is essential that you enter the comma that goes after the value, or alternatively type a space and then a comma, so that the other values are read from the file in the correct order. When you have finished typing the data-file, it should be checked visually on the screen. The next section describes how the data-file may be printed out in a more readable way to facilitate checking.

Printing a data-file for checking

The data in Figure 36.3 are not very easy to read, and formatting the information into a more ordered layout, and printing it out on paper would make checking much easier. To do this you should produce a file called CHECK, which when run under MailMerge will read the data file called MEMBERS, and print the information in an orderly way. The information stored in each record of the data-file is:

Number, Title, Full-name, Street, Town, First-name, Class, Subscription

The commands used in the file called CHECK are shown in Figure 36.4.

FIGURE 36.4 The commands in file CHECK to check the data-file called MEMBERS

```
..File to read MEMBERS file, and produce a formatted printout using MAILMERGE
.DF MEMBERS
.RV Number, Title, Full-name, Street, Town, First-name, Class, Subscription
.OP    (omit pagenumbers)
.CP 6  (start a new page if there are less than 6 lines left)

&Number&       &Title& &Full-name&      known as &First-name&
       &Street&
       &Town&
       Class of membership &Class&
       Subscription &Subscription& guineas
..file ends here
```

The purpose of these commands is described briefly below. The line beginning .. is merely a comment describing the purpose of the file. The .DF command defines the data-file as a file called MEMBERS. The .RV command reads in the eight variables stored in each record in the MEMBERS file. Note that the same names have been used for each of the variables as were used in the letter to the members, since these are self explanatory. There is no need for the variable names to be the same, and the names X1, X2, X3, ... X8 could be used equally well. The .OP command is to suppress the printing of page numbers at the bottom of each page, and the .CP 6 command causes a new page to be started if less than six lines remain on the current page. This has been included to prevent a data record from being split between two pages. The value six arises because the file includes one blank line after the .CP command, followed by five lines which will be printed. These include the eight variables which were read from the data-file, and a few words which are printed by way of explanation.

MailMerge may now be used to Merge-print the file CHECK. This is done by typing **M** in reply to the WordStar "No-File" menu, specifying the file to be Merge-printed as CHECK, and either pressing **ESCAPE** if the printer is ready, or going through all the printing questions if necessary. The output produced is shown in Figure 36.5.

Several records (in this case Golf club members) will be printed on each page, and simple mis-spellings may be detected. More important than this, errors such as a missing comma in the data-file can be detected quite easily. This would result in the data being printed out of place. It is strongly recommended that a newly typed or altered data-file is always printed in this way, since it is easier to detect and correct errors at this stage rather than printing hundreds of useless letters or envelopes.

FIGURE 36.5 Output from CHECK

1   Mr. A. Palmer   known as Arnold
        1 High Street
        Upper Missenden
        Class of membership Full
        Subscription two hundred guineas

2   Wing Commander J. Wilks   known as WingCo
        10 Castle Road
        Winchester
        Class of membership Country
        Subscription one hundred guineas

3   Miss Felicity Anne Winstanley   known as Anne
        Abercromby Manor, Palace Road
        Salisbury
        Class of membership Non-Playing
        Subscription fifty guineas

Printing sticky labels for mailing

It may be useful to print the names and addresses on sticky labels, which can be used for mailing something to the members or clients on the mailing list. A method similar to that used for the checking may be used. A file called LABELS should be produced using WordStar in the Non-Document edit mode.

The variables must be read in the same order as they were stored in the data-file, and the printed layout must be tailored to fit the size of the labels used. Assume that the labels are on a continuous roll, each measuring three inches across and two inches deep. Printing at ten characters to the inch, the longest line which will fit on a label is thirty characters. Printing at six lines to the inch, there is room for twelve lines on a label. The number of blank lines included before and after the variable insertions can be worked out once you decide how many lines of useful information you wish to print on the label. In this case there are three blank lines before the address, five lines of address and associated spaces, and four blank lines after the address, thus accounting for the twelve lines.

When printing labels it is usual to suppress the top margin and the bottom margin by including **.MT 0** and **.MB 0** commands, and to suppress page numbers with a **.OP** command. For example, the data-file called MEMBERS contains the information on the members of the Golf Club. Note that all the variables in a record must be read to keep the data in order, but there is no need to use all the variables in this letter. The variables stored in each record in the data-file are: Number, Title, Full-name, Street, Town, First-name, Class, Subscription

The **.DM** command displays a message on the screen, which shows the name being printed on the current label. This is useful to show how far the job has progressed. At the end of printing each label the screen is cleared with a **.CS** command. The whole set of commands needed are shown in Figure 36.6.

The output which is produced when this file is printed using MailMerge is shown in Figure 36.7. If the printing on the labels needs moving to the right, this can be achieved either by adding the appropriate number of spaces at the beginning of each line where a variable is printed, or alternatively a **.PO** command may be added to the LABELS file, with a suitable number after it to indicate the page offset required, that is the column where printing should start. This is discussed in chapter 26 - Dot commands.

FIGURE 36.6 Commands in the file LABELS

```
..file to print addresses from file MEMBERS on 3 x 2 in. sticky labels
.MT 0
.MB 0
.OP
.DF MEMBERS
.RV Number, Title, Full-name, Street, Town, First-name, Class, Subscription
.DM Label to &Title& &Full-name& now being printed
..Three blank lines before address


..Five lines used for the address
&Title& &Full-name&,

&Street&,

&Town&.
..Four blank lines after address


.CS
..file ends here
```

FIGURE 36.7 Sticky label printout

Mr. A. Palmer,

1 High Street,

Upper Missenden.

Wing Commander J. Wilks,

10 Castle Road,

Winchester.

Miss Felicity Anne Winstanley,

Abercromby Manor, Palace Road,

Salisbury.

Suppose that the labels were a different size, for example three inches wide by one inch deep. If the printer prints six lines per inch, there is room for exactly six lines on the label. In this particular case one line is needed for the person's name, one for the street name and one for the town name. This leaves three unused lines, which could be used for one blank line before the person's name, and two blank lines after the address.

Printing envelopes

A very similar procedure may be used to print directly on envelopes. A file called ENVELOPES should be produced to read the data file, and print the appropriate variables to give the name and address in a suitable format.

It is necessary to stop the printer as soon as one envelope has been printed, so that the next envelope may be inserted. This may be accomplished in two different ways. The first method is to define the "page" size as the length of one envelope, and when running MailMerge to go through the questions about the printing and answer YES to the question PAUSE BETWEEN PAGES? The alternative method is to put the ^C character in the file at the appropriate point, which has the effect of "pausing" the printer. The status line on the screen shows a message PRINT PAUSED, and the "No-File" menu is displayed. When a new envelope has been inserted in the printer, pressing P restarts the printer. If ^C is typed while editing a file, it will be interpreted as a command to scroll a screenful of information up. To enter ^C in the file, it is necessary to type ^P^C, when the display shows ^C, and that is what goes into the file.

It is suggested that the top and bottom page margins are set to zero with **.MT 0** and **.MB 0** commands as for the sticky labels. If the ^C method of stopping the printer is used, then it is recommended that the pagelength is set large enough to roll the envelope out of the printer after the address has been printed. The number of blank lines printed before the address may need adjusting to make the printing appear at the correct height on the envelope. Similarly the page offset value used in the **.PO** command may need changing. The suggested commands for the ENVELOPE file are shown in Figure 36.8.

FIGURE 36.8 Commands in the file ENVELOPES

```
..file to print envelopes using data from the MEMBERS file
.MT 0
.MB 0
.OP
.PL 40  Page length - adjust if necessary
.PO 10  Page offset - adjust if necessary
.DF MEMBERS
.RV Number, Title, Full-name, Street, Town, First-name, Class, Subscription
.. ^C on the next line will stop the printer to allow you to insert envelope
^C
..Three blank lines before address - adjust if necessary


..Three lines used for the address
&Title& &Full-name&,
&Street&,
&Town&.

.PA  end of "page", roll envelope out
..file ends here
```

Chapter 37.

PRINTING SEVERAL FILES AS A BOOK

It is possible to use WordStar to print several separate files as a complete document, or as a book. Two methods are described, one which is tedious, and another which imposes limits on the maximum size of the document. MailMerge works with WordStar to enhance its file handling capabilities. One particularly useful feature of MailMerge is described, where several files are chained together so that they are printed as if they had been merged into a single document. This method is simple, elegant, and imposes no limit on the maximum size. Other uses of MailMerge, such a printing multiple copies of the same document, and the production of customised letters, are described in the chapters 34, 35 and 36.

Chaining several files to print as a single document

It is quite common to prepare a large document, such as a book, as several separate chapters, each of which has been stored as a separate file on the disk. This is the sensible way to produce a large document, because it is much quicker to edit small files than very large ones, and also because it reduces storage problems on the disk and the possibility of "disk full" errors. It may be necessary to store files on more than one disk if the book is sufficiently large. With WordStar it is quite possible to print each file in turn, and with a little careful manipulation of page numbers you can obtain a set of pages which are numbered sequentially throughout. Using MailMerge, this can be printed in a single job, with the page numbers automatically numbered sequentially. Three methods of printing the book are described, two using WordStar on its own, and the better way using MailMerge.

Suppose the individual files to be printed together to make a book are called CHAPTER1.TXT, CHAPTER2.TXT, CHAPTER3.TXT , CHAPTER4.TXT and INDEX.TXT. Using WordStar the file CHAPTER1.TXT can be printed out. It is then necessary to find the last page number which was used. Suppose this was page 17, then CHAPTER2.TXT must be edited and the command .PN 18 inserted at the beginning of the file. When this file is printed, the pages will be numbered in sequence starting from page 18. Similarly when the last page number used for Chapter 2 is known, Chapter 3 can be edited with a suitable .PN instruction and then printed, and so on with Chapter 4, and then with the Index.

This is a long and tedious procedure, and if having done this some text is added or deleted in an early Chapter resulting in a change of page numbers, then all the .PN commands will have to be changed before reprinting the book.

The second way of printing the book under WordStar is to copy all the individual chapters into a single file, and then print the new file. To do this, WordStar should be called to create a new document file by typing **D** in reply to the "No-File" menu. Suppose that you choose the filename NEWBOOK.TXT for this file. Files may be read from the disk into the new file NEWBOOK.TXT using the block read command ^KR. This then asks for the filename. It should be noted that the files will be read from the currently logged-in disk drive. If the drive letter is included in the filename, the particular disk drive where the file is stored can be specified.

CHAPTER1.TXT	would look for CHAPTER1.TXT on the currently logged--in disk drive
A:CHAPTER2.TXT	would look for CHAPTER2.TXT on drive A:
B:CHAPTER3.TXT	would look for CHAPTER3.TXT on drive B:

and

Thus the separate chapters could be incorporated into one file by the commands shown in Figure 37.1.

142

FIGURE 37.1 Commands to produce file NEWBOOK.TXT

```
^KR
NAME OF FILE TO READ?   INDEX.TXT
^KR
NAME OF FILE TO READ?   CHAPTER4.TXT
^KR
NAME OF FILE TO READ?   A:CHAPTER3.TXT
^KR
NAME OF FILE TO READ?   B:CHAPTER2.TXT
^KR
NAME OF FILE TO READ?   CHAPTER1.TXT
```

Note that the filenames are in the reverse order, since after a block read the cursor is at the beginning of the block. The file NEWBOOK.TXT should now be saved on disk by typing ^KD.

The WordStar print option P can now be used to print the file NEWBOOK.TXT. (If you want each chapter to start on a new page, insert a .PA command at the end of each chapter to force a page throw). There are several disadvantages to this method. First the file NEWBOOK.TXT may be too large to fit onto a floppy disk. Plainly when using this method the maximum size of the document is the space available on a single disk. In addition, difficulties are created should you need to edit the new large file. At the most trivial this is because editing a large file will be very slow. Rather more serious, when editing a file there should be twice as much free space on the disk as the size of the file. (The reason for this is that when saving a file after editing, the newly altered file is first stored on disk with the same file name and the ending .$$$. At this stage there will certainly be two files present on the disk with the same file name, one with the ending .$$$ and the other with the ending .TXT. There may be three files on the disk with the same file name, if a .BAK file exists. Eventually the .BAK file is discarded, the original .TXT file is renamed with the ending .BAK, and the .$$$ file is renamed with the ending .TXT. Thus there must be at least sufficient space on the disk for the .$$$ file as well as the .TXT file. In addition to this, a number of scratch work files are produced on the disk by WordStar, which require further space. These scratch files are invisible to the user, that is they appear and disappear without the user being aware that they ever existed. They are nevertheless essential for the operation of WordStar - for example a scratch file is needed when moving backwards through a file, or when block move or block copy operations are performed).

If the MailMerge program is available on the WordStar disk (as a separate file called MAILMRGE.OVR), then the problem of printing several files to make a book can be handled more elegantly. First WordStar is run to produce a new command file called for example BOOK. To produce this file the **N** option should be selected from the "No-File" menu to edit a non-document file, rather than selecting **D** to edit the usual WordStar text files. This file is called a command file because it is made up either completely, or mainly of dot commands, rather than text. It contains a series of File Insert .FI commands to find the appropriate files, which must be stored on a floppy disk mounted on one or more of the disk drives in the computer. Thus .FI CHAPTER1.TXT would insert the file CHAPTER1.TXT into the printout, provided it is present on the currently logged-in disk drive. Assuming that the currently logged-in disk drive is B: then this command would have exactly the same effect as the command .FI B:CHAPTER1.TXT where the disk drive is specified as B:. In a similar way, the command .FI A:CHAPTER2.TXT would look for the file CHAPTER2.TXT on disk drive A:. Suppose that CHAPTER4.TXT is stored on a different disk from CHAPTER3.TXT. The word CHANGE must be included in the .FI instruction after the filename. When this command is reached, the computer will stop and display a message asking you to change the floppy disk. This feature means that the maximum size of a document is not limited by what will fit on one floppy disk.

The .FI command is explained more fully in chapter 39 - Special Dot Commands for MailMerge. The contents of file BOOK might be as shown in Figure 37.2.

FIGURE 37.2 Contents of the command file BOOK

```
.FI CHAPTER1.TXT
.FI A:CHAPTER2.TXT
.FI B:CHAPTER3.TXT
.FI CHAPTER4.TXT CHANGE
.FI INDEX.TXT
```

After entering the appropriate .FI commands, the file BOOK must be stored on disk by typing ^KD. Provided that all the individual chapter files are present, then MailMerge will print the collection of files as one document, with the pages numbered sequentially throughout. There is no need to insert .PN commands in each chapter. Should the document be altered subsequently, then any changes in page numbering will be handled automatically throughout the whole document. The book will be printed as one continuous document.

It is essential that each of the files printed has a **RETURN** at the end of the last line. If this is not so, the next .FI command will be printed as text at the end of the previous file, and apart from spoiling the printout of that chapter, it will result in the next chapter being missed out altogether.

With this arrangement, individual chapters will not start on a new page. If the chapter files are in fact standard paragraphs, as used for example in legal, insurance or business documents, this will produce a normal printed page. However if the files are really chapters of a book, steps must be taken to start each chapter on a new page. This might be achieved by putting a .PA command either at the beginning or at the end of each file, (to force printing to start at the top of a new page). However, it is easier to include the .PA commands in the command file BOOK rather than in the constituent files, as shown in Figure 37.3.

FIGURE 37.3 Alternative contents of the command file BOOK

```
.FI CHAPTER1.TXT
.PA
.FI CHAPTER2.TXT
.PA
.FI CHAPTER3.TXT
.PA
.FI CHAPTER4.TXT
.PA
.FI INDEX.TXT
```

For the moment, consider how to print the book when WordStar and MailMerge are on drive A: and the command file and all the data files are on drive B: (This means that the drive letters and the CHANGE command are not present in the command file). The simplest way to Merge-print the document, having made sure that the printer is switched on, loaded with continuous paper and positioned correctly, is to type **M** in response to the "No-File" menu. The screen changes and the menu displayed is shown in Figure 37.4. A question asks for the name of the file to be Merge-printed. When the file name is typed, in this case the command file BOOK, it is displayed after the question. At this stage if **ESCAPE** is pressed, the printer will immediately start to print - hence the need to get it ready beforehand.

A slightly more complicated way of Merge-printing this command file is to type **M** at the "No-File" menu, then type the filename (in this case BOOK, and press **RETURN**. A series of questions are displayed on the screen one by one,

144

allowing various print options to be selected. (Full details of the questions, the options available, and how to print a file in this way are given in chapter 34 – Producing Several Identical Copies of a Document).

FIGURE 37.4 The M command display

```
M       editing no file
 ^S=delete character    ^Y=delete entry     ^F=File directory
 ^D=restore character   ^R=Restore entry    ^U=cancel command

 NAME OF FILE TO MERGE-PRINT? BOOK


DIRECTORY of disk B:
 CHAPTER1.TXT   CHAPTER2.TXT   CHAPTER3.TXT   CHAPTER4.TXT   INDEX.TXT     BOOK
```

How to use files on several disks to make one book

The use of the CHANGE command has already been described above. It is worth considering the arrangement of files on the various disks to minimise the need for intervention by the operator when using several disks.

Suppose that CP/M, WordStar and MailMerge are on one disk in drive A:, that the command file BOOK together with the files CHAPTER1.TXT, CHAPTER2.TXT and CHAPTER3.TXT are all stored on a second floppy disk, and that the files CHAPTER4.TXT and INDEX.TXT are stored on a third floppy disk. The contents of the command file BOOK are shown in Figure 37.5.

FIGURE 37.5 The command file BOOK

```
.FI CHAPTER1.TXT
.PA
.FI CHAPTER2.TXT
.PA
.FI CHAPTER3.TXT
.PA
.FI CHAPTER4.TXT CHANGE
.PA
.FI INDEX.TXT CHANGE
```

The disk with CP/M, WordStar and MailMerge is put in drive A: and the disk with the command file BOOK and the chapters 1, 2 and 3 is put in drive B:. WordStar is loaded, the L command from the "No-File" menu is used to change the logged-in drive to B:, and the command file BOOK is Merge-printed. Chapters 1, 2 and 3 are printed out in the usual way. When the command .FI CHAPTER4.TXT CHANGE is encountered, a message is displayed on the screen:

Insert diskette with file B:CHAPTER4.TXT then press RETURN

The disk with chapter 4 and the index is then placed in drive B:, RETURN is pressed, and chapter 4 is printed. The computer now looks for the command file BOOK to see what to do next, and when it cannot find the file it displays the message:

Insert diskette with file B:BOOK then press RETURN

The disk with the file BOOK must now be replaced on drive B:. When RETURN is pressed, the next instruction read from this file is .PA to start a new page, and then the command .FI INDEX.TXT CHANGE is encountered. The CHANGE causes another message to be displayed:

Insert diskette with file B:INDEX.TXT then press RETURN

The disks must be changed back again. After printing this file, a message asks for the command file to be replaced:

Insert diskette with file B:BOOK then press RETURN

The job now finishes.

It can be seen that there is a lot of unnecessary disk changing because the command file is removed from the computer. Four disk changes were necessary for this fairly simple job.

A much better way of performing this task is to put the command file on drive A:, together with CP/M, WordStar and MailMerge, so that it is available at all times during the job. Note that with a computer with two drives it is generally best to keep the programs WordStar and MailMerge on drive A:, and restrict WordStar data files to drive B:. This case is an exception to the general rule. The command file now required is shown in Figure 37.6, and it can be seen that in this case there is only one CHANGE command.

FIGURE 37.6 New version of the command file BOOK

```
.FI CHAPTER1.TXT
.PA
.FI CHAPTER2.TXT
.PA
.FI CHAPTER3.TXT
.PA
.FI CHAPTER4.TXT CHANGE
.PA
.FI INDEX.TXT
```

Remember that you are running WordStar with B: as the logged-in disk drive, so when you want to Merge-print the command file present on drive A:, you must include the drive letter in the filename **A:BOOK.** Chapters 1, 2 and 3 will be printed, and a message will ask for the disk in drive B: to be changed. When this has been done, chapter 4 and the index will be printed. Done in this way, the whole book will be printed with only one disk change.

Chapter 38.

PRACTICE IN MERGING FILES

In this chapter you will print the four verses of Rudyard Kipling's poem "If" as if they were a single document. To do this you must produce a command file which will call up the individual files VERSE1.TXT, VERSE2.TXT, VERSE3.TXT and VERSE4.TXT which were typed and saved on disk in chapter 18 - Practice Using Files. When this has been done, the command file will be Merge-Printed. The steps are as follows:

1. Load WordStar and from the "No-File" menu type **N** open a non-document file, and call the file **MERGEIF.CMD**. (The ending .CMD is often used for command files).

2. The MailMerge command to find a file is **.FI**. The full stop **must** be in column 1, and each command must be on a separate line. Type the following commands:

   .FI VERSE1.TXT   (RETURN)
   .FI VERSE2.TXT   (RETURN)
   .FI VERSE3.TXT   (RETURN)
   .FI VERSE4.TXT   (RETURN)

   If the command file was left like this, then there would be no gap between the verses when this file was MergePrinted. To overcome this, introduce a blank line inbetween the **.FI** commands, so that a blank line will be printed. Add the author's name at the bottom, and the title at the top:

   ..beginning of file
   　　　　　^PB—IF—^PB

   .FI VERSE1.TXT   (RETURN)

   .FI VERSE2.TXT   (RETURN)

   .FI VERSE3.TXT   (RETURN)

   .FI VERSE4.TXT   (RETURN)

   　　　　　　　　Rudyard Kipling
   ..end of file

   Type **^KD** to save this file on disk.

3. To print the file, select the **M** option from the "No-File" menu, and in in reply to the question **NAME OF FILE TO MERGE-PRINT?** type **MERGEIF.CMD**. If you press **RETURN** you will have to answer the questions about printing which are explained in chapter 34 - Producing Multiple Copies of a Document. If all of the default answers are acceptable, and the printer is switched ON with paper loaded, you can press **ESCAPE** instead. The heading, the four files and the author's name will all be printed as if they were part of a single document.

Chapter 39.

SPECIAL DOT COMMANDS FOR MAILMERGE

MailMerge uses all the regular dot commands used by WordStar, which are described earlier in chapter 26 - Dot commands. There are a number of additional dot commands which apply only to MailMerge, and are in fact ignored by WordStar. These additional commands are tabulated below, (parameters enclosed in brackets are optional). A summary of the dot commands may be displayed on the screen at any time when a document is being edited by typing ^JD. There are six screenfulls of information, and the last one contains special dot commands for MailMerge.

Ask the operator to type the value of a variable .AV

The command has the general form:

.AV ("prompt",) name of variable (,length)

for example   **.AV Name**
or   **.AV "Type full name of customer", Name**
or   **.AV "Type 6 digit telephone number", Tel, 6**

The prompt is an optional message, enclosed by either single or double quotation marks, which will be displayed on the screen to tell the operator what value to type in. If the prompt is omitted, then the variable name followed by a question mark will be used as prompt. The name of the variable is from 1-40 characters long, must begin with a letter, and may contain only letters, numbers or hyphens. Spaces and other characters are not allowed. The length parameter is optional, and if present it defines the maximum number of characters which may be typed as the variable.

Clear Screen .CS

The general form of the command is:

.CS (message)

for example   **.CS**
or   **.CS Insert the next envelope**

The first example clears the screen of any previous messages, and in the second example the screen is cleared and the message "Insert the next envelope" is displayed at the top of the screen when the command is used.

File Insert .FI

The general form of this command is:

.FI filename (CHANGE)

for example   **.FI CHAPTER1**
or   **.FI CHAPTER2 CHANGE**

In the first example, the file specified by the filename is CHAPTER1, and this will be inserted in the document being printed out at the place indicated by the .FI command. Files inserted in this way **must** end with a RETURN, or you will corrupt the next command, or have problems if the document is printed repeatedly. The file will be used many times if it contains Data File .DF, Read Value .RV, or Repeat .RP commands. Unless the drive is specified as part of the filename, it is assumed that the file is present on the logged-in disk drive. For example for drive A: you would type A:CHAPTER1.

If the word CHANGE is present after the filename, then when this command is reached, a message will request a change of disks. The message specifies the name of the file required, and the disk drive on which it should be mounted. RETURN must be pressed when the correct disk has been inserted, in this case the one containing CHAPTER2. MailMerge then checks that the file is present, and then continues printing. When using this facility for changing disks, it is important that the disk removed does not contain any of the files required by WordStar itself, namely WSOVLY1.OVR and WSMSGS.OVR. With the recommended arrangement of CP/M and WordStar on drive A: and WordStar data files on drive B: this problem will not arise.

If the .FI command is the last line of the file, it is important that RETURN has been entered at the end of the line, or the file insert command will be ignored.

Data File .DF

The general form of this command is:

.DF datafile-name (CHANGE)

for example   .DF CUSTOMER
or   .DF CUSTOMER CHANGE

The first example specifies that the data file to be used is called CUSTOMER, and the second example requests a change of disks when this command is reached, so that the disk which holds the CUSTOMER file may be inserted. It is assumed that the file is present on the logged-in disk drive, but if it is on another drive this may be specified by putting the drive letter and a colon immediately before the filename, for example for drive C put C:CUSTOMER.

If the word CHANGE is present after the filename, then when this command is reached, a message will request a change of disks. The message specifies the name of the file required, together with the disk drive on which it should be mounted. RETURN must be pressed when the correct disk has been inserted, in this case the one containing CUSTOMER. MailMerge checks that the required file is now present, and then continues printing. When using this facility for changing disks, it is important that the disk removed does not contain any of the files required by WordStar itself, namely WSOVLY1.OVR and WSMSGS.OVR. With the recommended arrangement of CP/M and WordStar on drive A: and WordStar data files on drive B: this problem will not arise.

Read Variables .RV

The general form of this command is:

.RV variable1, variable2, variable3, ...

for example   .RV Name, Street, Town

This gives a list of the names of one or more variables which are to be read from the datafile previously specified, in the order given. For example, the variables could be Name, Street, Town and City for a set of customers, and the order and number of these variables read in must match the order and number of these terms stored in the datafile. If a particular variable is stored in the datafile, it must be included in the .RV line, regardless of whether or not it is used in the matrix letter. If more than one variable name is used in the command, the variables must be separated by a comma and may optionally be separated by spaces as well.

Repeat .RP

The general form of this command is:

.RP (number of times to be repeated)

for example   .RP
or   .RP 50

This command is useful to make MailMerge print a document many times when reading data from a datafile with a .DF command. In the first example, the document will be printed repeatedly until the data in the datafile is exhausted. In the second example it has been specified that the document should be printed 50 times, unless the data run out.

Note that .RP 0 prints the document once, the same as .RP 1. If the .RP command is the last line of the file, it is important that RETURN has been entered at the end of the line, or the repeat command will be ignored.

Display Message .DM

The general form of this command is:

.DM message

for example   .DM Load data file containing customers L to Z on drive B
or   .DM Letter to &Name& now being printed

This command makes MailMerge display a message on the screen at the appropriate time during the printing of a document. This can be useful to the operator, particularly if you want to give instructions about changing the disks in use (see .AV and .DF commands) or as in the second example where the variable Name which contains the customer's name is displayed, since this shows which letter is currently being typed, thus indicating the progress through the list of letters being printed.

Set Value .SV

The general form of this command is:

.SV variable,value assigned to the variable

for example   .SV Date,29th. February 1983

This command sets the value of the variable, in this case Date, to 29th. February 1983. A comma must separate the variable name and the data assigned to it. The variable called Date may now be printed anywhere in the document where it is specified by &Date&. This provides a means of setting a variable once in the file, rather than in several places. (Variables may also be set with .AV Ask for Value, and .RV Read Value commands).

PRINT-TIME LINE FORMING

MailMerge automatically reforms the line affected and also the rest of the paragraph after variable data has been inserted. This is discussed in chapter 35 - Producing Standard Letters. The print-time line former actually consists of two parts, the input scanner and the output formatter. The input scanner examines text from the file being printed with MailMerge before any variables have been inserted, to find the margins in use, the spacing, and whether the text is right justified or ragged. The output former processes the text after the variables have been inserted, and is responsible for the automatic reforming mentioned above. The Dot commands described in the rest of this chapter are not normally needed, but they may be useful to those advanced users who wish to control print-time line forming for themselves. Some possible reasons for wishing to do this are given below:

1. Wanting to suppress the automatic reforming of lines after variable data have been included. This means that output lines will be printed exactly like the input lines from the file, except that the variable references have been replaced by the contents of the variables.

2. Needing to produce a printout with a ragged right hand edge from text which has been right justified, or vice-versa.

3. Requiring a printout with different margins from those which were used when the file was originally produced by the editor.

Print-time line Forming .PF

The .PF command must have one of three endings: DIS, OFF, or ON. The default is .PF DIS, which leaves print-time line forming to MailMerge's discretion. This means that after a variable has been inserted, the text is reformed up to the next RETURN, which is generally the end of the paragraph. To prevent this happening, the command .PF OFF should be inserted. The command .PF ON turns the print-time line former on. This means that all text from this point on will be reformed, right up to the end of the document, unless another .PF command is encountered. When .PF is ON, changes may be specified to the left or right margins, the line spacing, or the justification, using a combination of the following five dot commands. **Unless .PF is ON, these five commands are inoperative.**

Right Margin .RM

The command must either be followed by a number between 1 and 240 which indicates the column number of the right margin when printing, or have the ending DIS. The latter is the default, and uses the same right margin for printing as was used in the input file. To print with a different margin than was used by the editor, for example to print with the right margin set at column 80 when the document produced by the editor used a right margin set at column 65, use:

```
.PF ON      (force print-time line forming on)
.RM 80      (force print-time right margin to column 80)
```

It should be remembered that if the margins are changed, page breaks will not occur in the printout at the same place as they were displayed on the screen by the editor. To change back to printing text with the same margins as in the input file, with discretionary reforming where variables have been inserted use:

```
.PF DIS     (discretionary print-time line forming)
.RM DIS     (if reforming lines is necessary, match the input)
```

Left Margin .LM

The command must either be followed by a number between 1 and 240 which indicates the column number of the left margin when printing, or have the ending DIS. The latter is the default, and uses the same left margin for printing as was used in the file. Setting the left margin should be carried out with great care if either a whole paragraph is indented, or a hanging paragraph with text to the left of the left margin are present.

Line Spacing .LS

This command must either be followed by a number between 1 and 9 to set the line spacing used at print-time, or have the ending DIS. The latter is the default, and prints using the same spacing as the input text. To print a file in double spacing when the input file has single spacing, use:

```
.PF ON    (force print-time line forming on)
.LS 2     (force double spacing)
```

Output Justification .OJ

This command must have one of three endings: ON, OFF or DIS. The ending ON produces a justified right margin, OFF produces a ragged right margin. The ending DIS, which is the default, produces a justified printout if the text in the input file is justified, and a ragged right edge to the printout if the text in the input file is ragged. To produce a printout with a ragged right edge from an input file containing text which has been right justified by the editor use:

```
.PF ON    (force print-time line forming on)
.OJ OFF   (force ragged right edge in printout)
```

To produce a printout which is right justified from a file which contains text with a ragged right edge use:

```
.PF ON    (force print-time line forming on)
.OJ ON    (force right justification of printout)
```

Input Justification .IJ

This command is to control the action of the input scanner in the rare circumstances that some unusual text confuses it. The command must have one of three endings: ON, OFF or DIS.

The ending ON interprets input as justified, follows any changes in right margin if .RM DIS is operating, and justifies the output if .OJ DIS is in effect.

The ending OFF interprets input as ragged. If line reforming is needed it finds the length of the largest line in the vicinity, and matches that if .RM DIS is operating.

The ending DIS looks at the input, and if it finds a constant right margin it prints justified, and if it finds small variations in the right margin it prints ragged.

Chapter 40.

CHECKING SPELLING

At least ten programs are available which will work with Word-Star to proof read a file to find spelling and typing mistakes. These vary greatly in their ease of use, speed, size of dictionary used, price, and the number of claimed mis-spellings which are in fact correctly spelled. The spelling checking program marketed by MicroPro is called SpellStar. This is an optional program, but has the advantage over other spelling checking programs that it works from within WordStar, rather than being merely compatible with it.

SpellStar proof reads a file of text produced by WordStar by checking the spelling of each word in the document against its own dictionary. Words in the file which can not be matched from the dictionary are marked as suspect. These may be genuinely misspelled, or may be the names or people, addresses or technical words which are not in the dictionary. You then have to examine the suspect words, and take appropriate action. There are essentially two different jobs. First how to check and correct a document, and second how to update the main dictionary, or create your own additional technical dictionary, so that SpellStar works more reliably next time. The two jobs of checking the spelling in a document, and maintaining the dictionary are examined in this chapter.

How to proof-read a document with SpellStar

SpellStar is sold as a separate program, and comprises two files. The first is called SPELSTAR.OVR, occupies 18K of space, and contains the spelling checking program. The second file SPELSTAR.DCT contains the standard dictionary of about 20,000 words, and occupies 98K of file space, or even more if you have extended the dictionary. The file SPELSTAR.OVR must be present on the disk in drive A: together with the WordStar program. The SpellStar dictionary file may also be present on this disk if there is enough space, but the dictionary file may be kept on a separate disk if necessary, and inserted in to drive A: when needed. The text file which you are going to check should be on drive B:.

Load WordStar and change the logged-in drive to B: in the usual way. Drive B: contains your text files. The WordStar "No-File" menu will be displayed on the screen. Before starting proof-reading and spelling checking, make sure that there is enough room on the disks. Temporary work files will be produced by SpellStar which are roughly as big as the file you intend to proof-read. Select the **R** option to run a program, and type the command STAT *.*. This will list the names and sizes of all the files on the logged-in drive B:, and the amount of free space on the disk.

To use SpellStar, type **S** to perform spelling checking from the "No-File" menu. A menu is displayed on the screen (Figure 40.1).

FIGURE 40.1

For spelling check, enter name of file to be checked.
(^R for the last file edited)

For dictionary maintenance, enter name of file
containing words to add to or delete from dictionary.

^S=delete character	^Y=delete entry	^F=File directory
^D=restore character	^R=Restore entry	^U=cancel command

NAME OF FILE TO CHECK / ADD TO DICTIONARY?

You should type in the name of the file you wish to proof-read. For the purpose of this example the file LETTER.TXT will be used. This file was last used in chapter 11 - Practice in Basic Editing, and should be on the disk in drive B:. Simply type the filename, and press **RETURN**. The SpellStar **Operations Menu** will then be displayed on the screen, as shown in Figure 40.2. (If you have just been editing a file with WordStar, and you then wish to proof-read it, the menu explains that if you type ^R, the filename will be displayed without you having to type it, then press **RETURN**). Alternatively you may try the spelling checker out using the sample text file called SAMPLE.TXT which is provided with SpellStar, or the file EXAMPLE.TXT which is provided with WordStar. Because these files are on drive A: you should type **A:SAMPLE.TXT** or **A:EXAMPLE.TXT** and press **RETURN.**

FIGURE 40.2 The SpellStar Operations Menu

```
SpellStar - Release 1.2 - Serial # XXXXXXXX
Copyright (C) 1981 MicroPro International Corporation

          O P E R A T I O N S

     C - Check spelling
     M - Maintain dictionary
     X - Exit to WordStar no-file menu

   Operation?

If your dictionaries are not on the current disk,
   insert the correct disk before continuing.
```

If the file SPELSTAR.DCT which contains the SpellStar dictionary is not present on drive A:, you must replace the disk in drive A: by one that has the dictionary. Later on you may create your own supplementary dictionary or dictionaries. If you wish to use a supplementary dictionary as well as the main one, both must be present on this disk. You will be instructed when to replace the original disk in drive A: at the end.

The operations menu offers you three choices, to check spelling, to add words to or delete words from the dictionary, or to leave SpellStar and return to the WordStar "No-File" menu. At this stage you want to check spelling, so type **C**, and the Spelling Check menu will be displayed (Figure 40.3).

FIGURE 40.3 The Spelling Check menu

```
        SPELLING CHECK CONTROLS           CURRENT VALUE

     D - Use another main dictionary   =   B:SPELSTAR.DCT
     S - Add supplemental dictionary   =
     F - Change file to be checked     =   B:LETTER.TXT
     W - Change work drive             =      B:

   <Return> - Start spelling check
        X    - Exit to Operations Menu

Control to change?
```

The present values for the names of the main dictionary to be used, the file to be checked, and the logged-in drive are displayed. If these are correct, press **RETURN** and start the spelling check. If these values are wrong, either exit to the Operations Menu by typing **X**, or type **D, S, F** or **W** to change the appropriate value(s) before pressing **RETURN** to start the spelling check.

The main dictionary used by default is SPELSTAR.DCT, which is the one provided. Normally you will not need to change this, and for this exercise no change is required. The menu shows that the dictionary is expected on drive B:, and it is actually mounted on drive A:. SpellStar is clever, and will look for the main dictionary first on drive B:, and if it cannot find it there it will then look for it on drive A:, provided that it has the file extension .DCT. There is therefore no need to change this. You may change it by typing D to "Use another dictionary", and then type **A:SPELLSTAR.DCT** and pressing **RETURN**. SpellStar then changes the entry to A:SPELLSTAR.DCT. Exactly the same result is obtained by typing **A:** and **RETURN**. (If later on you produce your own main dictionary called OXFORD.DCT, and want to use this instead of A:SPELLSTAR.DCT, you would type **D**, then **OXFORD** and **RETURN**. The entry will be changed to A:OXFORD.DCT). The file extension (file type) may also be changed without typing the whole filename. For example to change the dictionary from A:SPELLSTAR.DCT to A:SPELLSTAR.NEW you need only type **D**, then **.NEW** and **RETURN**. Remember if the file extension to the main dictionary is not .DCT then you must specify the correct drive where it will be found.

The next command **S** allows you to specify a supplementary dictionary, which will be used in addition to the main one. Since you have not produced one yet, you cannot use this feature at present. You will find it convenient later on to make several supplementary dictionaries. For example you might have supplementary dictionaries called CHEMIST.SUP containing technical chemical words and symbols, LEGAL.SUP containing legal phrases and words, MEDICAL.SUP for medical words, TAX.SUP containing words used when writing to the income tax inspector or your accountant, or BUSINESS.SUP containing business words. Alternatively you may make a supplementary dictionary for each firm you write letters to frequently, containing the address, and the names of people in your company and theirs, so that these do not get marked as possible mis-spellings. It is better to keep the main dictionary for common words, and use supplementary dictionaries for specialized words. The reason for this is simple. If you put all the words in one dictionary, proof checking would be rather slow because you would be checking through a whole lot of chemical names, and medical terms unnecessarily when checking a letter to your income tax inspector. This arrangement permits you to use one main dictionary and one supplementary dictionary at the same time on a document. Provided that the supplementary dictionary has the ending .SUP, SpellStar will look for it first on the logged-in drive, then on drive A:.

If SpellStar cannot find either the main or the supplementary dictionary, an error message is displayed. The reasons for this are:

(a) You have typed the wrong filename.
(b) If the dictionary has an ending other than .DCT or .SUP then the wrong drive may have been specified.
(c) You have inserted the wrong dictionary disk.

You should press **R** to restart, and correct the filename or drive letter, or insert the correct disk.

The command **F** allows you to change the name of the file to be proof-read. This may be of use if you have mis-typed the name of the file, but its main use is when you have completed proof-reading one file you can change the file name and then proof-read another file, and so on for a whole series of files.

SpellStar creates temporary files roughly as big as the one being proof-read, so there must be some space on the disks for these. By default, the work files are stored on the logged-in disk. The **W** command allows you to change the logged-in disk drive. This may be useful if there is not enough room for work files on the logged-in disk, since by changing the logged-in drive the work files can be sent to a different disk.

The command **X** is used to drop back one level, that is in this case back from the Spelling check menu to the Operations menu.

When you are ready to start proof-reading the file LETTER.TXT, press **RETURN.** The screen changes as shown in Figure 40.4.

FIGURE 40.4

SpellStar is now checking your document for misspelled words.

```
Number of words in document.......: 78
Number of different words.........: 57
Number of words in main dictionary: 21027
Number of words in supplement.....:
Number of dictionary words checked: 2584
Number of misspelled words........: 6
Total number of misspellings......:
```

First SpellStar counts the number of words in the file, and the number of different words. These totals are displayed in lines 1 and 2 on the screen, and the file LETTER.TXT contains 78 words, of which 57 are different.

After a pause, the number of words in the main dictionary and the supplementary dictionary are given in lines 3 and 4. The size of your main dictionary may differ slightly from the figure 21027 shown here if MicroPro, or your dealer have added or deleted any words, and it will certainly be different if you have done any dictionary maintenance on it. In this case, the size of the supplementary dictionary is blank because one was not specified.

There is another pause, and the number of dictionary words checked so far is displayed in line 5 on the screen. This number is updated at intervals 1000, 2000 ... and so on until checking is complete. This step may take some considerable time if you are working on a very long document. When checking is complete, the number of "misspelled" words is displayed in line 6. This is a misleading statement, and really means the number of words in the document which cannot be found in the dictionary or dictionaries used. This includes genuine spelling mistakes and typing errors, plus the names of people and places, abbreviations, technical words and uncommon words which are not in the dictionaries used. It would really be better to call them "unmatched" words. An extra message is displayed at the bottom of the screen, beneath the information in Figure 40.4. This is shown in Figure 40.5.

FIGURE 40.5

SpellStar has completed proofreading your document.

```
Enter  "L"  to list the misspelled words.
Enter <Return> to flag errors in your text.
Enter  "R"  to abandon the check and restart.
```

At this stage, SpellStar has found all the "misspelled" words, but has not marked them in the file. You may list the misspelled words, and then flag (mark) them in the file, or go straight to marking them in the file.

Next type **L** to list the words suspected of being misspelled. The list is shown on the screen (Figure 40.6):

If the list of "misspelled" words is more than will fit on the screen, the first screenful is displayed, and at the bottom are listed commands explaining how to continue:

"Space"=continue, "C"=continuous listing, "^L"=stop/start listing

Compound words with "hard" hyphens, that is hyphens you have typed, are treated as two words, and may be listed as "misspelled". "Soft" hyphens inserted when reforming a paragraph with hyphen help ON are ignored.

If the list is very large, you may have selected the wrong dictionary, and you should type **R** and abandon this check. The original text file will be unchanged, and you can repeat the spelling check with the correct dictionary.

FIGURE 40.6 List of "misspelled" words

```
PM ST TH EVANS SEATING ELIZABETH


Enter <Return> to correct errors, "R" to restart.
```

In the list of "misspelled" words produced (Figure 40.6), the words Evans and Elizabeth are proper nouns, and would not be in the dictionary. Seating looks correct, and the others pm st and th could either be abbreviations or genuine errors. To make sure, you should examine the "errors" in context. You should now press **RETURN** to mark the errors in the file. When this has been done, the total number of misspellings is filled in on the bottom line of Figure 40.4, as shown in Figure 40.7. In this case, the total number of misspellings is 7, and since the number of misspelled words is given as 6, it follows that one word is misspelled twice.

FIGURE 40.7

```
SpellStar is now checking your document for misspelled words.

Number of words in document.......: 78
Number of different words.........: 57
Number of words in main dictionary: 21027
Number of words in supplement.....:
Number of dictionary words checked: 2584
Number of misspelled words........: 6
Total number of misspellings......: 7
```
PM ST TH EVANS SEATING ELIZABETH
SpellStar has flagged the misspellings in the text.

If you changed disks at the beginning of this program, please insert the original disk before continuing.

Enter <Return> to correct errors, "R" to restart.

A message shows that SpellStar has flagged the misspellings in the text. Another message instructs you to replace the original disk in drive A: if you changed this for a disk with the dictionary. <u>It is essential that you put the correct disk back before continuing.</u>

The last line tells you to press **RETURN** to correct the errors, or **R** to restart. (If you type **R** then you go back to the Operations Menu Figure 40.2. You will not have changed the file you were checking in any way, and you will not leave any extra files on the disk). You should press **RETURN** to examine the errors, and correct them if necessary. There is a pause, and a file called LETTER.@@@ is produced which is the same as the file LETTER.TXT that you were proof-reading, except that "misspellings" are marked with ^@ before each

unmatched word. The first part of the .@@@ file is then displayed on the
screen as shown in Figure 40.8.

FIGURE 40.8 The file LETTER.@@@ with "misspellings" marked by SpellStar

                            1^@st. June 1984

        Dear Mr. ^@Evans,

            The school will be holding the
        annual Prize-giving ceremony on Saturday
        6^@th. July, at 2.30 ^@pm. in the School
        hall.

            Since your daughter ^@Elizabeth is
        amongst the prize winners, I am pleased
        to be able to invite you to join the
        special guests, who will be seated at the
        front of the hall.

            Since ^@seating is strictly limited, a
        reply would be appreciated before 10^@th.
        June, stating how many seats you require.

                    Yours sincerely,

                    Headmaster.

At the top of the screen the status line from WordStar is displayed, together
with a menu giving information on how to correct the file (Figure 40.9):

FIGURE 40.9

        B:LETTER.TXT PAGE 1 LINE 1 COL 27   ACTION(F/B/I/D/S)?

        F - Fix word   D - Add to dictionary
        B - Bypass word   S - Add to supplemental dictionary
        I - Ignore word

    L----!----!----!----!----!----!----!----!----!----!----!--------R

    The cursor is positioned just before the first "error", the **st** in the line
with the date 1**st**. June 1984, and the ^@ does not show for this word. On
terminals which support highlighting the **st** will appear either in inverse
video, or half intensity. The other "mistakes" will still have their ^@
markers. You must deal with this word by typing F, B, I, D or S. (The meaning
of these five commands is explained in subsequent paragraphs). When you have
"fixed" the word, SpellStar automatically moves the cursor to the next
"mistake". The ^@ preceding the next marked word disappears and the word is
highlighted. You fix that word, move to the next "mistake", and go through the
whole file making corrections as necessary.

For the moment, the cursor is flashing alternately at the word **st** and at the **(F/B/I/D/S)?** in the cursor line. You have to decide whether to alter the word, or leave it unchanged. Before actually doing anything, the meanings of the five possible commands F, B, I, D and S will be examined.

If the word is incorrect, then typing **F** will give you the chance to correct it. This takes you to the WordStar editor, and you may make alterations using the usual WordStar commands for moving the cursor, inserting or deleting text, or any other changes. The paragraph may need reforming with ^B after making alterations. This moves the cursor to the end of the paragraph, and if the cursor moves past any other flagged words, you must move it back. (^E moves the cursor back one line, ^QE moves the cursor to the top of the screen, and ^QR moves the cursor to the beginning of the file). When you have done this, type ^L to return to SpellStar and the cursor will automatically move on to the next misspelling. (If you type **F** and do not change the word, it will no longer be marked as incorrect).

The command **B** is used to bypass the word. This is used when you are not sure whether it is wrong, and would like to defer a decision about it. You can then come back and re-examine it later. The command is also used when the word is correct, but you are undecided whether to add it to a dictionary or ignore it. This decision can be deferred until later. When B is pressed, the ^@ marker is left in the file, and SpellStar automatically moves on to the next misspelling.

If the word which is marked is correctly spelled, then you do not want to change it, but you should consider whether to include it in a dictionary. There are three options:

1. If the word is an uncommon one, it is not worth putting it in the dictionary. This is because storing unusual words in the dictionary will make it very large, which will take up a lot of disk space, and increase the time taken to perform spelling checking. In this case you should type I to ignore the word.

2. If the word is a common one, likely to be used again, then you should type **D**. A file called LETTER.ADD contains the marked words, and the word will be marked with a D, so that when you subsequently do some dictionary maintenance it will be added to the main dictionary.

3. If you would like to add the word to a supplementary dictionary type **S**. It will be marked in the LETTER.ADD file with an S, and will be added to a supplementary dictionary when you do dictionary maintenance.

If for example you typed either D or S to the word **seating**, SpellStar will ask:

Add to dictionary:SEATING(Y/N)?

This gives you a chance to change your mind. When you type **Y** the cursor moves to the next "error". SpellStar stores approximately 20 words which were most recently ignored I or added with D or S, and if it finds these again it remembers what you want to do with the word, and does not ask you again.

Eventually you will reach the end of the file. If you have dealt with all of the "misspelled" words, type ^KD to save the corrected version of the file. You will then return to the WordStar "No-File" menu. The original unchecked file which was previously called LETTER.TXT is now renamed LETTER.BAK. The file LETTER.@@@ which you have just proof-read and corrected is now renamed LETTER.TXT. The file LETTER.ADD contains words that you want to add to the dictionaries, which are marked D or S to indicate whether you intend putting them in the main or the supplementary dictionary. Dictionary updating will be performed later.

If you bypassed any of the flagged words, you must type ^QL. The menu in Figure 40.10 then appears on the screen:

FIGURE 40.10

> To search for misspelled words, enter one of the following -
> RETURN=search forward, B=search backward, G=from start of file:

These commands allow you to go through the file again, dealing with any words that you bypassed the first time. Since the cursor is at the end of the file, pressing **RETURN** to search in a forward direction will not work. The command **B** will search the file backwards, that is from the end towards the beginning, stopping at each word which is flagged. The command **G** jumps to the beginning of the file, and searches for flagged words in the usual direction. At each flagged word you have the opportunity to Fix, Bypass, or Ignore the word, or to add it to either the main or a supplementary dictionary. When you have finished corrections, save the file with a ^KD command. You will then return to the WordStar "No-File" menu.

How to maintain or create a dictionary

From the WordStar "No-File" menu you must first type S to invoke Spell-Star. The menu shown in Figure 40.1 is displayed, and the important part is that it asks for the name of the file containing words to be added to or deleted from the dictionary. If you have previously run SpellStar to proofread a file, you will have produced a file with the ending .ADD, which contains a list of words to be added to the dictionary. Alternatively you can type a word file for yourself, or buy a separate dictionary on a disk. To update an existing dictionary, or to create a new one, you must have a word file. Type the name of this, for example **LETTER.ADD** and press **RETURN**.

The SpellStar Operations Menu is then displayed on the screen (Figure 40.2). If the dictionary is not on the disk in drive A:, you are now given the opportunity to change the disk. Previously you selected the C option to check the spelling in a file, but this time you should type **M** to maintain the dictionary. The dictionary maintenance menu is then displayed (Figure 40.11). If the current values displayed are all acceptable, press **RETURN** to start dictionary maintenance. Otherwise, you may change the values of the dictionary maintenance controls or options. Their meanings are discussed below.

FIGURE 40.11 The dictionary maintenance menu

	DICTIONARY MAINTENANCE CONTROLS		CURRENT VALUE
F	- Change word file to use	=	B:LETTER.ADD
D	- Change dictionary to update	=	B:SPELSTAR.DCT
U	- Change name of new or updated dictionary	=	B:
W	- Change work drive for sort	=	B:
	DICTIONARY MAINTENANCE OPTIONS		
N	- Create a new dictionary	=	NO
A	- Add words	=	NO
T	- Delete words	=	NO
C	- Combine add/delete	=	YES
S.	- Use "S" words from ".ADD" file	=	NO
L	- List dictionary words	=	NO

<Return> - Start dictionary maintenance.
    X   - Exit to Operations menu

Control or option to change?

Dictionary maintenance controls

The first line shows the name of the word file you specified, in this case LETTER.ADD. This will be used to update the dictionary. If you have typed the name incorrectly, then type **F**. A menu shows you the current filename, and invites you to type in the required change. The drive, the main filename, or the extension may be changed independently in the same way as described earlier for the spelling check menu (Figure 40.3).

The dictionary to be updated is shown as SPELSTAR.DCT. This is the standard SpellStar dictionary which is provided. It is expected on the logged-in drive B:, but as with the spelling checking, SpellStar will find the file even though it is mounted on drive A:. If you want to create a new dictionary, type **D** and then press the space bar to give a blank for the filename, and then **RETURN**. To alter a different dictionary from the one shown, type **D**. A menu shows you the current filename, and invites you to change the drive, filename, or extension, and then press **RETURN**.

The name of the new or updated dictionary is blank by default. If you are creating a new dictionary, and have used the **D** option above to get a blank filename, then you must use the **U** option to specify the name of the dictionary you are going to produce. A menu will help you as before. If the dictionary to update was specified in the **D** command line of the menu, then if the name of the new or updated dictionary is left blank (as it is by default), then Spell-Star will overwrite the old dictionary with the new one. If you do not want this to happen, you must either change the filename or extension, so that a different file will be produced, or you must change the drive so that the original dictionary is on one drive, and the new one on another. You may not have two files with the same name on the same disk drive.

SpellStar requires space for a temporary scratch file to sort the words to be added to the dictionary into order. This file is about the same size as the word file. By default this temporary file will be written on the logged-in drive, which is B: in this case. If there is insufficient space on this drive, an alternative drive may be specified by using the **W** option.

Dictionary maintenance options

The dictionary maintenance options are all toggles. Their default settings are displayed as YES or NO in the lower half of the menu, (Figure 40.11), and the setting of each can be reversed by pressing the appropriate key **N, A, T, C, S,** or **L**.

The most commonly used SpellStar option is **C**, which assumes that you intend to <u>add</u> <u>words</u> <u>to</u> <u>and</u> <u>delete</u> <u>words</u> <u>from</u> <u>an</u> <u>existing</u> <u>file</u>. Both adding and deleting are performed in the same operation. If a word present in the word file is not present in the dictionary, the word will be added. If the word is already present in the dictionary, SpellStar will delete it. To prevent accidental erasure, each word to be deleted is displayed, with the message:

This word is in the dictionary. Should it be deleted? (Y/N)?

You must type **Y** for yes or **N** for no, and this gives you chance to change your mind before the word is actually deleted. If you are using a .ADD file it will only contain words not found in the dictionary, so the possibility of deletions will not arise unless you have used one dictionary to make the .ADD file, and are using another dictionary in the maintenance run. If this happens, abandon the run by typing **X**.

If you only want to add words to an existing dictionary, and not to delete any, type **A**. The menu in Figure 40.12 will be displayed.

FIGURE 40.12

```
          A - Add words NO  Add all words in word file to
                            dictionary.  Enter <Y>es or <N>o.
```

The NO shows that the Add words feature is not ON. If you type **Y** the NO will change to YES, showing that the add words feature is now ON. At the same time the setting of the add/delete question in **C** is changed to NO. You might use this option if you are producing your own dictionary by using a whole text file to add to the dictionary. SpellStar will discard duplicate words.

If you are using a .ADD file to amend the dictionary, this may contain some words marked **D** to be added to the main dictionary and some marked **S** for a supplementary dictionary. By default the **S** supplementary option in the menu (Figure 40.11) is set to NO, so the supplementary dictionary will not be changed, but the words marked D in the .ADD file will be added to the main dictionary. To update the supplementary dictionary you should type **S**. This changes the S line on the menu (Figure 40.11) to YES, so that the supplementary dictionary is updated. Words marked S in the .ADD file will then be added to the supplementary dictionary.

The **T** option allows you to delete words only. This might be useful for example if you have prepared a file wrongly spelled words that you have put in the dictionary by mistake, or a file containing words with American spellings that you would like to remove from the dictionary.

The **N** option should be turned ON by pressing the **N** key if you wish to create a new dictionary, rather than updating an existing file. A menu is displayed when this key is pressed (Figure 40.13)

FIGURE 40.13

```
          N - New option:NO  Create a new dictionary using words
                             in word file.  Enter <Y>es or <N>o.
```

If you type **Y** the NO in this menu will change to YES, showing that the new dictionary option is turned ON, the setting of the **A** option will change to YES and the setting of the **C** option will automatically change to NO. This is because it is only possible to add words to a new dictionary, and not possible to delete them.

The **L** option allows you to see which words are being added to the dictionary. If you type **L**, the screen changes as shown in Figure 40.14.

FIGURE 40.14

```
   SpellStar is now creating or updating your dictionary:

        Number of words in word file........................:6
        Number of different words in word file.............:6
        Number of words in dictionary being updated.......:
        Number of words added to dictionary...............:
        Number of words deleted from dictionary...........:
        Number of words in new or updated dictionary......:

                                        [List of update words]
   PM ST TH EVANS SEATING ELIZABETH

   Enter <Return> to proceed, "R" to Restart
```

The number of words in the word file is counted and displayed. In this case there are six words. If you are using a .ADD file, the number of words will be either the D words or the S words depending on whether you are updating the main or a supplementary dictionary. Usually the number of different words will be the same, since SpellStar discards duplicates when making a .ADD file. If you are using a text file, there may well be duplicates, and the numbers will be different. If you are using a text file, the Add only toggle must be ON, or else you may start deleting the duplicate words unexpectedly!

A list of the words in the update file is displayed in the lower part of the screen. With a .ADD file, either the D or the S words will be displayed, depending on whether you are updating the main or a supplementary dictionary. The words have been sorted alphabetically by length, that is two letter words alphabetically, then three letter words alphabetically, then four letter words, and so on. They are arranged like this ready to integrate into the dictionary. If the word list is too large to fit on the screen, instructions are given at the bottom of the screen:

"Space"=continue, "C"=continuous listing, "^L"=stop/start listing

At the end of the list is the message:

Enter <Return> to proceed, "R" to Restart

If the list is not what you expected, press **R** to quit and go back to the Operations Menu (Figure 40.2). You can then go to the Maintenance controls (Figure 40.11), and choose the right word file before proceeding.

If all is well, press **RETURN**, and the maintenance run will proceed. Each time a word is added or deleted, SpellStar goes through every word in the dictionary. For this reason the run will continue for a short time after the last word in your word list has been added. The numbers start to fill in on the menu in Figure 40.14. The fourth line changes as words are added, the fifth line as words are deleted, line three shows how many words have been read from the original dictionary and line six shows how far the new file has been written. Because you selected the L option, SpellStar lists the words in the updated dictionary and stops after one screenful. You may examine the screenful, and press **space**, C or ^L to continue the updating.

"Space"=continue, "C"=continuous listing, "^L"=stop/start listing

Pressing the space bar moves on to the next screenful and stops again. Continuous listing results in scrolling, and ^L stops the listing of the dictionary and allows SpellStar to update the dictionary more quickly.

When the updating is complete, a message is displayed:

SpellStar has completed the dictionary maintenance.
Enter <Return> to return to WordStar, "R" to restart.

Pressing **RETURN** will take you to WordStar's "No-File" menu, and pressing **R** takes you to the SpellStar Operations menu (Figure 40.2), from where you can do more spelling checking, or dictionary maintenance.

After using SpellStar it is essential that you delete any unwanted files. If the old and new versions of the dictionary have different names, delete the old one once you are sure that the new version is correct. If you quit before completing a run, you may leave a .@@@ file. This should be deleted. Each time you do a spelling check you will produce a new .ADD file. You may wait until you have several of these before doing dictionary maintenance, but once this has been done they should be deleted.

Chapter 41.
INTRODUCTION TO CP/M

The essential hardware components to run CP/M on a micro-computer are examined. The purpose of an operating system is explained, and the functions of the main programs which make up CP/M are described. These are: (1) FDOS - the Functional Disk Operating System, which is made up of two parts, BDOS and BIOS, (2) CCP - the Console Command Processor, (3) a set of transient programs, and (4) BOOT which is used to load the system. The CCP contains five or six intrinsic commands, DIR, REN, ERA, TYPE, SAVE and in some cases USER. These are mentioned briefly here, but the next chapter 42 - CP/M Intrinsic Functions covers these in some detail. The transient programs generally available are STAT, PIP, SYSGEN, (FORMAT), MOVCPM, ED, ASM, DDT, LOAD, DUMP and SUBMIT. The first five of these are described in chapters 43 - 45.

CP/M stands for Control Program Monitor, and is the most popular and most widely used operating system for eight bit microcomputers. An operating system is a program - or a set of programs which make a set of electrical components communicate with each other and function as a computer. It also enables you to operate the computer, and control what it does. CP/M has gained such widespread acceptance that it has become the de-facto industry standard. Because it is so widely used, an enormous number of programs are available to run on CP/M machines, covering languages such as BASIC, FORTRAN, PASCAL and others, together with applications programs such as Wordprocessing packages, databases, inventory and stock control programs, games and so on. An offspring of CP/M called CP/M86 is widely used on sixteen bit microcomputers.

Hardware components required to run CP/M on a computer

A microcomputer controlled by CP/M must have a central processor, random access memory, (which is often called RAM or memory), a console device, at least one disk drive, and optionally a printer. The central processor and RAM constitute the heart of the microprocessor, and the other parts attached to this are regarded as peripheral devices. It does not matter whether a peripheral device is physically a separate piece of equipment in its own box, like a printer, or whether it is built into the same box as the computer, as the disk drives often are. The essential peripheral devices are the console and disks, though others such as a printer, graph plotter, paper tape reader or punch, or cassettes can be handled by CP/M as additional peripheral devices.

The central processor

The central processor or cpu is the component where the calculations are performed. This is a single silicon chip - usually a Z80, 8080 or 8085 chip for eight bit computers, or an 8088 or 8086 chip for sixteen bit computers. Computers based on other central processor chips such as the 6502 and 6800 can not run CP/M.

The memory

A microcomputer must have a minimum of 20K bytes of memory to run CP/M. This is to allow space to hold the operating system in memory, and to leave a small amount of space for the users own program. Larger user programs require more memory. 48K and 56K are quite common sizes, and the usual limit is 64K. A byte is the storage space required to store one character, and the computer term "K" refers to 1024 bytes, though often for simplicity this is approximated to 1000. The memory (RAM) is made up of a series of silicon chips. It must be remembered that RAM is "volatile", that is its contents disappear when the computer is turned off. This means that a program must be loaded from permanent store on disk into RAM every time that the program is to be run.

This operation is handled automatically by CP/M.

The console device

The console device is the means of getting information in to the computer, and of displaying messages or results from the computer. It may consist of a teletype, which is a typewriter keyboard combined with a printer. The keyboard allows information to be input into the computer, and the printer allows CP/M to output information. When a character is typed from the keyboard, it goes to part of CP/M called BIOS, which sends it to the program which is being executed, and the character is echoed back to the console printer. This allows you to see what you have typed. BIOS also transmits results from the computer, warning messages and error messages to the console printer so that they can be read. Alternatively the console device may be a video terminal often called a "glass teletype" in the USA, or a visual display unit (or vdu) in Britain. This comprises a keyboard for inputting information, and a cathode ray tube (television screen) for displaying messages from the computer. The keyboard has exactly the same layout as a typewriter keyboard, but there are several extra keys. The most important of these is the CONTROL key, which may alternatively be marked CTL or CTRL. The console may be a separate unit which plugs in to the computer, or it may be an integral part of the computer. Teletypes are mechanical printing devices, that run thirty to one hundred times slower than a vdu, are noisy, and are more likely to go wrong.

The disk drives

A CP/M based microcomputer must have at least one, and preferably two disk drives. The CP/M operating system must be loaded into the computer from a disk. The disk drive(s) may be housed in a separate unit connected to the computer, or they may be an integral part of the computer. Disk drives are used to read or write information semi-permanently in magnetic form on floppy disks. Disks are of two sizes: 8 inches in diameter, or 5.25 inches in diameter. There is a standard format for writing disks. It is IBM format single sided single density 8 inch. Unfortunately only a few computers use this format. It is unlikely that disks written on one make of computer can be read on a different make of computer, because of variations in (1) the size of disks, (2) single or double density recording, (3) the number of tracks recorded on a side, (4) single sided or double sided disks, (5) hard or soft sectoring of the disk, (6) the number of bytes per block and (7) the skew of blocks on the disk, The information stored may be a program, such as CP/M itself, WordStar, BASIC, or a user written program, or alternatively data may be stored. Disks are described more fully in chapter 2 - The Handling and Care of Floppy Disks. Computers which use cassettes are always very slow in reading or writing information from or to the tape, they read and write much less reliably than disks, and cannot run under CP/M.

The printer

A printer is called the "list device" by CP/M, and files, data, or the output from programs may be printed on paper to give "hard copy". The printer may be a line printer, a dot matrix printer, or a daisy wheel printer. A line printer prints a whole line at once, and may print at speeds of up to 1200 lines a minute. The quality of the printout is usually poor, but this sort of printer is useful when very large amounts of output are to be printed. Dot matrix printers are fairly fast, and commonly print 100-200 characters per second. Though some matrix printers boast "correspondence quality output", they print characters as a series of dots rather than fully formed characters, and most are of middle or low quality. Daisy wheel printers use fully formed characters which are hit one after another by a hammer. They give very high print quality - as good as an electric typewriter, but they are relatively very slow. A typical speed is 40 characters per second, but the range covers 10-80 characters per second.

CP/M does not require a printer, and if a teletype or other printing terminal is used as console device, then a printer is not needed. If a vdu is used as console, then a printer is highly desirable, otherwise no permanent printed output can be obtained.

The programs which make up CP/M

The CP/M operating system is a set of programs, that is software. It lets the microprocessor know what peripheral devices or hardware are present, and it acts as an interface between the microprocessor and any of the peripheral devices, between any two peripheral devices, and also between the microprocessor and you.

CP/M consists of four major groups of programs, each of which is subdivided into smaller programs. The four main areas are:

1. FDOS the Functional Disk Operating System

FDOS enables the executing program to manipulate files on the disks, and to communicate with the other peripherals. It comprises two main parts. The first is BDOS, short for Basic Disk Operating System, and the second part is BIOS the Basic Input and Output System. BDOS converts commands about CP/M files into instructions to read or write individual sectors on the disk. The instructions are passed to BIOS which executes them. BDOS is the same on CP/Ms for different machines, but the BIOS is different. These programs are invisible to the user, and you do not use them directly. Such programs are essential for communication between the keyboard and cpu, disks and cpu, cpu and vdu screen, or cpu and printer, and if they were not provided you would have to write these for yourself.

BDOS The basic disk operating system

BDOS implements a set of System Functions which are used by the executing program such as 'read a line from the keyboard' or 'create a file'. A disk file stores information and may contain a program which you have purchased, a program which you have written yourself, data such as a payroll or a list of customers names and addresses, or it may contain text such as letters, documents or books for Wordprocessing.

One disk may hold quite a large number of files. The maximum number on a floppy disk is frequently 64. Every file must have a unique filename, and BDOS keeps a directory which is a file on the disk where the name, the size and the location of each file on the disk is recorded.

Each disk is divided into a number of tracks, or concentric rings. A typical 8 inch IBM-compatible disk has 77 tracks, and each track is divided into 26 wedge shaped segments which are called sectors. 5.25 inch disks may have 35 or 40 tracks on each side, and may be divided into 10 or 16 sectors. The outermost track is number 0, the next is track 1, and so on. The entire CP/M operating system, including FDOS and CCP are stored on the outermost two tracks on the disk. When the computer is started up and CP/M is loaded, the entire system on these two tracks is copied into memory. The directory is stored on the next track, and the rest of the disk may be used to store transient programs and your files. (Under CP/M version 2.2 and later, the system may occupy more than two tracks).

BDOS locates a file by specifying the track and sector where the information is stored. The information on tracks and sectors is stored automatically in the directory by BDOS when the file is created, and is read automatically when the disk is logged-in. Thus users do not have to know anything about the tracks and sectors. BDOS gives the track and sector number to BIOS, which physically accesses the disk. Sometimes CP/M (that is BIOS) may find an error on the disk, and if so the faulty track and sector numbers are reported.

BDOS does not store a file as a set of contiguous blocks on one or more adjacent tracks on the disk. Blocks may be stored anywhere on the disk, and the directory keeps a plan of the location of each block, and the order in which they should be arranged. This is at first surprising, but there are two reasons for this apparently untidy storage pattern. First it is possible to extend a file dynamically, by adding some extra blocks on the end when needed. This means that there is no need to declare the size of the file when it is first created, no problem of wasting space through making the file too big and not filling it, nor any problem of making the file too big to fit into the declared space. The second reason why blocks are not adjacent is that having read one block, the central processor may take some time to move the information into the correct memory location, and during this time the disk may have rotated past the start of the next block. Thus the disk would have to complete a whole revolution before the next block could be read or written, making disk operations slow. To avoid this happening, blocks are deliberately offset or staggered, often by four blocks. BDOS looks after this for you.

Early versions of CP/M up to and including version 1.4 supported up to four disk drives. Versions 2.0 and later support up to sixteen disk drives. The drives are named in alphabetical order, the first drive being called A:, the second drive B:, and so on. When the system is first started, the active or logged-in disk drive is always A:, and this can be seen from the CP/M prompt of **A>** on the screen. To change to another drive, for example B:, type **B:** and press **RETURN**. (Since drive B: is now the logged-in drive, the CP/M prompt changes to **B>**). The colon is a vital part of the drive name, and without it the CCP thinks you would like to run a program of that name, rather than selecting a disk drive. When it cannot find the program it replies **B?** or **C?** depending on which drive you tried to select. If you attempt to select a drive which does not exist, you will obtain an error message **BDOS ERROR ON D: SELECT**. Typing any character will make CP/M reboot. Should you select a legal drive, but have no disk in it, or have the drive door open, then the system will hang up until you insert a disk, or shut the drive door, or reboot the system.

BIOS The basic input/output system

BIOS is the part of CP/M that actually transfers data between the microprocessor and the peripheral devices. BIOS sends characters to the vdu screen or printer, reads characters from the keyboard, and reads or writes sectors from or to a disk. Before reading or writing BIOS checks to see if the device is busy, and if so, it waits till the device is ready, before transferring data at the correct speed for the device. BIOS also checks the data for obvious errors, such as an incorrectly read disk.

2. CCP the Console Command Processor

This contains the programs to perform a number of built in or intrinsic functions which the user may call up by typing the appropriate command. These intrinsic functions are listed here, and are fully described in chapter 42 - CP/M Intrinsic Commands.

DIR Displays the directory of filenames present on a disk
REN Renames a file already present on the disk
ERA Erases a file from the disk
TYPE Types the contents of a file on the console
SAVE Saves the program or data in RAM in a disk file
USER This is only applicable to versions 2.0 and later,
and it changes the user number

3. The Transient programs

A number of transient programs are provided as part of CP/M. They exist as separate files on the disk, and can be loaded into the transient program area, and run when required. They are not held in memory all of the time like the built in (intrinsic) commands. The usual transient programs are listed here, and some of them are described in detail in later chapters.

STAT   Used to find the size of files on the disk, the amount of free space on the disk, information about the system and to display or change the assignment of peripheral devices.

PIP   Used for copying disk files.

SYSGEN   Writes the CP/M operating system on the outer two tracks of a disk. PIP cannot copy CP/M.

FORMAT   Formats brand new disks before they are used to store programs or data. It is essential that this is done for all 5.25 inch disks. It is also necessary on some (but not all) 8 inch disks.

MOVCPM   If when you first get CP/M it has not been configured by the dealer for your particular machine, then CP/M will not know where the top of memory is in your computer. Thus CP/M will not know where to load FDOS and CCP in memory, and to be safe it will probably load them low in memory in case the system does not have much RAM. This will reduce the size of the transient program area, and you will not use all of the memory present. MOVCPM is a program which helps you to alter, that is configure a version of CP/M to take advantage of all the memory present. MOVCPM must be used again if extra memory is added at a later date.

ED   This is an editor, which is very difficult to use. WordStar is infinitely better as an editor, but if you are editing programs remember to edit a **Non-Document File.**

ASM   Reads assembly language source files, and produces an 8080 machine code program from it.

DDT   The Dynamic Debugging Tool, which may be used to test, debug and alter machine code programs.

LOAD   Takes a hexadecimal file and produces a machine code file.

DUMP   Dumps the contents of a file in hexadecimal on the console.

SUBMIT   Submits a file of commands for batch processing.

4. BOOT the bootstrap loader

BOOT is a small program which is loaded into memory (RAM). It performs a special function in loading CP/M when first the computer is switched on.

At the start when the computer is switched on, the "volatile" RAM memory is empty, and so cannot help. A very small program is permanently stored in a Read Only Memory chip or ROM, and the program in this makes the central processor read the BOOT program from disk into the RAM memory, and then control is transferred to the BOOT program now stored in memory. BOOT makes the central processor read the entire CP/M system (BDOS, BIOS and CCP) into memory, and then transfers control to CCP. The main computer memory (RAM) is used as shown in Figure 40.1.

168

FIGURE 40.1   CP/M architecture and memory map

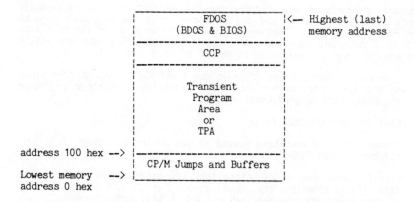

The memory from 0 to 100 hex is reserved by CP/M for jumps to BDOS and BIOS, and for buffers. The transient program area may be used for any transient program and data that you care to use. This could be one of the CP/M transient programs such as STAT or PIP, WordStar, or a BASIC interpreter and the BASIC program you have written. The sizes of the FDOS and CCP areas are fixed, and are big enough to hold these programs. The size of the TPA is the total amount of memory less 100 hex, less the space occupied by CCP and FDOS. Hence the size of the TPA varies from one computer to another. Transient programs may also use the space occupied by CCP thus for all practical purposes extending the TPA. These programs finish by reloading the CCP from disk to its original working position in memory.

Chapter 42.

CP/M INTRINSIC COMMANDS

There are essentially two different sets of commands in CP/M. The first set contains five or six intrinsic commands, which can be run at any time, because they are built in as part of the CP/M operating system, and are stored on the system tracks on the disk. The first five of the intrinsic commands DIR, REN, ERA, TYPE and SAVE, are available on all versions of CP/M, but the sixth intrinsic command which is called USER is only available on CP/M version 2.0 and later. The use of these commands is described briefly in this chapter. The second set of commands are the transient commands, which are really separate programs provided as part of CP/M, and which may be run from CP/M provided that the command is present as a separate command file on the system disk. The transient commands generally available are STAT, PIP, SYSGEN, (FORMAT), MOVCPM, ED, ASM, DDT, LOAD, DUMP and SUBMIT. FORMAT is not needed on all systems. The first five of these transient commands are described in the following chapters.

The directory command DIR

The DIR command is used to display the disk directory on the vdu or terminal. The directory is simply a list of all the files present on the particular disk. Suppose that the logged-in disk drive is A:, that is A: is the active drive, then the screen will show the CP/M prompt A>. When the command DIR is typed, and RETURN is pressed:

    A:DIR   RETURN

the directory of files present on drive A: is displayed on the screen. With CP/M versions 1.4 and earlier, the directory is arranged as a simple list:

```
A>DIR
A:PIP     COM
A:STAT    COM
A:WS      COM
A:WSMSGS  OVR
A:WSOVLY1 OVR
A:MAILMRGE OVR
```

The DIR command works very fast, and if a vdu is being used and there are a lot of filenames, some may scroll off the top of the screen before they can be read. This is particularly so with CP/M version 1.4. The listing may be stopped to allow the filenames to be read by pressing ^S, and the listing may be restarted by pressing ^S again, or any other key except ^C, which is used by CP/M to abort the job in progress.

With CP/M versions 2.0 and later, the directory is arranged as four columns of entries listed across the screen, separated by colons:

```
A>DIR
A: PIP     COM : STAT    COM : WS     COM : WSMSGS   OVR
A: WSOVLY1 OVR : MAILMRGE OVR
```

If a printout of the filenames is required, typing ^P before the DIR command echoes the listing on the screen to the printer. Since the printer works much slower than the vdu screen, the output will be slowed down. Everything which appears on the screen will continue to be printed until ^P is pressed again.

There are two ways of listing the directory of another disk drive, for example B:. First the drive you wish to examine may be included after the DIR command. Note that there must be one or more spaces between the command DIR and the drive name:

      A>DIR B: RETURN

The second way is to change the logged-in drive, then use the DIR command:

      A>B: RETURN
      B>DIR   RETURN

    Sometimes you need to know if a named file is present on a disk. One way of doing this is to list all the files present on that disk, and then examine the directory listing. The alternative is to make the computer do the searching, by using the DIR command with the filename as an argument, for example:

      A>DIR STAT.COM   RETURN

If the file STAT.COM is present on drive A: the screen will display:

      A:STAT.COM

If the file is not present the screen will display the message:

      NOT FOUND

In a similar way you can check if the file is present on drive B: either by:

or

      A>DIR B:STAT.COM   RETURN

      A>B: RETURN
      B>DIR STAT.COM   RETURN

It is possible to use the asterisk * as a "wild card" to indicate any number of ambiguous characters in the filename, or a question mark to indicate one ambiguous character in the filenames used. Consider the command:

      A>DIR *.COM   RETURN

The asterisk matches with any filename in the directory, hence all the files on the disk with the file type .COM will be listed on the screen:

A: PIP   COM : STAT   COM : WS   COM

or   A:PIP   COM
         A:STAT   COM
         A:WS   COM

The rename command REN

    The REN command is used to rename an existing file on the disk. Since the filenames are stored in the directory, CP/M does not have to copy the file itself, and merely changes the directory entry. The command is therefore very quick. The general form of the command is:

      REN newname = oldname

There _must_ be one or more spaces between the command REN and the new filename. Spaces are optional around the = sign, but spaces must not occur in file names.

Thus:

       A>REN LETTER.TXT=LETTER.BAK   RETURN
or   A>REN LETTER.TXT = LETTER.BAK   RETURN

will change the name of the existing file LETTER.BAK on drive A: to LETTER.TXT.
Note that the drive name may be specified as part of the filename.

       A>REN B:LETTER.TXT = B:LETTER.BAK   RETURN
       A>REN LETTER.TXT = B:LETTER.BAK   RETURN
       A>REN B:LETTER.TXT = LETTER.BAK   RETURN

In all these cases the file on drive B: is renamed. If different drives are
specified for two filenames, then CP/M will not rename anything, because REN
only alters a directory entry, and cannot copy the file from one drive to
another. If a drive name is specified for one file and not the other, CP/M
assumes that the same disk drive applies to both filenames.

If you try to rename a file which does not exist on the disk, then nothing
is altered, and the error message **NO FILE** is displayed on the screen. If you
choose a new filename which already exists on that disk, CP/M detects that you
are attempting to duplicate a filename, and assumes that you have made a
mistake. If this happens, nothing is renamed, but an error message **FILE EXISTS**
is displayed on the screen. File names on one disk must be unique, and CP/M
does not allow two files with the same name on the same disk. If you really
want to make the new file have this name, you must first erase the existing
file with that name using the ERA command, and then rename the required file.

The erase command ERA

The ERA command is used to erase filenames from the directory. This is
very quick, since only the directory is changed. Actually the directory entry
for that filename is marked as "erased", and though the contents of the file
still remain on the disk, they cannot be read by CP/M. This file space is no
longer reserved, and is made available for use. It will eventually be overwritten by other files. The general form of the command is:

      ERA filename

Note that there must be one or more spaces between the ERA command and the
filename, and that the logged-in disk drive is assumed unless the drive name
preceeds the filename. For example:

       A>ERA LETTER.BAK   RETURN
or   A>ERA B:LETTER.BAK   RETURN

The first command erases the file LETTER.BAK from the logged-in drive A:,
while the second erases the file from drive B:.

In the above cases, the filename is specific, and refers to a single file.
It is also possible to use "ambiguous" file references which refer to a number
of different files. Suppose that the disk contains the following files:
LETTER.TXT, LETTER.BAK, LETTER2, LETTER2.BAK, REPLY.BAK, ORDER.BAK and PIP.COM.
An asterisk * may be included in the filename, to indicate any number up to
eight ambiguous characters, or if an asterisk is included in the file type it
refers to up to three ambiguous characters. Consider the command:

       A>ERA *.BAK   RETURN

The * which replaces the filename will match with any filename, hence the
command would erase all files of any name from the disk provided that they had
the file type .BAK. Thus files such as LETTER.BAK, LETTER2.BAK, REPLY.BAK and
ORDER.BAK would all be erased. The files LETTER.TXT, LETTER2 and PIP.COM would

not be erased. Next consider the command:

>A>**ERA L*.BAK**   **RETURN**

This will erase all filenames beginning with L regardless of what other letters
if any make up the filename, so long as the file type or ending is .BAK. Thus
files such as LETTER.BAK and LETTER2.BAK would be erased, but the files
LETTER.TXT, LETTER2, REPLY.BAK, ORDER.BAK and PIP.COM would not be erased.
Next consider the command below:

>A>**ERA LETTER.***   **RETURN**

The asterisk replacing the file type means that absolutely any file type, which
could be blanks, or any one, two or three characters will match. This means
that the files LETTER.TXT and LETTER.BAK would both be erased. The files
LETTER2, LETTER2.BAK, REPLY.BAK, ORDER.BAK and PIP.COM would not be erased.
Next consider the command:

>A>**ERA *.***   **RETURN**

Since an asterisk for the filename means that any filename will fit, and an
asterisk for the file type means that any filetype will fit, this command will
erase all the files on the disk, irrespective of the filename or filetype.

If you attempt to erase a file which does not exist on the specified
drive, then CP/M versions 2.0 and later give an error message **NO FILE,** but
version 1.4 and earlier do not give an error message, so you will not know that
the file has not been erased unless the DIR command is used to check the
directory.

Attempts to erase files from a disk which is write protected (that is a
write protect tab is present on 5.25 inch disks, and the tab is absent on 8
inch disks) will give a **BDOS ERROR.** Pressing any key will reboot the system.
Similarly attempting to erase a file from a disk which is R/O (read only) will
cause a similar **BDOS ERROR.**

The TYPE command

The TYPE command displays the contents of a file on the console device
attached to the computer, which may be a vdu or a printing terminal. If a vdu
is used, a copy of the file may be printed if the ^P command is typed either
before the **TYPE** command, or alternatively after **TYPE** and the filename, but
before pressing **RETURN.** The file must contain printable ASCII characters,
which may be text, numbers stored as ASCII characters, or the source of a
program. Files with the ending .COM contain non-printing characters, and if
the TYPE command is used on them they will produce garbage on the screen, may
ring the bell, produce inverse video or scroll backwards! Fortunately this
does not damage either the file or the terminal. Even though WordStar data
files contain text, they also contain control characters, and so the TYPE
command does not work satisfactorily on them. Users should use the WordStar
edit function to examine such files on the screen, or the WordStar print
function to print such a file, rather than using the CP/M TYPE command.

The general form of the command is:

TYPE filename   RETURN

There must be one or more spaces between the TYPE command and the filename.
The disk drive may optionally be included in the filename, for example:

>A>**TYPE README.DOC**   **RETURN**
or   A>**TYPE B:STARTREK.BAS**   **RETURN**

The display of the file will first fill the vdu screen, and then scroll off the top of the screen continually until the end of the file is reached. This is not very helpful if you want to read something at the beginning or the middle of the file. The display may be stopped at any point by pressing ^S, thus allowing time to read what is on the screen. The display may be started again by pressing ^S or any other character except for ^C which aborts the job. When the TYPE command is actually in progress, it may be aborted by pressing any key except ^S.

The SAVE command

The SAVE command is used to copy the contents of memory (RAM) from the Transient Program Area, into a disk file. This is only of use if you are writing or altering an assembler language program, or if you are regenerating the CP/M system itself. It is included here for completeness. The general form of the command is:

SAVE number filename

One or more spaces must be present between the command SAVE and the number, and also between the number and the filename. The number is the number of pages of data to be written to the file. Under CP/M a page is 256 bytes of data.

With CP/M version 1.4 and earlier, the SAVE command may destroy the contents of memory, (the Transient Program Area), so a file may be saved once only. With CP/M version 2.0 and later, the Transient Program Area is not changed in any way by the SAVE command, so the same program may be saved under several separate filenames, on several separate disks, or under several different user numbers.

The USER command

CP/M version 2.0 and later allows 16 different user numbers to be specified. These are user numbers 0, 1, 2, ... 15 inclusive. Each file is associated with a user number. If you totally ignore user numbers then all files will have the user number 0. On first booting up the system (cold boot), CP/M puts you in user number 0. Thus commands such as DIR will list all the files on the disk, just as with the earlier versions of CP/M. The user number may be changed, for example to 3 with a command:

A>USER 3   RETURN

Any number between 0 and 15 may be used. In this case 3 has been selected as the active user number. This means that CP/M has moved to another part of the directory, and files associated with user number 0 can no longer be accessed. If you now create a file it will have the user number 3. The DIR command will only list files in the active user number, (3 in this case), hence any files in user number 0, or any user number other than 3 will not be displayed. CP/M only recognises filenames which belong to the currently selected active user number. Thus REN will only rename files in user number 3, ERA will only erase files in user number 3, and TYPE and SAVE will only work on files in user number 3. This user number will remain in effect either until it is changed with another USER command, or until the system is "cold-booted" again.

The main use of user numbers is to simplify matters when different users store files on the same disk. This is important with multi-user versions of CP/M. Provided that each user uses a different user number, they can list the directory of just their own files, rather than all the files on the disk. It also reduces the possibility of accidentally erasing or altering files belonging to someone else. It is also useful to separate different classes of work which may be done by either the same user, or different users. For example, all files to do with Wordprocessing might be put in one user number, the accounts in another user number, and all BASIC programs in another. With the increasing use of hard disks, which have an enormous amount of storage space - commonly from 3 Megabytes up to 26 Megabytes, a means of subdividing the filespace is essential.

If the file store is subdivided into different user numbers, it will inevitably be necessary to copy files from one user number to another, using the CP/M file copying program PIP.COM. This is described in chapter 44, but the special application of copying files between different user numbers is described below. First there is the problem of how to get the program PIP from user number 0 into our current user number 3. Then there is a second problem of how to use PIP to copy files into user number 3 from other user numbers.

How to copy PIP.COM from user number 0 into user number 3

1. Cold boot the system, so that you are in user 0, or if the system is up and running, change to user number 0 with a **USER 0** command.

2. Run the program STAT to find the size of the program PIP.COM. To do this type:

   >   A>STAT PIP.COM   RETURN

   and the computer replies
   ```
   Recs  Bytes  Ext  Acc
    58    8K     1   R/W A:PIP.COM
   ```

   The size of PIP is 8K, or 32 pages of 256 bytes. It is essential that you check this for yourself, since the size may change in other versions.

3. Since there is no direct method of copying PIP from user number 0 to user number 3, you must copy PIP from user number 0 into memory, and then save the contents of memory in user number 3. This is done as follows:

A>PIP	RETURN	load PIP into memory
*	RETURN	exit from PIP
A>USER 3	RETURN	change to user number 3
A>SAVE 32 PIP.COM	RETURN	save 32 pages from memory as a file called PIP.COM in user number 3.

How to copy files from one user number to another

Now that you have a copy of PIP in the required user number, (3), and you are associated with this user number, it is easy to copy files into this user number. The general form of a command using PIP is:

>   PIP newfilename = oldfilename[options]

In this case you should specify the user number where the old filename is stored, using the G option and the user number in square brackets after the filename. For example to copy the file WS.COM into the currently logged in user number (3) from user number 0 type:

>   A>PIP WS.COM=WS.COM[G0]   RETURN

or to copy the file STAT.COM into the currently logged in user number (3) from user number 5 type:

>   A>STAT.COM=STAT.COM[G5]   RETURN

Chapter 43.

THE STAT COMMAND

CP/M contains both intrinsic and transient commands. The six intrinsic commands DIR, REN, ERA, TYPE, SAVE, (and USER) built in as part of the CP/M operating system, are described in the previous chapter. The transient commands are separate programs which may be run from CP/M provided that the command is present as a separate command file (.COM file) on the system disk. A transient command is actually a machine code program, which is automatically copied from disk into memory by CP/M and then executed as a command. The transient commands generally available are STAT, PIP, SYSGEN, (FORMAT), MOVCPM, ED, ASM, DDT, LOAD, DUMP and SUBMIT. FORMAT is not needed on all systems. Though the transient commands all exist as files on the disk, and have filenames which end .COM, this is not typed when the file is executed as a command, but it must be typed when the file is copied or erased. The program STAT is described in this chapter, PIP is described in the next (chapter 44), and SYSGEN, FORMAT and MOVCPM are described in chapter 45.

Uses of the program STAT

STAT.COM is a program provided as part of the CP/M package, which can be used both to display and also to change the status of the disks, of individual files, of the peripheral devices and in later versions of the users too. Differences between early and later versions of CP/M are given.

1. Disk status

If the command STAT is typed, the read/write status of each disk will be displayed together with the amount of free space on the disk. For example if the command is typed as soon as you have logged-in, CP/M versions up to 1.4 will display something like:

       A>**STAT**   **RETURN**
       A:R/W, Space: 160k

Drive A: has read and write status (R/W), and files on this disk may be read, written or erased. There is 160k of free space on this disk. Until drive B: is accessed, CP/M does not know that it exists. To examine the disk in drive B: you should type **STAT B:**. If you have previously accessed drive B:, for example by typing **DIR B:**, reading a file from B: or changing the logged-in drive to B: then the STAT command will show the free space on both drives. When a drive is first accessed, a header table is read from the disk directory and stored in memory. This table contains the information about the names, sizes and position on the disk of the various files.

To find if there is enough free space on a disk to write a new file, then the command **STAT A:**, or **STAT B:** should be typed, depending on which drive you are interested in. A message like the one below will be produced:

       Bytes Remaining On A: 160k
or
       Bytes Remaining On B: 95k

All of the files on one disk (for example drive B:) may be set as read only (R/O) to prevent the files being accidentally erased or overwritten, by typing the command:

       A>**STAT B:=R/O**   **RETURN**

Read only status simply means that files can be read, but nothing can be written or erased from this disk. If you attempt to write on this disk, an error message will appear:

BDOS ERROR ON B: R/O

The system then waits until any key is pressed, when the system automatically warm boots, and all disks are given R/W status. The R/O status has thus been destroyed, and files may now be written or erased. If you want R/O status, then you must re-establish it with another STAT B:=R/O command.

The file protection features have been enhanced in CP/M versions 2.0 and later. Individual files may be protected with R/O status, as well as for the disk as a whole. Thus certain files may be protected, but other files on the same disk may have R/W status, and you may write to or erase these files. To set a named file to R/O status, type:

    STAT filename $R/O   RETURN

Note that there must be at least one space between the command STAT and the filename, and also between the filename and the $R/O. The filename may be preceded by the drive letter and a colon. The file remains read only even if ^C is typed. To change the status of a R/O file back to R/W, type:

    STAT filename $R/W   RETURN

2. File status

STAT may be used to display the size of a file, or a group of files. The general form of the command is **STAT filename.** The drive letter and a colon may precede the filename. For example:

    A>STAT WS.COM   RETURN

would look for the file WS.COM on the logged-in drive (A: in this case), or:

    A>STAT B:WS.COM   RETURN

would look for the file on drive B:. The display with CP/M versions 1.4 and earlier is shown below:

    A>STAT WS.COM   RETURN

    RECS BYTS EX D:FILENAME.TYP
    124 16K 1 A:WS.COM

This shows that the file WS.COM contains 124 records, occupies 16k of file-space, and uses one disk extent. A disk extent is a 16k block, and unknown to the user the directory has an entry for each 16k. Thus a file between 16k and 32k in size has two extents, and a file between 32k and 48k has three extents. The layout is slightly different with CP/M 2.0 and later, and shows in addition Acc the "access", that is whether the file has read and write status, or read only status. If the filename is enclosed in parentheses it has "system status". This is explained later.

    A>STAT WS.COM   RETURN

    Recs Bytes Ext Acc
    124   16k   1 R/W A:WS.COM
    Bytes Remaining On A: 160k

Generalised filenames may be used in the STAT command. The asterisk is a "wild card" which matches any filename on the disk. In a similar way, a question mark may be used to fit any single letter in the filename. For example the command below will list all files with the ending .COM:

            A>STAT *.COM   RETURN

        RECS BYTS EX D:FILENAME.TYP
        256 32K 2 A:INSTALL.COM
        124 16K 1 A:WS.COM
         58   8K 1 A:PIP.COM
         41   6K 1 A:STAT.COM

The layout is slightly different for CP/M version 2.0. The most general command is:

            A>STAT *.*   RETURN

This matches any filename, and any extension, so that the size of every file on the disk is listed.

    In CP/M version 2.0 and later individual files may be given read only R/O or read and write R/W status. This is described in the section on Disk status above. In addition a file may be declared as a SYSTEM file. For example:

        A>STAT PIP.COM $SYS   RETURN

    This makes the file PIP.COM on drive A: into a system file. This does not mean that it is now part of the operating system. It still exists as a file on the disk as before, it may have R/W or R/O status, but it will not be listed by the DIR command. This may be useful if the file is always present on all of your disks, and shortening the directory listing will make other files easier to find. The SYSTEM status may be removed, and the file listed in the directory again by the command:

        A>STAT PIP.COM $DIR   RETURN

    Another enhancement with CP/M version 2.0 is the argument $S which may be appended to a command to display the file SIZE in records. This is identical to the number of records shown under RECS for the usual sequential type of files, but is different for random access files which may be used in data-bases. An example of the command is:

        A>STAT WS.COM $S   RETURN

        Size Recs Bytes Ext Acc
        124   124   16k   1 R/W A:WS.COM
        Bytes Remaining On A: 160k

3. Peripheral device assignments

    CP/M can communicate to the outside world through four "logical devices" in addition to the disks. Some or all of the "logical devices" may be used as channels for the input and output of information. The four "logical devices" are:

    (1) **CON** - the operators console. This is the device that the Console Command Processor (CCP) reads commands from, and is the place where the CCP sends messages.

    (2) **LST** - this is the output listing device. Most programs send data which is to be printed to this device.

    (3) **RDR** - this stands for "reader" and is an input device which is used by

some programs.

(4) **PUN** - this stands for "punch". It is an output device used by some programs.

Programs may read information from the console, or from the reader, and they may output information to the console, the list device or the punch. The real devices such as a teletype or a vdu, and a printer which are actually connected to the computer must be associated with these "logical devices". BDOS has a table which links "physical devices" with the "logical devices". The console is likely to be either a teletype printing terminal, or a vdu. The list device could be a printer, or it could be the console if a printing terminal is used as console. A paper tape reader, or a cassette recorder could be attached to the reader device, and a papertape punch or a cassette recorder could be attached to the punch device. If you change the devices, or add an extra one, CP/M can be changed to accommodate the peripherals you wish to attach. The command:

STAT DEV: **RETURN**

may be used to find out the current device assignments. Note that there must be at least one space between the command STAT and the argument DEV:, and that the colon is essential, or STAT will look for a file called DEV. The output will look something like:

      STAT DEV: **RETURN**
      CON: is CRT:
      RDR: is TTY:
      PUN: is TTY:
      LST: is LPT:

These device assignments may be changed with a command of the form:

      STAT logical-device = physical-device

For example if the console is changed to a teletype, and a paper tape punch is added, the following commands should be typed:

      STAT CON: = TTY:
      STAT PUN: = PTP:

or several devices (two in this case) may be changed in one line:

      STAT CON:=TTY:,PUN:=PTP:

(On some computers BIOS ignores the device specifications and always uses the same devices, hence changing the logical assignment with STAT has no effect).

The physical devices permitted are:

Console devices
TTY: teletype-like printing terminal
CRT: cathode ray terminal (vdu)
BAT: used when batch processing - all input is from the RDR device, and all output is sent to the LST device. There is no operator intervention.
UC1: a user-defined console

Listing devices
TTY: teletype-like printing terminal
CRT: cathode ray terminal (vdu)
LPT: line printer, dot matrix printer, or daisy wheel printer
UL1: user-defined listing device

Reader devices
TTY: teletype-like printing terminal
PTR: paper tape reader or cassette
UR1: user-defined reader
UR2: user-defined reader

Punch devices
TTY: teletype-like printing terminal
PTP: paper tape punch or cassette
UP1: user-defined punch
UP2: user-defined punch

A list showing all of the possible physical devices which may be assigned to each logical device can be displayed by typing the command **STAT VAL:**. It should be remembered that these devices are only names given by CP/M to different input/output channels, and they may not physically correspond to a peripheral of the same name. Later versions of CP/M (2.0 and later) also show five extra lines giving a summary of all the STAT command formats, as shown below:

```
Temp R/O disk: d:=R/O                        ) STAT options list
Set Indicator: d:filename $R/O $R/W $SYS $DIR )      only
Disk Status  : DSK: d:DSK:                   )       on
User Status  : USR:                          )     CP/M 2.0
Iobyte Assign:                               )     and later
CON: = TTY: CRT: BAT: UC1:
RDR: = TTY: PTR: UR1: UR2:
PUN: = TTY: PTP: UP1: UP2:
LST: = TTY: CRT: LPT: UL1:
```

4. User status - Only on CP/M versions 2.0 and later

If the command **STAT USR:** is typed, then the current user number is displayed, together with information about which user numbers have stored files on the logged-in disk. For example:

A>**STAT USR:**   **RETURN**

ACTIVE USER : 2
ACTIVE FILES: 0 2 13

A>

This shows that you are logged-in as user number 2, that the logged-in disk drive is A:, and that this disk contains files for user numbers 0, 2, and 13. The DIR command may be used to display a list of files that are in user number 2 (the currently logged-in user number) just by typing DIR. To display the filenames for other user numbers, you must first change the logged-in user number with for example a **USER 0** command, and **DIR** will then list files in user number zero. (Remember that files declared SYSTEM files will not appear in the directory listing, but may be displayed by the command **STAT *.*** and appear in parentheses).

More on disk status

An infrequently used command is **STAT DSK:**. This displays the technical details of all of the disk drives in the system. If a drive letter and a colon precede the filename, then information on the one specified drive is given. Unless you change or add extra disks, then this information will not change for

your particular computer. The details shown below are for a North Star double
density, double sided disk.

A>STAT A:DSK: **RETURN**

    A: Drive Characteristics
 2720: 128 Byte Record Capacity
  340: Kilobyte Drive Capacity
   64: 32 Byte Directory Entries
   64: Checked Directory Entries
  256: Records/ Extent
   16: Records/ Block
   40: Sectors/ Track
    2: Reserved Tracks

This drive has a capacity of 2720 records; each record is 128 bytes long,
giving 340k bytes storage. The directory can hold 64 entries. The number of
Checked Directory Entries is the number of entries which the system will check
to see if a new disk has been inserted in the drive. This is usually all the
directory entries. There are 256 records on each extent, 16 records per block,
40 sectors per track, and 2 reserved tracks.

Chapter 44.

THE PIP COMMAND

The peripheral interchange program called PIP is used to transfer files from one peripheral device to another, and it is one of the most widely used CP/M transient commands. Its most common use is for making a copy of a file on the same disk, or for copying one file or a whole series of files from one disk to another. Files may also be transferred from disk to an output device such as CON:, LST: or PUN:, and information may be input from an input device such as CON: or RDR: into a disk file. PIP may be used to concatenate files, that is join several files together into a new file. Lastly by using certain optional parameters, PIP may be used to modify files systematically as it copies them, for example to add line numbers, or to convert a file to capital letters. It is worth remembering that PIP makes no changes to the original file(s), which are exactly the same after running PIP as they were before. Any changes made will appear in the new file produced.

Use of PIP to copy files

The transient command PIP may be used at any time when the CP/M prompt A> or B> is displayed, provided that the file PIP.COM is present on the logged-in disk, and is available to your user number. All transient commands require the file to be loaded into memory (the transient program area) before it can be executed. CP/M does this automatically. The general form of the command is:

PIP new-filename = original-filename[parameters]   RETURN

There must be one or more spaces between the command PIP and the new filename. Either of the file names may be preceded by the drive letter and a colon, but if these are omitted, then the logged-in drive is assumed. Spaces are optional around the equals sign. The parameters are optional, and are discussed later, but if they are present they must be enclosed by square brackets.

Suppose that drive A: contains the file PIP.COM, and is the logged-in drive, and that you wish to copy the file called STAT.COM from drive A: to B:. This is done by the following commands:

A>PIP B:STAT.COM = A:STAT.COM   RETURN

Here the new file is specified on drive B: and is called STAT.COM. Since the new filename is the same as the original filename, the new filename may be omitted:

A>PIP B: = A:STAT.COM   RETURN

Because the logged-in drive is A:, this need not be specified in the original file name:

A>PIP B: = STAT.COM   RETURN

Suppose that the logged-in drive is A:, that PIP.COM is on drive B:, and you wish to copy the file LETTER.TXT from drive B: to A:. This is done by:

A>B:PIP A:LETTER.TXT = B:LETTER.TXT   RETURN

or   A>B:PIP A: = B:LETTER.TXT   RETURN

or   A>B:PIP LETTER.TXT = B:LETTER.TXT   RETURN

Note that since PIP.COM is on drive B:, the command must be B:PIP in each case. Since the new filename is the same as the original filename, this need not be specified. The newfile is on drive A: which is the logged-in drive, so this need not be specified. However, either the drive or the filename must be specified - you may not omit both.

Suppose that drive A: is the logged-in drive, and it contains the files PIP.COM and LETTER1.TXT. If you wish to make a backup copy of LETTER1.TXT on the same disk, and call it LETTER1.BAK, this may be done as follows:

     A>A:PIP A:LETTER1.BAK = A:LETTER1.TXT   RETURN

or   A>PIP LETTER1.BAK = LETTER1.TXT   RETURN

Note that the drive letters may be omitted throughout because all the files are on the logged-in drive.

CP/M permits the use of general filenames with an asterisk to match any number of characters in either the filename or the extension, or a question mark to match with any one one character. Thus if PIP.COM is on drive A:, the command:

     A>PIP B: = A:*.COM   RETURN

will copy all the files which have the extension (that is end with) .COM from drive A: to drive B:. In a similar way the command below will copy all the .COM files present on drive B: onto drive A:.

     A>PIP A: = B:*.COM   RETURN

Part of a filename may be specified explicitly, and the rest filled in by either a * or the appropriate number of ? characters. For example, the files WSU.COM, WS.COM, WSOVLY1.OVR and WSMSGS.OVR could all be copied from drive A: to drive B: by the following commands:

     A>PIP A: = B:WS*.*   RETURN

or   A>PIP A: = B:WS??????.*   RETURN

or   A>PIP A: = B:WS??????.???   RETURN

Note that a filename is padded with spaces and stored as eight characters, if you have not used eight characters, and in a similar way the extension is always stored as three characters.

The most general filename *.* will match any filename and any extension, and this may be used to copy all the files from one disk to another. In the example below, all the files present on drive A: are copied onto B:

     A>PIP B: = A:*.*   RETURN

Input from or output to a logical or physical device

In much the same way as the disk drive may be specified in a PIP command, a logical or a physical device may also be specified. Logical and physical devices are described in chapter 43 - The STAT Command. The most important logical devices are CON: the console, and LST: the list device, but there are also RDR: the reader device and PUN: the punch device. For example, assuming that the file PIP.COM is on drive A:, the command below will copy the file LETTER1.TXT from disk A: to the console device. If the console is defined as a teletype, the file will be printed. If the console is a vdu the file will be displayed on the screen.

```
A>PIP CON: = LETTER1.TXT                        RETURN
```

In a similar way the file may be copied to the list device by the command below, and if a printer is connected to this, the file will be printed.

```
A>PIP LST: = LETTER1.TXT                        RETURN
```

A copy of a file may be sent to the punch device, which may be physically connected to a paper tape punch, a card punch or a cassette recorder, or may be being used for batch operation by the command:

```
A>PIP PUN: = LETTER1.TXT                        RETURN
```

Lastly, information may be read in from the reader device, and stored as a file on the disk. This is often useful for importing programs from other machines, and the physical device attached is usually a paper tape reader, a card reader, or a cassette recorder, but it may also be used for batch work. A command to input information into a new disk file called GAME is shown below:

```
A>PIP GAME = RDR:                               RETURN
```

Some special parameters

A special device name PRN: may be used in PIP commands. This is very similar to the device LST: which is used to send the file to the printer. The difference is that PRN: expands tabs to 8 character columns, numbers lines, and inserts a form feed to start a new page every 60 lines. An example is:

```
A>PIP PRN: = LETTER1.TXT                        RETURN
```

The parameter NUL: may be appended to a PIP command to send 40 null characters (ASCII code 0) to the output device. This is useful when sending a file to a paper tape punch. For example:

```
A>PIP PUN: = ACCOUNTS.BAS,NUL:                  RETURN
```

In special circumstances you may send an end of file marker ^Z to the device, by appending ,EOF: to the command, though this is done automatically by PIP. Also the PIP program may be patched to permit the use of a special input device INP: or a special output device OUT:.

Errors and aborting a run

If a PIP command is typed which is invalid for some reason, then copying does not even start. An error message will be displayed - either **"INVALID FORMAT"** if you have got the syntax wrong, or **"NO FILE"** if you have spelt the filename incorrectly or used a filename which does not appear on the disk.

If the command is copying from one disk file to another, there is no way of stopping it once it has started. If however the copying operation involves other devices such as CON:, LST: or PRN: then copying may be stopped by typing ^S (in the same way as the screen display can be stopped), and re-started by pressing any character except ^C. The command may be aborted by pressing any key except ^S, and the message **ABORTED: filename** is displayed.

Concatenation of text files

PIP may be used to combine two or more files into a single file, and this process is called concatenation. The original file(s) which may be on different disks if necessary, are processed in the order specified, and added at the end of the new file which is being created. The original files must contain only printable ASCII characters, which excludes machine code in .COM files, and WordStar data files (which contain numerous non-printing control characters). The original files must also end with the usual end of file marker CONTROL-Z (^Z), which is put there automatically by CP/M. During the process of concatenation, all the end of file markers except for the last one are discarded from the new file, so that it only has one, and that is at the end. The general form of the command for concatenation is:

A>PIP A: = file1,file2,file3,file4   RETURN

The filenames must be specified explicitly, and must not contain any general characters * or ?. The drive letter and a colon may be included in the filename where necessary. Suppose for example you would like to concatenate the following files in the order given, into a file called NEW.BAS on drive A:.

		Name of file	Drive
1.	main program	MAIN.BAS	A:
2.	input subroutine	INPUT.BAS	B:
3.	checking subroutine	CHECK.BAS	B:
4.	plotting subroutine	PLOT.BAS	A:

This can be done by the following command:

A>PIP NEW.BAS = MAIN.BAS,B:INPUT.BAS,B:CHECK.BAS,PLOT.BAS   RETURN

Before doing this it is wise to run STAT to make sure that there is enough room for the new composite file on the disk. Another way of concatenating files is to specify the first file in the list as the new composite file. This reduces the amount of disk space needed, but remember that the original (small) MAIN.BAS file will not exist after the run:

A>PIP MAIN.BAS = MAIN.BAS,B:INPUT.BAS,B:CHECK.BAS,PLOT.BAS   RETURN

Concatenation may be used to list several files with a single command:

A>PIP LST: = file1,file2,file3,file4   RETURN

Multi-line commands

All of the PIP commands used so far have comprised one line commands with RETURN pressed at the end of the line. If several different commands are to be carried out one after another, this method is slow because PIP has to be loaded from disk for each single line command, and control returns to the operating system when the command has been executed. An alternative method is to load PIP once, carry out as many commands as required while retaining PIP in memory, and getting rid of PIP and returning to the operating system only when you are finished. This is done by typing PIP and pressing RETURN.

A>PIP   RETURN
*

PIP replies with an asterisk as a prompt rather than the usual CP/M prompt A> or B>. You may now give a series of commands to copy files. When each command is completed, PIP gives another prompt *, and the next command may be typed. When all the commands have been executed, you get a prompt *, and must press RETURN to leave PIP and return to CP/M, when the prompt A> is obtained:

A>PIP   RETURN
*A: = B:PROGRAM1.BAS   RETURN
*A: = B:LETTER.TXT   RETURN
*A: = B:STAT.COM   RETURN
*   RETURN
A>

This multi-line feature allows files to be copied on disks which do not have the command file PIP.COM. Suppose that the CP/M system and PIP.COM are on disk 1, that you would like to copy a file onto disk 2, and that the file to be copied is called MAILLIST.TXT and is present on disk 3. Neither disk 2 or disk 3 contains PIP. First boot the system with disk 1 in drive A: and disk 2 in drive B:. If the system was already running and you have changed disks, press ^C to log the disks in. Then type **PIP** and press **RETURN** to load PIP from disk 1 into memory. Then when the PIP prompt * is displayed, remove disk 1 from drive A: and insert disk 3 in this drive. Type the command

B:=MAILLIST.TXT   **RETURN**

and the copy will be made. If copying is complete, return to CP/M by pressing **RETURN**. If you wish to copy another file from disk 3, this can be done in the same way, before you return to CP/M. Remember that you may not write on disk 3, because it is write protected, since it has not been logged-in. Alternatively, you may insert disk 4 into drive A:, and copy files from that onto disk 2.

Special parameters for PIP

There are a large number of different parameters which may optionally be specified to modify the new file produced by PIP. One or more of these parameters may be used in a single PIP command, provided that they are enclosed in square brackets, and follow immediately after the original-filename.

PIP new-filename = original-filename[parameters]   RETURN

[V] Verify. This makes PIP verify that a file has been copied correctly from one disk file to another. It will not work if a device is specified. The new file is read and compared with the original file, to ensure that no copying errors have occurred. This is essential with important programs, but does make copying slow.

[U] Upper case. This converts each lower case (small) letter to an upper case letter.

[L] Lower case. This converts each upper case letter to a lower case (small) letter.

[E] Echo all transfers operations to the console.

[B] Block mode transfer. PIP puts data into a buffer until it reads an X-OFF character (^S) from the device. It then clears the buffer, and puts new data in the buffer, and so on. This is useful when reading data from a paper tape reader or a cassette.

[Qs^Z] Stop copying when the string s (terminated by Control-Z) is found.

[Ss^Z] Start copying when the string s (terminated by Control-Z) is found.

[Dn] Delete characters which extend past column n. May be used with narrow printers.

[N] Add Line numbers starting from one to each line copied. A colon is inserted after the linenumber.

[F] Remove Form-Feed characters from the file. These do not occur in WordStar text files.

[Pn] Include page ejects every n lines. If n is omitted or equals one then page ejects occur every 60 lines.

[**Tn**] Expand Tab characters (Control I) to every nth column during transfer. Tabs do not occur with WordStar Document file mode, but may occur in Non-Document file mode. CP/M usually expands tabs to every 8th column.

[**O**] Object file transfer, for non-ASCII files. PIP ignores the normal CP/M end of file marker.

[**H**] Used for copying Hex files. PIP checks the validity of the each record and removes non-essential characters.

[**I**] Ignore ":00" records in a hex file.

[**Z**] Zero the parity bit on input for each ASCII character.

The following three functions were introduced with CP/M 2.0:

[**Gn**] Allows you to copy the named file from another user number n, where n is in the range 0 - 15.

[**W**] Allows files specified as R/O to be overwritten without being questioned on the console.

[**R**] Allows a file designated as a system file to be read, and copied by PIP.

Chapter 45.

THE FORMAT, SYSGEN AND MOVCPM COMMANDS

Three CP/M transient commands are described in this chapter. FORMAT is not standard CP/M, though most versions of CP/M have it. It is used to format, that is to initialise a brand new floppy disk before you try to write any files on it. Some 8 inch disks are pre-formatted at the factory before you buy them. Others 8 inch disks need formatting, and all 5.25 inch disks must be formatted before use. The CP/M operating system must be present on the outer two tracks of the floppy disk which is used to boot the system initially. SYSGEN is a program which will copy the system tracks containing a working copy of the operating system from one disk to another, so that the new disk may be used to boot the system. MOVCPM is used to change the size of CP/M, which may need doing initially if it has not been done by your dealer, and will only need doing again if you increase the amount of memory in your computer.

FORMAT

The transient program FORMAT.COM is not a standard part of CP/M, but is now provided with many versions, and is used to format, that is write on new floppy disks, before they are used to store data files and programs. All new disks must be formatted before they are used to store files. This may have been done for you at the factory, or you may have to do it for yourself. You must consult your computer documentation to find out whether you need to format disks for your machine, since there is no general rule about this.

Most 8 inch floppy disks are formatted at the factory where they were made, and sold as IBM format single sided single density, or sometimes double density. While these may be used straight away on many computers, others with 8 inch disks require that you format new disks for yourself on your own computer before using them. All 5.25 inch disks must be formatted by the user. The program FORMAT.COM is provided with CP/M on many systems to format brand-new floppy disks.

Unfortunately the program FORMAT.COM is different on each computer, and the messages and questions it asks vary from machine to machine. The instructions given here provide only a general guide, and may be different on your machine.

Load the system, and type **DIR** to list the directory of drive A: to make sure that the program FORMAT.COM is present. Insert the brand-new floppy disk which is to be formatted in to drive B:. Type **FORMAT** and press **RETURN**. A message is displayed on the screen such as **FORMAT Version 2.3** ...... and asking for the drive number. On most computers you should type **B**, but some refer to the drives by number and in this case you type **2**. The exact procedure now varies considerably from one machine to another. Some may ask if you have a hard disk, if the floppy disk is single or double density, or if the disk is single sided or double sided. If you are asked these questions you must answer them as directed, and eventually a message tells you to press carriage return to format the disk. When this is done, the disk light on drive B: comes on, and the stepper motor in the disk drive can be heard clicking regularly for half a minute or so. Some show a series of asterisks on the screen indicating how many tracks on the disk have been formatted. Some versions of FORMAT then return you to CP/M with the system prompt **A>**, while on others a message on the screen asks if you wish to run the FORMAT program again.

SYSGEN

The CP/M transient program SYSGEN.COM is stored as a file on the master

CP/M disk. It allows you to copy the system tracks containing the operating system itself from one disk to another, and is required because PIP copies files but not the system tracks. The procedure for doing this is given below:

1. Boot the system with a disk containing a working copy of the operating system and the file SYSGEN.COM in drive A:. Put the disk you wish to copy an operating system on to in drive B:. This may be a new (empty) disk, which has been formatted if necessary, or it may be a disk which already contains some data files. SYSGEN does not alter the directory or existing files in any way. If there is already a copy of CP/M on the system tracks of disk B: (perhaps an out of date version), then this will be overwritten.

2. Type **SYSGEN** and press **RETURN**, and a message will appear on the screen similar to that in Figure 45.1.

FIGURE 45.1

A>**SYSGEN**
SYSGEN VERSION 3.0
SOURCE DRIVE NAME (OR RETURN TO SKIP)

3. In this case you wish to read the system tracks from the disk in drive A:, so type **A**. You do not need to type a colon or press RETURN. Another message is displayed:

SOURCE ON A, THEN PRESS RETURN

The program waits and allows you time to change the disk in drive A: if necessary, though in the present case you already have the correct disk mounted, so you should press **RETURN**. If you do change the disk, do not cold boot or warm boot(^C), simply press RETURN.

4. There is some disk activity. The system tracks are read from drive A: and stored in memory, (actually in the transient program area), and another message is displayed:

FUNCTION COMPLETE
DESTINATION DRIVE NAME (OR RETURN TO REBOOT)

The program waits for you to specify the drive which contains the disk on to which you wish to copy the system tracks. In this case it is drive B:, so you must type **B** without a colon or RETURN.

5. Yet another message is displayed:

DESTINATION ON B, THEN TYPE RETURN

The program will wait until you have inserted the required disk in drive B:, and you then press **RETURN**. In this case the correct disk is already mounted, so press **RETURN** straight away. There is some disk activity.

6. When the system tracks have been written on to the new disk, a message is displayed:

FUNCTION COMPLETE
DESTINATION DRIVE NAME (OR RETURN TO REBOOT)

These messages are the same as those in paragraph 4. The FUNCTION COMPLETE message indicates that the system tracks have been written to the new disk. You may remove the disk from drive B: and insert another disk, and by repeating paragraph 5 you can write the system which you stored in the TPA on to this disk. The process may be repeated for a whole set of disks if required. When you have processed all the disks, type **RETURN**. This warm boots the system, gives a system prompt **A>** on the screen, and waits for the next command.

7. If you only have one disk drive in your system, you can still use SYSGEN, and you must specify drive A: as the source drive as previously, but you must then specify drive A: as the destination drive, and remove the master disk and insert the new disk before you press **RETURN**.

It is worth re-stating the point that the system tracks on a disk cannot be used to store files. They either contain a working CP/M system, or are left blank. It can do no harm to use SYSGEN to copy the operating system on to all of your disks, that is on to disks containing programs and disks containing data files. The advantage of doing this is that you can boot the system from any disk.

Errors when using SYSGEN

There are three errors which you may make when using SYSGEN. These are:

(a) typing something which is not recognised as a drive letter
(b) typing a drive letter which could exist under CP/M, but which does not exist on your machine.
(c) typing a valid drive letter, but not putting a disk in the drive, or failing to shut the door to the disk drive.

If you type something which is not recognised as a drive letter, for example a number, a character such as + or *, or a control character, then with CP/M 1.4 one of the following error messages will be displayed on the screen:

> INVALID DRIVE NAME (USE A, B, C OR D)
> SOURCE DRIVE NAME (OR RETURN TO SKIP)

or

> INVALID DRIVE NAME (USE A, B, C OR D)
> DESTINATION DRIVE NAME (OR RETURN TO REBOOT)

You simply retype the drive letter correctly, and the system tracks are copied. The messages with CP/M version 2.0 are slightly different, and on some systems the disk drives are identified by numbers rather than letters.

If your system has drives A: and B:, and you type in a letter C for the destination drive letter. CP/M 1.4 recognises four drives A to D, and CP/M 2.0 recognises sixteen drives A to P, so C seems correct, and a message appears:

> DESTINATION ON C, THEN TYPE RETURN

If you notice that you have made a mistake, you can terminate the SYSGEN run by pressing ^C (CONTROL and C). If you press **RETURN** you will either find that the system "hangs", that is the computer is totally lost, and the keyboard has no effect at all, or you may get a disk error. The system should be cold-booted, and SYSGEN run again.

If you type a valid drive letter, but have not inserted a disk, or have not shut the drive door, you will either crash the system, or get a disk error message, depending on your system. If you get a disk error, insert the disk or shut the drive door and press **RETURN**. Otherwise you must cold-boot the system.

MOVCPM

The transient program MOVCPM.COM is used to move the CP/M system from disk into memory, and then alter the size of CP/M itself. This is done to take advantage of all the memory (RAM) in your computer so that the transient program area TPA is as large as possible. You may tailor CP/M to any required size. This may need to be done when first you get your computer and CP/M, but unless you are familiar with CP/M it is best done by your dealer or a friend. You will only need to run MOVCPM again if you expand the memory in your computer, or on rare occasions you may run MOVCPM because you want to construct a special (smaller) CP/M so that you can run a transient program which requires a reserved area at the top of memory.

If the system is running, and the CP/M prompt **A>** is displayed on the screen, then provided the program MOVCPM.COM is present on the disk in drive A:, you can run the program by typing **MOVCPM** and pressing **RETURN**. Assuming that you have 64K of memory in your system, the messages displayed on the screen will be similar to Figure 45.2:

FIGURE 45.2

```
A>MOVCPM
      CONSTRUCTING 64K DOS VERSION 2.0
      64K DOS VERS 2.0

      A>
```

(On some systems there may be a question ENTER Y FOR HARD DISK SYSTEM. If you have a hard disk type **Y**, otherwise press **RETURN**).

This command constructs the maximum size of CP/M which is possible for your computer, (in this case 64K), **and executes it immediately.** Thus any further work done in this computer session will use the new (larger) version of CP/M. Note that the working version of CP/M in memory has been changed, but the version stored on disk is unchanged. The effect of running MOVCPM is shown in Figure 45.3.

FIGURE 45.3   The memory map before and after using MOVCPM

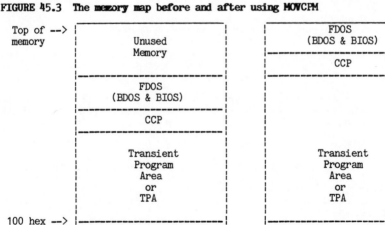

| Top of --> | Unused | | FDOS |
| memory | Memory | | (BDOS & BIOS) |

The MOVCPM command may optionally have two parameters after it. The first of these allows you to specify the size, that is the amount of memory which CP/M may occupy in K bytes. If you have 48K bytes of memory, you could type **MOVCPM 48** to construct a 48K version of CP/M. This would in fact be no different from typing **MOVCPM**, and letting the program work out the maximum size. However, you might physically have 64K bytes of memory in your computer, but have a disk board which uses a memory address just above 58K, so you would type **MOVCPM 58** to construct a 58K version. If you let the program work out the maximum size, you would get a 64K version, and there would be a conflict between your program and the disk board using memory above 58K. This might crash the system, cause unexpected disk activity, or give incorrect results. In the same way, a high memory address may be used on some computers to access a video board, or a floating point arithmetic board, and in such cases memory conflicts should be avoided by specifying the size of CP/M you require. The same procedure is used if you have a special program which requires a reserved memory area at the top of memory.

The second optional parameter to MOVCPM is an asterisk ***** which is used when you want the changed version of CP/M to remain in the transient program area, so that you can copy the new version on to the system tracks of a disk. In this way you can save the latest changed version, and will not have to change CP/M each time you use it. Thus typing **MOVCPM 48 *** would make the computer read CP/M from the system tracks of the logged-in disk into memory, change it to a 48K version, and then display the message:

READY FOR "SYSGEN" or "SAVE nn CP/Mxx.COM"

The computer will wait for you to type SYSGEN, or to type a SAVE command. Both alternatives are discussed below. (Instead of typing **MOVCPM 48 *** you could have typed **MOVCPM * *** which would construct the maximum size CP/M, and then wait for you to type SYSGEN or SAVE).

If you want to copy the new version of CP/M onto the system tracks of one or more disks, so that you will automatically boot up the new version on future occasions, type **SYSGEN** and press **RETURN.** The following messages are shown:

A>**SYSGEN**
SYSGEN VERSION 3.0
SOURCE DRIVE NAME (OR RETURN TO SKIP)

Since the new version of CP/M is already loaded in the TPA, you do not want to read it from disk, so you do not type a drive letter, but simply press **RETURN.** The next message asks for the destination drive:

DESTINATION DRIVE NAME (OR RETURN TO REBOOT)

If you type a drive name, the new CP/M will be written to that disk, and a message FUNCTION COMPLETE will appear when this has been done. You may repeat the process for other disks if required, and finally press **RETURN** to leave SYSGEN and reboot CP/M from the logged-in disk.

After running MOVCPM you obtain the message:

READY FOR "SYSGEN" or "SAVE nn CP/Mxx.COM.

Instead of using the SYSGEN command, you may use a SAVE command if you wish to create a **.COM** file on the disk containing the CP/M system you have just produced in the TPA. You might wish to do this if you want to change CP/M for yourself using DDT, or if you wish to DUMP the system. Not many people will want to do this, and you must be expert at 8080 assembler language. This is beyond the scope of this book. To do the SAVE you should type:

SAVE nn CP/Mxx.COM   and press **RETURN**

The values of "nn" and "xx" must be copied exactly from the "READY FOR SYSGEN" message shown on the screen. "nn" is the number of pages which you must save, and this varies from machine to machine. "xx" is the size of CP/M that you have constructed.

Appendix 1.

BACKING UP THE CP/M MASTER DISK

Before starting to work with CP/M you should duplicate the factory master disk. There are two main stages involved in copying an entire CP/M system disk. First the operating system itself must be copied, and then the CP/M utility programs must also be copied. The steps involved in doing this are set out below.

1. Switch the mains on for both the computer and the vdu. Then insert the factory master disk with the CP/M operating system and the CP/M utility programs into drive A: and boot the system. Different computers have slightly different procedures for turning on the system, so be sure to follow exactly the instructions for your computer. A sign-on message should appear on the screen, which will give the **CP/M version number**, and a few lines below this a prompt **A>** appears.

2. Type the command **DIR** and press **RETURN** to display the directory of files stored on this disk. Check that the programs FORMAT.COM, SYSGEN.COM and PIP.COM are present.

Before being used to store information, a floppy disk must first be formatted. To do this, the disk must be inserted into a computer, and a special program run to write something on the disk. 8 inch floppy disks are normally formatted at the factory where they were made, and so they may be used straight away on many computers. Some computers with 8 inch disks, and all computers with 5.25 inch disks require that you format new disks for yourself on your own computer before using them. The program FORMAT.COM is not a standard part of CP/M, but is provided with many CP/M's to format brand-new floppy disks.

The second program SYSGEN.COM is needed to copy the CP/M operating system itself onto the new disk, since this is not stored as a normal file, and occupies the outermost two tracks on the disk. These two tracks are reserved especially for the CP/M system, and this space on the disk cannot be used for storing programs or data files. For this reason you might as well put the CP/M operating system on each disk you use.

The third program PIP.COM is used to copy files, (which may be either programs or data), from one disk to another.

3. Insert a brand-new floppy disk into drive B:. If your computer uses factory formatted 8 inch disks, ignore the rest of this paragraph, and move to paragraph 4 below. Otherwise, the disk must be formatted so that it can store data properly. On most computers this is achieved by typing **FORMAT** and pressing **RETURN**. A message is displayed on the screen such as **FORMAT Version 2.3** ...... and asking for the drive number. Type **B.** The exact procedure varies from one machine to another. On some computers the program may ask if the disk is single or double density, and then if the disk is single sided or double sided. A message then instructs you to press carriage return to format the disk. When this is done, the disk light on drive B: comes on, and the stepper motor in the disk drive can be heard clicking regularly for half a minute or so. With some versions you then get a CP/M system prompt **A>**, whereas others display a message on the screen which asks if you wish to run the FORMAT program again to format another disk, or to exit from the program back to the operating system.

4. The next step is to copy the CP/M operating system itself onto the outer two tracks of the new disk. This is done by typing **SYSGEN** and pressing **RETURN**. The messages, and what you should type in reply are shown in Figure A1.1.

FIGURE A1.1 Messages when using SYSGEN

Message displayed on screen   Type this in reply

A>   **SYSGEN** and press **RETURN**
SYSGEN VER 3.0
SOURCE DRIVE NAME (OR RETURN TO SKIP) **A** and press **RETURN**
PLACE SOURCE DISK ON A, THEN TYPE RETURN press **RETURN**
FUNCTION COMPLETE
DESTINATION DRIVE NAME (OR RETURN TO REBOOT) **B**
DESTINATION B THEN TYPE RETURN   press **RETURN**
FUNCTION COMPLETE
DESTINATION DRIVE NAME (OR RETURN TO REBOOT) press **RETURN**
A>

5. Finally, there are a number of utility programs on the CP/M system disk, and these should be copied on to the new disk. The screen should be displaying the prompt **A>**, and to copy all of the files on the disk from drive A: to drive B: you must type:

   PIP B:=A:*.*[V] and press **RETURN**

The name of each file will appear on the screen as it is copied, and the prompt **A>** will appear when the copying operation is complete.

  Remember to label the disk, stating the contents (eg. CP/M + all utilities), whether the disk is a master copy, a backup copy or a working copy (eg. working copy), and the date.

  Further information is given in chapter 45 - The FORMAT, SYSGEN and MOVCPM Commands, and chapter 44 - The PIP Command.

Appendix 2.

NOTES ON INSTALLING WORDSTAR

The factory master disk containing WordStar contains the program WSU.COM. This stands for WordStar Uninstalled. The file WSU.COM will not actually work until it has been installed, that is set up or altered to run with your particular terminal and printer. A program called INSTALL is provided which will automatically do this for you in most cases. Usually installation is performed by selecting choices from menus. When WordStar is installed, it is stored on disk as another file called WS.COM, and it is this installed version which you must copy onto your working disk, together with the files WSMSGS.OVR and WSOVLY1.OVR. The installation procedure is best done by your dealer, but it can be performed by beginners without too much difficulty provided that their particular terminal and printer are listed in the menus. If this is not so the WordStar program must be patched to make it work. This task is beyond the capability of a beginner, and you are advised to get your dealer, or someone who understands WordStar to carry out the installation procedure.

Preliminaries

1. First load CP/M and if necessary on your system run the program FORMAT to format a new disk.

2. Copy the CP/M operating system onto the first two tracks of the new disk using the CP/M transient program called SYSGEN. (See Appendix 1).

3. Copy the CP/M programs PIP.COM and STAT.COM from the master CP/M disk onto the new disk using the CP/M program PIP.

4. Copy the programs WSU.COM, WSMSGS.OVR, WSOVLY1.OVR and INSTALL.COM from your master WordStar disk onto the new disk using PIP.

Your master CP/M disk and master WordStar disk are now safe, and we will work with the copy just made. Insert this in drive A:, and press ^C (Control C).

Installation - sorting out the files used

Type **INSTALL** and press **RETURN** to run INSTALL. The program takes several seconds to load, then a copyright message is displayed, and you are asked:

Do you want a normal first time installation of WordStar?
(Y = yes; N = display other options):

Type **Y**, and the following message is displayed:

This will INSTALL the WSU.COM on the current drive, save the result on file WS.COM on the current drive, and then run the INSTALLed WordStar.   **OK (Y/N):**

Type **Y**, and a choice of terminals appears on a menu.

Choice of terminal

At the time of writing, some nineteen different terminals are listed in three menus, and the number increases with each new release of WordStar. If your terminal is listed in the menu, type the appropriate letter, otherwise type the code to look at the next menu which shows more terminals. Either type the letter for your terminal, or if it is not shown on the menu type Z for none of the above. In this case you need help from someone who understands the technical manual for your terminal, and can use the patcher routine at the end of INSTALL to put the correct cursor control codes for your terminal into the WordStar program.

After you have typed the code letter for a terminal, INSTALL displays a message confirming your selection of the terminal, and asking **OK (Y/N):**. Provided that you are happy with this, type **Y**, when you will move on to installing the printer. If you have made a mistake, type **N**, and you will repeat the terminal selection.

Choice of printer

At the time of writing, nine different classes of printers are listed in the menu. If your printer is listed, type the appropriate letter. INSTALL displays a confirmatory message and explains anything special about your selection, and then asks **OK (Y/N):**. Provided that you are happy with this, type **Y**, when you will move on to the next menu on communications protocol. If you have made a mistake, type **N**, and you will repeat the printer selection. If your printer is not listed, it can almost certainly be made to work with selection **A** Any Teletype-like printer. If you know that your printer can backspace, try option **C**.

Communications protocol

Printers may be connected to the computer either through a parallel port, or through a serial port (RS 232 connection). We will consider serial printers here. Printers are all relatively slow. Most daisy wheel printers are capable of 40 characters per second, though the range is 25 - 80 cps). Dot matrix printers may go up to 200 cps. If the computer transmits information to the printer slower than the printer's maximum, then there is no need for a communications protocol. We really want to make the printer work at its maximum speed. If the computer transmits information faster than the printer can print, then the printer buffer will overflow and some information will be lost. There are two ways of preventing this loss of data. First there may be a hard wire connection between the printer and the computer which carries a printer busy signal to stop the computer sending any more information when the printer's buffer is full. Transmission will start when there is room in the buffer. The second way is to have a communications protocol whereby the printer talks to the computer, and the computer talks to the printer through the usual three wires for transmitting data, receiving data and ground. There are two such protocols.

Protocols give the user better response than a printer busy signal when concurrently editing and printing.

1. **ETX/ACK.** The computer transmits a fixed number of characters to the printer followed by an **ETX** character. When the printer has printed all the characters up to the **ETX** it transmits an **ACK** character back to the computer to say that it is ready for more data. The computer then sends another block of data followed by **ETX** ... and so on. WordStar requires to know how big the blocks should be. If the printer buffer is less than 256 characters then a change must be made with the Patcher at the end of the installation.

2. **XON/XOFF.** The computer sends data to the printer, and when the printer buffer is full it sends an **XOFF** character to stop the computer. The printer continues printing and when there is room for more data in the buffer, the printer transmits an **XON** character to the computer to restart transmission.

If the computer transmits data at 300 baud or slower (30 cps. or less), then most printers will run satisfactorily without implementing a protocol or hard wiring printer busy. Many printers will print faster than 30 cps. and to take advantage of this a faster baud rate (typically 1200 baud for a daisy wheel printer and 9600 baud for a matrix printer) is needed together with either a protocol or a printer busy signal to stop the computer outrunning the printer.

The communications protocol menu asks you to choose **EXT/ACK, XON/XOFF** or no protocol, and then confirms your selection and prints **OK (Y/N)** as before. When you reply **Y** the driver menu is displayed.

Choice of driver

WordStar offers a choice of how the printer is to be driven. For installations not using a protocol, then L for the CP/M List device should be used, because this is the simplest. If a protocol is required then the List device is not suitable as CP/M does not allow characters to be read from the List device. Unless the user has a good knowledge of BIOS I/O drivers, then direct port access (P) and User Installed driver subroutines (S) should not be used.

If your machine has the IOBYTE in CP/M fully implemented, then by using STAT it is possible to redefine which peripheral you wish to use as Console. WordStar takes advantage of this and allows the printer to be accessed as the "Primary Console (TTY:)" device, or the "Secondary Console (CRT:)" device. Either may work if your CP/M has the IOBYTE implemented - try them.

If the IOBYTE is not implemented, and you do not know how to define the printer I/O ports, and you do not know how to write driver subroutines, then you are not able to implement a protocol. Either get your dealer to do it for you, use a printer busy line, or drive the printer more slowly.

Patcher

For use only by the cognoscenti who want to customise their working version of WordStar. For first-time installation bypass the Patcher by typing **Y** in response to the questions "Are the modifications to WordStar now complete".

Appendix 3.

PRODUCING A WORKING DISK CONTAINING CP/M & WORDSTAR

On computers with two floppy disks, the best arrangement for word-processing is to have a working disk with CP/M and WordStar on one drive, and the WordStar data files containing text on the other. This working disk may be produced by following the steps in Appendix 1 to copy CP/M onto the disk, then following the steps given below to copy WordStar onto the disk:

a) Place the new working copy of the CP/M disk (produced by following the instructions in Appendix 1) in drive A:, and place the master copy of WordStar in drive B:.

b) CP/M reads and remembers information from the directories of the disks present in the disk drives when the system is booted up and first used. If the disks actually present in the disk drives are changed then this information will no longer refer to the disks currently in the drives, and problems will follow if you try to write to the disks. To overcome this problem, ^C must be pressed after changing the disks. This operation is called "warm-booting" the system, (as opposed to "cold-booting" which is the operation to activate the computer when first it is switched on). It is important to make sure when either "warm-booting" or "cold-booting" the system that the disk in drive A: has the CP/M system written in the first two (system) tracks on the disk, or failure will occur.

c) Type **DIR B:** to list the directory of the master WordStar disk in drive B:. This is to check that the files which you would like to copy onto the new disk are actually present. Provided that WordStar has been installed for use with the particular vdu and printer attached to your computer, the actual WordStar program should be present as a file called WS.COM. Two other files are also needed, and these are called WSMSGS.OVR and WSOVLY1.OVR.

d) The next step is to copy the required files from the master disk in drive B onto the new working copy in drive A:. This is done using the CP/M file copying program called PIP.COM, as shown below:

The screen should show the prompt **A>**
Type **PIP**   and press **RETURN**
The system loads PIP which replies with the prompt *****
Type **A:=B:WS.COM[V]**   and press **RETURN**
                                 This copies the file called WS.COM on drive B:
                                 into a new file with the same name on drive A:
                                 The [V] makes the computer verify, that is
                                 check the new file against the original file
                                 to ensure that it has been copied correctly.
The prompt ***** indicates that copying and verification are finished
Type **A:=B:WSMSGS.OVR[V]**   and press **RETURN**
                                 This copies and verifies the file WSMSGS.OVR
The prompt ***** indicates that copying and verification are finished
Type **A:=B:WSOVLY1.OVR[V]**   and press **RETURN**
                                 This copies and verifies the file WSOVLY1.OVR
The prompt ***** indicates that copying and verification are finished
Then press the **RETURN** key to finish with the program PIP, and the
      computer will reply with the usual system prompt **A>**.

Finally remember to label the new disk. Further details of the use of PIP can be found in chapter 44 - The PIP Command, near the end of the book.

Appendix 4.

THE ^J HELP MENU

At any time when a file is being edited, the Help menu can be displayed on the screen by typing ^J.

```
^J      B:EXAMPLE  PAGE 1 LINE 1  COL 1              INSERT ON
                  < < <    H E L P   M E N U      > > >
                                    |              |   --Other  Menus--
  H  Display & set the help level   | S  Status line  | (from Main only)
  B  Paragraph reform (CONTROL-B)   | R  Ruler line   | ^J Help   ^K Block
  F  Flags in right-most column     | M  Margins & Tabs | ^Q Quick  ^P Print
  D  Dot commands, print controls   | P  Place markers | ^O Onscreen
                                    | V  Moving text   | Space bar returns
                                    |              | you to Main Menu.
L----!----!----!----!----!----!----!----!----!----!----!--------R
```

^JH This displays the current help level on the screen, and allows you to change it if required. The help level has a value 3, 2, 1 or 0. With a high number, more information will be displayed on the screen in the form of menus, but in consequence less text from the document you are preparing will show on the screen, and also WordStar will work more slowly. The help levels are described in detail in chapter 22 - Changing the Help Level.

The remaining commands all generate explanations on the screen, and these are briefly examined in turn. Many of the explanations cover several screensful, and pressing the space bar, or any key displays the next screenful. To stop going through all the instructions, and to return to the point in the file which you were editing, press ^U followed by **ESCAPE.**

^JB This displays three screensful on reforming paragraphs, and the automatic hyphenation which may occur when reforming text.

^JF This gives one screen of information explaining the flag characters which appear at the right of the screen when you are editing a file.

^JD Six screensful of information are given on print control characters and dot commands. These include an explanatory page, three pages of information on the common dot commands, one on special characters which may be used in headers and footers, and a final page on special dot commands used by MailMerge. Two chapters, 26 - Dot Commands, and 39 - Special Dot Commands for MailMerge cover these in detail.

^JS This gives two screensful which explain the information displayed in the status line

^JR A single screenful explains what the markings on the ruler line mean, and how to change the margins and tabs in the ruler. This subject is covered further with the command ^JM, and in detail in chapter 28 - On-Screen Formatting - Margins, Tabs and Ruler.

^JM This gives five screensful on setting margins, line spacing and justification, tabs, and using columnar tabs. These are explained in detail in chapter 28 - On-Screen Formatting - Margins, Tabs and Ruler, and chapter 29 - More On-Screen Formatting - Line Functions and Toggles.

^JP This gives two screensful explaining about using place markers. This is described in chapter 15 - Advanced Cursor Movements and Scrolling Text.

^JV This gives a single screenful explaining how to move a block of text, and is covered in chapter 30 - Manipulating Blocks of text.

^JI This command is not on the menu, but it gives two screensful which summarize some of the common editing commands. These are covered in chapter 10 - Basic Editing, chapter 15 - Advanced Cursor Movements and Scrolling text, and chapter 16 - Editing - The Find andReplace Commands.

Appendix 5.

THE ^K BLOCK MENU

The ^K menu can be displayed by typing ^K when a file is being edited.

```
^K      B:EXAMPLE  PAGE 1 LINE 1  COL 1                    INSERT ON
                   < < <    B L O C K  M E N U    > > >
 -Saving Files-  | -Block Operations-  | -File Operations- | -Other Menus-
S Save & resume  | B  Begin  K  End    | R Read    P Print | (from Main only)
D Save--done     | H  Hide / Display   | O Copy    E Rename| ^J Help ^K Block
X Save & exit    | C  Copy   Y  Delete | J Delete          | ^Q Quick ^P Print
Q Abandon file   | V  Move   W  Write  | -Disk Operations- | ^O Onscreen
 -Place Markers- | N  Column off (ON)  |L Change logged disk| Space bar returns
0-9 Set/hide 0-9 |                     |F Directory on (OFF)| you to Main Menu.
L----!----!----!----!----!----!----!----!----!----!----!--------R
```

The **first column** lists the four commands for saving files. These are:

^KS This command saves the file currently being edited on to the disk, and continues editing the same file.

^KD This saves the file being edited, and returns to the "No-File" Menu.

^KX This saves the file on disk, leaves WordStar, and returns to the CP/M operating system.

^KQ This abandons the file which was being edited, and returns to the "No-File menu.

The use of these four commands is fully described in chapter 12 - Saving Files.

Place markers may be set in a file by typing ^K0, ^K1, ^K2, ... or ^K9. It is then possible to jump to any specified place marker by typing the equivalent command ^Q0, ^Q1, ... or ^Q9. The use of place markers is explained near the end of chapter 15 - Advanced Cursor Movements and Scrolling Text.

The **second column** gives the commands for handling blocks of text. These are fully described in chapter 30 - Manipulating Blocks of Text, but are also listed below:

^KB is used to mark the beginning of a block at the current cursor position, or to delete the beginning marker if the cursor is at the marker.
^KK is used to mark the end of a block.
^KH is a toggle to hide the marked block, or if typed a second time to re-display it.
^KC is the command to copy (that is duplicate) a marked block.
^KV is the command to move a marked block from one place to another.
^KY caused the marked block to be deleted.
^KW is used to write a marked block to a disk file.
^KN is a toggle to switch <u>column</u> blocks ON or OFF.

The **third column** gives commands concerning file and disk operations.

^KR This command is used to read another file from the disk, and insert it in the file which is being edited, at the cursor position. This is useful for inserting files containing standard paragraphs into a document, or for inserting a block which had been previously been written to a disk file with a ^KW command.

^KO This command is for copying a disk file, either to another disk, or to a file on the same disk but with a different name.

^KJ Is a command for deleting a disk file.

^KE Is used to rename a disk file.

These WordStar commands perform the same functions as CP/M does with PIP for copying files, ERA for erasing files, and REN for renaming files. There are two big differences with the WordStar commands. First they are run from within WordStar, so that if you run short of disk space in the middle of a job, it is possible to copy a file on to another disk and then erase the original file, or to erase a backup file, in order to make some more space on the disk, and then save your file from memory on to disk. If you had to return to CP/M to do this, then the file being edited in memory would be lost. Second the WordStar commands are much easier to use. The CP/M commands work provided that you get the syntax of the commands exactly correct without any help. In contrast, WordStar prompts you with a message which ask you to type the name of the file you wish to erase, rename, or copy, and for the new filename where appropriate.

^KL This command changes the logged-in disk drive. This is normally set with an L command from the "No-File" menu, but if difficulties are encountered through running out of disk space, changing the drive which is logged-in may allow you to save the file currently in memory.

^KF If the file directory is displayed, this command switches the display OFF. If the display is OFF, this command turns it ON. Commands like this which reverse something are called toggles. Being able to examine the directory while you are actually editing may be useful if you need to know the name of a file so that it can be included into the present file, or erased to make some space on the disk. (The file directory can also be switched OFF or ON by typing the command F when at the "No-File" menu). Since the directory occupies quite a lot of the screen, which would be better used to display text, it is good to be able to switch the display of the directory ON and OFF as required.

Using some of these advanced commands
(The logged-in drive is B: and contains a file called INDEX)

Message on the screen	What you type	
	^KF	(switch file directory ON so you can see the file names)
	^KO	(command to copy a file)
NAME OF FILE TO COPY FROM?	**INDEX**	
NAME OF FILE TO COPY TO ?	**A:INDEX**	
		(the file called INDEX on the logged-in drive B: is copied on to the disk in drive A:)
	^KJ	(command to delete a file)
NAME OF FILE TO DELETE?	**INDEX**	(delete file INDEX from the logged-in drive B:)
	^KF	(switch display of file directory OFF again)

Appendix 6.

THE ^O ON-SCREEN FORMATTING MENU

The on-screen formatting commands are all given in the ^O menu, which may be displayed by typing ^O when a file is being edited.

```
^O     B:LETTER.TXT   PAGE 1 LINE 1 COL 01              INSERT ON
                < < < O N S C R E E N   M E N U   > > >
-Margins & Tabs-  | -Line Functions-  | -More Toggles-  | -Other Menus-
L Set left margin |C Centre text      |J Justify   off (ON)|  (from Main only)
R Set right margin|S Set line spacing |V Vari-tabs off (ON)|^J Help  ^K Block
X Release margins |                   |H Hyph-help off (ON)|^Q Quick ^P Print
I Set N Clear tab|    ----Toggles----  |E Soft hyph on (OFF)|^O Onscreen
G Paragraph tab   |W Wrd wrap off (ON)|D Prnt disp off (ON)|Space Bar returns
F Ruler from line |T Rlr line off (ON)|P Pge break off (ON)|you to Main Menu.
L----!----!----!----!----!----!----!----!----!----!----!--------R
```

The first column in this menu lists the functions to do with margins and tabs. These are described briefly here, and are fully explained in chapter 28 - On-Screen Formatting - Margins, Tabs and Ruler.

^OL & ^OR are used to set the left and right margins of the page

^OX   is used when you wish to type outside these margins

^OI & ^ON are used to set tabs in the ruler line, or to remove them

^OG   this indents the left margin for the next paragraph

^OF   substitutes a special ruler stored in the file for the default one

The second and third columns in this menu list some line functions and some toggles. These commands are described briefly here, and more fully in chapter 29 - More On-Screen Formatting - Line Functions and Toggles.

^OC centres the text on the cursor line

^OS sets the line spacing to single, double or triple spacing

^OW turns word wrap OFF or ON again

^OT turns the display of the ruler line on the screen OFF or ON again

^OJ turns justification of the right edge OFF to give a ragged margin, or ON again to give a straight edge

^OV switch the variable tabs OFF ie. ignore tabs in the ruler, or ON again

^OH switch the automatic hyphenation of long words OFF, or ON again

^OE switch soft hyphens ON (hyphens typed will be soft) or OFF (hard hyphens)

^OD this alternately hides or displays control characters on the screen

^OP turn the display of page breaks on the screen OFF, or ON again

Appendix 7.

THE ^P PRINT MENU

The Print menu can be displayed on the screen any time that a document is being edited by typing ^P. The commands are summarized below, and are described in chapter 23 - Special Print Effects.

```
^P      B:LETTER.TXT  PAGE 1 LINE 1 COL 01              INSERT ON
                   < < <   P R I N T   M E N U   > > >
      ——— Special Effects ———  |  -Printing Changes-  |  -Other  Menus-
   (begin and end) | (one time each)  | A Alternate pitch  | (from Main only)
   B Bold D Double | H Overprint char | N Standard pitch   |^J Help  ^K Block
   S Underscore    | O Non-break space| C printing pause   |^Q Quick ^P Print
   X Strikeout     | F Phantom space  | Y Other ribbon color|^O Onscreen
   V Subscript     | G Phantom rubout | —User  Patches—    |Space Bar returns
   T Superscript   | RET Overprint line| Q(1) W(2) E(3) R(4) |you to Main Menu.
   L----!----!----!----!----!----!----!----!----!----!----!--------R
```

The first column contains commands which produce common print enhancements, and the command must be entered both before and after the text to be enhanced.

^PB produces bold type **like this,** which is used for main headings.

^PD gives double strike **like this,** which is used for headings.

^PS causes text to be underlined <u>like this.</u>

^PX produces ~~strikeout,~~ that is crossed-out text.

^PV is used for subscripts, for example water H_2O

^PT is used to produce superscripts, for example x^2.

The second column has commands which also produce special print effects, but these are only entered once.

^PH causes the last character to be overprinted.

^P RETURN causes the last line to be overprinted.

^PO this gives a non-break space, that is a space which will not be used to break two words, even if they fall at the end of a line.

^PF and **^PG** are called phantom space, and phantom rubout respectively, and can be used to print special characters on some daisy wheel printers.

The third column has commands which cause printing changes:

^PA and **^PN** may be used on some printers to change to the alternate pitch, (default 12 characters per inch) and back again to the normal pitch (10 characters per inch).

^PC is used to make the printer pause, generally to allow the daisy wheel to be changed, or a new envelope to be inserted.

^PY is used on some printers to change colour, for example from black to red, if a two colour ribbon is fitted.

Appendix 8.

THE ^Q QUICK MENU

The Quick menu may be displayed any time editing is in progress by typing
^Q. It contains powerful commands for moving the cursor, which are quicker
than those given in the Main menu. In addition, it contains commands for
deleting text and finding or substituting text.

The ^Q Quick Menu

```
^Q      B:EXAMPLE  PAGE 1 LINE 1 COL 1              INSERT ON
                  < < <    Q U I C K   M E N U    > > >
        ——Cursor Movement——  | -Delete- |  ——Miscellaneous——  | -Other  Menus-
S left side   D right side  |Y line  rt|F Find text in file  | (from Main only)
E top scrn    X bottom scrn |DEL lin lf|A Find & Replace      |^J Help  ^K Block
R top file    C end file    |L Find Misspelling              |^Q Quick ^P Print
B top block   K end block   |Q Repeat command or             |^O Onscreen
0-9 marker    Z up    W down|  key   until   space           |Space bar returns
P previous    V last Find or Block|  bar  or other key       |you to Main Menu.
L————!————!————!————!————!————!————!————!————!————!————R
```

The cursor moving commands are more fully explained in chapter 8 - Simple
Cursor Movements, and chapter 15 Advanced Cursor Movements and Scrolling Text.
They are briefly described below:

^QD   This command moves the cursor to a position one character past the last
character displayed on that line. (This is not usually the extreme right
of the screen, unless you have set the right margin to column 80).

^QS   This command moves the cursor to the extreme left of the present line.

^QE   This moves the cursor to the top line of text shown on the screen. (This
is not the same as moving to the top of the screen, since the status line
and possibly the Main Menu and the ruler line may be displayed. The
cursor can only move within the text area of the screen, and not into the
ruler, menus or status line.

^QX   This command moves the cursor to the next to bottom line of the screen.
Under WordStar the cursor never stays on the bottom line.

These four commands are easy to remember because they use a diamond of keys on
the keyboard, (Figure A8.1), and the position in the diamond is related to the
movements left, right, top and bottom.

FIGURE A8.1 The diamond of keys for Quick cursor movements

(cursor to top of text area of screen)
^QE

(cursor to left side) **^QS**   **^QD** (cursor to right side)

^QX
(cursor to bottom of screen)

^QR   This command moves the cursor to the top (beginning) of the file.

^QC   This moves the cursor to the bottom (end) of the file.

^QB This moves the cursor to the marker at the beginning of a block.

^QK This moves the cursor to the marker at the end of a block.

^Q0, ^Q1, ... Q9 move the cursor to the place markers ^K0, ^K1, ... ^K9 which have been put in the file.

^QZ This command scrolls text up off the top of the screen continuously, so that you can read nearer the end of the file. The speed of scrolling can be changed from its starting value of 3, by typing a number from 1, the fastest to 9, the slowest.

^QW This scrolls text downwards off the bottom of the screen continuously, so that you see nearer the beginning of the document. The speed of scrolling can be changed in the same way as for ^QZ.

^QP This command moves the cursor to the position it **Previously** occupied before the last command. This is particularly helpful following a command which moves the cursor a long way, for example after using ^KS to save and re-edit a file, or after using ^B to reform a long paragraph.

^QV When used after a Find or Replace command, this moves the cursor to the position it occupied before the last command. If you mis-type the string you are searching for with Find or Replace, then you will get a "NOT FOUND" message. In these circumstances the **^QV** command is very useful since it returns you to the place where you started the search, so that you can type the string correctly and do the Find or Replace again.

^QY This deletes the character under the cursor and the characters to the right, up to the end of the line.

^Q DEL This deletes the line to the left of the cursor.

The next two commands are considered in detail in chapter 16 - Editing - the Find and Replace Commands.

^QF This command will Find a specified string.

^QA This command Finds a specified string and Replaces it by another string.

^QL This is a SpellStar command.

^QQ This command makes WordStar repeat the next command entered, and the speed may be changed in the same manner as for the ^QW and ^QZ scrolling.

Appendix 9.

SUMMARY OF EDITING COMMANDS

^A	move cursor left one word	^OC	Centre the text on cursor line
^B	reform paragraph	^OD	turn Display of control characters
^C	scroll up one screenful		on screen OFF/ON
^D	move cursor one character right	^OE	turn "soft" hyphen entry OFF/ON
^E	move cursor up one line	^OF	set margins & tabs from line
^F	move cursor right one word	^OG	indent paraGraph (paragraph tab)
^G	delete character under cursor	^OH	turn Hyphen help OFF/ON
^H	delete character to left of cursor	^OI	set a tab
^I	tab	^OJ	turn Justification OFF/ON
^J	display HELP menu	^OL	set Left margin
^K	display BLOCK menu	^ON	remove a tab stop
^L	repeat last find or replace	^OP	turn display of Page breaks OFF/ON
^M	same as RETURN	^OR	set Right margin
^N	insert "hard" carriage return	^OS	set line spacing
^O	display ON-SCREEN menu	^OT	turn ruler display OFF/ON
^P	display PRINT menu	^OV	turn variable tabs OFF/ON
^Q	display QUICK menu	^OW	turn word Wrap OFF/ON
^R	scroll down one screenful	^OX	margin release
^S	move cursor one character left		
^T	delete word to right of cursor		
^U	interrupt	^P RETURN	overprint the last line
^V	turn insert ON/OFF	^PA	Alternate pitch (on some printers)
^W	scroll down one line	^PB	produces **Bold type**
^X	move cursor down one line	^PC	makes the printer pause
^Y	delete whole line	^PD	produces Double strike
^Z	scroll up one line	^PF	phantom space
		^PG	phantom rubout
^JB	explain reforming of paragraphs	^PH	overprint the last character
^JD	list print directives	^PM	overprint the last line
^JF	explain "Flags" at right of screen	^PN	Normal pitch (on some printers)
^JH	change the Help level	^PO	enter a non-break space
^JI	command index	^PS	produces underScored text
^JM	explain Margins and tabs	^PT	produces superscripts
^JP	explain use of Place markers	^PV	produces subscripts
^JR	explain the Ruler line	^PX	produces strikeout
^JS	explain the Status line on screen	^PY	some printers change ribbon colour
^JV	explain moVing text		
		^Q0 - ^Q9	move cursor to marker 0-9
^K0 - ^K9	set/hide place markers 0-9	^QA	find a string & replace by another
^KB	mark/hide beginning of Block	^QB	move cursor to beginning of Block
^KC	Copy a block of text	^QC	move cursor to the end of the file
^KD	editing Done - save file	^QD	move cursor to right end of line
^KE	rEname a file	^QE	move cursor to the top of screen
^KF	turn File directory ON/OFF	^QF	Find a specified string
^KH	Hide/display the marked block	^QK	move cursor to end of blocK
^KJ	delete a file	^QP	move cursor to Previous position
^KK	mark/hide end of a blocK		before the last command
^KL	change the Logged-in disk drive	^QQ	repeat the next command
^KN	ordinary block/column block toggle	^QR	move cursor to beginning of file
^KO	cOpy a file	^QS	move cursor to left Side of screen
^KP	Print a file	^QV	move cursor to its position before
^KQ	Quit edited version of file		the last command
^KR	Read a file & insert in document	^QW	scroll down continuously
^KS	Save and re-edit the present file	^QX	move cursor to bottom of screen
^KV	moVe a block of text	^QY	delete from cursor to end of line
^KW	Write a marked block to a file	^QZ	scroll up continuously
^KX	save file and eXit to CP/M		
^KY	delete the marked block		

Appendix 10.

SUMMARY OF THE DOT COMMANDS

(The commands marked *** work only on printers which support micro-spacing).
(The parameter **n** must be a whole number).

Command	Function	Units	Default value
Vertical spacing and layout			
.LH n ***	Line Height	1/48 inch	8 (48/8 = 6 lines per inch)
.PL n	Paper Length	lines	66 lines = 11 inches
.MT n	Margin at Top	lines	3 lines = 3/6 = 0.5 inch
.MB n	Margin at Bottom	lines	8 lines = 8/6 = 1.33 inches
Page breaks			
.PA	start a new PAge		
.CP n	Conditional Page	lines	
.PO n	Page Offset	columns	8 columns = 8/10 = 0.8 inch
Page numbers			
.PN n	Page Number		1
.OP	Omit Pagenumbers		
.PC n	Page number Column	columns	col. 33 (centre of 65 col. page)
Headings and footings			
.HE message	Heading		blank
.HM n	Heading Margin	lines	2 lines = 2/6 = 0.33 inch
.FO message	Footing		contains page number
.FM n	Footing Margin	lines	2 lines = 2/6 = 0.33 inch
Miscellaneous			
.. message	Comment		
.IG message	Comment		
.UJ n ***	microjustification	0 = OFF) 1 = ON)	ON (adds micro-spaces to justify the right margin)
.SR n ***	Subscript and superscript roll	1/48 inch	3 = 3/48 inch
.BP n	Bidirectional Print	0 = OFF) 1 = ON)	ON (prints left to right, then right to left)

Line heights *** only on printers which support micro-spacing

Command	lines/inch	Command	lines/inch	Command	lines/inch
.LH 1	48.0	.LH 8	6.0 (single)	.LH 16	3.0 (double)
.LH 4	12.0	.LH 9	5.3	.LH 18	2.6
.LH 6	8.0	.LH 10	4.8	.LH 20	2.4
.LH 7	6.8	.LH 12	4.0	.LH 24	2.0 (triple)

Character spacings (pitch) *** only on printers which support micro-spacing

Dot command	Pitch characters/inch	Dot command	Pitch characters/inch
.CW 6	20	.CW 13	9.2
.CW 7	17.1	.CW 14	8.6
.CW 8	15	.CW 15	8
.CW 9	13.3	.CW 16	7.5
.CW 10	12 (alternative-pitch)	.CW 17	7
.CW 11	10.9	.CW 20	6
.CW 12	10 (normal pitch)	.CW 24	5

SPECIAL DOT COMMANDS FOR MAILMERGE

Command	Function	Meaning
.AV var1, var2	Ask Variable	stop and ask the operator to type the value of the variable(s) var1, var2 ...
.SV variable	Specify Variable	sets the value of a variable in the file
.FI filename	FIle	specifies name of a file which is to be inserted & printed at this point
.DF filename	Data File	gives name of file to be used to read data from
.RV var1, var2	Read Variable(s)	specifies the names and order of the variables var1, var2 ... which are to be read from the previously named data file
.RP n	Repeat	repeats data file n times, or until all the records have been read
.DM message	Display Message	displays the message given on this line on the screen
.CS	Clear Screen	clear the screen of messages
.PF ON	Print time- -line Forming	must be ON/OFF/DIS.
.RM n	Right Margin	reset Right Margin to col. n at print time
.LM n	Left Margin	reset Left Margin to col. n at print time
.LS n	Line Spacing	reset Line Spacing to n at print time
.OJ	Output- -Justification	must be ON/OFF/DIS. Changes the justification of text at print time.
.IJ	Input- -Justification	must be ON/OFF/DIS. Used only for unusual text, & controls whether input text is interpreted as justified or ragged

Appendix 11.

DIFFERENCES BETWEEN WORDSTAR VERSIONS 1, 2 & 3

The main changes introduced with WordStar version 2.2 since version 1.0 are:

1. Hyphen help. When reforming paragraphs WordStar may stop and offer you
    the option of hyphenating a long word which will not fit on the current
    line. WordStar will suggest where to put the hyphen, but you may put it
    somewhere else if you wish. This feature avoids getting too much empty
    space on a line.

2. Soft hyphens were introduced. These will only print if they occur at the
    end of a line, but provide a convenient place where long words may be
    split into two.

3. Print control toggle ^OD. This toggle allows you to hide any characters
    which will not print, (such as ^B for bold, ^S for underscored, etc.), so
    that the layout on the screen is exactly as the document will be printed.

4. Paragraph indent. A new command ^OG temporarily moves the left margin to
    the next tab stop. This is useful for indenting a whole paragraph, or in
    producing hanging paragraphs.

5. Decimal tab stops have been introduced, to facilitate the lining up of
    decimal points in columns of figures.

6. A new program called MergePrint was introduced, to work in conjunction
    with WordStar. It allows multiple copies to be printed. It also allows a
    number of separate files to be "boilerplated", that is chained together at
    print time. This removes the necessity to actually merge them into a
    single file before printing. In addition it allows data insertion points
    to be defined within the text of a document. This is particularly useful
    for inserting information such as names and addresses into standard
    letters. This information may either be typed, or read from a data file.

The main changes introduced with WordStar version 3.0 since version 2.2 are:

1. The menus have been revised to make them easier to read. The commands
    have been regrouped to make it easier to find the information.

2. Horizontal scrolling has been introduced. This makes it possible to view
    a document which is wider than the screen, laid out as it will be printed,
    rather than having a long line split on two or more lines of the screen.
    This means that you can see on the screen whether text is properly aligned
    and if the margin is justified. If your lines of text are longer than the
    screen width, WordStar displays a "screen-window" showing the part of the
    document with the cursor. The window changes automatically as you enter
    text or move the cursor. If you keep to lines short enough to display on
    the screen then you will not see any difference from earlier versions.

3. Block moves have been introduced for vertical columns of data. To change
    from the usual horizontal block mode, which allows you to move sentences
    or paragraphs, type ^KN. This puts you in vertical block mode, and
    vertical columns may be marked, copied, moved or deleted. This is
    valuable for rearranging tables of data. Note however that a vertical
    block cannot be written to file, or read from a file, whereas normal
    blocks can. Typing ^KN again toggles you back to normal block mode.

4. A spelling correction program called Spellstar has been introduced, which can be called directly from the "No-File" menu in WordStar.

5. When printing a document, you may now answer some of the questions and then press **ESCAPE** to accept the default values for the remaining questions. Previously the choice was to press **ESCAPE** at the beginning to accept the default values for all of the questions, or to answer them all.

SUMMARY OF EDITING COMMANDS

^A move cursor left one word
^B reform paragraph
^C scroll up one screenful
^D move cursor one character right
^E move cursor up one line
^F move cursor right one word
^G delete character under cursor
^H delete character to left of cursor
^I tab
^J display HELP menu
^K display BLOCK menu
^L repeat last find or replace
^M same as RETURN
^N insert "hard" carriage return
^O display ON-SCREEN menu
^P display PRINT menu
^Q display QUICK menu
^R scroll down one screenful
^S move cursor one character left
^T delete word to right of cursor
^U interrupt
^V turn insert ON/OFF
^W scroll down one line
^X move cursor down one line
^Y delete whole line
^Z scroll up one line

^JB explain reforming of paragraphs
^JD list print directives
^JF explain "Flags" at right of screen
^JH change the Help level
^JI command index
^JM explain Margins and tabs
^JP explain use of Place markers
^JR explain the Ruler line
^JS explain the Status line on screen
^JV explain moVing text

^K0 - ^K9 set/hide place markers 0-9
^KB mark/hide beginning of Block
^KC Copy a block of text
^KD editing Done - save file
^KE rEname a file
^KF turn File directory ON/OFF
^KH Hide/display the marked block
^KJ delete a file
^KK mark/hide end of a blocK
^KL change the Logged-in disk drive
^KN ordinary block/column block toggle
^KO cOpy a file
^KP Print a file
^KQ Quit edited version of file
^KR Read a file & insert in document
^KS Save and re-edit the present file
^KV moVe a block of text
^KW Write a marked block to a file
^KX save file and eXit to CP/M
^KY delete the marked block

^OC Centre the text on cursor line
^OD turn Display of control characters
     on screen OFF/ON
^OE turn "soft" hyphen entry OFF/ON
^OF set margins & tabs from line
^OG indent paraGraph (paragraph tab)
^OH turn Hyphen help OFF/ON
^OI set a tab
^OJ turn Justification OFF/ON
^OL set Left margin
^ON remove a tab stop
^OP turn display of Page breaks OFF/ON
^OR set Right margin
^OS set line spacing
^OT turn ruler display OFF/ON
^OV turn variable tabs OFF/ON
^OW turn word Wrap OFF/ON
^OX margin release

^P RETURN overprint the last line
^PA Alternate pitch (on some printers)
^PB produces **Bold type**
^PC makes the printer pause
^PD produces Double strike
^PF phantom space
^PG phantom rubout
^PH overprint the last character
^PM overprint the last line
^PN Normal pitch (on some printers)
^PO enter a non-break space
^PS produces underScored text
^PT produces superscripts
^PV produces subscripts
^PX produces ~~strikeout~~
^PY some printers change ribbon colour

^Q0 - ^Q9 move cursor to marker 0-9
^QA find a string & replace by another
^QB move cursor to beginning of Block
^QC move cursor to the end of the file
^QD move cursor to right end of line
^QE move cursor to the top of screen
^QF Find a specified string
^QK move cursor to end of blocK
^QP move cursor to Previous position
     before the last command
^QQ repeat the next command
^QR move cursor to beginning of file
^QS move cursor to left Side of screen
^QV move cursor to its position before
     the last command
^QW scroll down continuously
^QX move cursor to bottom of screen
^QY delete from cursor to end of line
^QZ scroll up continuously

SUMMARY OF THE DOT COMMANDS

(The commands marked ******* work only on printers which support micro-spacing).
(The parameter **n** must be a whole number).

Command	Function	Units	Default value

Vertical spacing and layout
.LH n ***	Line Height	1/48 inch	8 (48/8 = 6 lines per inch)
.PL n	Paper Length	lines	66 lines = 11 inches
.MT n	Margin at Top	lines	3 lines = 3/6 = 0.5 inch
.MB n	Margin at Bottom	lines	8 lines = 8/6 = 1.33 inches

Page breaks
.PA	start a new PAge		
.CP n	Conditional Page	lines	
.PO n	Page Offset	columns	8 columns = 8/10 = 0.8 inch

Page numbers
.PN n	Page Number		1
.OP	Omit Pagenumbers		
.PC n	Page number Column	columns	col. 33 (centre of 65 col. page)

Headings and footings
.HE message	Heading		blank
.HM n	Heading Margin	lines	2 lines = 2/6 = 0.33 inch
.FO message	Footing		contains page number
.FM n	Footing Margin	lines	2 lines = 2/6 = 0.33 inch

Miscellaneous
.. message	Comment		
.IG message	Comment		
.UJ n ***	microjustification	0 = OFF) 1 = ON)	ON (adds micro-spaces to justify the right margin)
.SR n ***	Subscript and superscript roll	1/48 inch	3 = 3/48 inch
.BP n	Bidirectional Print	0 = OFF) 1 = ON)	ON (prints left to right, then right to left)

Line heights ******* only on printers which support micro-spacing

Command	lines/inch	Command	lines/inch	Command	lines/inch
.LH 1	48.0	.LH 8	6.0 (single)	.LH 16	3.0 (double)
.LH 4	12.0	.LH 9	5.3	.LH 18	2.6
.LH 6	8.0	.LH 10	4.8	.LH 20	2.4
.LH 7	6.8	.LH 12	4.0	.LH 24	2.0 (triple)

Character spacings (pitch) ******* only on printers which support micro-spacing

Dot command	Pitch characters/inch	Dot command	Pitch characters/inch
.CW 6	20	.CW 13	9.2
.CW 7	17.1	.CW 14	8.6
.CW 8	15	.CW 15	8
.CW 9	13.3	.CW 16	7.5
.CW 10	12 (alternative-pitch)	.CW 17	7
.CW 11	10.9	.CW 20	6
.CW 12	10 (normal pitch)	.CW 24	5

SPECIAL DOT COMMANDS FOR MAILMERGE

Command	Function	Meaning
.AV var1, var2	Ask Variable	stop and ask the operator to type the value of the variable(s) var1, var2 ...
.SV variable	Specify Variable	sets the value of a variable in the file
.FI filename	FIle	specifies name of a file which is to be inserted & printed at this point
.DF filename	Data File	gives name of file to be used to read data from
.RV var1, var2	Read Variable(s)	specifies the names and order of the variables var1, var2 ... which are to be read from the previously named data file
.RP n	Repeat	repeats data file n times, or until all the records have been read
.DM message	Display Message	displays the message given on this line on the screen
.CS	Clear Screen	clear the screen of messages
.PF ON	Print time-line Forming	must be ON/OFF/DIS.
.RM n	Right Margin	reset Right Margin to col. n at print time
.LM n	Left Margin	reset Left Margin to col. n at print time
.LS n	Line Spacing	reset Line Spacing to n at print time
.OJ	Output-Justification	must be ON/OFF/DIS. Changes the justification of text at print time.
.IJ	Input-Justification	must be ON/OFF/DIS. Used only for unusual text, & controls whether input text is interpreted as justified or ragged

Duplicate page - to be torn out and kept near the computer

SUMMARY OF EDITING COMMANDS

^A	move cursor left one word	^OC	Centre the text on cursor line
^B	reform paragraph	^OD	turn Display of control characters
^C	scroll up one screenful		on screen OFF/ON
^D	move cursor one character right	^OE	turn "soft" hyphen entry OFF/ON
^E	move cursor up one line	^OF	set margins & tabs from line
^F	move cursor right one word	^OG	indent paraGraph (paragraph tab)
^G	delete character under cursor	^OH	turn Hyphen help OFF/ON
^H	delete character to left of cursor	^OI	set a tab
^I	tab	^OJ	turn Justification OFF/ON
^J	display HELP menu	^OL	set Left margin
^K	display BLOCK menu	^ON	remove a tab stop
^L	repeat last find or replace	^OP	turn display of Page breaks OFF/ON
^M	same as RETURN	^OR	set Right margin
^N	insert "hard" carriage return	^OS	set line spacing
^O	display ON-SCREEN menu	^OT	turn ruler display OFF/ON
^P	display PRINT menu	^OV	turn variable tabs OFF/ON
^Q	display QUICK menu	^OW	turn word Wrap OFF/ON
^R	scroll down one screenful	^OX	margin release
^S	move cursor one character left		
^T	delete word to right of cursor		
^U	interrupt	^P RETURN	overprint the last line
^V	turn insert ON/OFF	^PA	Alternate pitch (on some printers)
^W	scroll down one line	^PB	produces **Bold type**
^X	move cursor down one line	^PC	makes the printer pause
^Y	delete whole line	^PD	produces Double strike
^Z	scroll up one line	^PF	phantom space
		^PG	phantom rubout
^JB	explain reforming of paragraphs	^PH	overprint the last character
^JD	list print directives	^PM	overprint the last line
^JF	explain "Flags" at right of screen	^PN	Normal pitch (on some printers)
^JH	change the Help level	^PO	enter a non-break space
^JI	command index	^PS	produces underScored text
^JM	explain Margins and tabs	^PT	produces superscripts
^JP	explain use of Place markers	^PV	produces subscripts
^JR	explain the Ruler line	^PX	produces ~~strikeout~~
^JS	explain the Status line on screen	^PY	some printers change ribbon colour
^JV	explain moVing text		
^K0 - ^K9	set/hide place markers 0-9	^Q0 - ^Q9	move cursor to marker 0-9
^KB	mark/hide beginning of Block	^QA	find a string & replace by another
^KC	Copy a block of text	^QB	move cursor to beginning of Block
^KD	editing Done - save file	^QC	move cursor to the end of the file
^KE	rEname a file	^QD	move cursor to right end of line
^KF	turn File directory ON/OFF	^QE	move cursor to the top of screen
^KH	Hide/display the marked block	^QF	Find a specified string
^KJ	delete a file	^QK	move cursor to end of blocK
^KK	mark/hide end of a blocK	^QP	move cursor to Previous position
^KL	change the Logged-in disk drive		before the last command
^KN	ordinary block/column block toggle	^QQ	repeat the next command
^KO	cOpy a file	^QR	move cursor to beginning of file
^KP	Print a file	^QS	move cursor to left Side of screen
^KQ	Quit edited version of file	^QV	move cursor to its position before
^KR	Read a file & insert in document		the last command
^KS	Save and re-edit the present file	^QW	scroll down continuously
^KV	moVe a block of text	^QX	move cursor to bottom of screen
^KW	Write a marked block to a file	^QY	delete from cursor to end of line
^KX	save file and eXit to CP/M	^QZ	scroll up continuously
^KY	delete the marked block		

Duplicate page - to be torn out and kept near the computer

SUMMARY OF THE DOT COMMANDS

(The commands marked *** work only on printers which support micro-spacing).
(The parameter n must be a whole number).

Command	Function	Units	Default value
Vertical spacing and layout			
.LH n ***	Line Height	1/48 inch	8 (48/8 = 6 lines per inch)
.PL n	Paper Length	lines	66 lines = 11 inches
.MT n	Margin at Top	lines	3 lines = 3/6 = 0.5 inch
.MB n	Margin at Bottom	lines	8 lines = 8/6 = 1.33 inches
Page breaks			
.PA	start a new PAge		
.CP n	Conditional Page	lines	
.PO n	Page Offset	columns	8 columns = 8/10 = 0.8 inch
Page numbers			
.PN n	Page Number		1
.OP	Omit Pagenumbers		
.PC n	Page number Column	columns	col. 33 (centre of 65 col. page)
Headings and footings			
.HE message	Heading		blank
.HM n	Heading Margin	lines	2 lines = 2/6 = 0.33 inch
.FO message	Footing		contains page number
.FM n	Footing Margin	lines	2 lines = 2/6 = 0.33 inch
Miscellaneous			
.. message	Comment		
.IG message	Comment		
.UJ n ***	microjustification	0 = OFF) 1 = ON)	ON (adds micro-spaces to justify the right margin)
.SR n ***	Subscript and superscript roll	1/48 inch	3 = 3/48 inch
.BP n	Bidirectional Print	0 = OFF) 1 = ON)	ON (prints left to right, then right to left)

Line heights *** only on printers which support micro-spacing

Command	lines/inch	Command	lines/inch	Command	lines/inch
.LH 1	48.0	.LH 8	6.0 (single)	.LH 16	3.0 (double)
.LH 4	12.0	.LH 9	5.3	.LH 18	2.6
.LH 6	8.0	.LH 10	4.8	.LH 20	2.4
.LH 7	6.8	.LH 12	4.0	.LH 24	2.0 (triple)

Character spacings (pitch) *** only on printers which support micro-spacing

Dot command	Pitch characters/inch	Dot command	Pitch characters/inch
.CW 6	20	.CW 13	9.2
.CW 7	17.1	.CW 14	8.6
.CW 8	15	.CW 15	8
.CW 9	13.3	.CW 16	7.5
.CW 10	12 (alternative-pitch)	.CW 17	7
.CW 11	10.9	.CW 20	6
.CW 12	10 (normal pitch)	.CW 24	5

Duplicate page – to be torn out and kept near the computer

SPECIAL DOT COMMANDS FOR MAILMERGE

Command	Function	Meaning
.AV var1, var2	Ask Variable	stop and ask the operator to type the value of the variable(s) var1, var2 ...
.SV variable	Specify Variable	sets the value of a variable in the file
.FI filename	FIle	specifies name of a file which is to be inserted & printed at this point
.DF filename	Data File	gives name of file to be used to read data from
.RV var1, var2	Read Variable(s)	specifies the names and order of the variables var1, var2 ... which are to be read from the previously named data file
.RP n	Repeat	repeats data file n times, or until all the records have been read
.DM message	Display Message	displays the message given on this line on the screen
.CS	Clear Screen	clear the screen of messages
.PF ON	Print time--line Forming	must be ON/OFF/DIS.
.RM n	Right Margin	reset Right Margin to col. n at print time
.LM n	Left Margin	reset Left Margin to col. n at print time
.LS n	Line Spacing	reset Line Spacing to n at print time
.OJ	Output--Justification	must be ON/OFF/DIS. Changes the justification of text at print time.
.IJ	Input--Justification	must be ON/OFF/DIS. Used only for unusual text, & controls whether input text is interpreted as justified or ragged

INDEX

216